Where to watch birds in

Thames Valley & The Chilterns

THE *WHERE TO WATCH BIRDS* SERIES

Where to Watch Birds in Bedfordshire, Berkshire, Buckinghamshire, Hertfordshire and Oxfordshire
Brian Clews, Andrew Heryet and Paul Trodd

Where to Watch Birds in Cumbria, Lancashire and Cheshire
Jonathan Guest and Malcolm Hutcheson

Where to Watch Birds in Devon and Cornwall
David Norman and Vic Tucker

Where to Watch Birds in Dorset, Hampshire and the Isle of Wight
George Green and Martin Cade

Where to Watch Birds in East Anglia
Peter and Margaret Clarke

Where to Watch Birds in France
Ligue Française pour la Protection des Oiseaux

Where to Watch Birds in Ireland
Clive Hutchinson

Where to Watch Birds in Italy
Lega Italiana Protezione Uccelli

Where to Watch Birds in Kent, Surrey and Sussex
Don Taylor, Jeffrey Wheatley and Tony Prater

Where to Watch Birds in Scotland
Mike Madders and Julia Welstead

Where to Watch Birds in Somerset, Avon, Gloucestershire and Wiltshire
Ken Hall and John Govett

Where to Watch Birds in South America
Nigel Wheatley

Where to Watch Birds in Southern Spain
Ernest Garcia and Andrew Paterson

Where to Watch Birds in Wales
David Saunders

Where to Watch Birds in the West Midlands
Graham Harrison and Jack Sankey

Where to Watch Birds in Yorkshire and North Humberside
John Mather Second edition 1995

Where to watch birds in

Thames Valley & The Chilterns

Brian Clews and Paul Trodd

Third Edition

Christopher Helm
A & C Black · London

Third edition 2002
Second edition 1995
First edition 1987

Line drawings by Gary Claydon, Gavin Haig, Julian Smith, Andrew Chick and Marianne Taylor

Christopher Helm, an imprint of A & C Black Publishers Ltd., 37 Soho Square, London W1D 3QZ

0-7136-5953-X

A CIP catalogue record for this book is available from the British Library

A & C Black uses paper produced with elemental chlorine-free pulp, harvested from managed sustainable forests.

Printed and bound in Great Britain by Creative Print and Design (Wales), Ebbw Vale

CONTENTS

FOREWORD

Since the days of Lloyd George, British Prime Ministers have sought solace and inspiration away from the hurry-and-scurry of Westminster by retiring to their country retreat set in the calming, picturesque Chilterns. The undulating hills surrounding Chequers make a tranquil sanctuary whatever the season. In summer, their verdant coating of Beech woodland is a reminder of how England may have looked a thousand years ago. As autumn golds fade to austere winters, the bare trees and rising chalk escarpments still typify all that is captivating about the English countryside.

In the shadow of the Chilterns, the region's other great natural feature, that grand old lady of all British rivers, the Thames, slowly and incessantly goes about her business, draining the nation's most populated watershed into the North Sea.

The fact that the Chilterns and Thames Valley lie less than an hour's drive from London, are straddled by some of the densest tracts of suburbia, carved mercilessly by our busiest motorways and yet still retain their rural charm, adds to their enduring quality. It also makes them an exciting and accessible destination for the birdwatcher.

To think, however, this book is about birding woodland and river valleys – even though Hawfinch, Wood Warbler, Redstart, and Nightjar are among the birder's most highly sought species – would be an error. The relentless forces of progress, in other words, Man's uncontrollable impulse to change everything around him, have seen the creation of a diverse range of valuable and productive habitats: clay and chalk pits, gravel workings, reservoirs, farmland, water meadows, even rubbish tips, all create precious niches for birds to prosper.

Fifteen years ago the significance of the region and its birds was recognised in Where to Watch Birds in Bedfordshire, Berkshire, Buckinghamshire, Hertfordshire & Oxfordshire (Helm). Since then, the Chilterns and the Thames Valley have seen some remarkable changes. The M25 has made an indelible mark across the landscape, but not far from the noise of rush-hour traffic the melancholy 'chups' of Tree Sparrows can still be heard. High above the hurly-burly of the M40, the unmistakable shape of Red Kites is today as much a feature of motorway driving as traffic cones and delays. This book will help you find such sites, the little-known oases and havens where birds thrive and birders can enjoy all that is good about the very heart of rural England.

Stuart Winter

ACKNOWLEDGEMENTS

A work of this nature would be less complete but for the invaluable assistance of many people. In particular, the authors would like to thank the many wardens, rangers and park officials who aided our survey work. Numerous organisations have also been instrumental in our quest for details of sites and sensitive breeding species, including all five county councils, the county recorders, the county Wildlife Trusts, the RSPB and the Forestry Commission. The Bird Clubs of Bedfordshire, Buckinghamshire, Berkshire and Hertfordshire, the Berkshire Bird Bulletin Group, North Bucks Birders, Oxford Ornithological Society and the Banbury Ornithological Society and their respective committees have all made important contributions and the authors thank them deeply.

Of the many individuals who contributed, special thanks are due to the following for site information, proof reading and a variety of supporting functions.

Bedfordshire: John Adams, Peter Almond, Ian Dawson, Rob Dazley, Graham Wilton Jones, Dave Kramer, Richard Lawrence, Boo Mathews, Barry Nightingale, Dave Odell, Martin Palmer, Peter Smith, John Trew and Mike Williams.

Berkshire: Bruce Archer, Derek Barker, Fraser Cottington, Richard Elston, Stephen Graham, Pat Martin, Brendan McCartney (Berkshire Birding), Mike Smith, Ian Twyford and Mike Wicker.

Buckinghamshire: Rob Andrews, Graham Atkins MBE, Steve Brooke, Chris Bullock, Paul Earle, Andy Harding, Steve Jones, Trevor Lawson, Alan Madge, Keith Mitchell, John Schmidt, Andrew Stevenson, Joan Thompson, Bob Tunnicliffe, Mike Wallen and Nicky Wheeler.

Hertfordshire: Lynne Atkinson, Gwyneth Bellis, Garry Elton, Jack Fearnside, Mike Ilett, Judith Knight, Lee Marshal, Don Otter, Jim Terry and Barry Trevis.

Oxfordshire: Rod d'Ayala, Keith Blaxhall, John Brucker, Dave Dunford, David Green, Neil Lambert, Ian Lewington, Barbara Nunn, Simon O'Sullivan, Mike Rogers, Thomas Stevenson, Jon Uren, Toni Whitehead and Ivan Wright. Also to Andrew Heryet for his original research for the first edition.

The authors are particularly indebted to Stuart Winter for his foreword to this book and also to the five artists, Andrew Chick, Gary Claydon, Gavin Haig, Julian Smith and Marianne Taylor for the line drawings. Special thanks too go to Hazel Clews and Patricia Trodd for moral support and a variety of support work during the eighteen months the project took to complete.

INTRODUCTION

At first glance, any birdwatcher finding themselves relocated to the Thames and Chiltern counties, or holidaying there, may wonder if there are any birds to be found anywhere. Landlocked and home to some three and a half million people, with end-to-end traffic jams, busy motorways, business parks and noisy airports, an impression of a wildlife-free urban jungle is easy to obtain. But it only takes a footpath leading away from the housing estate, a track across nearby farmland or a stroll through a promising copse or wood to change that view entirely. These five counties possess in fact an amazing mosaic of habitat, much of it off the beaten track, to embrace and fascinate any and all who want to experience the joys of the countryside. Yes, it may mean hearing the hum of traffic alongside an otherwise-idyllic lake, or even the scream of jets overhead a stoic woodland, but it seems that much of the wildlife does not mind this and we suddenly realise that nature is indeed on our doorstep. All is not lost!

The hundreds of migrating Honey Buzzards which swept down the eastern half of England in an unprecedented invasion during September 2000, would have looked down on the region and seen a great variety of habitats, first encountering the prairies of rape and cereals growing above a bed of clay and flint, which form the base of the northern edge of the region, where partridges and a few summering Quail are to be found. They would have then looked longingly at the Oak woodlands that abut the Great Ouse as it meanders across Buckinghamshire and Bedfordshire, and the heathland resting on lower greensand with its conifer-clad ridges, home to the Lady Amherst's Pheasant. Hertfordshire's damp Oak and Hornbeam compartments will have looked equally alluring. Those which drifted south and east over the region would have noted large reservoirs and gravel pits painted with ducks and geese, and refuse tips dotted with a myriad gulls near the sprawling extremities of the nation's capital, and the attractive habitat clinging to the valleys of the Thames, Great Ouse, Colne and Lee river systems. Along these verdant valleys, marshes, reed swamp and water-meadows will have glistened in the sunshine, their riparian sojourners moving to adjacent watercress beds and sewage treatment works when all else is frozen. The huge expanse of Windsor Great Park and its adjacent Gorse-clad heaths would also have looked most inviting, with Hertfordshire's patches of Oak and Hornbeam giving way to Berkshire's dry coniferous woods.

Yet those which found themselves taking a more south-westerly track across the region would have noted the great chalk scarp overlooking the Vale of Aylesbury and the middle Thames area, capped with the remnants of old Beech forests, now in the form of 'hangers' and a productive feeding ground for Brambling and other finches. Even some of the steeper inclines find themselves subject to the plough in this sector, but the steepest parts still provide a home for herb-rich pasture. Here, sheep and Rabbit combine to keep the sward short and the Hawthorn at bay, enabling Skylark, pipits, wagtails and buntings to haunt these sacred pastures, often joined by wintering raptors such as Hen Harrier and Short-eared Owl. This dramatic Berks. and Oxon. downland scene is occasionally broken by invading scrub, especially on the gentler slope towards the Thames, and here remnant Corn Bunting, Barn Owl and Stone Curlew exert their tenuous grip.

Since earlier editions of this book, the Chiltern countryside has become dotted with hundreds of metal telephone masts and several thousand new houses, and many more are to follow. But there have been gains too, with the huge area of Greenham Common air base returned to nature and the creation of a major new waterway in the form of the Berks. and Bucks. flood alleviation channel, both offering new opportunities for natural habitat to evolve, to the benefit of our birds. And the entire region has benefited from one of the most significant conservation stories of the twentieth century: the return of the Red Kite. Extinct in England for some one hundred and fifty years, the reintroduction scheme has led to about 100 pairs producing over 200 young each year, and the continuing spread of this magnificent raptor throughout the Chilterns counties.

In addition to the birds, the region also boasts a wealth of ornithological expertise. The Bird Room of the Natural History Museum can be found at Tring, whilst at Oxford the Alexander Library in the Edward Grey Institute for Field Ornithology is one of the finest collections of bird books in Britain. Europe's largest conservation organisation, the Royal Society for the Protection of Birds (RSPB) is based at Sandy in Bedfordshire and is responsible, among other things, for the management of over 150 nature reserves nationwide. At a more local level, there are many active RSPB member groups, whilst the younger birdwatcher is well catered for by the RSPB's junior sections, Wildlife Explorers and Phoenix. All five counties have their Nature Conservation Trusts and many of their reserves are featured heavily in this book. The County Trusts really are the grass roots of local conservation, indeed without their valuable work much of the region's landscape and natural history heritage would have been lost. For a minimal membership fee, access is granted not only to regional reserves but also to most of the 1,300 nature reserves managed by the Trusts throughout Britain. Additionally, the region has a large number of very active bird clubs and natural history societies with ornithological branches. These groups do much valuable work documenting the local avifauna, organising field trips and providing ample scope for learning and discussion. Today's birdwatchers are indeed fortunate in having this plethora of knowledge at their disposal. Do make full use of it, as this can only lead to a greater understanding and appreciation of the region's avifauna and habitats.

So it can be seen that the region does indeed offer both the experienced and aspiring birdwatcher much variety of habitat in which to explore this fascinating pastime, with the benefit of excellent road and rail facilities to enable every corner of these diverse counties to be explored. We do hope this book helps to maximise the reader's enjoyment.

County Recorders

Having visited a location, any records one has made can be very valuable in assessing the overall picture of birdlife in the region. Therefore, please pass on details of your sightings to the respective County Bird Recorder, either immediately after your visit or at the end of each year. Records should ideally be presented in Voous classification order and accompanied, if possible, with a grid reference to facilitate easy processing. Indicate clearly any records which you feel should remain confidential and this will be respected.

Bedfordshire	Dave Odell, 'The Hobby', 74 The Links, Kempston, Bedford, MK42 7LT
Berkshire	Peter Standley, 'Siskins', 7 Llanvair Drive, South Ascot, Berks. SL5 9HS
Buckinghamshire	Andy Harding, 15 Jubilee Terrace, Stony Stratford, Milton Keynes, MK11 1DU
Hertfordshire	Mike Ilett, Nobland Green Farm, Wareside, Herts. SG12 7SJ
Oxfordshire	Ian Lewington, 119 Brasenose Drive, Didcot, Oxon. OX11 7BP

Birdwatcher's Code of Conduct

1. The welfare of birds must come first.
2. Habitat must be protected.
3. Keep disturbance to birds and their habitat to a minimum.
4. When you find a rare bird think carefully about whom you should tell.
5. Do not harass rare migrants.
6. Abide by the bird protection laws at all times.
7. Respect the rights of landowners.
8. Respect the rights of other people in the countryside.
9. Make your records available to the local bird recorder.
10. Behave abroad as you would when birdwatching at home.

Key to Symbols

MAIN ROADS	▬▬▬▬	DECIDUOUS WOODLAND	
MINOR ROADS	▬▬▬	CONIFEROUS WOODLAND	
FOOTPATHS	·············	MARSHLAND	
RAILWAY TRACK	+++++++++		
BUILDINGS	■ OR □	FLOWING WATER	
HIDE	●	STILL WATER	
PARKING	P5 OR P10 etc.	MUD FLAT OR SANDBAR

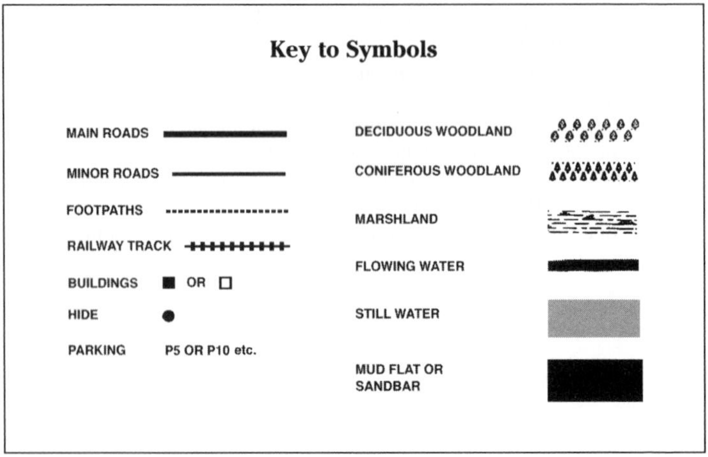

HOW TO USE THIS BOOK

THE REGION

The region under discussion in this book consists of the counties of Bedfordshire, Berkshire, Buckinghamshire, Hertfordshire and Oxfordshire. Each of the five counties is discussed separately, in alphabetical order, as a complete section.

Each county is preceded with a county map with the relevant main sites plotted to give the reader a rough idea where the sites are in relation to main towns. Each main site has its own map and, in addition, a six-figure grid reference for use in conjunction with the Ordnance Survey 1:50,000 series of maps. Main sites are described in alphabetical order; where further sites are discussed within a main site (for example, Colne Valley), subsidiary headings and maps are used to indicate the division.

At the end of each county section, additional sites are listed and grid references given. These are briefer accounts of how to get to them and what to expect when there.

Measurements

Road distances throughout are given in kilometres, with the mile conversion afterwards in parentheses; all other measurements in the book are stated in metric first with imperial in parentheses second. Conversions are approximate.

Habitat

A brief account of each main site's general features, habitats and topography, along with its size and status, if any (for example, Site of Special Scientific Interest (SSSI), Local Nature Reserve (LNR), etc.), is given. It may include a note of the other forms of wildlife present. Even the most blinkered birdwatcher would find it hard to ignore a riot of colourful wildflowers and their related butterflies in summer at certain downland sites. Attempts have been made to give the latest information on gravel pit description and access but it is acknowledged that working pits may change significantly in a short space of time.

Access

Directions are given from the nearest main road, directing the reader to the relevant car park, lay-by or viewpoint. These directions should be used in conjunction with the related site map. The Ordnance Survey six-figure grid reference used throughout will help the reader to pinpoint the site. (For anybody unsure of how to read these references, a simple guide is given on the inside back cover of any of the Ordnance Survey 1:50,000 series of maps.)

Details of the facilities that exist at the site are outlined as well as details of where to apply for information or, if necessary, a permit. (For further information see also the Useful Addresses section of this book.) Railway stations are also mentioned if they are within reasonable walking distance of the site discussed.

Unless otherwise stated, it is important that birdwatchers remain on the permitted rights of way and also observe the Code of Conduct at all times. Failure to do so may jeopardise the opportunities that exist.

The best time of day to visit is included and relates mainly to activities of the general public when they conflict with those of the birdwatcher. Generally speaking, the peak hours of bird activity are at dawn and dusk, although this is less applicable, for example, during the winter at a reservoir or gravel pit.

Species

This forms the main section of each site, where species most likely to be seen throughout a typical year are discussed in detail. A note or two may mention any past rarities that have occurred or what could be seen if observer coverage were to be intensified. Very common species are not dealt with except where high numbers are likely to occur.

Birds, however, are fickle creatures, subject to the vagaries of weather, disturbance and habitat change; for these reasons a site that one year harbours a particular species may not be as good in subsequent years. The names of birds used in this book follow the practice of earlier editions, but it is acknowledged that some species are now being referred to, for example, as Northern Wheatear, and Common Redstart.

Calendar

This section forms a summary of events from the species account, allowing the reader a succinct point of reference as to what season or month a particular species can be expected. Some degree of overlap may occur at certain times of the year, as some species linger into the subsequent period.

THE SITES

The choice of sites for inclusion in this book was drawn up following discussion with local birdwatchers, and the various conservation bodies active in the region, since it was necessary to exclude any sites sensitive to additional disturbance by visitors. Unfortunately, much site survey time was lost due to the outbreak of foot-and-mouth disease. Allowing for these criteria, the authors hope that from their research, coupled with years of local experience, the information presented is accurate and that no glaring omissions have been made. Should errors be noted, the authors would be pleased to hear of them. Sites have also been chosen to ensure geographical spread, a range of different habitats and a selection of species to satisfy birdwatchers of all abilities and experience.

Similarly, the authors would be pleased to hear from any observers who consider a site worthy of inclusion in future editions, bearing in mind the basic criteria already mentioned. Please address any correspondence to the publishers, A&C Black (Publishers) Ltd, 37 Soho Square, London W1D 3QZ.

GLOSSARY OF TERMS

In writing this book, the authors have attempted to minimise the use of technical terms but several have been utilised. The general meaning of these words or phrases is explained below. Several abbreviations are also expanded.

BBOWT	Berkshire, Buckinghamshire & Oxfordshire Wildlife Trust
BOS	Banbury Ornithological Society
Carr (or Carse)	Waterside scrub
Corvid	A member of the crow family (usually referring to Carrion Crow, Rook or Jackdaw)
Crepuscular	More likely found at dusk or perhaps dawn
Dabbling Duck	Species that use a surface-feeding technique (e.g. Mallard)
Diurnal	Active during daylight (e.g. Little Owl)
Diving Duck	Species that feed on underwater vegetation or creatures (e.g. Tufted Duck)
Escarpment	Steep face of a ridge or plateau
Fall	Arrival of large numbers of birds on migration, usually occasioned by weather conditions preventing onward progress
FC	Forestry Commission
FE	Forest Enterprise
Feral	An introduced species (e.g. Canada Goose)
Hirundine	One of the martins or the Swallow
HMWT	Hertfordshire & Middlesex Wildlife Trust
Leaf Warbler	More correctly, Phylloscopus warblers (including such species as Willow Warbler, Chiffchaff and Wood Warbler)
Nocturnal	Active during the hours of darkness
Passage	Referring to a bird on migration which may visit a location during its journey
Passerine	A term used to describe any small bird encountered on land (as against seabirds, etc.)
Pelagic	A bird of the open sea
Phylloscopus	'Correct' term for Leaf Warbler (see above)
Raptor	Birds of prey which hunt in daylight (e.g. Kestrel or Sparrowhawk, but not including owls)
Redhead	Referring to female or juvenile Goosander, Red breasted Merganser, Smew and Goldeneye
Reeling	A bird song resembling a fishing reel winding (e.g. Grasshopper Warbler)
Ringtail	Female or juvenile harriers (Hen or Montagu's)
Riparian	Inhabitant of river banks
'Roding'	Boundary territorial flight of Woodcock
RSPB	Royal Society for the Protection of Birds
RSPCA	Royal Society for the Prevention of Cruelty to Animals
SAC	Special Area of Conservation

Sawbill	Member of the family including Goosander, Red breasted Merganser and Smew
SPA	Special Protection Area
SSSI	Site of Special Scientific Interest
STW	Sewage Treatment Works
Sylvia Warbler	Warblers of bushes and scrub (e.g. Whitethroat, Garden Warbler, Blackcap and Dartford Warbler)
TABG	Theale Area Bird Group
TAVR	Territorial Army Volunteer Reserve
Thermal	A column of rising air caused by unequal heating of the land
Wader	Birds of estuaries, mudflats and wet meadows, usually long-legged and long-billed (e.g. Redshank, Curlew)
Wild Swans/Geese	As against feral species, and excluding Mute Swan (e.g. Whooper Swan, Brent Geese)
Winter Thrushes	Fieldfares and Redwings, but also Mistle or Song Thrushes when flocked in winter
Wreck	A fall of exhausted birds, due to exceptional storms. Occasionally results in arrivals of petrels and auks well inland
WTBCN	Wildlife Trust for Bedfordshire, Cambridgeshire, Northamptonshire & Peterborough

USEFUL ADDRESSES

National Associations

British Trust for Ornithology (BTO)
National Centre for Ornithology
The Nunnery
Thetford
Norfolk
IP24 2PU

Ramblers Association
2nd Floor,
Camelford House,
87–90 Albert Embankment
London
SE1 7TW

English Nature
Northminster House
Peterborough
PE1 1UA

Royal Society for the Protection of Birds (RSPB)
The Lodge
Sandy
Bedfordshire
SG19 2DL

Forestry Commission/Forest Enterprise
231 Corstophine Road
Edinburgh
EH12 7AT

Wildfowl and Wetlands Trust (WWT)
Slimbridge
Gloucester
GL2 7BT

National Trust
36 Queen Anne's Gate
London
SW1H 9AS

Woodland Trust (WT)
Autumn Park
Dysart Road
Grantham
Lincolnshire
NG31 6LL

County Associations

Bedfordshire

Bedfordshire Bird Club
Miss Sheila Alliez
Flat 67, Adamson Court
Hillgrounds
Kempston
Bedfordshire
MK42 8QT
www.bedsbirdclub.org.uk

The Wildlife Trust for Beds, Cambs, Northants & Peterborough
(Bedford Office)
Priory Country Park
Barkers Lane
Bedford
MK41 9SH
www.wildlifetrust.org.uk/bcnp

(There are RSPB groups at Bedford,Biggleswade and Luton.)

Berkshire

BBOWT
Hasker House
Woolley Firs
Cherry Garden Lane
Maidenhead
Berkshire
SL6 3LJ
www.wildlifetrust.org.uk/berksbucksoxon

Berkshire Bird Bulletin (monthly)
Brian Clews
118 Broomhill
Cookham
Berkshire
SL6 9LQ

Newbury District Ornithological Club
Jim Burnett
44 Bourne Vale
Hungerford
Berkshire
RG17 0LL

Reading Ornithological Club
Mike Smith
5 Nabbs Hill Close
Tilehurst
Reading
Berkshire
RG31 4SG
www.roc.care4free.net/

(There are RSPB groups at East Berkshire, Reading, Wokingham and Bracknell.)

Berkshire Birder's Web Sites

www.berksbirds.co.uk
http://members.aol.com/berksbirds/index.htm

Buckinghamshire

Amersham Birdwatching Club
Mary Mackay
26a Highfield Close
Amersham
Buckinghamshire
HP6 3HG

North Bucks Birders
Andy Harding
15 Jubilee Terrace
Stony Stratford
Milton Keynes
MK11 1DU

Buckinghamshire Bird Club
Roger Warren
Bakery Lodge
Skirmett
Henley-on-Thames
Oxon
RG9 6TD
www.hawfinches.freeserve.co.uk

(There are RSPB groups at Aylesbury and Milton Keynes.)

Hertfordshire

Hertfordshire Bird Club
Jim Terry
46 Manor Way
Borehamwood
Hertfordshire
WD6 1QY
www.fly.to/hertsbirdclub

Welwyn & Hatfield District Council
Council Offices
The Campus
Welwyn Garden City
Hertfordshire
AL8 6AE

Hertfordshire & Middlesex Wildlife Trust
Grebe House
St Michael's Street
St Albans
Hertfordshire
AL3 4SN

Lee Valley Regional Park Authority
Abbey Mills
Highbridge Street
Waltham Abbey
Essex
EN9 1BZ

(There are RSPB groups at Chorleywood, Harpenden, Hemel Hempstead, Hitchin, Hoddesdon Potters Bar, St Albans, Stevenage and Watford.)

Oxfordshire

Banbury Ornithological Society
Tony Clark
11 Rye Close
Banbury
Oxon
OX17 7XG

Oxford Ornithological Society
David Hawkins
The Long House
Park Lane
Long Hanburgh
OX8 8RD
http://members.tripod.co.uk/OOS/index.htm

Berkshire, Buckinghamshire & Oxfordshire Wildlife Trust
The Lodge
Armstrong Road
Littlemore
Oxford
OX4 4XT
www.wildlifetrust.org.uk/berksbucksoxon

Senior Warden
Farmoor Reservoir
Farmoor
Oxon
OX2 9NS

(There are RSPB groups at Oxford and Didcot.)

Bird and Wildlife Hospitals

Berkshire Wildlife Rehabilitation Unit (birds of prey only)
Clive Palmer
8 Mill Lane
Padworth
Berkshire
RG7 4JU
(Tel. 01189712781)

RSPCA Southridge Animal Centre
Packhorse Lane
Ridge
Potters Bar
Hertfordshire
EN6 3LZ
(Tel. 08704 427104)

Lisa Sharp
Maidenhead
(birds and small mammals)
(Tel. 01628 628013)

Blackwater Wildlife Rescue
(near Camberley)
(Tel. 01276 31477)

Milton Keynes Wildlife Hospital
Mr & Mrs V Seaton
150 Bradwell Common Boulevard
Milton Keynes
MK13 8BE
(Tel. 01908 604198)

St Tiggywinkles
Sue & Les Stocker MBE
Aston Road
Haddenham
Aylesbury
Buckinghamshire
HP17 8AF
(Tel. 0844 292292)

Kestrel Lodge Bird Hospital
David Chandler
101 Sheridan Avenue
Caversham
Berkshire
RG4 7QB
(Tel. 0118 947 7107)

Swan Lifeline, Berkshire
(national coverage)
(Tel. 01753 431667.)

Swan Sanctuary, Surrey
(national coverage)
(Tel. 01784 431667.)

Bradwell Common Wildlife Hospital
Mr & Mrs V Seaton
150 Bradwell Common Boulevard
Milton Keynes
MK13 8BE
(Tel. 01908 604198)

Merrist Wood College, Guildford
Surrey & south Berks
(Tel. 01483 884072 for advice only)

Permits

Hansons Aggregates
Dix Pit Complex
Stanton Harcourt
Oxfordshire
(01865 882211)

(Wytham Woods)
The Conservator, Wytham Woods
Sawmill Yard
Keeper's Hill
Wytham
Oxfordshire
OX2 8QQ

RMC Angling
RMC House
The Square
Lightwater
Surrey
GU15 5SS
(01276 453300)

Thames Water Plc
14 Cavendish Place
London
W1G 9NU
(0207 636 8686)

BEDFORDSHIRE

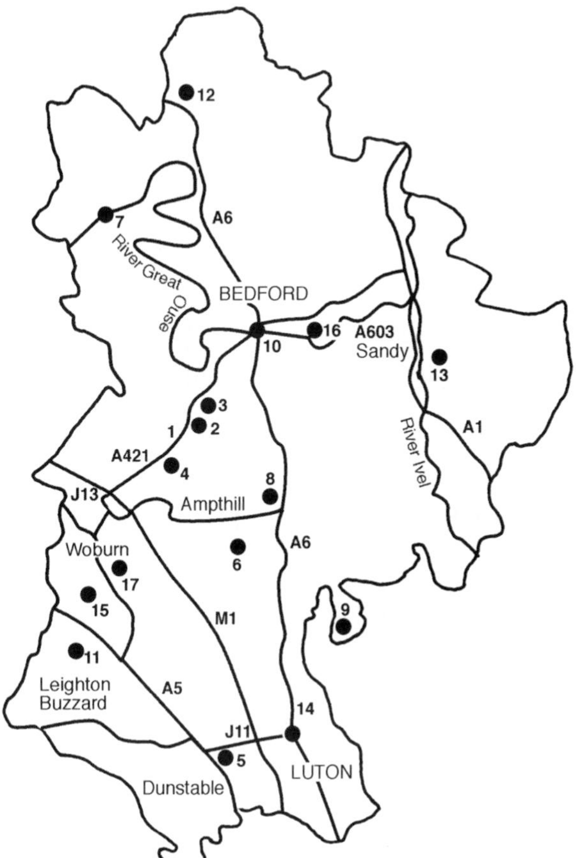

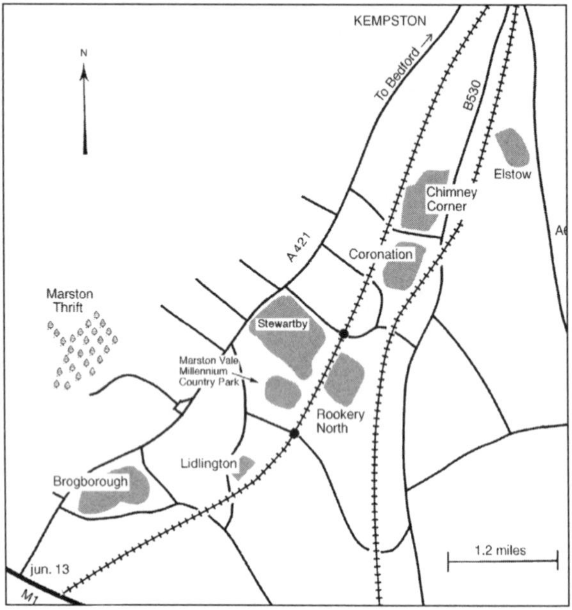

1 BEDFORD CLAY PITS

To the south-west of Bedford lies a series of pits, some worked and some exhausted, formed by the excavation of Oxford clay for the brick industry. Together, these pits constitute the largest area of open water in the county and are of particular importance to wintering wildfowl, roosting gulls and to a lesser degree passage and breeding waders.

Stewartby and Brogborough Lakes are the largest of the flooded pits and are both treated as main sites, along with the newly created Marston Vale Millennium Country Park. The remaining pits are discussed later in this section.

The birdwatcher should be aware that several pits in the Marston Vale are strictly out of bounds, particularly if being actively worked or used as landfill sites.

Yellow Wagtail

2 MARSTON VALE MILLENNIUM COUNTRY PARK

OS ref. TL 003 415

Habitat

The forest of Marston Vale is one of 12 new community forests established in England with the aim of improving the environment for both people and wildlife. Literally millions of pounds have been spent on the project centred at Marston Moretaine, south-west of Bedford, including the creation of a new Wetland Reserve. An old, deep-water clay pit, Millbrook Pillinge, has been incorporated into the reserve to complement the newly created shallow lagoons and a 16-ha reedbed. Open wet grassland (40 ha) with surrounding bunds and extensive tree planting completes the scene. There are two bird hides, and a number of observation points (difficult to access at the time of writing) from the bunded Wetland Reserve.

Access

From the A421, between junction 13 of the M1 and Bedford, turn off at Marston Moretaine and follow the signs to Lidlington. The main entrance (open 10:00–18:00 hrs daily) into the country park is signposted off Station Road and leads to the car park. When closed park near Millbrook Station or around Stewartby Lake and follow the signs. Trains stop within walking distance of the park at Stewartby and Millbrook on the Bedford to Bletchley branch line (Silverlink 08705 125240).

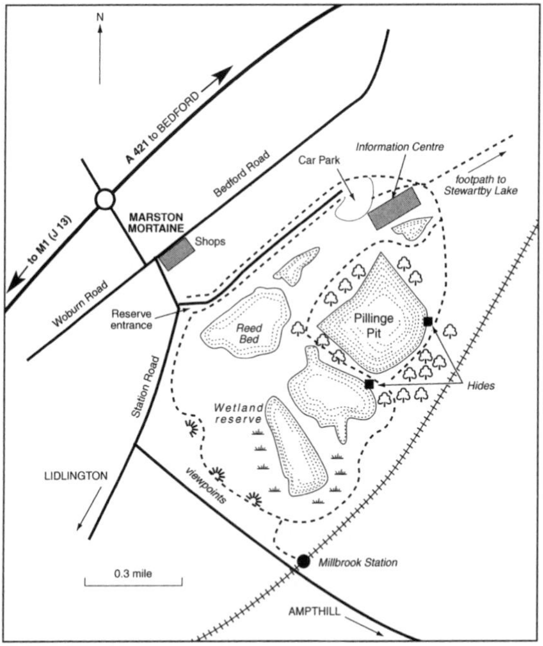

A spacious information centre is well equipped with toilets, a café and shop, plus a children's play area and exhibition room. A list of planned events can be obtained in the foyer, along with details of cycle hire and a bird sightings chalkboard. Permits for access into the Wetland Reserve can be bought for £2.50. The perimeter path links into Stewartby Lake and is firm enough for wheelchair users; footpaths into the Country Park Wetland Reserve, even though the two hides have ramps, are unsuitable for wheelchairs.

There is also a website: www.marstonvale.org and the site phone number is 01234 762607.

Species

Opened in a blaze of publicity in April 2000, Marston Vale Millennium Country Park, has fast become an important site within the Bedford clay pit complex and is the only significant area in the Vale actively managed for wildlife. Wildfowl and waders are the site's mainstay with a variety of resident passerines taking advantage of the new plantations and grassland.

Winter birding is centred mainly on The Pillinge lake which plays host to large numbers of Pochard, Tufted Duck and Coot, alongside lesser numbers of Great Crested and Little Grebes, Cormorant, Gadwall and the occasional Goldeneye. Shoveler and Teal occur on the shallow wetlands where there is also the chance of Snipe and Lapwing. Kestrel and Sparrowhawk are resident and in recent winters Peregrine and Merlin have hunted locally. The grasslands beside the access road are good for Skylark, Meadow Pipit, finches and buntings, and Stonechat may be seen on dead weed stems beside the newly planted reedbed. Winter thrushes can be found just about anywhere, while Grey Heron and Kingfisher find plenty of still water in which to fish.

Shelduck and Redshank are often the first wetland indicators of spring while Wheatear and Chiffchaff are in the vanguard of true summer migrants. Little Ringed and Ringed Plovers arrive from late March onwards, and have bred, along with declining numbers of Redshank and Lapwing. The spring wader passage is light with Common Sandpiper, Greenshank and Dunlin to be expected, although scarcer species will no doubt turn up as the site develops, such as Ruff, godwits, Curlew and Whimbrel. Willow Warbler, Whitethroat and Blackcap are well represented in the scrub around the site and are joined by Lesser Whitethroat and Garden Warbler by late April. A few Turtle Dove and Cuckoo also occur and by early May Hobby arrive with the Swifts.

Summer is typified by warbler activity, particularly Whitethroat, Sedge and Reed Warblers, while out on the grasslands Skylark and Yellow Wagtail can be found. Common Terns drift over from nearby clay pits and prospecting Oystercatcher are often noted. Shoveler breed and in 2000 a pair of Garganey successfully reared young. Little Egret has also been recorded.

During August the wader passage includes Common and Green Sandpipers joined by the occasional Wood Sandpiper, Greenshank, Ruff and Dunlin. Of the larger species, which tend to be fly-overs, both species of godwit have been noted, as well as Curlew and Whimbrel. Into September and the prospect looms of something rarer such as Little Stint or Curlew Sandpiper. Fence lines should be checked for Whinchat and the pools for Grey Wagtail. As autumn progresses Goldfinch and Linnet flocks congregate on the rough ground, while Siskin and Redpoll should benefit from the many Alders and Birch trees planted around the site. An overhead passage of Chaffinch, larks and pipits is noted while Goldcrest join the roving tit flocks.

The country park has the potential to be a top wader site, if the water levels can be correctly managed and the general public can be prevented from wandering at random in the wetland area. An early morning visit is recommended to miss the majority of disturbance, mostly from dog-walkers. If all proceeds as planned the site should attract breeding waders such as, Lapwing, Ringed and Little Ringed Plovers, Redshank and maybe even Snipe and Oystercatcher; it can be surely only a matter of time before a real rarity is found.

Calendar

Resident: Great Crested and Little Grebes, Cormorant, Grey Heron, Sparrowhawk, Kestrel, Lapwing, Kingfisher, Green and Great Spotted Woodpeckers, Skylark, Meadow Pipit, finches and buntings.

November–February: Pochard, Tufted Duck, Coot, Gadwall, Shoveler, Teal, Goldeneye, chance of Peregrine or Merlin, Snipe, gulls, winter thrushes, Goldcrest, Stonechat, finch and bunting flocks.

March–May: Shelduck, Hobby, Little Ringed and Ringed Plovers, Redshank, Common Sandpiper, Greenshank, Dunlin, chance of rare wader, Swift, Turtle Dove, Cuckoo, hirundines, pipit and wagtail passage, Wheatear, warblers.

June–July: breeding birds, Oystercatcher, hirundines, chance of Garganey.

August–October: Passage waders – sandpipers, Greenshank, Dunlin, Ruff; chance of rarity, Grey Wagtail, Whinchat, thrushes, hirundines, warblers, Goldcrest, Redpoll, Siskin, finch flocks.

3 STEWARTBY LAKE COUNTRY PARK

OS ref. TL 005 425

Habitat

Stewartby Lake itself covers 116 ha (287 acres) and the Country Park site 128 ha (318 acres). The water area is sub-leased to the Stewartby Water Sports Club by the county council and during the summer much disturbance takes place from water-skiers, yachting and powerboats. It is for this reason that an early morning visit is advisable, especially in April when migration is likely to turn up a few surprises. In winter late afternoon is the best time to watch the gull roost; Stewartby Lake is one of the premier gull-watching sites in the region.

Initially brackish, and in places very deep, the water has taken many

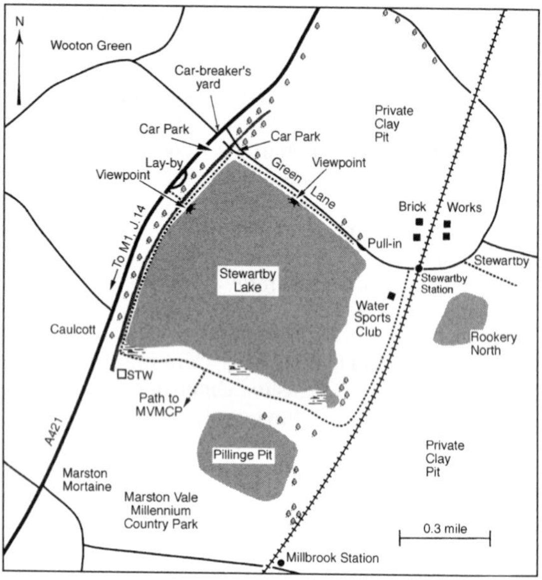

years to establish an aquatic vegetation. The margins vary from brick rubble on the northern edges to marshy shallows in the south, where an area is set aside as a nature reserve. A steep, wooded bank separates the lake from a stream along the south-western edge and, opposite, an open grassy area leads down to a concrete slipway, providing somewhere for passage waders and wagtails to stop off. The hillocks to the south are vegetated with rough grass, sedge and scrub, and an adjacent sewage works is also of interest.

Access

Equidistant between Bedford and junction 13 of the M1 motorway, the lake is located 1.5 km (1 mile) north-east of the village of Marston Moretaine just off the A421. A car park is signposted off Green Lane but parking space can be found in a lay-by on the main road at Caulcott for watching the gull roost. Access is via a footbridge over a stream to a raised clearing beside the lake, where a platform is due to be constructed. Alternatively take the Stewartby road, Green Lane, which runs along the north-eastern boundary of the lake, parking near the entrance to the car breaker's yard, or travel further along the lane to a lay-by near the entrance to the Water Sports Club. Trains on the Bedford to Bletchley branch line stop at Stewartby station within five minutes walk of the site (Silverlink 08705 125240).

Check the grass for waders and passerines, especially in spring and autumn. A circular walk is marked out allowing access around the lake and also links to the Marston Vale Millennium Country Park.

Species

For much of the year Stewartby Lake can seem incredibly mundane, with just the ubiquitous Coot breaking the monotony of the stark man-made landscape. Nevertheless some of the best birdwatching in the county can be experienced here, given the correct weather conditions.

When winter strikes with a vengeance, icing over the surrounding brick pits, Stewartby stays comparatively ice-free, attracting a wide cross-section of wildfowl, sometimes in large numbers. Consequently, during January and February, if a cold spell is forecast be prepared for almost anything. Three species of diver have been recorded in these circumstances but all are exceptionally rare. Great Crested Grebe numbers swell to over 100 with a chance of the scarce Red-necked Grebe in their midst; Black-necked and Slavonian have also occurred. At times these rarer grebes stay close to the bank, so persistent scanning is required to pick them out. Little Grebe can be seen all year, their numbers peaking into double figures during the winter, with a few pairs breeding amongst the small patches of reeds. By January Mute Swan numbers can build up to over 50.

Canada Geese frequent the fields towards Marston Moretaine and included in their ranks are an assortment of Barnacle and Greylag, most of feral origin, but Barnacle Geese have bred at adjacent clay pits. Cormorant find the fishing much to their taste and often perch atop the many buoys, drying their wings. Shag have occurred in the past and the boom by the ski-ramp is a favoured spot. One or two Snipe normally find the boggy ground of the nature reserve to their liking.

The most common duck are Mallard, Tufted Duck and Pochard with smaller numbers of Teal and Gadwall. During cold spells a noisy flock of Wigeon can be expected, commuting between the lake and nearby fields to graze. A flight of Shoveler may come and go, the drakes resplendent in their breeding plumage, but are only scarce visitors whereas Ruddy Duck and Goldeneye are noted more regularly. All sawbills are rare here. Another duck often noted during the spring is the Shelduck.

As dusk approaches a large gull roost assembles, with birds returning from a day spent foraging on nearby refuse tips. The roost consists mainly of Black-headed Gull, with correspondingly lower numbers of other common species. During most winters a few Glaucous, Iceland and Mediterranean Gulls are found. Diligent searching in recent years has revealed examples of Yellow-legged Gull and most excitingly, in 2001, Bedfordshire's first ever record of Laughing Gull.

The scrub alongside the stream invariably attracts a few Goldcrest mingled in amongst the hyperactive tit flocks and very occasionally a

Cormorant

Firecrest. In the taller Alders, Siskin can be seen, along with Redpoll and Goldfinch. Water Rail can be heard, but rarely seen, in the small reedbeds along the southern margin and the sewage works is worth checking for pipits, wagtails and wintering Chiffchaff. The rank grassland has attracted Short-eared Owl in the past but Kestrel and Sparrowhawk are now more likely. Kingfisher can be encountered anywhere around the lake, with the steep banks providing ideal nest sites during the breeding season.

A good indication of spring is Chiffchaff and Blackcap calling energetically from the bushes along the lane, with Willow Warbler later, during the first week of April. The short turf near the Water Sports Club is perfect for a Wheatear and even more attractive to Yellow Wagtail. Counts of around 50 have been made from the lay-by in mid-April but have declined in recent years. Meadow Pipit and Pied Wagtail have also declined. Continental wagtail races sometimes occur, with Blue-headed and White Wagtails most likely to be found.

The grassy lawn near the jetty is the main area suitable for passage waders and is best checked out as early as possible due to disturbance. Redshank are early arrivals from March onwards and flocks of Lapwing are often present, while Little Ringed and Ringed Plovers pass through in April. Dunlin and Common Sandpiper are other regular visitors, the latter showing a preference for the brick rubble banks. Waders scarce to the county that have put in an appearance have included Ruff, Sanderling, Whimbrel and Bar-tailed Godwit, but these really are the exceptions to the rule. In September 1993, Bedfordshire's third Purple Sandpiper was found on the yachting slipway.

Over the lake hirundines arrive; a trickle at first, building up to several hundred by the end of April, by which time the first Swifts can be expected along with an attendant Hobby. Common Scoter, migrating across central England, occasionally pause awhile but are now less than annual. April is the best spring month for Little Gull and Kittiwake but, as with the scoter, both gulls may only stay for a few hours. Early May is a good time of year for species richness at Stewartby Lake as summer migrants arrive in force. Occasional records of Grasshopper Warbler have featured on passage and in recent years Nightingale have bred.

Most exciting of all for the inland birdwatcher is the passage of terns, sometimes in exceptionally high numbers. Common Tern are the most abundant, wheeling noisily overhead and plunge-diving for small fish. The closely related Arctic Tern can also be expected en-route to their northern breeding grounds; having wintered in the South Atlantic they make the longest migration flight of any bird. The elegant Black Tern can be seen over the lake, occasionally in large numbers; heavy rainstorms can briefly drive down migrating terns. Sandwich and Little Terns, although rare, occur almost annually.

Scrub warblers busily rear their young amongst the thickets on the western perimeter, with Sedge and Reed Warblers along the southern margin reedbeds. The wires along Green Lane is a good site for the decreasing Turtle Dove, while Cuckoo fly over, more often heard than seen. Both common species of woodpecker regularly breed on site.

The autumn passage is less dynamic, with similar species to those in spring but in drabber, non-breeding plumages. Tern numbers can be good in August and September with the year's crop of juveniles swelling numbers considerably, both White-winged Black and Whiskered Tern (2001) have occurred at Stewartby. Gale force westerlies during September and October make this the time of year for an inland seabird 'wreck', with an outside chance of Leach's Petrel and Grey Phalarope. In the gale of October 1987 the county's only Sabine's Gull was recorded. Gannet, Storm Petrel and Fulmar have all been noted in late autumn following strong blows. If winds persist through the season the likelihood of a skua appearing increases (and with it the expected debate as to the identification!); Pomarine, Long-tailed and Great Skuas have all been recorded.

Calendar

Resident: Grey Heron, Little and Great Crested Grebes, Cormorant, Mute Swan, Canada Goose, Mallard, Sparrowhawk, Kestrel, Moorhen, Coot, Kingfisher, Green and Great Spotted Woodpeckers, common tits and finches.

December–February: Common grebes increase, chance of rare grebes, wild swans rarely, Wigeon, Gadwall, Teal, Shoveler, Pochard, Tufted Duck, Goldeneye, sawbills rare, Ruddy Duck, Snipe, large gull roost with chance of Yellow-legged, Glaucous, Iceland and Mediterranean Gulls, Water Rail, Grey Wagtail, Goldcrest, Chiffchaff, Redpoll, Siskin and buntings.

March–May: Shelduck, Common Scoter (scarce), Hobby, Little Ringed and Ringed Plovers, Lapwing, Redshank, Dunlin, Common Sandpiper, chance of rare waders, chance of Kittiwake and Little Gull, Common, Arctic and Black Terns, Turtle Dove, Cuckoo, Swift, hirundines, Yellow Wagtail, Meadow Pipit, Wheatear, Whinchat, common warblers.

June–July: Waders return in July, otherwise quiet.

August–November: Waders, terns, Meadow Pipit, Grey Wagtail, hirundines mass in September. Chance of rare seabirds blown in by autumn gales in October.

4 BROGBOROUGH LAKE **OS ref. SP 978 395**

Habitat

Brogborough Lake and its associated peripheral habitats, together form an area similar in size, at about 120 ha (300 acres), to the previous location, making it the second largest lake in the Marston Vale. It is a deep and, in places, steep-sided clay pit with less surface water disturbance than Stewartby Lake. The margins are bordered mainly by scrub with a poplar shelter belt along the northern side, several reedbeds (main one in south-west corner) and rank grass. A small tree-clad island offers limited sanctuary to roosting waterfowl and Cormorant. Windsurfers generally range over the eastern half of the lake and there is limited seasonal fishing.

Access

Leave the M1 motorway at junction 13, taking the A421 towards Bedford. The lake is 3 km (2 miles) from the M1 just past the village of

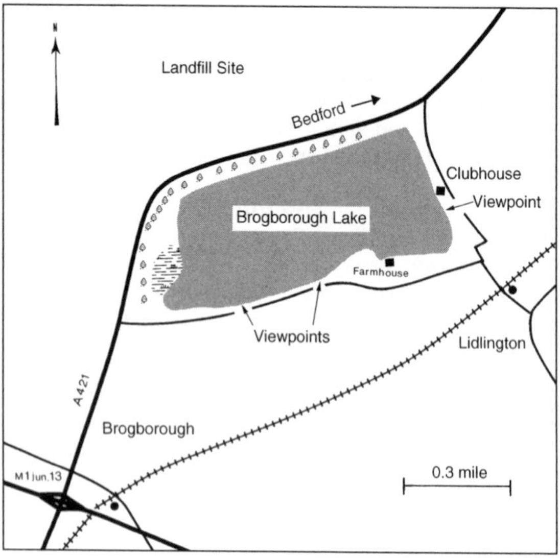

Brogborough. Although there is no general public access to the site, the lake can be scanned from selected viewpoints along the southern and eastern banks where public footpaths meet the lake. For gull-watching approach along the southern side on the road to Lidlington, parking carefully along the lane by gaps in the hedgerow.

To view the eastern end of the lake access is via a footpath adjacent to the entrance to the Brogborough Board Sailing Club. Do not park on the main A421 on the north-west side or, under any circumstances, in the Shanks and McEwan lorry turn lay-by.

Silverlink trains on the Bedford to Bletchley branch line stop at Lidlington station which is a 15-minute walk from the lake (08705 125240).

Species

Winter birding at Brogborough Lake is dominated by gull-watching from mid-afternoon onwards as gulls arrive from surrounding refuse tips to roost. Due to a combination of elevation and light, the south-west corner offers good viewing conditions for searching the massed ranks through a telescope. Among the many thousands of commoner species there are regular sightings of Glaucous, Iceland and Mediterranean Gulls, plus a recent record of Ring-billed Gull. A small tree-clad island is used for roosting by 50–60 Cormorant (numbers have topped 100 in the past), and large numbers of Pochard, Tufted Duck, Great Crested Grebe and Coot cover the surface water. Brogborough Lake is the county stronghold for Goldeneye with up to 50 regularly present most winters; sawbills are generally rare with Goosander the most likely.

Inevitably, over the years, locally rare wildfowl have occurred, the most likely being Red-crested Pochard and Scaup, while Long-tailed and Ferruginous Ducks and the county's first Eider have also been noted. Of the three scarce grebes the Red-necked is the most regular, one remaining into the spring when it attained full breeding plumage. The reedbed is worth checking as a bunting roost contains small numbers of the declining Corn Bunting; Bittern and Bearded Tit have rarely occurred, while Water Rail and Kingfisher are frequent visitors.

As spring approaches, the large flocks of ducks and gulls gradually disperse leaving the lake to the resident breeders and passage migrants; Shelduck are regularly noted with one or two pairs nesting in the surrounding vale some years. Common Scoter and Little Gull pass through in variable numbers, while the more weather related occurrences of Kittiwake can be expected during March or April, particularly after strong northerly winds. In early March the lake is a good place to try for an early Sand Martin, with Swallow and House Martin following a few weeks later. Around the margins check for early warblers, particularly Sedge and Grasshopper Warblers, and Nightingale sometimes sing from scrub near the reedbed. The short grass of the windsurfers' car park often attracts parties of Yellow and alba wagtails.

The highlight of spring passage is the arrival of terns, attracted to Brogborough's large sheet of still water to pause awhile and feed. Common Tern breed elsewhere in the clay vale and as a result are ever present from May to September. For the more discerning birder Arctic Tern are almost annual and flocks of Black Tern can briefly appear on weather fronts, normally on an easterly airflow.

Summer is generally quiet with migrant species such as Cuckoo and Turtle Dove evident and, strangely, Green Woodpecker in the thin shelter belt. Reed Warbler breed in the Phragmites, where occasionally Ruddy Duck are noted, and common wildfowl nest around the margins.

The early autumn passage is similar to the spring movement as terns and Little Gull move through, and roosting hirundines may attract a hunting Hobby. Later in the season, following persistent gales, the lake is as good as anywhere in the county to check for storm-blown seabirds. Over recent years Fulmar, Great and Pomarine Skuas, Velvet Scoter and Leach's Petrel have all occurred. Other local rarities recorded at Brogborough Lake have included Night Heron, Gannet, Bean Goose and Firecrest.

Late autumn features flocks of winter thrushes and Goldcrest, while tits forage around the scrubby margins. The adjacent farmland is worth checking for finches, Skylark and partridges.

Calendar

Resident: Common grebes and wildfowl, Sparrowhawk, Kestrel, Green Woodpecker, Kingfisher, common tits, finches and buntings.

December–March: Occasional Red-necked Grebe, Cormorant, large numbers of Pochard, Tufted Duck, Goldeneye and Coot, sporadic Scaup, Red-crested Pochard and sawbills, large gull roost including chance of Glaucous, Iceland and Mediterranean Gulls, occasional Kittiwake, Water Rail and bunting roost.

April–June: Shelduck, chance of Common Scoter, Common, Arctic and Black Terns, Little Gull, Cuckoo, Turtle Dove, Nightingale, and passage warblers.

July–August: Hobby at hirundine roost. Reed Warbler and scrub warblers.

September–November: Passage terns and gulls, chance of storm-blown seabirds, wintering gulls and wildfowl begin to arrive. Goldcrest and winter thrushes.

BEDFORD CLAY PITS – Additional Sites

We now turn to the other pits in the Marston Vale which, with Stewartby Lake CP and Brogborough Lake, form an area generally known as the Bedford Clay Pits. Access to the pits is often restricted and in the case of the active landfill sites totally prohibited. Most, however, can be viewed from nearby roads or existing public footpaths. The Bedford Clay Pits comprise an area of great political sensitivity where there is much local opposition to further landfilling.

Chimney Corner Clay Pit (OS ref. TL 037 443)

A large irregular-shaped lake lying just north of Kempston Hardwick with a shallow lake further north. Sometimes attracting passage waders to the muddy edges, it can be partially viewed from the B530; park in Manor Road by the Chimney Corner pub. Colonies of Common Tern and Black-headed Gull breed on the raised islands while Greylag and Canada Geese nest on the dry hillocks. This pit has attracted scarce diving duck in the past such as Scaup, Red-crested Pochard and Red-breasted Merganser.

Coronation Clay Pit (OS ref. TL 030 430)

Approach the pit from the south, through Stewartby village, parking in Magpie Avenue at TL 025 425. Follow the track across a field, down the side of a hedgerow and over a ditch. Scan the partially flooded pit from surrounding footpaths on the east and west sides.

In winter expect the usual variety of ducks and gulls on the water and clay ridges while the scrub to the north has held Short-eared Owl. Spring passage can be good for terns and waders. Grasshopper Warbler breed and Nightingale are often heard. Depending upon the changeable water levels Redshank, Little Ringed Plover and Common Tern may also breed. It is a particularly good site for Hobby throughout the summer, and small numbers of Yellow-legged Gull regularly occur in early August. County rarities have included Temminck's Stint, Knot, Garganey, Pectoral Sandpiper and Pomarine Skua.

The future of this site is uncertain but development plans have included turning at least part of the site into a nature reserve.

Elstow Clay Pits (OS ref. TL 045 456)

Situated 1.5 km (1 mile) south-west of Elstow and once the proposed site for the dumping of low-level nuclear waste. A series of small pits and rough grassland with a refuse tip that attracts a few gulls in the winter; check thoroughly as Glaucous have been noted. A road at the southern end, west of the A6, affords views across the lake that usually holds small numbers of wintering duck; Black-throated Diver, Ferruginous Duck, Scaup and Slavonian Grebe have been seen here.

Lidlington Clay Pit (OS ref. TL 000 401)

A tiny pit with open water and several small reedbeds. Small numbers of wintering wildfowl, and once a Bittern; Velvet Scoter and Scaup have occurred. Summer breeders include Reed and Sedge Warblers and Reed Bunting.

View from the lay-by. Also check the nearby fields in winter for swans, gulls, plovers and the occasional raptor.

Rookery North Clay Pit (OS ref. TL 018 420)

A strictly private pit viewed only from a well-marked public footpath that runs to the south of Stewartby village. Park in the lay-by near the station, as if visiting Stewartby Lake, cross over the railway line, c.200 m east towards the village, and follow the footpath. Limited views can be had across an area of open water, islands and shallows, with rough grassland to the south.

In the winter it is good for Cormorant, grebes, ducks and gulls. Passage waders occur, depending on the water levels, while Redshank and Lapwing nest nearby. Hobby and Kestrel hunt over the rough grass and Common Tern fish the pit. Various warblers, finches and buntings breed.

Another highly sensitive site with an uncertain future. The southern pit is strictly out of bounds.

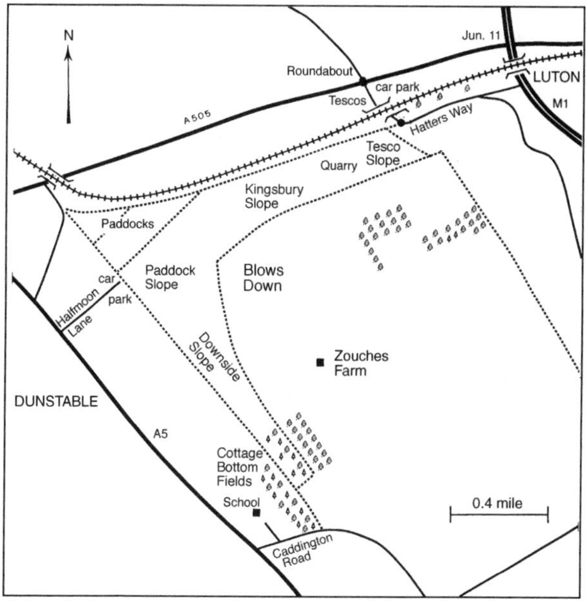

5 BLOW'S DOWNS

OS ref. TL 033 215

Habitat

Sandwiched between Dunstable to the west and the M1 motorway to the east lies a 2.5 km (1.5 mile) long escarpment slope of the Chilterns known locally as Blow's Downs. A maximum elevation of 230 m (695 ft) is attained, making this site one of the highest in the county. As its name implies, it is a windy area and the early morning observer is advised to wear warm, windproof clothing. Some classic open downland still remains due to the combined grazing of Rabbit, cattle and the scrub clearing activities of the Blow's Downs Conservation Group. Contrasting with the short turf are several areas of mixed Hawthorn, Blackthorn and Elder scrub, a plantation of assorted deciduous and coniferous trees and a stand of mature beech bordering the railway line to the north-east. A disused chalk quarry is a good viewpoint for observing overflying migrants, and is occasionally used by a local ringing group. The paddocks to the north-west are attractive to feeding passerines, particularly chats and pipits.

Hare, Fox, Muntjac, Stoat and Badger are all resident and Slow-worm can sometimes be encountered on warm summer days basking in the sheltered quarry bottom. The usual variety of plants typical of calcareous soil and their associated butterflies are found here too, including Bee Orchid and Chalkhill Blues, especially along the steeper slopes and at Cottage Bottom Fields.

For further information on Blow's Downs visit the impressive website at www.fly.to/blows.downs

Access

Exit at junction 11 of the M1 and take the A505 west toward Dunstable. At the first roundabout, turn left up Skimpot Road by Tesco's superstore and park in the Ladbrokes Casino car park (or alongside the roundabout in Hatters Way if visiting on a Sunday morning). Walk up to the railway line following a track under the bridge, through a kissing gate and onto the downs at Tesco's Slope. If visiting early in the morning follow the fence above the roundabout cutting, taking the obvious gully to the hilltop, and then walk west with the sun behind you. Keep to the top track, checking the scrub and downland regularly on Kingsbury and Paddock Slopes respectively. Carry on through the scrub and then head south-east to Cottage Bottom Fields checking Downside Slope en-route. Backtrack following the electricity grid lines toward the paddocks. A footpath running parallel with the railway line will complete the circuit back to the bridge.

An alternative access point is from the A5. Drive south from Dunstable town centre for 1 km (0.6 mile), turning left up Half Moon Lane. Park at the end of the road and continue on foot. There are good bus links from Luton main line railway station to Dunstable town centre.

Public access is virtually unlimited across Blow's Downs. As all the migrants turn up here, there is no need to venture into the private woods near Zouches Farm. The local conservation group, Wildlife Trust and District Council have erected a number of footpath signs, information boards and stiles. The majority of the downland habitat has been designated a SSSI, which could be important in the near future as a part of the site is under threat from a proposed by-pass.

Species

Although primarily a migration watchpoint, Blow's Downs presents something of interest throughout the year. The most exciting period is the spring passage with Ring Ouzel, Redstart and Wheatear regularly appearing, sometimes in good numbers. In recent years increasing numbers of raptors have been noted, Common Buzzard being the most regular, but also Red Kite and Goshawk.

During the winter months check out the mixed flocks of Yellowhammer and finches that feed amongst the straw around the horse sheds on

Ring Ouzel

the paddocks. A thorough search can often be rewarded with a Reed Bunting. The Beech stand near the Tesco's roundabout attracts flocks of Chaffinch in hard weather to feed on the mast, along with the possibility of Brambling. Mixed passerine flocks consisting of tits, including Long-tailed, Marsh and Willow, Goldcrest and finches forage ceaselessly amongst the scrub at this time of year. Blow's Downs is also a good site for the declining Bullfinch.

The most impressive spectacle of the year can be the winter roosting activities of large flocks of Starling, but recently numbers have dwindled, roosts may also shift locally from year to year. Visit an hour before sunset when sub-roosts form on nearby rooftops and trees prior to the main assembly in the downland scrub. Other common species joining the throng include House Sparrow, Collared Dove and thrushes on the periphery, while a Sparrowhawk may be on the lookout for a late meal. Owls are reported intermittently from this site and no doubt one day a lucky watcher will find a roost of Long-eared Owl hidden amongst the Hawthorn.

Spring passage begins in mid-March with the arrival of Wheatear on the open downs and paddocks. Numbers of 20 plus have been regularly recorded, but they soon move on following a clear night. Black Redstart are next to arrive, occurring almost anywhere along the ridge until the end of April, but with a special preference for the paddocks. They favour the vantage points of barbed wire fences and stables and flick down to feed, exposing their shimmering orange tail. If a high pressure weather system predominates over Europe in early April a fall of passerines can be expected with Blackcap, Chiffchaff and Willow Warbler in the vanguard. Stonechat are occasionally noted in the paddocks or along the fence bordering the railway line and have overwintered.

Throughout April Ring Ouzel can be encountered anywhere along the ridge, the best areas being the scrub and open grass at Tesco's and Kingsbury Slopes and around the old chalk quarry. Do not enter the quarry as this only disturbs the birds, but instead scan from above and the reward can be protracted views of Ring Ouzel feeding in the quarry bottom. Single figure groups have been recorded here, and in some years the passage continues into May. By mid-April Redstart arrive, the males first in flashy breeding plumage; careful checking in the sheltered hollows and gullies around mid-morning is the best time to find one. The distinct 'tsweep' flight call of passage Yellow Wagtail can be heard and sometimes they pause to feed amongst the livestock.

Tree Pipit also can be identified by their diagnostic flight call, at once telling them apart from the more numerous Meadow Pipit, whose numbers on passage may reach 100 in a day in early April. The former pipit no longer stays to breed but the Meadow Pipit still nests on the open downland around the quarry and in the long grass of the paddocks. Grasshopper Warbler has also been lost as a breeding bird but occasionally turns up on passage when its distinctive 'reeling' song aids detection. Listen out for Whitethroat across the scrub-clad slopes, along with smaller numbers of Garden Warbler and Lesser Whitethroat. The bluebell woods above Cottage Bottom Fields are good for Chiffchaff, Willow Tit and the occasional passage Nightingale.

Towards the end of April Whinchat may occur on the paddocks fencing, and along the old railway line. Passage Cuckoo and Turtle Dove begin to appear, but in ever decreasing numbers, and hirundines are more regularly noted. As May approaches passage slows down and all that can be expected is a trickle of late-arriving Spotted Flycatcher. Some years the spring rush brings in a local rarity. Pied Flycatcher, Firecrest and Hobby are typical but should not be expected and are normally the reward of local birders, who spend many hours on the downs in spring. Past rarities have included Dotterel, Waxwing and Snow Bunting and more recently Dartford Warbler.

In summer, an early morning visit is essential to avoid the disturbance of picnickers and walkers who flock here on warm days. Linnet and Yellowhammer nest on the open scrub while Sparrowhawk and Hobby are often seen hunting nearby. Kestrel likewise, although their hunting technique is different, the birds hovering in pursuit of small rodents. Cottage Bottom Fields is a good area to visit at this time of year for chalkland plants and butterflies and a chance of Turtle Dove 'purring' from overhead wires. Summer is a busy time for warblers, with many pairs raising two broods. Their song is much subdued towards the end of the period as they fatten up in readiness for the long haul south.

The autumn passage is typically more extended and not as exciting as the spring. A trickle of Redstart, Wheatear, Ring Ouzel, warblers and hirundines filter along the ridge. Whinchat numbers peak in late August in the paddocks, with Stonechat a month or two later, and there is usually a flock of Goldfinch feeding on weed seeds. As October closes the first flocks of Redwing and Fieldfare arrive from the boreal forests of the north, nervously gorging on the year's crop of Hawthorn berries. Blackbird and Song Thrush move in from the Continent and Goldcrest join the tit flocks.

Calendar

Resident: Kestrel, Sparrowhawk, Mistle Thrush, Willow, Marsh and Long-tailed Tits, Bullfinch, Yellowhammer.

December–February: Possible eared owls, Common Buzzard, winter thrushes, Starling and pigeon roost, Stonechat, occasional Brambling and Reed Bunting.

March–May: Late March to late April, gull passage, Wheatear, Black Redstart, Ring Ouzel, Chiffchaff, Blackcap and occasional Stonechat. Throughout April, Meadow and Tree Pipits, Yellow Wagtail and Willow Warbler. Mid-April to early May, Hobby, Turtle Dove, Cuckoo, hirundines, Redstart, Whinchat, Grasshopper Warbler, Lesser

Whitethroat, Garden Warbler and Spotted Flycatcher. Waders overhead: Lapwing, Curlew and Golden Plover most likely. Best chance of rarity in April, Quail, Pied Flycatcher and Firecrest.

June–July: Breeding passerines, Skylark, Meadow Pipit, Willow Warbler, Sylvia warblers, finches and Yellowhammer.

August–November: Passage migrants, Whinchat and Wheatear around Paddocks followed by Stonechat and occasional redstarts. Large finch flocks form, particularly Goldfinch, winter thrushes, Goldcrest, influx of Blackbird.

6 FLITWICK MOOR

OS ref. TL 046 354

Habitat

Flitwick Moor is situated where the River Flit crosses an inlier of impermeable clay in the Lower Greensand Ridge, forming, at 31 ha (79 acres), Bedfordshire's largest expanse of valley fen or carr. The moor has become much drier over recent years, although an attempt has been made to arrest the situation by controlling the underground springs with dams and sluices forming a mosaic of wet habitats. Oak, Ash and Birch can be found on the drier parts, with Alder and willows growing in the wet, more open areas, alongside sedge and reed. The moor has a rich flora, especially in the surrounding wet meadows, and an insect population which includes some nationally rare species of sawfly. Peat was formerly extracted from the moor, and the iron-rich springs that rise in the reserve were once bottled and sold as a blood tonic. Flitwick Moor is a relic example of a unique habitat in the region and is recognised as such by its status as a SSSI.

The wet meadows and arable land along the Maulden by-pass are worthy of attention, particularly during winter floods, for Snipe, ducks and gulls. The broad verges often attract hunting Barn Owl, while Little Owl can be found perched on roadside posts.

Access

From Flitwick town centre take the road east towards Greenfield. After 0.8 km (0.5 mile) turn left into Maulden Road and head north for a further 0.8 km (0.5 mile) to Folly Farm, opposite a small industrial estate. Turn right alongside the farm and follow the unmetalled road to the small car park. Take the main track into the wood and on to the wooden bridge. Cross over the bridge and the most interesting part of the moor, the reed swamp, is on both sides of the track. Carry on into the meadow following the River Flit path, which leads back to Greenfield Road or through the wood to the car park. Alternatively, turn south along Maulden Road, off the A507 Maulden by-pass, and left into the site by the farm.

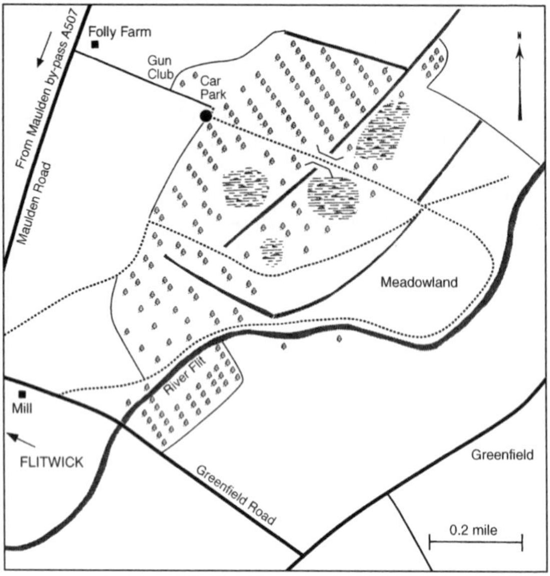

The moor is within easy walking distance of Flitwick railway station, on the main Bedford to King's Cross, St Pancras line.

Species

A visit to this site can be productive at any time of the year but, as with most woodland, springtime brings a peak of activity with the arrival of the summer migrants. Small flocks of Siskin and Redpoll can be found throughout the wood during the winter, especially in the Alders along the river. Other agile finches reaping the seed harvest are Goldfinch and Greenfinch. The wet meadows bordering the River Flit are good for wintering Snipe and the occasional passing Grey Heron. The river itself usually harbours a couple of Grey Wagtail, smart birds with a sharp flight call and yellow 'ringed' tail. They are mainly a winter visitor from hill country, but in recent years have become established as a breeding species near the old mill where the turbulent water is to their liking. Teal and Mallard are typical dabbling ducks of the wetter parts of the moor, a few pairs of the latter staying on to breed.

Water Rail can be seen and heard throughout the year but towards the end of winter they become more active as they establish their breeding territories. Flitwick Moor is one of the few regular breeding sites in the county for this crepuscular species; a good spot is by the wooden bridge near the reed swamp in the north-east corner. A variety of squeals and grunts betrays their presence, and with patience it is possible to catch a glimpse as they move amongst the dead reeds and tangle of bushes; however, beware the mimicry of both Moorhen and Song Thrush. Another species most active at dawn and dusk from April to July is the Woodcock, whose distinctive 'roding' display flight can be seen or heard over the wood.

With the onset of warmer weather summer migrants start arriving with, as always, Chiffchaff and Blackcap first. Willow Warbler are not far behind but do not breed in any great numbers. Sedge Warbler on the other hand are perfectly suited to this habitat and are soon setting up territories in the open marsh and river's edge, song-flighting vigorously from any vantage point. The closely related Reed Warbler arrive in May and haunt the small reedbeds scattered throughout the moor. Cuckoo frequently parasitises the warbler and can sometimes be seen flapping amongst the reeds in an effort to locate a nest. The swamp-loving Grasshopper Warbler is now only a sporadic visitor to the moor. Other warblers scattered throughout the site are Whitethroat in the hedgerows, Lesser Whitethroat in scrub and Garden Warbler in the wood.

Yellow Wagtail are now encountered mainly on spring passage with one or two pairs occasionally summering. Other common riparian species like Moorhen and Reed Bunting are present, and a pair of Kingfisher can usually be seen along the Flit, where suitable banks allow them to breed. In spring Willow Tit sing amongst the Birch, the many soft Elders offering good breeding sites for this hole-excavating tit.

In summer the wood is alive with juvenile tits and warblers as the season's broods are calling and feeding amongst the cover. Good views are obtainable from any of the footpaths bisecting the wood. All three species of woodpecker are resident, with the scarce Lesser Spotted showing a preference for the waterside willows.

Birds of prey present are Hobby, Kestrel and Sparrowhawk in the daylight hours with Tawny Owl at night and a slim chance of Barn Owl along the river. If visiting at dawn or dusk, check the posts along Maulden Road for Little Owl; by staying in the car a close approach is often allowed.

To summarise: Flitwick Moor is at its best around dawn on a fine May morning. Arrive an hour before sunrise and walk slowly through the wood stopping at the open marshes to listen for crepuscular specialities. Beware of hungry mosquitoes during the summer months.

Calendar

Resident: Sparrowhawk, Kestrel, Water Rail, Moorhen, Tawny Owl, Little Owl (around Folly Farm), Kingfisher, Green, Lesser Spotted and Great Spotted Woodpeckers, Grey Wagtail, Marsh and Willow Tits, Treecreeper, Redpoll and Jay.

Water Rail

December–February: Grey Heron, Teal (rare), Snipe, Woodcock (a pair or two breed), Siskin, Magpie roost, winter thrushes, finches and occasionally buntings.

March–May: Turtle Dove (scarce), Cuckoo, Yellow Wagtail, Mistle Thrush, Grasshopper Warbler (rare), Sedge and Reed Warblers, Sylvia warblers, Chiffchaff, Willow Warbler and Reed Bunting.

June–July: Breeding passerines.

August–November: Warblers depart, tits start to flock together, roosting Woodpigeon.

7 HARROLD ODELL COUNTRY PARK

OS ref. SP 958 567

Habitat

Harrold Odell Country Park is another example of how to turn an exhausted gravel pit into a multi-recreational area suitable for wildlife. The habitats on offer are similar to Priory Country Park in Bedford, although the island on the main lake is more attractive to waders. The smaller water to the south is heavily fished and of little interest to the birdwatcher, unlike the nearby reed swamp and willow scrub which is a hive of activity the year round. The park also includes a 1.2 km (0.75 mile) stretch of riverbank and meadows alongside the Great Ouse, bordered with established willows and Alders. Amphibians abound during springtime in the still waters and Grass Snake are regularly seen here and along the river. Mink are becoming an all too familiar sight throughout the Ouse Valley, having largely replaced the indigenous Otter and Water Vole.

Access

From Bedford town centre north along the A6, turn left after 4 km (2.5 miles) towards Oakley. Follow the lane through to Harrold passing through the villages of Pavenham and Carlton. Just north of Carlton the road bridges the river; the entrance to the park is a further 100 m (110 yds) on the right. Once inside the gate, park near the visitors centre, complete with toilets (wheelchair accessible), and check the sightings board. A restaurant (Truly Scrumptious Tearooms) has recently opened in the visitors centre.

A footpath encircles the main lake, taking in the hide, with tracks branching off through the reed swamp and down to the river. The Bell in Odell village is highly recommended for its pub lunches.

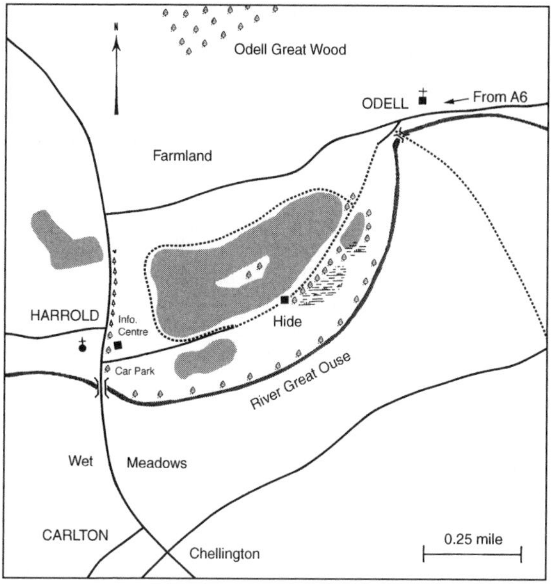

Species

The focal point of interest to the birdwatcher, whatever time of year, is the island, as it affords refuge from human disturbance allowing birds to rest in comparative safety. During the winter hundreds of feral Greylag and Canada Geese noisily congregate towards evening following daytime forays on surrounding farmland. Odd escapees, such as Barnacle and Bar-headed Goose are often found, while sporadically genuinely wild geese such as White-fronts and Pink-feet have been seen overhead.

Out on the water variable numbers of duck are present, Mallard, Gadwall, Tufted Duck and Pochard being most numerous, with occasional Shoveler and Shelduck. Smew periodically occur in small numbers but rarely stay long, and Goosander are fairly regular between December and February when a Red-crested Pochard sometimes appears. The early morning observer can often be rewarded with a flock of Wigeon grazing on the meadow or lakeside grass, at times numbering 300 strong. Goldeneye are present from late autumn to early spring along with a large pack of several hundred Coot. The wet meadow attracts Snipe and Teal, while the arboreal Siskin and Redpoll feed on cones situated atop the riverside Alders. The reed swamp attracts a variety of passerines to roost at dusk, including buntings and finches. Water Rail regularly winter and the secretive Bittern is sometimes encountered.

Spring commences with the arrival of Sand Martin over the water and Wheatear around the grassy edges. Redshank and Little Ringed Plover are now almost lost as breeding birds but are present on passage alongside a few Dunlin and Common Sandpiper. Periodically, unusual coastal species such as Turnstone, Sanderling or Oystercatcher appear but can never be predicted and rarely stay long. Groups of terns pass through, mainly Common at first with Black Tern a little later in the season. Most passerines are less obvious, although warblers drifting north feed among the willow scrub and scattered timber. Small flocks of Yellow Wagtail haunt the open meadow beside the fishing lake along with an assortment of Pied Wagtail and Meadow Pipit.

Summer breeders include all the normal resident riparian species as well as a colony of Reed Warbler among the Phragmites and a few pairs of Yellow Wagtail in the surrounding fields; Grey Wagtail can be found along the river. The ebullient Sedge Warbler ranges across the park nesting within rank vegetation, whereas the more retiring Whitethroat prefers drier scrub. The island is a hive of activity with small colonies of Cormorant and Grey Heron nesting in the willows; Harrold Odell Country Park was the first breeding site for Cormorant in Bedfordshire. Common Tern nest on the purpose-built tern rafts, beside a motley selection of duck in eclipse plumage. Hobby regularly hunt over the wetland for insects and martins, and nest nearby on open countryside.

A drawn-out wader passage sets in from late summer onwards with Greenshank and the occasional Ruff enlivening proceedings. Curlew and Whimbrel may pass overhead calling but rarely settle. Common and Green Sandpipers scuttle around the margins and one or two marsh terns in dowdy autumn dress may move through. Kingfisher are more obvious in late summer as the juveniles disperse in search of a territory and wildfowl, in eclipse plumage, increase in number. Winter thrushes and Skylark can occur on the open grass as passage Goldcrest and warblers move south.

County rarities at Harrold Odell Country Park include Slavonian Grebe, Great Northern Diver, Caspian Tern and Little Egret.

Calendar

Resident: Great Crested and Little Grebes, feral geese, Mute Swan, Tufted Duck, Mallard, Coot, Cormorant, Grey Heron, Kingfisher, woodpeckers, Grey Wagtail, tits including Willow, common finches and buntings.

December–February: Bittern (rare), chance of wild geese, Gadwall, Wigeon, Teal, Shoveler, Pochard, Shelduck, Goldeneye, Smew (rare), Goosander, Snipe, winter thrushes, Goldfinch, Siskin, Redpoll, chance of Stonechat.

March–May: Sand Martin, Wheatear, Redshank, Little Ringed and Ringed Plovers, Common Sandpiper, Common Tern, Black Tern (rare), Cuckoo, hirundines, wagtails, warblers, Meadow Pipit.

June–July: Riparian breeders, Hobby, Swift, breeding warblers, returning waders, Kingfisher more obvious.

August–November: Sandpipers, Greenshank, possible Ruff, Curlew or Whimbrel, hirundines, passage terns, pipits, larks, warblers, wagtails and winter thrushes, Goldcrest.

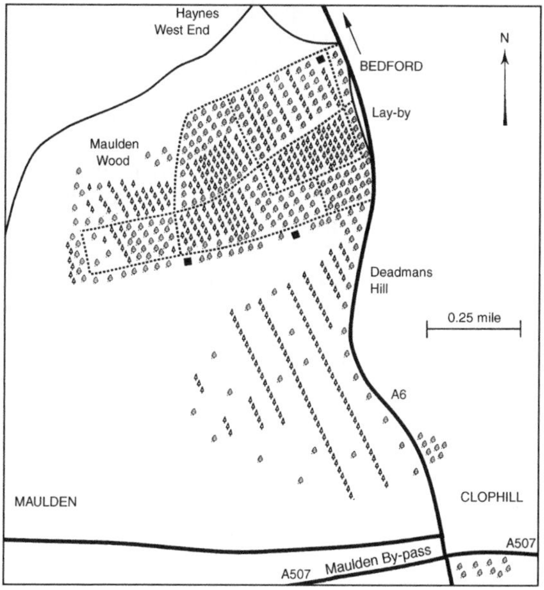

8 MAULDEN WOOD

OS ref. TL 070 390

Habitat

Maulden Wood, a part of Ampthill Forest, is a plantation-type wood owned by the Forestry Commission. Varying stages of growth help to create some diversity of habitat, but little of the typical greensand woodland remains. Oak and Ash comprise the main blocks of deciduous trees and support the majority of species. The pine plantations are almost impenetrable and of little use to birds apart from serving as good winter roost sites. The young plantations are the most rewarding for the birdwatcher, forming an ever-changing patchwork throughout the wood. Surrounding fields are always worthwhile checking, particularly on the southern perimeter where the view on a warm spring morning can be stunning.

This site has had well over 300 species of moths recorded within its boundaries so consequently, during the summer months, a local moth group is frequently active. Gathered around their mercury-vapour lamps, they make an eerie sight when encountered late at night.

Access

Maulden Wood is situated 1.5 km (1 mile) north of Clophill and to the west of the A6. Access is from a lay-by, where there is ample car parking space. The Forestry Commission have marked trails covering the entire wood. An early morning visit is essential to avoid dog-walkers and noise pollution from the nearby A6.

Species

Bedfordshire is the stronghold for Lady Amherst's Pheasant, with Maulden Wood being a particularly good place to hear the unique trisyllabic croaking call of this naturalised species. Introduced from China around 1900, they have spread out from their original release site at Woburn to colonise a number of woods along the Greensand Ridge. A resident species, it is more easily seen in the winter dashing across firebreaks and sometimes, with luck, feeding amongst the Oak litter. In spring, their call is heard from deep cover as the males set up territories. They remain elusive through the summer, keeping well into dense undergrowth and are only rarely seen, mostly at dawn and dusk.

All three species of woodpecker are represented, with the Great Spotted being the most common. Lesser Spotted are easier to see in early spring when calling and favour the more mature Oaks, looking for dead wood and drumming posts. Green Woodpecker are normally heard 'laughing' throughout the wood or seen bounding across clearings; the field near the forester's cottage, with plenty of anthills, makes for good feeding.

Resident raptors include Kestrel, Sparrowhawk and increasing numbers of Common Buzzard. The Tawny Owl is plentiful, and highly vocal, across the woodland complex where it breeds in purpose built nest boxes. Little Owl can also be found on surrounding farmland.

The main arrival of common warblers takes place from the middle of April, and the wood is soon alive with their song. This is a good time for a dawn chorus visit, when you could expect to see, but mostly hear, between 30 to 40 species in a couple of hours. A few pairs of Tree Pipit and Grasshopper Warbler can sometimes be found, but numbers fluctuate annually, with none at all showing in some years. Today, the Nightingale is no longer guaranteed, despite the habitat being suitable, and both Wood Warbler and Redstart are rare passage migrants.

Woodcock and Redpoll are both typically associated with greensand woodland, their numbers increasing in the winter. A few pairs of each stay on to breed, with Woodcock easily seen at dawn and dusk quartering the wood, performing their 'roding' display flight. Redpoll are much less predictable and are often seen flying in circles calling frantically, seemingly unable to decide exactly just where they are heading for!

All six species of tits are present along with the highly vocal Nuthatch and the not so obvious Treecreeper. The two 'black-capped tits' are easier to identify in spring by their distinctive songs. Two long distance

Willow Tit

migrants, the Turtle Dove and Cuckoo, are represented, but in ever decreasing numbers, along with a few Spotted Flycatcher.

Bird song progressively tails off through the summer, and a visit on a warm afternoon can be very dull indeed, with adults feeding late broods and juveniles moulting. Once the summer visitors have departed, the resident passerines have the wood to themselves and can fatten up in preparation for the coming winter. Mixed flocks of tits and Goldcrest roam the wood in search of food, while winter thrushes feed on nearby meadows. Corvids are plentiful and the woodland ponds have a resident Moorhen or two.

Not the best wood in the region, but ease of access, coupled with a relatively small size makes it worth a visit during the spring for a good selection of common woodland birds, with a winter visit for Lady Amherst's Pheasant and the chance of Crossbill.

Calendar

Resident: Kestrel, Sparrowhawk, Common Buzzard, Lady Amherst's Pheasant, Woodcock, Tawny and Little Owls, Green, Great Spotted and Lesser Spotted Woodpeckers, Mistle Thrush, Goldcrest, Willow and Marsh Tits, Nuthatch, Treecreeper, Jay, Redpoll.

December–February: Lady Amherst's Pheasant easier to see, Crossbill occasionally, tit flocks, winter thrushes.

March–May: Mid-April for Cuckoo, Turtle Dove, Tree Pipit, Grasshopper Warbler occasionally, Garden Warbler, Blackcap, Chiffchaff, Willow Warbler, Whitethroat, Lesser Whitethroat, Nightingale (rare). From mid-May, Spotted Flycatcher.

June–July: Breeding passerines.

August–November: Flocks of small mixed passerines roam the wood. Roosting pigeons, corvids and thrushes into winter.

9 PEGSDON HILLS

OS ref. TL 120 295

Habitat

Pegsdon Hills is one of the finest examples of a chalk downland habitat remaining in Bedfordshire today. It was purchased by the Wildlife Trust in 1992 following a public appeal and donations from various countryside and conservation bodies. The reserve covers 79 ha (195 acres) of which 25 ha (65 acres) is a SSSI. Much of the open downland is sheep-grazed, including the medieval cultivation terraces, known as lynchets, which are of archaeological interest, but outside the reserve boundary.

Scrub, hedgerows and a small woodland add to the biodiversity, but the most challenging aspect of the management plan is to restore an

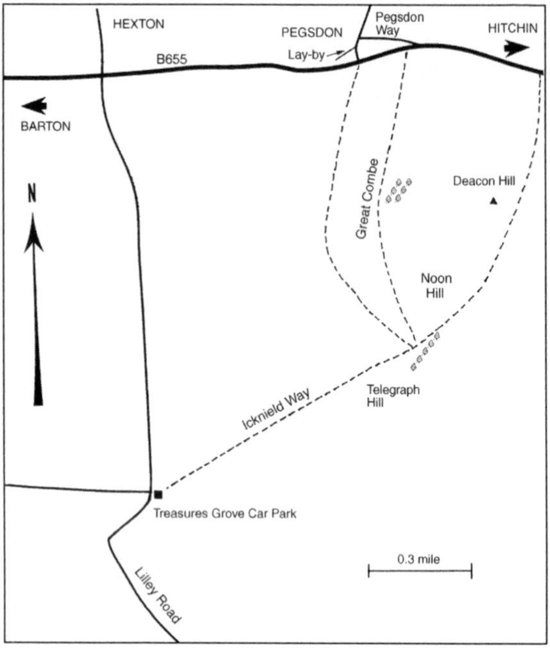

adjacent arable field to native grassland; a small area has been set aside to grow the flowering 'weeds' of arable land. Pegsdon Hills supports a rich variety of typical calcareous plants and their dependant insects; a visit one warm morning in June is recommended for the best results. On a fine day the view northwards across the Bedfordshire countryside from Deacon Hill is unparalleled, with the county town of Bedford and the Lower Greensand Ridge both visible in the distance.

Access

The reserve is located between Hitchin and Barton-le-Clay on the southern side of the B655 near the village of Pegsdon. Park considerately in Pegsdon Way, or in the small lay-by just off the T-junction. Carefully cross the busy B655 and read the information board, entering the reserve via the kissing gate. Follow the footpath towards the coombe and the various side tracks which lead up through the scrub; the ancient Icknield Way borders the southern side of the reserve and is a popular route with ramblers. A circular route is well-marked. Parking at the 'Treasures' Grove car park on the Lilley Road at TL 109 283 is only advisable early morning; evening car break-ins are commonplace. Follow the bridleway towards Telegraph Hill and beyond.

Species

In the 1960s the Great Combe at Pegsdon Hills was the last regular breeding site in Bedfordshire for Red-backed Shrike, with Stone Curlew occasionally nesting on the surrounding fields and open downland. Even though both are now long gone their ghosts linger on, and while there seems little chance of the former species returning, the latter has been noted on passage here and elsewhere on the chalk hills; a check on bean or pea fields is recommended during April and May when you might also find Dotterel. Lapwing have recently returned to breed on a prepared stony field on Noon Hill.

The combination of rough grass and scrub is attractive to resident birds of prey: Kestrel, Sparrowhawk, Common Buzzard, Little and Tawny Owls all breed in the vicinity and Barn Owl has been noted recently. The Long-eared Owl finds favour here too but is never easy to observe. Whether encountered at roost in winter, or in the breeding season, it should not be approached; unfortunately there have been several unsavoury instances over the years of disturbance from birders at this site. Both species of partridge haunt the arable fields while Meadow Pipit and Skylark are omnipresent, varying in numbers with the seasons. Corn Bunting are more likely to be found singing from exposed perches on nearby barley fields. The hills may initially appear to be an unlikely place to find woodpeckers but all three species have been recorded on site with the tiny Lesser Spotted the scarcest. Resident passerines can be found in the scrub including Marsh and Willow Tits, Bullfinch and the ever present Yellowhammer.

With the arrival of spring an increase in Meadow Pipit is noted as passage birds move through. Wheatear occur in small numbers on the open slopes while the occasional Ring Ouzel keeps closer to the hawthorn scrub. From mid-April onwards Swallow pass overhead along with wagtails and the first Tree Pipit and Cuckoo. Early Chiffchaff and Blackcap are followed by Willow Warbler, the commonest breeding species on the hills, and by the end of April the noisy scrub warblers arrive. Turtle Dove and Hobby are noted into May, with the latter species occasionally nesting in the area.

The summer months are dominated by breeding activity as the resident finches and migrant warblers raise multiple broods; declining numbers of 'purring' Turtle Dove profit from the weedy fields and thickets. Tree Pipit breed in the broken scrub along the steeper slopes and occasionally a Grasshopper Warbler will nest in a bramble patch. The small wood holds a pair or two of Spotted Flycatcher, and Woodcock often display over the wooded hillside; Redstart has bred once but is mainly a rare migrant. The liquid call of the Quail is also infrequently heard. Chattering flocks of Goldfinch and Linnet are a feature of late

Long-eared Owl

summer as the young feed on weed seeds, making obvious prey for hunting Sparrowhawk and Hobby.

The more protracted autumn passage attracts a few Whinchat, Stonechat and Wheatear to pause a while and often the sharp flight note of the Grey Wagtail can be heard among the passing Yellows. As the warblers fall silent, moult and surreptitiously depart for another year, the hills seem strangely quiet. October brings winter thrushes, finches, Goldcrest and Skylark moving through and the possibility of Common Buzzard drifting over from nearby woodland.

The winter months are mainly quiet with roving tit flocks foraging in the scrub, finches feeding on dead seed-heads and large flocks of Woodpigeon and Stock Dove on the open fields. Lapwing and the occasional group of Golden Plover also haunt the nearby arable land. The small mixed wood sometimes attracts Chaffinch and a few Brambling to feed, depending on the size of the beech mast crop, and Crossbill have been recorded in the pines. The scrub is home to roosting birds during the long winter nights, most noticeably Fieldfare, Redwing and Yellowhammer. Over the years at Pegsdon Hills and across the surrounding countryside, the occasional ringtail harrier and Short-eared Owl have occurred, but both are the exception to the rule. Common Buzzard, however, are regularly noted.

Calendar

Resident: Kestrel, Sparrowhawk, Common Buzzard, Grey and Red-legged Partridges, Stock Dove, Little, Tawny and Long-eared Owls, Green, Great Spotted and Lesser Spotted (rare) Woodpeckers, Skylark, Meadow Pipit, tits including Marsh and Willow, finches, Yellowhammer and Corn Bunting.

November–February: Lapwing and Golden Plover, possible Short-eared Owl, Hen Harrier and Merlin (rare), winter thrushes, roosting passerines, Goldcrest, occasional Brambling.

March–May: Meadow Pipit passage, Wheatear, Ring Ouzel (scarce), Swallow, warblers and finches on passage, Hobby, Turtle Dove, Cuckoo.

June–August: Breeding activity. Turtle Dove, warblers, finches (including Goldfinch, Linnet and Bullfinch), Yellow Wagtail, Grasshopper Warbler (rare), Tree Pipit, Spotted Flycatcher (scarce), Woodcock, hunting raptors, Quail (rare).

September–October: Whinchat, Stonechat (scarce), Wheatear, passage Skylark, warblers, Blackbird and winter thrushes, Goldcrest, finch and bunting flocks.

10 PRIORY COUNTRY PARK OS ref. TL 071 495

Habitat

Despite its close proximity to Bedford town centre, Priory Country Park, formerly known as Barkers Lane gravel pits, regularly attracts a wide range of birds within its 500 ha (200 acres), 200 ha of which are still water. The main feature is an old gravel pit combining well-vegetated margins of Phragmites and willows with fishing swims and an overgrown island. To the north-east corner of the lake are two smaller interconnecting finger lakes with much rank vegetation and dead timber, proving attractive to many forms of wildlife and ideal for ringing operations. A long hedgerow to the west borders a large open field with scattered trees and bushes. Elsewhere many clumps of sallow and other native trees have been planted with surrounding buffer zones of uncut grasses to form an attractive country park. There is a wheelchair-friendly hide set in a small reedbed on the southern side.

Sweeping around the southern half of the main lake is the River Great Ouse with varying bank cover and many fine old willows along the towpath. Meadows to the south at Fenlake frequently flood to varying degrees attracting, in winter, numbers of gulls and ducks. In summer the smaller lakes harbour many forms of aquatic insect life among the marshy patches. Mink, Fox and Muntjac are regularly noted and recently Otters have been seen along the river.

Restricted views across a sewage works and adjoining farmland completes the array of habitats. A newly installed cycle path leading to Willington is worthwhile exploring as it passes by a series of working gravel pits, known locally as Octagon Farm, which has Sand Martin colonies and attracts passage waders.

Access

The two main access points are on opposite sides of the lake, with ample car parking facilities at both; an additional overflow car park is available near the main entrance (turn left shortly after entering the park) for use at the busy weekend period. For immediate access to the lake take the A428 Goldington Road east from Bedford town centre, turning right after 2 km (1.25 miles) down Newham Avenue (A5140). Travel a further 0.75 km (0.5 mile) and turn left along Barkers Lane, between a garage and playing fields. Another 0.75 km (0.5 mile) and the entrance to the car park is on the right, over the New Cut bridge. Ahead in the large field is the visitors centre, where information sheets concerning nature trails and guided tours can be found, plus a shop and toilet facilities. A motorised 'Easy Rider' is available for the disabled at the centre. School parties and societies are catered for; anyone wishing further information should contact the Warden on 01234 211182. A chalkboard has the latest bird sightings regularly updated, and the annual bird report is available from the shop. Please report any unusual sightings to the visitors centre.

For the southern entrance near the river, head along the A603 Sandy road from Bedford turning left after 3 km (2 miles) at the roundabout (signposted) with the new A421 southern by-pass, directly opposite Cardington Cross. Once in the car park a series of footbridges will even-

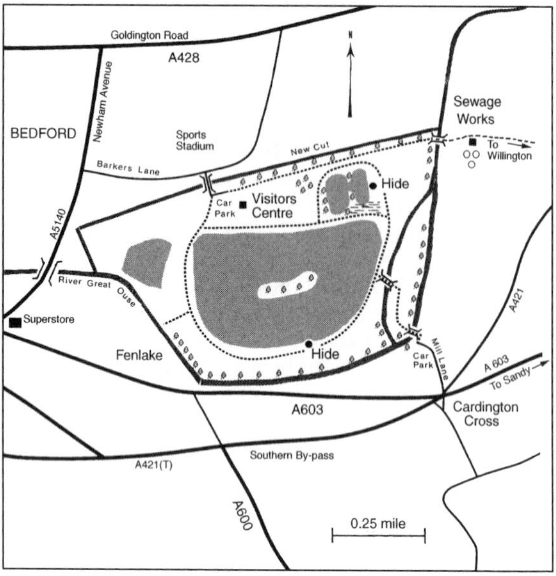

tually lead to the lake. Being a multi-recreational area many different water sports and pastimes are practised, e.g. canoeing, fishing and sailboarding. The park can be busy, particularly on warm summer days, making an early morning visit essential.

Species

This site's main virtue is a wide range of species on offer at all times of the year, especially in springtime; over 200 species have now been recorded in the park. Migrating birds seem to follow watercourses and the Great Ouse is no exception with the lake attracting passage waders for brief resting periods. However, lack of an exposed shingle spit or bar on the island means that most simply circle low over the water and then continue their journey. Nonetheless some do stop off occasionally around the shoreline or on undisturbed grassy areas surrounding the lake.

Winter wildfowl are most obvious on the main lake with varying numbers of Mallard, Pochard, Tufted Duck, Shoveler and Coot present throughout the season. Packs of noisy Wigeon come and go and a scattering of Gadwall are noted from late autumn into the new year. Small numbers of Goldeneye can be seen with Goosander more likely at the turn of the year. Scaup, Pintail and Smew are rare and Ferruginous Duck has wintered recently. When the meadows across the river at Fenlake flood small numbers of Snipe probe for worms, with Jack Snipe turning up rarely, normally towards spring. Dabbling duck such as Mallard and Teal sift through the vegetable matter, while the opportunist Black-headed Gull pester any Lapwing flocks. Similar conditions sometimes prevail between the two arms of the river near the sewage works. Great Crested Grebe (50 plus) and Little Grebe are regular in winter but other grebes are scarce and mainly recorded on passage. Grey Heron can be seen sentinel-like on the island all year round along with

Cormorant, which are present on most days. The marshier parts of the finger lakes suit the secretive Water Rail and once a Great Grey Shrike hunted this area preying heavily on small passerines. Wintering Chiffchaff are now a feature of the park. The sewage works is worth checking from the public footpath for finches and buntings, including Corn, with a chance of Stonechat. In recent winters large numbers of Lapwing and Golden Plover have congregated in the fields beyond the sewage works.

Chiffchaff and Wheatear are usually the first spring migrants on land with Sand Martin over the water. Into April and the tempo increases as Willow Warbler and Meadow Pipit pass through. Blue-headed and White Wagtails are sometimes recorded among the commoner Yellow and Pied Wagtails; however, flava wagtails are much less numerous nowadays. Thorough scrutiny of the pipit/wagtail flock is always challenging and can sometimes be rewarded with a Water Pipit; Grey-headed Wagtail has also been noted here.

Out on the lake terns start arriving, mostly Common with an occasional passage of Arctic and sporadically Little or Sandwich. Small groups of Black Tern tend to occur later in the season, particularly when the wind is from an easterly vector with rain. The highly oceanic Kittiwake and dainty tern-like Little Gull are noted just about annually. Hobby move in with the Swifts, and Osprey are becoming a regular feature during both passage periods.

Great Spotted and Green Woodpeckers both breed in the park and are regularly seen or heard. Kingfisher haunt the river along with Reed Bunting and Moorhen – Priory CP is one of the best places in the county for seeing Kingfisher. Back on the lake hirundines swarm over the surface and Common Sandpiper flit around the margin. Cuckoo return, along with good numbers of Reed Warbler, but the nervous Turtle Dove is in steep decline along with Spotted Flycatcher. The damp thickets around the finger lakes have increasingly attracted Nightingale in recent years.

Summer is a season of much disturbance by the public although an evening visit can be worthwhile as Hobby often dash in to hunt martins or dragonflies. Masses of Swift wheel and tumble overhead while riparian breeders busily feed their fledglings; there are particularly high breeding populations of Blackcap, Reed, Sedge, Garden and Willow Warblers. An Oystercatcher may fly over from nearby gravel pits where breeding has recently occurred and Grey Wagtail can be seen down by the slalom course feeding young.

A trickle of returning waders in late summer, such as Green Sandpiper and Greenshank, lead into a more protracted passage period with similar species to spring, though never as dynamic. A few Whinchat pass through and more Grey Wagtail are seen along the river or canoe course. Thrushes, tits and Goldcrest are typical late autumn birds with an overhead passage of Skylark, pipits and finches. Look out for wintering Redpoll and Siskin feeding on the riverside Alders.

Priory Country Park is a well watched site and thus has a habit of turning up county rarities. In recent years the following have been noted: Ferruginous Duck, Red-necked Phalarope, Caspian Tern, Bee-eater, Red-backed Shrike, Yellow-browed Warbler, Cetti's Warbler and Penduline Tit. Most remarkable of all, however, was one of the only inland records of Radde's Warbler, caught and ringed at the finger lakes in October 1991.

Calendar

Resident: Great Crested Grebe, Cormorant, Grey Heron, Kingfisher, Great Spotted and Green Woodpeckers, Grey Wagtail, tits, finches and buntings.

December–February: Grebe numbers increase, feral geese, Wigeon, Gadwall, Teal, Pintail, sawbills (other than Goosander) scarce, Shoveler, Tufted Duck, Goldeneye, Pochard, Water Rail, Snipe, Lapwing and Golden Plover, Stonechat, Goldcrest, Chiffchaff, winter thrushes.

March–May: Shelduck, common passage waders (mostly overhead), Little Gull, Kittiwake, Common and Arctic Terns (from April), Black Tern (May), hirundines, pipits and wagtails, Wheatear and Chiffchaff (from end March). Common warblers, Nightingale, Cuckoo, Reed Warbler, Hobby, chance of Osprey.

June–July: Breeding riparian species, sometimes Common Tern, Oystercatcher, hunting Hobby, Swift, returning waders.

August–November: Sandpipers, terns, wagtails, pipits, Whinchat, warblers depart, wildfowl increase in November, winter thrushes, passage Skylark and thrushes, Redpoll, Siskin, finches and Goldcrest.

11 STOCKGROVE COUNTRY PARK & RAMMAMERE HEATH

OS ref. SP 920 294

Habitat

Straddling the Beds./Bucks. border, on the Greensand Ridge, this large block of mixed woodland is owned and managed by the local authority and the Greensand Trust. The heavily used country park to the south of the Brickhill Road has an ornamental lake and brook complete with visitors centre, toilets and a tearoom (open at weekends and Bank Holidays). The deciduous Bakers Wood complements nearby pine plantations and open parkland with gorse and scrub.

North of the Brickhill Road is Kings Wood National Nature Reserve, a mixed semi-natural woodland and, the jewel in the crown, due to much hard work by the Greensand Project Group, Rammamere Heath, a classic greensand heath with heather and Birch scrub. The heath is on a slope affording good views across the canopy of Bakers and Kings Woods.

Access

Stockgrove Country Park is situated at Heath and Reach, just north of Leighton Buzzard. Take Woburn Road out of town and turn left into Brickhill Road; the country park is 1 km (0.75 mile) on the left. Park by

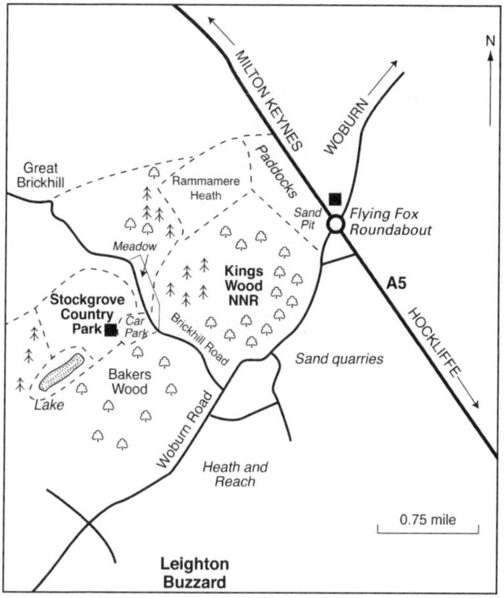

the visitors centre in the car park, or along the lane if full. A network of paths gives good access north and south of the Brickhill Road. From the A5 turn south at the Flying Fox roundabout and follow the signs to the country park off the Woburn Road.

Species

Most birders visit Stockgrove in winter for the large flock of Mandarin Duck present on the ornamental lake, where counts of 50 plus are regularly noted, amongst the Moorhen and Coot. The track down to the lake is good for finches, Nuthatch and tits, including Marsh Tit, attracted to food laid out on fence posts. Willow Tit are now rare with Kings Wood being the best area. All three species of woodpecker are present but, as always, Lesser Spotted is the most difficult, the best chance of detecting one being in late winter when drumming commences. The Alders around the bridge can attract Redpoll, Siskin and Goldfinch, while in a good year Crossbill can be found just about anywhere, the pines near the car park being a good spot in the past. Woodcock, Tawny Owl and Stock Dove are all resident and the farmland to the north is worth checking for Little Owl, Lapwing, Skylark, winter thrushes and partridges.

On a still spring morning the top of Rammamere Heath is a good vantage point to watch for displaying raptors. Sparrowhawk, Kestrel and Common Buzzard are most likely with a reasonable chance of Goshawk and from May onwards, Hobby. The heath regularly attracts a passing Woodlark, where they have bred in the past, and several pairs of Tree Pipit. Linnet, Bullfinch, Yellowhammer, Reed Bunting and Mistle Thrush all breed on site. By late April most of the spring migrants have arrived, including the warbler tribe. Willow Warbler and Whitethroat are most common followed by Blackcap, Chiffchaff, Garden Warbler and small numbers of Lesser Whitethroat. Wood Warbler and Redstart

Woodlark

are occasional visitors and Firecrest have been noted. Spotted Flycatcher is now scarce but a few pairs can still be found in Bakers Wood.

Stockgrove Country Park is very busy with picnickers during the summer and is best visited as early in the day as possible. An evening visit is worthwhile too as the heath may yield a hunting Hobby or, with future management, a Nightjar. Turtle Dove are occasionally seen on the farmland where wire fencing can attract a passage Whinchat.

The autumn period is generally quiet with the resident species flocking together and large flocks of pigeons and corvids using the conifers to roost.

Calendar

Resident: Mandarin Duck, Sparrowhawk, Kestrel, Common Buzzard, Moorhen, Coot, Woodcock, Stock Dove, Tawny and Little Owls, three woodpeckers, Mistle Thrush, Jay, Jackdaw, Nuthatch, Treecreeper, tits (including Marsh and Willow), Goldcrest, finches and buntings.

December–February: Mandarin flock, Skylark, Meadow Pipit, winter thrushes, Redpoll, Siskin and Crossbill.

March–May: Displaying raptors, Hobby, Woodlark, Tree Pipit, warblers, Spotted Flycatcher, occasional Wood Warbler and Redstart.

June–August: Summer breeders, chance of Nightjar and Turtle Dove.

September–November: Tit flocks, thrushes, Goldcrest, roosting pigeons and corvids.

12 STRAWBERRY HILL FARM, KNOTTING GREEN

OS ref. TL 005 626

Habitat

Set amongst the intensively farmed arable lands of north Bedfordshire this incredible site evokes memories of the 1930's farming depression. During the early 1990s the local farmer signed on to a 20-year set-aside plan, under the Countryside Stewardship Scheme, and 142 ha (350 acres) of prime farmland was removed from cereal production. Various governmental and conservation bodies monitor the regeneration process, which if left unchecked, will result in long-term tree cover.

Land drains have been blocked, forming boggy areas adjacent to a small brook and grasses left uncut. Despite some scrub growth the farm is primarily grassland, bordered with banks, hedgerows, and paddocks near the buildings. In summer the fields are ablaze with wild flowers, including large stands of teazel, while in winter the dead grasses and seed-heads attract a wealth of wildlife. There are several mature Oak and Ash trees in surrounding boundaries.

Access

The farm is situated in the tiny hamlet of Knotting Green just south of the Northamptonshire border. Take the signposted lane to Knotting off the A6 and after 1.6 km (1 mile) park between the first house on the right and Strawberry Hill Farm, near the red telephone box. A well-worn public footpath, by the paddock, leads out into the field. Although there

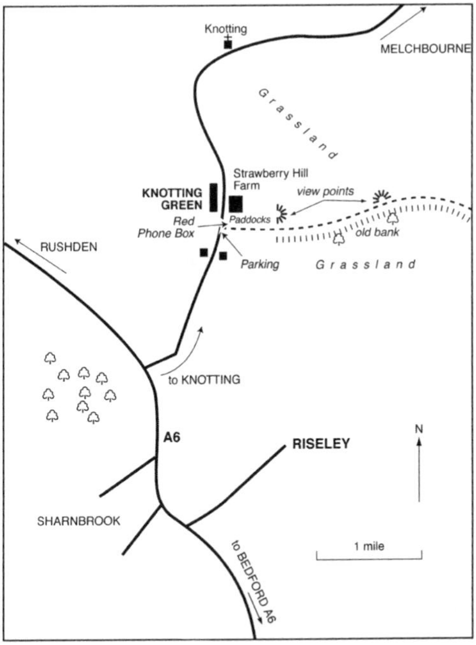

is a network of footpaths crossing the farmland, most birders simply walk ten minutes or so to the first old Oak tree along the bank, as this causes less disturbance, and scan the grassland vista. There are few spots quite like it in the barley belt of southern England, where a birder can stand and be surrounded by a sea of unimproved grassland.

Species

Although primarily a winter site for birds of prey, a visit at any time of year is worthwhile providing the weather is relatively dry and still; avoid wet and windy days. Barn Owls are omnipresent with one or two pairs breeding in the old farm buildings. They leave their roost at dusk and can often be seen flighting over the paddock before moving out across the grass to hunt. Having a protracted breeding season owls often occur in broad daylight in order to hunt rodents for hungry owlets, particularly in the summer.

Little Owl can sometimes be seen on fence posts around the farm, but a resident Tawny Owl is far more difficult to observe. Most winters bring a Short-eared Owl and in some years, probably related to vole numbers, a small group may be present hunting over the fields on bright winter afternoons. Hen Harrier and Merlin are rare, but almost annual visitors, in contrast to the resident Sparrowhawk and, at times numerous Kestrel. Other winter raptors that have occurred are Peregrine and Common Buzzard.

With the abundance of weed seed, large flocks of Goldfinch are attracted to teazel and thistle, while Linnet, Yellowhammer, Reed and Corn Buntings all feed and roost locally. Stonechat are visible on calm days perched atop umbellifers and Bullfinch move furtively through the roadside scrub. Both species of partridge are present with the Red-legged more likely to be seen running along the main track. Winter thrushes visit periodically while Skylark and Meadow Pipit are present all year. Strangely, in such an open habitat, Green and Great Spotted Woodpeckers are regularly noted.

Chiffchaff and Wheatear are typical spring harbingers while loose

Hen Harrier

flocks of Meadow Pipit pass overhead. During April Swallow arrive and are soon nesting around the farm buildings. The resident finches, buntings and Skylark all breed in good numbers but it is when the warblers arrive that the site really comes alive. Whitethroat is the most common, followed by Lesser Whitethroat, Sedge and Willow Warblers. Grasshopper Warbler can be heard singing from the damper patches and the Stonechat are replaced by a May Whinchat passage.

Summer is worth a visit to experience the good numbers of breeding birds, particularly our former common farmland species such as Skylark and Linnet. Cuckoo are attracted to parasitise the nesting Meadow Pipit, and Turtle Dove can still be heard 'purring' from hedgerow cover. Around the farm buildings a pair of Spotted Flycatcher usually find safe refuge. Hobby hunt over the grassland and most years Quail are present. Recent exciting developments have been the presence of Curlew as a potential coloniser.

By autumn the grassland seeds attract large numbers of finches and buntings, with attendant raptors, while overhead Lapwing are on the move. Any sparrow flocks should be checked for the, now rare, Tree Sparrow. Tit flocks and Goldcrest can be found around the paddock scrub and chats return to the grassland.

Calendar

Resident: Sparrowhawk, Kestrel, Stock Dove, Barn, Tawny and Little Owls, Grey and Red-legged Partridges, Green and Great Spotted Woodpeckers, Skylark, Meadow Pipit, Mistle Thrush, tits, finches and buntings.

November–February: Short-eared Owl, chance of Hen Harrier and Merlin, winter thrushes, Stonechat, Yellowhammer, Goldfinch, Linnet, Reed and Corn Buntings.

March–May: Hirundines, Wheatear, Whinchat, Whitethroat, Sedge and Grasshopper Warblers.

June–August: Breeding farmland birds, Curlew, Turtle Dove, Hobby, Cuckoo, Quail, Barn Owl active in late afternoon.

September–October: Passage of finches, Skylark, Meadow Pipit, Stonechat and Whinchat, chance of Common Buzzard.

13 THE LODGE

OS ref. TL 188 478

Habitat

The headquarters of the RSPB is situated in one of Bedfordshire's finest examples of lowland heath to have survived the ravages of the twentieth century. The site has been managed to allow a good selection of both animal and plant life to prosper and is justifiably rated a SSSI.

As part of Sandy Warren, this 42 ha (104 acre) reserve's most precious asset is its relict heathland. Here, heather is allowed to flourish alongside fine small grasses and bracken, although the latter is controlled to prevent it smothering the entire heath. Heathland is also being recreated, where pine plantations have been removed. The woodlands vary from areas of native Oak, Birch and Scots Pine to several small conifer plantations. The more formal gardens in front of the house abound with exotic trees and shrubs making ideal roost sites in winter.

Water is a scarce commodity on heathland so the construction of several small pools, one of which is overlooked by a hide, adds an important element to the reserve's habitats.

Among the mammals are a variety of rodents, including the unusual Yellow-necked Mouse and two colonies of Long-eared Bat. Through the summer months Grass Snake and Common Lizard can be noted on ponds and heath respectively; the reserve also supports a small population of reintroduced Natterjack Toad. The Purple Hairstreak butterfly occurs around the Oak canopy, and in the garden many more species are attracted to the Buddleias. Dragonflies and damselflies are often abundant in the summer.

Biggleswade Common to the south of the reserve is worthy of exploration for a variety of farmland birds.

Access

The Lodge lies 2.5 km (1.5 miles) south-east of the small town of Sandy (east of the A1) on the B1042 Sandy to Cambridge road. Approaching from the town, turn right at the reserve signpost. The car park is on the left after 50 m. The chalet-style building at the entrance houses the shop, reception and information centre. A number of well-marked nature trails are laid out, one with an accessible hide suitable for disabled visitors. There is also a picnic area and toilets. Parking for the disabled is available further down the drive near the main building.

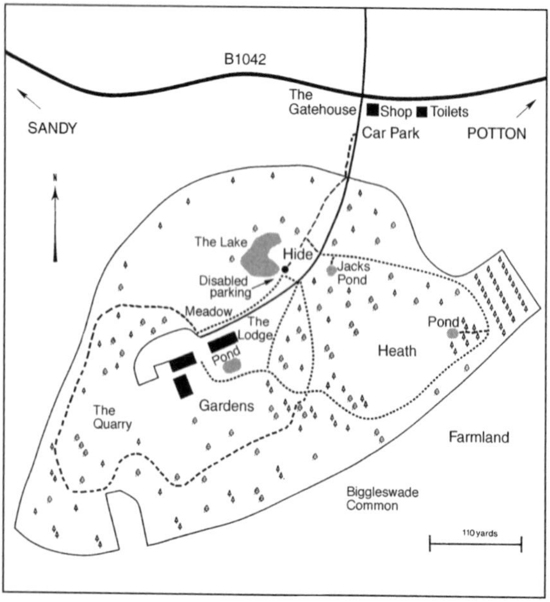

Winter Thrushes

The reserve is open all year from dawn to dusk. The shop is open from 09:00 until 17:00 hrs on weekdays and 10:00 until 17:00 hrs at weekends.

Species

Resident passerines abound at The Lodge making it an ideal site for the beginner to learn the basics of bird identification. The plantations and other scattered conifers attract good numbers of Coal Tit and Goldcrest, both birds typically associated with the Lower Greensand Ridge. Occasionally Crossbill occur, usually in small parties but more regularly Siskin and Redpoll are noted, especially in winter, sometimes drinking at Jack-'s Pond. At this time of year the available cover is exploited at dusk with finches and thrushes streaming in to roost in thick evergreen shrubs such as rhododendron; while Meadow Pipit prefer ground cover on the heath. Common Buzzard, Sparrowhawk and Kestrel are all resident.

Spring is an ideal time for watching woodpeckers, as all three species are at their most vocal. Green Woodpecker can often be seen bounding across the heath, while the two spotted woodpeckers 'drum' from dead timber; the Lesser Spotted is very elusive, but in recent years a pair have bred near the car park. Nest boxes are strategically positioned around the reserve and, in the breeding season, the majority are tenanted by Blue and Great Tits as well as Nuthatch, which characteristically plaster mud around the entrance hole as if it were a natural cavity. The thin call of Treecreeper is commonly heard as it spirals, mouse-like, up a tree trunk, extracting insects from the bark with its fine bill.

Our familiar songsters are soon joined by summer visiting warblers and the woodlands are quickly alive with their song. Blackcap and Garden Warbler are present in good numbers amongst the canopy, while Whitethroat can be found on heathland scrub and adjoining farmland hedgerows. The occasional Nightingale may be heard on Biggleswade Common to the south. Chiffchaff and Willow Warbler are numerous, the latter more so, but Wood Warbler is only recorded as a rare passage migrant. Tree Pipit arrive, song-flighting from isolated pines while Redpoll chatter overhead in search of nest sites high up in conifers. At dusk Woodcock display over the treetops and Tawny Owl can be heard. Hobby are regularly noted on the reserve and nest on adjacent farmland. Cuckoo parasitise common woodland birds, while the final long distance migrant to arrive, the Spotted Flycatcher, can still be found around the gardens, although in ever decreasing numbers. The scarce Firecrest has also bred.

The lake merits attention during the summer as birds come down to drink, especially pigeons and doves. A passing Grey Heron may be present or even a Kingfisher. More likely are pairs of breeding Moorhen and Mallard leading their obedient offspring in search of food. In late summer, if there is exposed mud, a migrating Green Sandpiper or Snipe might drop in to feed, while hirundines hawk low over the water for insects.

As the summer passerines depart and tits flock together, finches feed on the abundant weed seeds. With autumn well under way the first winter thrushes arrive, sometimes feeding on the lawn, but most passing overhead. Great Grey Shrike have wintered in the past, ranging over Biggleswade Common and along the old railway line. Flocks of Chaffinch are joined by small numbers of Brambling in search of food among the leaf-litter, their numbers varying annually.

The Lodge is best in spring when the full flavour of a greensand wooded heath can be appreciated, with perhaps a winter visit for finches and the chance of Crossbill. The likelihood of a rarity is remote, but an impressive number of species of raptor have been recorded flying over including Osprey, Honey Buzzard and Marsh Harrier.

Calendar

Resident: Grey Heron occasional visitor, Mallard, Common Buzzard, Sparrowhawk, Kestrel, partridges on farmland, Moorhen, Woodcock, Stock Dove, Tawny Owl, Kingfisher occasional, Green and Spotted Woodpeckers, Jackdaw, Jay, tits, Nuthatch, Treecreeper, Mistle Thrush, Goldcrest, finches including Redpoll.

December–February: Roosting passerines at dusk, Meadow Pipit, tit flocks, occasional winter raptors and Great Grey Shrike, Siskin and Brambling, winter thrushes, Crossbill occasionally.

March–May: Common warblers, Hobby, passing Wood Warbler. Tree Pipit, Cuckoo, Turtle Dove, hirundines, occasional chat or Wheatear on farmland, Spotted Flycatcher from mid-May.

June–July: Breeding passerines.

August–November: Snipe and Green Sandpiper on lake if muddy. Masses of juvenile tits, warblers and finches, occasional passage Pied Flycatcher and Redstart.

14 WARDEN & GALLEY HILLS NATURE RESERVE

OS ref. TL 091 261

Habitat

Situated on the northern outskirts of Luton, Warden and Galley Hills, the former rising to 195 m (640 ft), have still managed to retain some of their downland mystique. The Hills are owned by Luton Borough Council and managed for wildlife by Luton Museum Service. Sheep-grazing has been reintroduced on Galley Hill after a gap, benefiting the calcareous plants and dependant insects. The Hawthorn scrub is kept in check by local conservation groups and the Museum Service throughout the winter months. The eastern dip-slope is arable land and of limited interest. The South Bedfordshire Golf Course to the west adds to the variety of habitats with clumps of trees and open fairways. North of the old Icknield Way the scene is open farmland with a small stand of conifers tucked in by Galley Hill. The area was renotified as a SSSI in 1986 and the reserve lies within the Chilterns Area of Outstanding Natural Beauty.

Brown Hares are still relatively abundant on hill and field alike and it is not unusual to see 10 to 20 performing on the open 'prairies' towards the A6. A visit to the nearby John Dony Field Centre in Hancock Drive, Bushmead is recommended, where a photographic display and a large scale topographical model of the area can be viewed. The centre is open from 09:30 to 16.45 hrs weekdays, and 09:30 to 13.00 hrs on Sundays.

Access

Head north out of Luton along the A6 turning right after 3 km (2 miles) down Warden Hill Road. Park at the top of the road in a small pull-in near the entrance to Cardinal Newman School. Access onto the hills is unrestricted with many well-trodden tracks criss-crossing the site. A couple of footpaths bisect fairways on the golf course, so beware of low flying golf balls!

An alternative route to Galley Hill is to carry on north along the A6 to the Streatley roundabout and turn right towards Hexton. Drive for 2 km (1.25 miles) and park near an old farm track on the right. This runs south towards the plantation, crossing the Icknield Way near Galley Hill. For a more adventurous hike the ancient Britons' road can be followed north-east across the county boundary with Hertfordshire to Deacon Hill south of Pegsdon.

Species

The Hills are indeed desolate-looking in the dead of winter when most bird activity is centred around the golf course and on the fields adjoining New Farm. Coveys of both Grey and Red-legged Partridges can be seen scratching about in the winter barley or oil-seed rape, with large numbers of Feral Pigeon and Woodpigeon, a scattering of the more compact Stock Dove and the inevitable Collared Dove. Large flocks of Lapwing and smaller numbers of Golden Plover feed undisturbed except when harried by passing Black-headed Gulls. Corn Bunting are resident with occasional small groups; this nationally declining species is still relatively common on the open farmland surrounding the

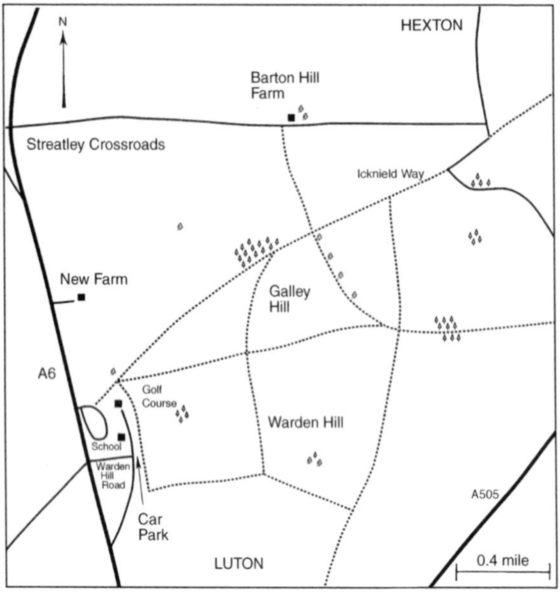

reserve. They usually form part of a larger mixed flock of Yellowhammer, Greenfinch, Linnet and the occasional Reed Bunting. The latter have recently taken to breeding away from wetland sites and a pair or two sometimes remain in the fields behind Galley Hill. Sparrow and finch flocks should be checked out for Tree Sparrow, nowadays more in hope than expectation.

Raptors are often reported along the whole range of hills from Luton to Pirton, and no doubt with increased coverage many more would be found. The resident Kestrel and Sparrowhawk are sometimes joined in winter by a Common Buzzard or more rarely a Goshawk or ring-tailed harrier. Little Owl hunt over the golf course and farmland while Tawny are more common further north around wooded Hexton.

Migrants pass along the ridge in spring making this site potentially as exciting as Blow's Downs. Although more difficult to work, regular watchers are rewarded with small numbers of Wheatear on the fairways and occasional Black Redstart and Ring Ouzel on the hilltops. The usual passage of warblers occurs with many Willow Warbler and a few Whitethroat staying to breed. Variable numbers of Meadow and Tree Pipits can be expected, the former regularly breeding, the latter sporadically. Quail are irregular visitors in late spring to the surrounding fields of barley, when their presence is betrayed by a distinctive and highly ventriloquial, trisyllabic whistle. Eared owls are rarely noted and Long-eared Owl occasionally nested during the 1990s.

The summer period is busy for breeding passerines such as Skylark, pipits, buntings and finches. Being close to Luton, Warden Hill is popular with walkers on warm summer days making a birdwatching visit inadvisable.

Autumn passage is typical of much of the Chiltern Hills from the August build-up of warblers and the chance of Whinchat, to November winter thrushes. Rain and mist during October can bring with it a fall of common migrants such as thrushes, chats, Meadow Pipit and Goldcrest.

Warden Hill, and particularly the downs running north-east to Pirton, are underwatched, thus presenting the pioneering birder in search of pastures new a genuine challenge.

Calendar

Resident: Sparrowhawk, Kestrel, Red-legged and Grey Partridges, Tawny and Little Owls, Skylark, common finches, Corn Bunting, Yellowhammer, Reed Bunting.

December–February: Possible winter raptors, eared owls, Lapwing, Golden Plover, pigeon and dove flocks.

March–May: Wheatear, possible Black Redstart and Ring Ouzel, Meadow and Tree Pipits, Cuckoo, Willow Warbler, Whitethroat, hirundines.

June–July: Quail late May to early June (irregular), breeding passerines.

August–November: Sylvia warblers and Whinchat in August, pipits, Goldcrest, winter thrushes October–November.

15 WEST WOBURN WOODS

OS ref: SP 925 337 (Wavendon Heath car park)

Habitat

West Woburn Woods is the collective name for a large block of mixed woodland straddling the Beds./Bucks. border on the Greensand Ridge. The main birding areas are Wavendon Heath, Charle, Back, Buttermilk and Lowes Woods. Conifer plantations comprise the majority of the woodland but there are some decent broadleaf stands at Charle Wood. The ever expanding Woburn golf course is at the centre of the complex and there is little remaining heathland.

Wavendon Heath is primarily coniferous, but with regular clear-felling briefly creating a more heath-like habitat. A series of derelict ponds is important in dry weather and the sandy soil makes for a good show of broom during the spring.

Charle Wood is now largely fragmented by the recent extension to the golf course but has retained some of its older trees. South of the lane the mixed plantations of Buttermilk and Lowes Woods harbour a fast declining population of Lady Amherst's Pheasant. Adjacent farmland, if left as stubble, can be good for winter finch flocks.

Access

The complex is sandwiched between Little Brickhill on the A5 and Woburn on the A5130. For Wavendon Heath either park at the top of Church Lane, Aspley Heath or in the car park along the lane to the golf course off the Woburn Road, where a network of paths leads through

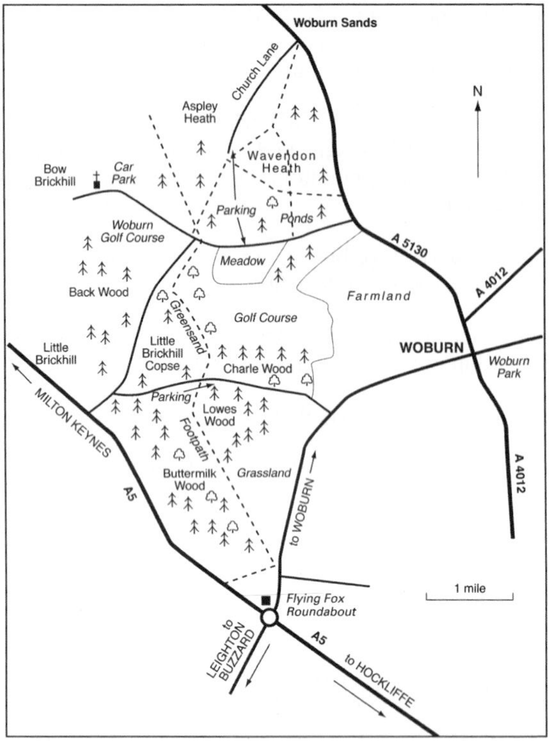

the woodlands. Back Wood can be worked from the car park near Bow Brickhill church.

For Charle, Lowes and Buttermilk Woods park in the lay-by on the county boundary at SP 925 328 and follow the footpath signs. This is particularly important south of the lane where the Greensand Ridge path runs through the private Lowes and Buttermilk Woods. There have been a number of unsavoury incidents over the years between visiting birders and a local gamekeeper. Avoid visiting on Saturdays during the shooting season from November–February.

Species

The main species sought after in the West Woburn Woods is the elusive and declining Lady Amherst's Pheasant where there are probably no more than ten calling males. The best area to search is from the Greensand Ridge path which bisects Buttermilk and Lowes Woods. Scan from the crossroads during early morning or evening and check every pheasant that comes into view. Back Wood and Wavendon Heath have one or two males with a few more scattered across Charle Wood and the golf course. Do not bother to visit on wet days or from May to October when the vegetation is too tall.

Winter holds the usual mixed flocks of tits, finches, Treecreeper, Nuthatch and Goldcrest. Both species of black-capped tit occur as do all three woodpeckers; although, typically, Willow Tit and Lesser Spotted Woodpecker are difficult to find. Woodcock are regularly flushed from the woodland floor, Brambling visit in variable numbers feeding on beech mast with Chaffinch in Charle Wood.

In early spring high ground at Wavendon Heath is worth scanning for raptors over the canopy. Sparrowhawk and Kestrel are common with increasing sightings of Common Buzzard and Goshawk. A migrant Woodlark may pause on any clear-felled areas and Redpoll can be expected 'buzzing' overhead. Woodpeckers are busy establishing territories by drumming and Mistle Thrush song rings out across the trees. Scrub and leaf warblers move in from mid-April and there is still a slim chance of a Grasshopper Warbler in the damper plantations of Buttermilk Wood.

The new plantations at Wavendon and Lowes Wood are good for breeding Linnet, Yellowhammer and Reed Bunting, while the small population of Tree Pipit may attract a summering Cuckoo. Wood Warbler has irregularly summered in Birch trees near Aspley Heath and Redstart are thinly scattered across the woods with a preference for the older pines in Charle Wood; Spotted Flycatcher are now scarce everywhere. On the heath watch out for overhead Sand Martin that nest in the sand quarry across the Woburn Road. Long-eared Owl and Nightjar have bred in the past and may return in the future.

Autumn is generally a quiet time of year but Tawny Owl can be highly vocal as young birds disperse to find a territory. Large numbers of pigeons roost in the woods and Crossbill may appear. Woodcock numbers are at a peak with the arrival of continental migrants.

Calendar

Resident: Sparrowhawk, Kestrel, Common Buzzard, Goshawk, Lady Amherst's Pheasant, Woodcock, Stock Dove, Tawny Owl, possible Long-eared Owl, Green, Great Spotted and Lesser Spotted Woodpeckers, Skylark, Mistle Thrush, Goldcrest, tits (including Willow and Marsh), Nuthatch, Treecreeper, Redpoll, Yellowhammer and Reed Bunting.

November–February: Winter thrushes, mixed passerine flocks, Brambling, Siskin.

March–May: Cuckoo, Woodlark (scarce), Sand Martin, Tree Pipit, Redstart, leaf and scrub warblers, chance of Wood and Grasshopper Warblers.

Lady Amherst's Pheasant

June–July: Hobby, Nightjar (occasionally), Spotted Flycatcher.

August–October: Roosting pigeons, chance of Crossbill, migrant Woodcock.

16 WILLINGTON GRAVEL PITS

OS ref: TL 105 502 (car park)

Habitat

A series of working and exhausted gravel pits in the Ouse valley 3.5 km (2 miles) east of Bedford which is linked by a cycle track and public footpath (Bedford to Sandy Country Way) from Priory Country Park. Surrounded by a screen of windbreak poplars, some of the pits have small islands and reedbeds and there is plenty of shallow edge habitat for waders. A large, open sheep-grazed field contrasts with lush summer growth along an arm of the Great Ouse.

Willington Dovecote, owned by the National Trust, backs on to market garden land, alongside a churchyard and rural gardens. There is another chain of pits, known as Octagon Farm, to the west plus more arable farmland; in all, the cross section of habitats makes for a wide variety of species. Visit in early May for a list of around 80 species.

Access

From the A421, Bedford southern by-pass, take the A603 east towards Sandy and turn left after 3.5 km (2 miles) down Balls Lane signposted Willington loop road. At the T-junction turn left and park near the dovecote in Church Lane; there is a small car park at the end of the lane which only holds two cars.

Access across Willington Gravel Pits is restricted but most of the site can be adequately viewed from footpaths; birders should not encroach upon the sheep fold. A fisherman's path which runs close to the main pit affords elevated views, from a mound on the southern flank, over the lake. The track skirts around the western and northern shores of the lake and although strictly speaking out of bounds, most fisherman are tolerant of birdwatchers.

Species

Willington Gravel Pits is one of the best wetlands in Bedfordshire for wildfowl and waders and holds something of interest throughout the year. 'Trapped' in the Ouse watercourse between two 'A' roads any future housing development is unlikely, although further pits could spring up just about anywhere. The site has a long list of county rarities and an established history of Barn Owls inhabiting the Tudor dovecote.

The mound is a good vantage point for scanning wintering wildfowl on the main lake, with Shoveler, Gadwall and Goldeneye amongst the common diving ducks, Coot, Little and Great Crested Grebes and Cormorant. Rare grebes such as Red-necked have occurred while Smew

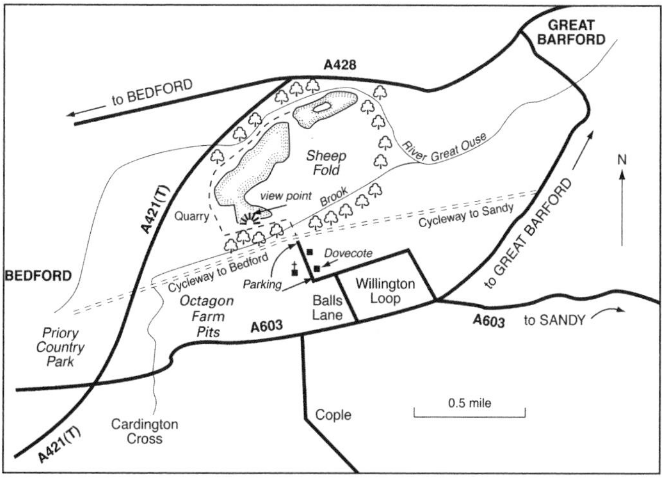

and Goosander appear most winters. A large flock of whistling Wigeon, Teal and feral geese graze the field, the latter comprising mainly Canada and Greylag with the odd feral Barnacle or White-front in their ranks. Wild swans are rarely noted here at either end of the winter periods. Golden Plover and Lapwing move up and down the valley but eventually end up on the field at some stage during the day, alongside winter thrushes, Skylark, Linnet and Meadow Pipit. All three buntings are resident but Corn Bunting is in decline.

Snipe can be flushed from any damp patch while Green and Common Sandpipers have wintered around the main lake. Scan from the bridge over the stream for Siskin, Redpoll and Goldfinch in the Alders and Kingfisher and Grey Wagtail along the river. Tit and finch flocks can usually be seen from here plus the two common woodpeckers.

Spring passage commences in early March with the arrival of Sand Martin which stay to breed in large colonies around the workings. Pipit numbers increase and should be checked for Rock or Water Pipit as a number of the former have been noted recently. Shelduck, Chiffchaff and Wheatear appear on lake, wood and field respectively whilst Little Ringed Plover and Redshank quickly establish territories. A few pairs of Lapwing nest on the field and Oystercatcher has been a recent addition to the breeding list. Ringed Plover, Common Sandpiper, Greenshank and Dunlin are regular on passage with a late spring rarity such as Sanderling, Turnstone or a godwit typical.

By early May hirundines and Swift swarm over the lake, Yellow Wagtail feed among the sheep, Common Tern are busy fishing after their long migration and Hobby arrive. All the common warblers are represented including Grasshopper Warbler (listen from the bridge), and Nightingale are heard most years. Cuckoo are vocal until midsummer and a few Turtle Dove can be found on the market garden fields. When weather conditions are favourable Black Tern can be expected.

Summer birding is all about breeding activity plus the chance of a rare early/late wader. At dusk wait by the dovecote for Barn Owls exiting the top slats to hunt. They often leave in broad daylight when feeding well-grown owlets. An evening stroll by the lake is a delight with

Barn Owl

warblers busily feeding nestlings, terns carrying fish and Sand Martin twittering at nest holes.

Autumn waders include good numbers of Greenshank, Common and Green Sandpipers with a chance of Little Stint or something rarer. Lapwing and Golden Plover return to the sheepfold and terns move down the valley. Winter wildfowl return and by October thrushes, larks, pipits, wagtails and pigeons are passing overhead.

Willington Gravel Pits is quite simply one of the best birdwatching sites in Bedfordshire and, being relatively underwatched, has much still to offer.

Calendar

Resident: Great Crested and Little Grebes, Cormorant, Greylag Goose, Grey Heron, Shoveler, Gadwall, Tufted Duck, Sparrowhawk, Kestrel, partridges, Stock Dove, Barn Owl, Kingfisher, Green and Great Spotted Woodpeckers, Skylark, Meadow Pipit, Grey Wagtail, Mistle Thrush, Treecreeper, tits, finches and buntings including Redpoll, Bullfinch and Corn Bunting.

December–February: Wildfowl peak, Goldeneye, Pochard, Wigeon, Teal, chance of Smew, Goosander, rare grebe, feral geese, Snipe, Golden Plover, Lapwing, Green Sandpiper, gulls, Redwing and Fieldfare.

March–May: Shelduck, Hobby, Oystercatcher, Little Ringed and Ringed Plovers, Dunlin, Redshank, Greenshank, Common Sandpiper, rare passage waders, Common and Black Terns, Cuckoo, Turtle Dove, Swift, Sand Martin, wagtails and pipits, Wheatear, Nightingale, warblers including Grasshopper Warbler.

June–September: Moulting ducks and geese, Lapwing, passage waders, sandpipers, Greenshank, departing Swift, hirundines and Hobby, Wheatear, Whinchat, warblers, pipits and wagtails on passage.

October–November: Returning wildfowl, plovers, terns, gulls, finches and buntings, winter thrushes.

17 WOBURN PARK

OS ref. SP 951 332 (car park)

Habitat

The small Georgian town of Woburn is acknowledged as one of the most important historic towns in England; the nearby Abbey has been the home of the Dukes of Bedford for over 350 years. The 1400 ha (3,000 acre) deer park is predominantly a mixture of grassland, managed by grazing, interspersed with woodland belts and stands of ancient parkland Oaks. Several lakes and ponds, some tree-fringed and with islands, are scattered throughout the site, the most important being Basin Pond, Eversholt Lake and Drakelow Ponds, the latter sometimes have muddy margins in late summer.

There are six species of deer in the park including the world's largest breeding herd of Pere David's Deer, and the tiny Muntjac which has colonised much of southern England through escapes from Woburn. Whatever time of year, Woburn Park must rate as one of the most beautiful areas to birdwatch in the entire region.

Access

Woburn Park is situated between the M1 and the A5, just south-east of Milton Keynes. From the A5 at Hockliffe take the A4012 towards Woburn and park in the car park in Park Street, opposite the church; from junction 13 of the M1 approach via Husborne Crawley on the A4012. Approaching from Hockliffe there is also limited parking in the lay-by at Ivy Lodge; care should be taken here as the traffic speed is invariably fast. From the car park opposite the church turn right towards a gatehouse, cross over the cattle grid and scan the Drakelow Ponds either side of the road; a waymarked footpath by the gatehouse passes to the rear of one of the ponds and through an open wooded area.

The main access point to the Park is at Ivy Lodge where all the good

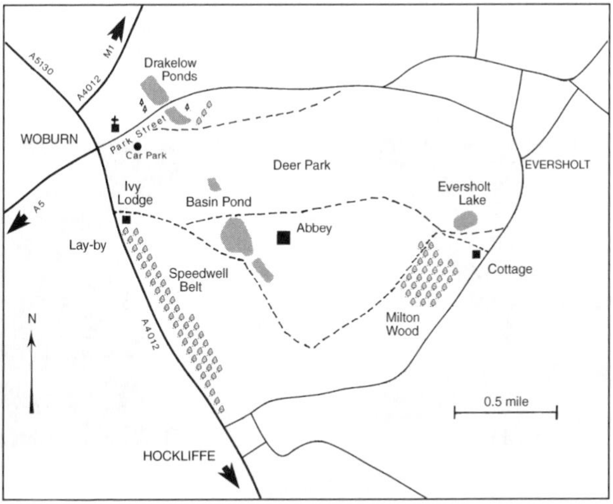

birding locations can be viewed from public footpaths: Speedwell Belt, Basin Pond, Milton Wood and Eversholt Lake. For a brief visit to the latter lake, park carefully in Eversholt village and walk back along the lane picking up the footpath by the old Tudor cottage. Woburn Park is far more accessible today than in former times but the birdwatcher should be reminded of the importance of staying on the waymarked trails, as many of the woods are private and there is game shooting in the winter period.

When parked opposite the church take time out to visit the Parish Church of St. Mary The Virgin across the road, where a magnificent stained glass window depicting 58 species of bird ('all that were to be found in the Park') commemorates the life of Mary, Duchess of Bedford, 1865-1937, who was an eminent ornithologist of her time. A postcard of the window is available from the church.

Species

The key species that most local birders visit Woburn for are the naturalised Mandarin Duck and the winter visiting Goosander. There is a resident population of anything up to 50 Mandarin Duck and normally about 20 wintering Goosander that frequent the tree-fringed margins and islands of the various lakes and ponds. Eversholt Lake and Basin Pond are consistently the best places to find both ducks, but they can turn up almost anywhere. In recent winters Goosander have been regularly noted at the larger of the two Drakelow Ponds. A winter visit to Eversholt Lake will also pay dividends, usually in the form of a mixed flock of Siskin, Redpoll and Goldfinch, feeding in the Alder canopy around the lake. On the more open Basin Pond, Pochard, Wigeon, Shoveler and Gadwall are regular amongst the commoner waterfowl, plus large numbers of Mute Swan, often with exotics such as Black Swan and Ruddy Shelduck. Lapwing, winter thrushes, feral geese or gulls on the surrounding fields are worthy of a second glance. The road bridge overlooking the Pond is a favourite spot for Kingfisher and Grey Wagtail, while the occasional Green Sandpiper can be seen around the margins. Common Buzzard now breed and are regularly seen in the park and surrounding woodlands.

Woburn Park's permanent deer pasture, infested with anthills and molehills, supports high concentrations of parkland species such as Mistle Thrush, Jackdaw and Green Woodpecker, all of which feed on the rich invertebrate fauna. The great variety and age of the parkland

Mandarin

timber provides abundant nesting sites for the aforementioned species, as well as Little Owl, Stock Dove, Nuthatch, Treecreeper and the two spotted woodpeckers. Milton Wood supports Willow and Marsh Tits and Tawny Owl, while the occasional cock Lady Amherst's Pheasant can sometimes be heard in the conifers and rhododendrons around Drakelow Ponds. Woburn Park was the original release site for this spectacular Asiatic pheasant.

Spring passage commences in March with the arrival of hirundines over the still waters, Wheatear on the pasture and Chiffchaff in the woodlands. Shelduck may be noted on the Basin Pond, while into April a Common Sandpiper may flit around the edge; Redshank, Greenshank and Oystercatcher have been recorded and with regular watching other waders would no doubt be encountered. Yellow Wagtail pass through, some staying on to breed, likewise Tree Pipit, Grasshopper Warbler (Milton Wood), Cuckoo and declining numbers of Turtle Dove.

During the summer months warblers abound and Spotted Flycatcher are as common here as anywhere in the county. Woodcock display overhead and Hobby hunt insects over the parkland; Sparrowhawk and Kestrel both breed. Large flocks of Mistle Thrush and Starling are often a feature of early summer.

The return passage is similar but more protracted than in spring, with a reasonable chance of a tern. Whinchat are likely in late August on exposed fence lines and any mud on Drakelow Pond could yield a wader or two. Check through the eclipse ducks as Garganey have been noted.

Woburn Park's great strength as a birding site is its ability to offer consistently good birdwatching throughout the seasons. A visit to this much underwatched site is thoroughly recommended, particularly in late winter and early summer.

For the Bedfordshire birder with a sense of history Woburn Park holds a special significance, as it was here in the early part of the twentieth century that the Duchess of Bedford, more popularly known as the Flying Duchess, made her many contributions to ornithology; she also erected the county's first bird hide in the 1920s.

Calendar

Resident: Great Crested Grebe, Gadwall, Cormorant, Grey Heron, Mandarin Duck, Sparrowhawk, Lady Amherst's Pheasant (scarce), Woodcock, Common Buzzard, Stock Dove, Little Owl, Kingfisher, three species of woodpecker, Mistle Thrush, Marsh and Willow Tits, Nuthatch, corvids, Goldcrest, Crossbill (irruptive).

December–February: Feral geese, Wigeon, Tufted Duck, Pochard, Teal, Goosander, Lapwing, Green Sandpiper, gulls on fields, Grey Wagtail, Meadow Pipit, winter thrushes (variable), Siskin, Redpoll.

March–May: Shelduck (has bred), Common Sandpiper, Cuckoo, Turtle Dove, Tree Pipit, Yellow Wagtail, Wheatear, hirundines, warblers.

June–July: Spotted Flycatcher, Swift, breeding warblers and finches, Hobby.

August–October: Passage waders and terns possible, Whinchat.

ADDITIONAL SITES

Ampthill Park (OS Ref. TL 027 385)

A large municipal public park on the Greensand Ridge with open fields, scattered timber and mixed woodland, north-east of Ampthill off the B530. Ample car parking with good access and many footpaths. Visit early morning. A wide cross-section of resident passerines including three woodpeckers and Marsh Tit. In spring, Tree Pipit, Wood Warbler and Firecrest have been noted on passage. There are good numbers of breeding leaf and scrub warblers in the summer as well as a few Spotted Flycatcher. In the winter check out the finch flocks for Brambling and Redpoll and the playing fields for Redwing and Fieldfare.

Barton Hills NNR (OS ref. TL 090 300)

A classic piece of sheep-grazed chalk downland east of the A6 at Barton-le-Clay and a National Nature Reserve. Roadside pull-ins give minimal parking along the B655 where public footpaths lead south onto the hills. There is parking in Church Road, off Hexton Road, by the church where the footpath runs alongside a chalk stream, which is good for wintering Grey Wagtail. Typical downland species breed such as Lapwing, pipits, Skylark, Linnet and Yellowhammer. Spring brings Wheatear, Ring Ouzel, warblers and Whinchat. Very underwatched, spring passage could be similar to Blow's Downs as Redstart, Pied Flycatcher and Firecrest have all been recorded. Barton Hills and the surrounding farmland is a reliable site for Grey Partridge. In the autumn check from hilltops for passing raptors and an overhead passerine passage.

Biggleswade Common (OS ref. TL 192 472)

A large section (120 ha) of common land to the south of The Lodge, Sandy that is well served by public footpaths. Approach down Stratford Road and follow the footpath signs. Good for finches and buntings in the winter (Twite in recent years) and warblers in the spring. Hobby, Cuckoo, Yellow Wagtail and Turtle Dove are summer visitors. Warren Villas NR is nearby and both sites are accessible from the Kingfisher Way public footpath.

Blunham Lake (OS ref. TL 159 511)

An old pit in the Ivel Valley just north of Sandy. Park along the A1 northbound at TL 163 509 and follow the track to the lake. A collection of pinioned wildfowl (Whooper Swan, Goldeneye and Ruddy Duck) attract small numbers of genuine wild winter ducks; Ferruginous have been recorded. Unfortunately tree growth around the margins has made viewing progressively more difficult. In winter the nearby market garden fields are worth checking for partridges, plovers and finches.

Bramingham Wood (OS ref. TL 066 259)

Located on the northern outskirts of Luton and surrounded by housing estates on all sides, this Woodland Trust reserve receives a great deal of human pressure from the local populous. However, local volunteers undertake sterling conservation work in the form of coppicing etc. to give this deciduous wood the vital clearings required for a more diverse flora and fauna to prosper. The usual woodland birds are found, including Nuthatch, Treecreeper, woodpeckers and Spotted Flycatcher, while both Tawny Owl and Sparrowhawk are resident.

Bromham Lake Local Nature Reserve (OS ref. TL 028 515)

An old gravel pit situated in a meander of the river Great Ouse. Managed by the local authority this small wetland reserve (10 ha) has tern rafts, a wildflower meadow and willow scrub complete with a wheelchair-friendly hide overlooking the lake. For access take Lower Farm Road east out of Bromham village and park before the railway track opposite the reserve entrance. Study the information board and follow the footpaths.

Over 100 species have been recorded with regular records of Hobby, Jack Snipe, Turtle Dove, Barn Owl and Redpoll. In the summer Common Tern nest and there is a wide selection of warblers and finches. Great Crested Grebe, woodpeckers and Grey Wagtail are resident and Kingfisher are regularly seen. The site has an impressive wildflower list and a good selection of dragonflies.

Cardington Airfield (OS ref. TL 090 469)

The two massive airship hangers at Cardington dominate the skyline for miles around. For the birder the grass airfield is of interest, particularly in the winter months when large flocks of winter thrushes, Golden Plover and Lapwing can occur; passing Hen Harrier, Short-eared Owl and Merlin have been recorded and, once, a Grey Plover. For the airfield, view from the old railway bridge, on the lane running south-west out of Cardington village, or from the A600 between Shortstown and Cotton End. Resident Grey Partridge and Corn Bunting, although in decline, still occur in limited numbers, whereas, what was once a good site for Tree Sparrow now has none.

Coopers Hill Local Nature Reserve (OS ref. TL 028 376)

Owned by Ampthill Town Council and managed by the Wildlife Trust this 12 ha (31 acres) greensand heath is one of the few remaining and is probably the best example of its type in Bedfordshire. The heather is rotationally cut and the bracken and Birch scrub controlled to prevent it choking the heath. The reserve is on the edge of Ampthill, bounded by Woburn Road, Station Road and the A507 by-pass. Park in the lay-by on Woburn Road or the small car park by the entrance to the Alameda and follow the waymarked tracks across the heath. The usual greensand birds prevail including Tree Pipit and Green Woodpecker; Wood Warbler has been noted on passage. A good early morning local patch site for anyone living in Ampthill and ideal to tie in with nearby Ampthill Park.

Dunstable (OS ref. TL 005 195) & Whipsnade (OS ref. SP 998 188) Downs

A scenic and much visited section of the Chiltern Hills, with the highest point in the county at 242 m (794 ft) and magnificent views across the Vale of Aylesbury countryside.

The county council maintains Dunstable Downs where there is ample parking off the B4541, plus toilets and a visitors centre. Hang-gliding and conventional gliding attract crowds of people at weekends during fine weather, when the site is best avoided. The usual mix of downland pipits, Skylark and buntings are present with a passage of Wheatear and Ring Ouzel. Willow Warbler and Whitethroat are common summer breeders while winter brings passerines to roost, including a sizeable collection of Magpie and some winter thrushes. Check out the gliding club field for Wheatear in spring and Golden Plover and Lapwing in winter.

Whipsnade Down is owned by the National Trust and is adjacent to the world-famous Whipsnade Wildlife Animal Park. Part of the downs are sheep-grazed and are superb for butterflies and chalk flora. Similar birds to Dunstable Downs plus a large corvid roost attracted to offal at a nearby pig farm. In spring check out the bare field within the Animal Park boundary, from the car park, for Wheatear and nesting Lapwing, and the fence line for Little Owl; Stone Curlew has been noted on passage. A good vantage point to look for raptors and passing gulls.

Dunstable Sewage Treatment Works (OS ref. TL 003 245)

A working industrial site owned by Anglian Water and managed jointly with the Bedfordshire Natural History Society for waders and wildfowl. Access is strictly by permit only, via the Society, but on the first Sunday of each month from 08:00 to 12:00 hrs the site is wardened allowing general access. For group visits contact the warden, Paul Trodd (01582 898369), in advance or the Society. The sewage works is to the east of the A5 just north of Dunstable. Take the Thorn road off the A5 and the entrance is on the south side, opposite Thorn.

A hide overlooks a scrape, a feeding station and four lagoons. Wintering wildfowl are joined by Water Rail and Snipe, while spring brings Common Tern, Little Ringed Plover and Redshank. Good numbers of warblers breed and the early autumn wader passage is noteworthy, particularly in August when all three common species of sandpiper can occur.

East Hyde (OS ref. TL 128 172)

An old water meadow along the River Lea between Luton and Harpenden. Park on the bridge over the river between the B653 and the railway line on the Bedfordshire/Hertfordshire county boundary. Scan the river, meadow and small marsh. Good in winter for feral geese, Golden Plover (on farmland), Snipe (occasional Jack), Teal, Gadwall, Kingfisher, Redpoll and Siskin. Little Egret has also been recorded.

Felmersham Gravel Pits (OS ref. SP 991 583)

A chain of old pits covering 21 ha (52 acres) of the Ouse Valley between the villages of Felmersham and Sharnbrook in north Bedfordshire. Owned by the Wildlife Trust and a SSSI this site is of particular interest to the botanist. Park in the small reserve car park by the lane. Typical riparian birds abound with good numbers of warblers in the summer. Bittern have occurred in the past and the county's first Purple Heron was recorded here. A likely site for colonisation by Cetti's Warbler in the future. Very underwatched and an ideal local patch.

Girtford Gravel Pits (OS ref. TL 153 505)

A chain of mature gravel pits along the River Ivel between Sandy and Blunham, partially viewed from the new Kingfisher Way public footpath. Park in the fishermen's car park by the old iron bridge at the above map reference and explore along the waymarked public footpaths beside the river. Scan across the pits to the east of the river for wildfowl and the shallower pit to the west (known locally as South Mills) for the occasional wader. The watercourse itself is good for Kingfisher, Grey Wagtail, warblers, Turtle Dove and Redpoll. A number of rarities have occurred here over the years, including Night Heron, Collared Pratincole and Red-rumped Swallow.

Grovebury Farm Sand Pit (OS ref. SP 923 233)

A working sand pit that can be viewed from a public footpath on the southern side of the A505 Leighton Buzzard by-pass. Park carefully along the by-pass by the footpath sign and scan the lake for terns, Shelduck, Goosander, Cormorant and the occasional wader. The Grand Union Canal is nearby and passes through wet meadows at the hamlet of Grove off the B488. Check for Grey Wagtail, Kingfisher, Corn Bunting and, in the summer, Yellow Wagtail.

Home Wood (OS ref. TL 140 463)

A predominantly coniferous wood owned by the Forestry Commission. Park carefully along the lane from Northill and keep to the waymarked tracks. As the wood is well away from main roads there is little noise pollution. A dawn chorus visit in May is highly recommended for singing Nightingale, 'roding' Woodcock, 'purring' Turtle Dove and 'reeling' Grasshopper Warbler. There is a good range of common woodland species and the surrounding area supports Barn and Little Owls, so check out fence lines at dawn or dusk.

Houghton Regis Chalk Pit (OS ref. TL 015 233)

An old marl lake with a reedbed and willow scrub, designated as a SSSI yet threatened by development. Park in Townsend Farm at the entrance to the industrial estate at the above map reference, and walk across the A5120 Houghton Road following the waymarked footpath between the fishing lake and the pit. Views from the public footpath are restricted. The pit is supposedly private, but is widely accessible to local people; dog-walkers, motor cyclists, fishermen and ravers all treat it as public open space. An early morning trip is advisable to miss the aforementioned.

In winter a late afternoon visit should yield Water Rail, Snipe, Jack Snipe and a mixed bunting roost, while in the summer warblers abound; check the northern chalk cliffs for Little Owl. Passage can be good and the site has produced a number of county rarities over the years, such as Red-throated and Black-throated Divers, Temminck's Stint, Hoopoe and Wryneck. A fabulous site in June for Spotted Orchids in the marsh.

Ivel Valley Walk

Known as the Kingfisher Way this well-marked public walkway runs 34 km (21 miles) from Baldock in Hertfordshire to Tempsford. The Bedfordshire section from Arlesey to Tempsford passes along the rivers Ivel and Great Ouse and through a mix of wet meadows and gravel pits. Most of the old mill races, such as those at Jordan's Mill and Langford have breeding Grey Wagtail, and Kingfisher are regularly seen, Twin Bridges, near Blunham being a particularly good spot (OS ref. TL 155 519). The full length of this walk takes in the following 'Additional Sites': Biggleswade Common, Blunham Lake, Langford Lakes, South Mills and Warren Villas NR.

For further details on the Kingfisher Way contact the Ivel Valley Countryside Project, based at Biggleswade Library.

Langford Lakes (OS ref. TL 184 402)

A chain of old gravel pits, now mainly used by fishermen, in the Hiz valley between Langford and Henlow. Views across the lakes are restricted as most are privately fished. Park by the Boot public house and explore along the footpath to the south and the mill area to the north for typical riparian species such as Kingfisher and Grey Wagtail; Osprey have occurred on passage.

Leagrave Marsh (OS ref. TL 060 248)

The source of the River Lea. Park by Five Springs tower block off Wauluds Bank Drive, Luton and follow the footpath beside the river, scanning the marsh and small Alder and Beech wood. A winter site for roosting Tawny Owl, Kingfisher, Snipe, Grey Wagtail, Redpoll and Siskin; check the Beeches for Brambling amongst the Chaffinch. One of the few remaining sites in the county where Water Vole are almost guaranteed.

Marston Thrift (OS ref. SP 972 415)

An ancient Ash and Oak wood on clay just to the north of Brogborough Lake. Turn off the A421 at the sign to Wood End, parking in the small car park at the end of the lane. Visit in spring and early summer for all six species of tits, three woodpeckers, warblers and the occasional Nightingale in the coppiced area. Good site for woodland butterflies.

Millbrook Woods (OS ref. TL 005 375)

A large block of mainly pine plantation woodlands, and a golf course, on the Greensand Ridge either side of the A507 Ampthill to Woburn road. Park in lay-bys along the road and follow the footpath signs across the golf course and along the Greensand Ridge Footpath through Moneypot Hill plantation. A few Lady Amherst's Pheasant still survive, while Tree Pipit and Redpoll breed; the occasional Redstart, Siskin and Crossbill have been recorded. Common Buzzard and Goshawk are regularly seen in this area.

Odell Great Wood (OS ref. SP 960 590)

A large damp gamekeepered Oak wood. Approach along the bridlepath from Odell village. Avoid visiting during the shooting season, especially on Saturdays. A good cross-section of deciduous woodland birds including Nightingale and Woodcock. Common Buzzard are now regular. An ideal site to visit in conjunction with nearby Harrold Odell Country Park.

Potton Wood (OS ref. TL 250 500)

Located 3 km (2 miles) east of the village of Potton off the B1040 towards Cockayne Hately. Park by the water tower and follow the footpath sign into the wood. A damp, mainly deciduous wood with the usual range of woodland birds, but most notable in spring and summer for its small population of Nightingale. Visit at dawn or dusk for the best impact.

Radwell Gravel Pits (OS ref. TL 015 575)

Approach down a narrow lane from Radwell village and park near the entrance to the old works. The pits are private but a public footpath bisects the site affording views over the water and along the river.

Waders and terns pause awhile on passage. Formerly a good site for breeding Sand Martin. Little Ringed Plover and Common Tern breed. Check the fields for wagtails and chats in spring and autumn. Chance of Hobby in summer. In winter view the flooded meadows towards the A6 from the railway bridge footpath. Large flocks of geese, ducks, plovers, winter thrushes and the occasional party of wild swans visit.

Roxton Gravel Pit (OS ref. TL 158 537)

A private gravel pit that can be viewed from nearby footpaths. Park at the bottom of Ford Lane, east of the village, and follow the footpath south beside the River Ivel. Good for a variety of wetland species including passage waders and breeding terns.

Swiss Gardens, Old Warden (OS ref. TL 148 448)

A woodland near the ornamental Swiss Gardens good for resident species, including Tawny Owl, Marsh Tit and Lesser Spotted Woodpecker. A reliable site for the latter species which is often located near the toilet block. Park in the Shuttleworth Collection, Old Warden Aerodrome car park and follow the footpath opposite.

The surrounding woodlands form the so-called 'Raptor Triangle' of Old Warden, Northill and Southill and can be viewed from roadside lay-bys. Common Buzzard breed and Red Kite often occur. Barn and Little Owls are regularly seen around Shuttleworth Agricultural College and the market garden fields towards Caldecote are worth checking for Golden Plover, Grey Partridge and Corn Bunting.

Tiddenfoot Waterside Park (OS ref. SP 913 239)

A small, mature sand pit with open water and willow scrub. Take Mentmore Road from Leighton Buzzard, parking in the car park at the above map reference. The park is a good local patch for anyone living in the town. Typical riparian birds are present and the willow scrub has turned up Bearded Tit, Nightingale and Firecrest recently, along with a Long-tailed Duck on the lake. Traditionally a good site for Willow Tit.

Totternhoe Knolls (OS ref. SP 979 220)

A chalk grassland SSSI managed by The Wildlife Trust primarily for its botanical interest. For the birder the site is worth a visit from June to August for a chance of Quail in the old lime quarry field (near the car park) to the rear of the site. Now infilled, and usually planted with barley, panoramic views over the surrounding countryside may yield the fast disappearing Turtle Dove. Corn Bunting, for the time being, are easy to see and hear; the 'fat bird of the barley' remains widespread in the Totternhoe and Eaton Bray district. From mid-morning onwards on a fine summer's day pay a visit to the reserve proper for classic chalkland flora, including several species of orchid, and associated butterflies.

For Totternhoe take the B489 from Dunstable towards Tring and follow the signs to Totternhoe and 'Nature Reserve'. Park in the car park off Castle Hill Road and follow the many waymarked tracks.

Warren Villas Nature Reserve (OS ref. TL 182 475)

A former gravel pit and recently designated nature reserve in the Ivel Valley to the south of Sandy. Sandwiched between the river and the A1 the site is accessible via a bridge from the Kingfisher Way footpath and could be tied in with visits to the nearby Biggleswade Common and The

Rook

Lodge, Sandy. Good for winter wildfowl and passage for waders, hirundines and wagtails. In the summer warblers, Common Tern, Hobby and resident breeders such as Kingfisher and Grey Wagtail can be seen. Ring-necked Duck has also occurred.

Wyboston Lakes (OS ref. TL 175 575)

A series of old gravel pits sandwiched between the A1 and the B1043 in the Ouse Valley, south of St Neots. Access is signposted off the southbound A1. A good bet in the winter months for wildfowl, including sawbills, and the occasional oddity such as divers, Common Scoter, Scaup and Eider. If anything, an underwatched area that could yield much more if worked on a regular basis. Spring brings terns, a few passage waders, wagtails, warblers and hirundines.

BERKSHIRE

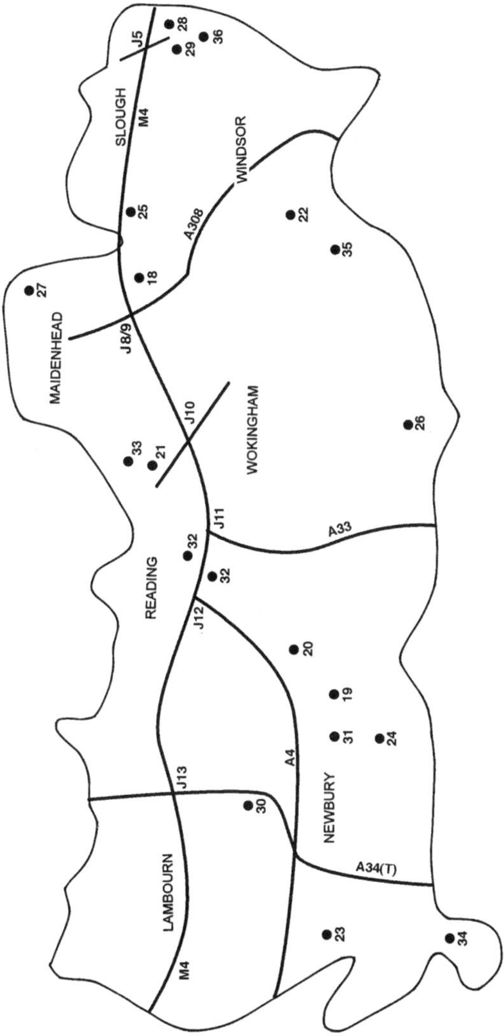
J5
28
29
36
SLOUGH
M4
WINDSOR
25
A308
22
35
18
27
MAIDENHEAD
J8/9
WOKINGHAM
J10
26
33
21
J11
A33
32
READING
32
J12
20
19
31
24
A4
J13
NEWBURY
30
A34(T)
LAMBOURN
23
34
M4

18 BRAY GRAVEL PIT

OS ref. SU 915 785

Habitat

The main water body is a well-established lake of some 29 ha (50 acres), nestling between the River Thames and the M4, and fashioned to serve the said motorway with gravel. An adjacent area, comprising two main pools and semi-submerged vegetation, has been more recently made accessible, and has attracted some good species. There is also a BBOWT reserve in the form of a small pool, with maturing vegetation, good for flora but perhaps too 'intimate' to attract anything other than the commoner species. Paddocks and a marina complete the surroundings of what remains a somewhat underwatched area.

Access

Vehicular access is from the A308 Maidenhead to Windsor road, near junction 8/9 of the M4, along the unmade lane to Monkey Island. Follow the signs to the windsurfing club, using the new car park just before the club buildings or parking at the reserve end near the motorway. Buses pass the end of Monkey Island Road, and the nearest railway station is Maidenhead, 3.2 km (2 miles) north. The main pool can be circumnavigated, via the footpath beside 'The Cut'. Halfway along this path, there is a small bridge across The Cut leading to the quieter pools beyond.

Species

Although not historically a haven for rarities, this is a site worth visiting any time of the year. Small rafts of duck, including good numbers of Great Crested Grebe, two or three Goldeneye, occasional Goosander and increasing numbers of Cormorant, reside in winter. At this time,

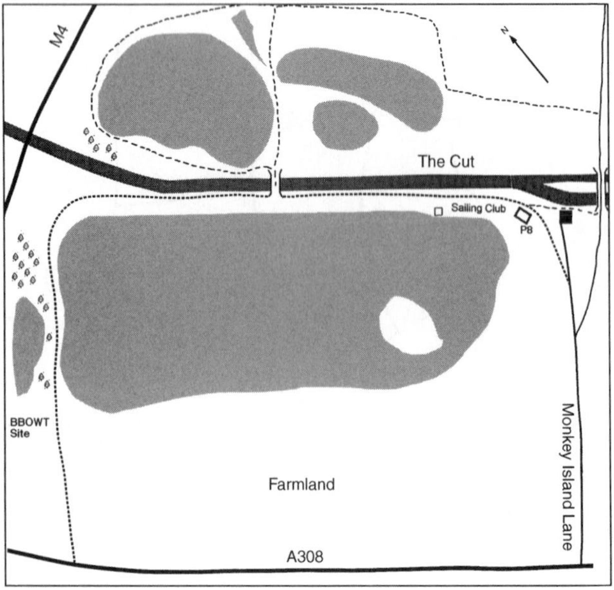

Kingfisher

and during passage, waders will be attracted to the worked area north of The Cut. The mature hedge along The Cut will yield Yellowhammer in winter and summer species such as Chiffchaff, Willow Warbler, Blackcap and occasional Lesser Whitethroat. Marsh Warbler has been noted here too. The Cut itself is favoured by Little Grebe, Water Rail and Kingfisher, the latter also often discovered at the BBOWT reserve. In spring, passage birds may well include Black Tern, and Arctic Tern, lurking amongst the Common Tern which once nested before removal of the rafts. The raucous calls of Ring-necked Parakeet seem out of place amongst the more musical utterances of Skylark and Reed Bunting around the adjacent wastelands.

Several hundred Lapwing, similar numbers of Woodpigeon, many Meadow Pipit and occasional Grey Partridge use the arable land near the main lake during the colder months, with up to 300 Golden Plover often in close association.

Probably the better area to investigate is the new site beyond The Cut, available since about 1998. The larger of the two lakes has an island used by loafing ducks and passage waders such as Common Sandpiper and Little Ringed Plover. Maturing reedbeds are used by Reed and Sedge Warblers and breeding Little Grebe. Previous visitors have included Shag, Slavonian and Red-necked Grebes, a Brent Goose, almost annual Smew, a Red-crested Pochard, Ferruginous Duck and Common Scoter. Other passing waders have been Curlew, Ruff, Oystercatcher, Bar-tailed Godwit, Spotted Redshank, Wood Sandpiper and Jack Snipe. Other rarities have included White and Blue-headed Wagtails and Black-eared Wheatear was once reported. Summertime hirundines on a feeding foray will regularly attract a Hobby or two, and once caught the attention of a passing Red-footed Falcon in June 2000.

The oft-threatened widening of the M4 project is currently shelved and this remains a pleasant site to visit, with the potential that anything might turn up.

Calendar

Resident: Great Crested and Little Grebes, Grey Heron, common ducks, Water Rail, Coot and Moorhen, occasional Grey Partridge, Sparrowhawk, Ring-necked Parakeet, Pied and Grey Wagtails, common tits and finches.

December–February: Chance of rarer grebes such as Slavonian, rafts of winter duck, Goldeneye, Smew and Pintail almost annual, with Goosander becoming regular, numerous Cormorant, sizeable gull roost, chance of Jack Snipe, Green Sandpiper, large flocks of mixed finches, Long-tailed Tit and also winter thrushes.

March–May: Wader activity likely to include Little Ringed Plover, Redshank, Greenshank, Dunlin and Snipe. Teal and prospect of Garganey. Early returning terns including Arctic and Common. Passage Yellow Wagtail.

June–July: Common Tern feeding, large numbers of hirundines and Swift, Cuckoo, possibility of Hobby, Reed and Sedge Warblers.

August–November: Still larger gatherings of House Martin and Swallow prior to migration, gull numbers increase, prospect of passage waders north of The Cut, arrival of Redwing and Fieldfare.

19 BRIMPTON GRAVEL PIT

OS ref. SU 570 655

Habitat

When extraction work ceased in 1980 it left a 4-ha (10-acre) site, surrounded by farmland and pasture, to naturally regenerate. There are two pools: one a small, round pond, the other a more significant water, bordered by mature vegetation in places, with more open banks to the west. The northern sector of this latter pit has a substantial flooded area which, apart from attracting riparian species, also serves to push the peripheral footpath further away from the water's edge. Despite this well-used path, the site has attracted a remarkable number of species, its record being partly due to the regular recording of a small number of local birdwatchers, particularly G E Wilson.

Access

The pools lie south of the road between Woolhampton and Midgham, and are locally know as Shalford Lakes. Driving past the south-bound road leading to Midgham station, one continues for approximately 1 km (0.6 mile) at which point the lakes are seen on the right. Continue past the pools to a point where a rough lay-by on a sharp right-hand bend is encountered. Unfortunately, anglers now have preference, so no parking inside is allowed, and it is now only possible to walk along the eastern boundary of the site.

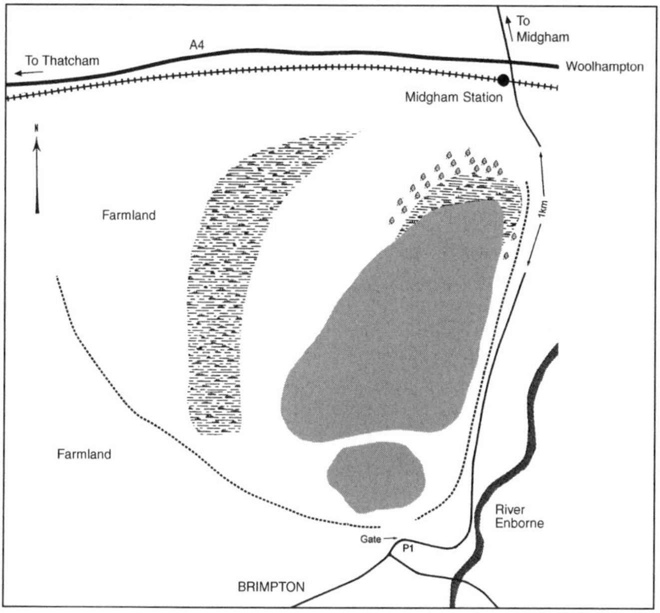

Species

Over 100 species have been recorded here in recent times. The water itself hosts all-year species such as Little and Great Crested Grebes, Mute Swan, Coot and Tufted Duck. It is worth checking Little Grebe carefully as both Red-necked and Black-necked Grebes have been known to make winter visits, as did a Black-throated Diver on one occasion. A January visit might be rewarded with rarer geese passing through. Winter ducks may include Teal, whilst Pintail, Common Scoter or Ruddy Duck are reasonable prospects, and springtime might result in a passing Garganey.

In summer, Swift and hirundines congregate in good numbers to feed, affording opportunities to compare House Martin and Sand Martin at close quarters. This activity ensures occasional sightings of the dashing Hobby, which continues to increase in the region. Common Buzzard too encroached into the area as the millennium closed. Common Tern fish for hungry youngsters raised elsewhere whilst related species have included Arctic, Black and Little Terns. Mature vegetation in the northern sector attracts summer visiting warblers, including Reed and Sedge, which in turn make the site popular with Cuckoo. Even Grasshopper Warbler is not unheard of here. Blackcap, Whitethroat, Lesser Whitethroat and Chiffchaff can be anticipated and passage Whinchat are a possibility. Resident Reed Bunting can be numerous. Amongst the rarer species which have sampled this sector has been Bearded Tit and, on one remarkable occasion, the UK's 19th record of Penduline Tit. The surrounding bankside and marshy areas will hold Pied and occasional Grey Wagtails at any time, with Yellow Wagtail in summer. Water Rail lurk in the denser vegetation.

The rougher adjacent pastures attract Lapwing, but waders such as Snipe, Redshank, Greenshank, Common and Green Sandpipers, seem now only occasional visitors, usually on autumn passage. Past years have produced Grey Plover, Bar-tailed Godwit, Ruff, Whimbrel and Curlew, and Spotted Redshank has visited, but agricultural activity right to the pool edge has curtailed the activity of waders in recent times. Many Meadow Pipit feed in this area, 170 once having been patiently counted. Tree Sparrow are probably a thing of the past now but both Stonechat and Whinchat could be expected in either passage period. Wheatear, however, seems to be more prominent in the spring.

Other notable visitors to the area in recent times include Great Northern Diver, Scaup, Red Kite, Osprey, Peregrine and Merlin, Long-eared Owl, Hoopoe, Water Pipit, Pied Flycatcher, Great Grey Shrike and the county's first ever Siberian Stonechat. Perhaps the rarest record has been the visit of a Sociable Plover. In summary, a small site that may appear quiet on some visits, but with the potential for surprises.

Calendar

Resident: Little and Great Crested Grebes, Grey Heron, Mute Swan, Mallard, Tufted Duck, Coot, Moorhen, Reed Bunting, common birds of the field.

December–February: Possibility of rarer grebes, movement of grey geese, Wigeon, Gadwall and Pochard in small numbers, occasional Teal, wandering Redshank, Lapwing and Snipe, large numbers of Meadow Pipit. Rarer visitors include Pintail and Ruddy Duck.

March–May: Possibility of passage terns, occasional Grey Plover, Ruff, Curlew or Spotted Redshank. Wandering local Common Buzzard. Large numbers of hirundine species.

June-July: Reed and Sedge Warblers breeding along with resident species and other summer warblers, prospect of Cuckoo.

August–November: Second passage less obvious than the first, but gatherings of Swift and hirundines before departure. Green and Common Sandpipers possible. Gulls more plentiful.

20 BURGHFIELD & PADWORTH COMMONS

OS ref. SU 635 653

Habitat

Encompassed by Padworth, Ufton Nervet, Burghfield and Mortimer is an area of common land and woods of varying maturity covering some 300 ha (750 acres). Some plantations have been felled in recent years, succeeded by younger trees, ranging from areas of carr, on Padworth Common, through young conifer compartments at Ufton Court, to more established stands in the vicinity of Four Houses Corner. Timber management is carried out by the Englefield Estate, with an emphasis on conservation; indeed there is a small 'reserve' area near Ufton Court where creatures as diverse as Glow-worm and Roe Deer are found. South of this area is a deciduous woodland and a small pool and, on the Hampshire border, a reclaimed gravel pit. Padworth Common itself has been established by Newbury District Council and, save for a stand of Scots Pine, is entirely open with emerging Birch and shrubbery. The boundary of the common with Hampshire is a mature Gorse hedgerow which provides a dense nesting facility for several species.

Access

The general area is 6.5 km (4 miles) south of Theale and the nearest main road connections are junctions 11 and 12 of the M4. Other than popular off-road parking in the Burghfield Common area, there are no 'official' car parking areas. However, there are places along the lanes serving the area to leave a vehicle. Stratfield Mortimer hosts an adjacent main line railway station. Pedestrian access is reasonably good over much of the area, although permitted access to parts of the Englefield Estate (01189 323748) is restricted to one or two public footpaths and main tracks.

Species

This significant area of woods and common land provides a good range of species throughout the year. Whilst the winter scene is one of foraging tits and finches, and farmland gatherings of winter thrushes and corvids, the warmer months herald the songs of Yellowhammer, Whitethroat and many other species. Parts of the deciduous woodlands around Ufton look like they ought to tempt passage Nightingale or Redstart to stop over. Tawny Owl will already be into their breeding cycle by the time these, and other summer visitors arrive and there is the enhanced prospect of seeing Crossbill in the more mature conifers during any irruption. The heathland area welcomes Whinchat during April. Wandering Barn or Short-eared Owls are seen in the general area from time to time, but the Little Owl is resident in the Ufton sector, and probably elsewhere too. Green and Great Spotted Woodpeckers also frequent the same region and Lesser Spotted Woodpecker are probably more common than records suggest.

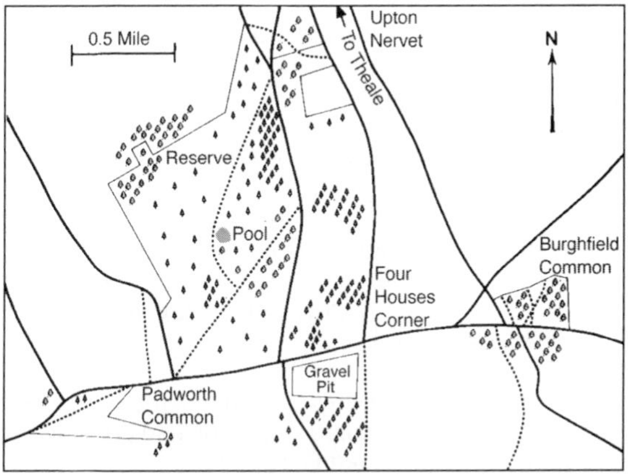

By late May the avian scene for the next few weeks is set. With possible encounters with Nightingale in the Padworth area and occasional singing Woodlark from across the Hampshire border, a definite summer flavour is taken on. Whitethroat are fairly common, their scolding 'chack' call from dense bushes or Gorse meaning you are too close to a nest. Linnet are found over much of the area and Garden Warbler frequent the Burghfield and Ufton regions. Willow Warbler sing from Birch or conifer and more mature woodland patches will be used by Chiffchaff and Blackcap. Coal Tit, Long-tailed Tit and Goldcrest breed in the more thickly planted softwood stands. Woodcock have been seen 'roding', but their status is uncertain.

If one bird in particular enhances the summer setting, however, it is the Tree Pipit, some of which stay on to nest. They may be found near Ufton or Burghfield and more regularly on Padworth Common where treetops and power lines alternate as song perches. Every birdwatcher has a favourite songster and for many this may well be the Nightingale. However, whereas this species delivers its melody from the depths of bushes, the Tree Pipit has a proclivity for delivering its lyrics during a prolonged obvious and elaborate song-flight.

The mature conifer compartments near Four Houses Corner can hold large numbers of Goldcrest and Coal Tit, whilst the open heathland opposite has Willow Warbler, Chiffchaff and, around the edges, Spotted Flycatcher. Another bird which can be expected almost anywhere here is the Cuckoo. The small woodland pool shown on the map usually hosts Moorhen and one or two Little Grebe, but any strange 'bird' calls in early spring at the pool side will be frogs calling. Sparrowhawk breed in the trees around the pool.

These sights and sounds are curtailed in autumn and for a while the area may be rather quiet, the deciduous woodlands being slightly more active than the coniferous stands. Groups of Redpoll build up, 20 or so being typical, and Siskin appear, their squeaky contact calls harmonising with those of mixed tit flocks working through the wood. The marshy conditions on and around Padworth Common become favourable for wintering Snipe and Lapwing, and beyond the Gorse hedge, Golden Plover may be overwintering. And so for a while, local birdwatchers revert to nearby gravel pits for their winter watching, but considering the good mixture of habitat, the commons are probably underwatched and merit greater attention in any season.

Calendar

Resident: Little Grebe, occasional Sparrowhawk, Kestrel, Grey Partridge, Pheasant, Lapwing, Snipe, probably Woodcock, Collared Dove, Tawny and Little Owl, Skylark, possibility of Woodlark, Meadow Pipit, Pied Wagtail, Goldcrest, Marsh and common tits, Nuthatch and Treecreeper. Linnet, chance of irregular Crossbill.

December–February: Possibility of Golden Plover and Snipe, Tawny Owls courting, numbers of Rook and Jackdaw increase, winter thrushes at woodland edge, mixed tit flocks in evergreen sectors, Siskin and Redpoll in suitable woodland.

March–May: Early-breeding species ensconced, more summer warblers on site by late April, as with Cuckoo. Tree Pipit and possible Nightingale by early May followed by Spotted Flycatcher.

June–July: Main breeding period, chance of churring Nightjar or reeling of Grasshopper Warbler. Hobby possible.

August–November: Passage activity not too evident, but winter thrushes may arrive before end of November. Possibility of overwintering Chiffchaff or Blackcap.

21 DINTON PASTURES & LAVELL'S LAKE

OS ref. SU 780 725

Habitat

Dinton Pastures Country Park was established by Wokingham District Council in 1979 following extensive mineral extraction. This had resulted in seven lakes in an area of some 100 ha (250 acres), half of this being water, between the River Loddon and the Emm Brook. After intensive landscaping, the area has matured greatly through the nineties. The main expanse, Black Swan Lake, is the only one on which water sports are permitted. It has two islands which some species use for breeding. White Swan Lake, the second largest, is well stocked for fishing. Sandford Lake was established as a wildlife area and possesses gravel pits, shallows and small islands suited to gulls and waders, viewed from a small hide. The remaining, smaller pools are in rather quieter corners of the park and are more marshy, tree-lined and secluded. Tern rafts have been successful on Sandford Lake. There are areas of scrub and old meadowland supporting a range of wild flowers, including Loddon Lily. A golf course provides open grassland, and there are stretches of established hedgerow at various points around the park.

Adjacent Lavell's Lake is a nominated conservation area and the Friends of Lavell's have constructed footpaths, hides and wader scrapes on this 16-ha (40-acre) site beside an existing reedbed. Maintaining water levels has been a problem over recent years but effective sluicing in 2001 will improve control. This, combined with the opening up of adjacent flood meadows, will serve to improve the area for dabbling ducks, waders and Grey Heron still further. Ongoing thinning of trees and foliage may also attract more pipits, wagtails, chats and Redstart.

Access

The site is north-west of Wokingham, the main entrance being off the B3030, Davies Street, approximately 180 m (200 yds) north of the bridge over the A329(M). By road, the area is served by the M4 (junction 10), taking the A329(M) towards Reading, the A329 to Wokingham, and turning left onto the B3030. Alternatively, from the A4 at Twyford, travel south on the A321, turning right to the B3030 at Hurst.

The main car park at the Country Park holds some 70 vehicles but

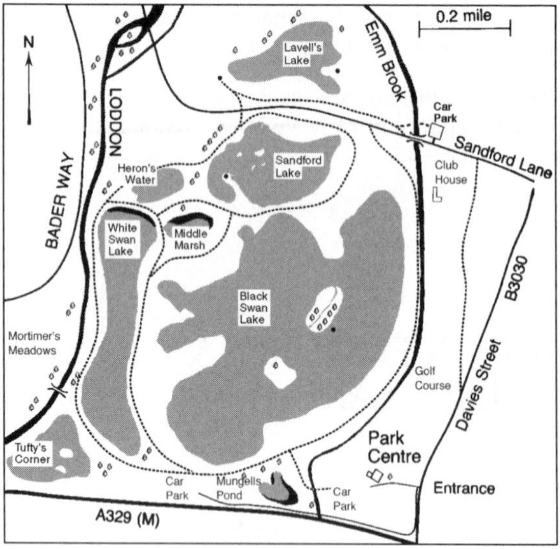

overflow parking is available in the angler's car park. A parking charge is levied at weekends in summer. There is pedestrian access to the pastures at two locations: near Sandford Mill to the north and over the Loddon footbridge near Tufty's corner to the south-west. Lavell's is served by a separate car park for about 30 vehicles in Sandford Lane.

The nearest railway station is at Winnersh approximately 1 km (0.6 mile) away and local buses pass the main entrance. The Park Centre comprises an information office (0118 934 2016), Warden's and administrative facility, lecture rooms, study rooms, toilets and a small refreshment area. The management run a programme of sports and educational activities throughout the year, including birdwatching, but also natural history subjects, mammal study, photography, conservation and many others. A new Natural History Centre was constructed in the nineties. Access to the only hide on Sandford Lake is unrestricted and the same applies to the two hides provided on Lavell's Lake, and many paths facilitate wheelchairs.

Species

Since regular records at Dinton were commenced, the species count has risen to over 170 and whilst many may only make irregular appearances, the combination of lakes and mature trees and hedgerows guarantees a good variety at any time. A day at the park in April can yield as many as 80 species. As with all such locations, the waters are most active in winter, the bushes and vegetation in summer. At the beginning of the year, waterfowl numbers build up on all of the main lakes and Dinton Pastures may be unusual in having Gadwall outnumbering Mallard and even Tufted Duck. Some 300 of this delicately marked duck were present in January 2000, always seemingly in pairs rather than as a flock and, in hard weather, following Mute Swan closely for scraps of weed the swans bring to the surface. The swans themselves often number in the high eighties, partly because the local Swan Rescue Service releases treated birds in the park for recuperation.

Rafts of some 100 Pochard accumulate, particularly on White Swan and Sandford Lakes, whilst double that number of Wigeon occur on Black Swan Lake. A few Shoveler and Goldeneye can be seen throughout January and February, the latter occasionally in double figures, but March sees the build-up of Canada Goose flocks which, along with Common Gull, have learned to come to bread, providing excellent opportunities for photography. An earlier Dinton specialty, the Egyptian Goose, has reduced in numbers somewhat, having spread out over adjacent sites.

Black Swan's southern island is often guarded by up to 100 Cormorant, perched on a large dead elm tree in the middle, sometimes accompanied by Grey Heron. Elsewhere, Mungell's Pond and the River Loddon are worth checking for Little Grebe and Water Rail. Whilst near the Loddon, scanning bankside Alders may be rewarded at this time of year by a flock of Siskin, occasionally interspersed with a few Redpoll, followed by groups of Goldfinch, especially at Mortimer's Meadows and the weir above Heron's Water. Pied and Grey Wagtails can usually be seen near the sports club buildings, or at Tufty's Corner, whilst Kingfisher can be expected anywhere on the site, especially on Emm Brook and the islands on Black Swan Lake.

Lavell's Lake has matured after landscaping work, and the wader scrape is likely to prove increasingly successful. The two good hides are well positioned; please fill in the log book on every visit. Already, Snipe, Common and Green Sandpipers are regularly seen, with occasional Redshank. A particularly good year for Greenshank was 2000. Ringed and Little Ringed Plovers, Ruff, Wood Sandpiper, Turnstone and Jack Snipe have been recorded as has Temminck's Stint, along with rare visits from Smew, Pintail, Ruddy Duck and Woodcock. Increasing numbers of Teal can be seen here, nowadays anything up to 100. Overwintering Bittern are regularly encountered, and the most recent rarities include Spotted Crake and a splendid Purple Heron, the county's sixth, which graced the location for a day or two. Golden Plover can be expected amongst flocks of Lapwing on Lea's Scrape on the meadows beyond, viewed from the south bank of the Loddon.

As spring advances, the flocks of winter thrushes and Teal give way to passage migrants. Wheatear and Yellow Wagtail pass through regularly, usually seen on or near the golf course. Common and Green Sandpipers may well be seen from the Sandford Lake hide and, when water levels are low, around the sandy banks of the two Swan Lakes. Both species of godwit have made appearances and Curlew and Whimbrel

Tufted Duck

pass through on occasions. Whilst Water Pipit and Tree Pipit are less frequent as the foliage has matured, Whinchat can still be located at this time, perhaps along Emm Brook on fence posts or exposed twigs, and Redstart has become almost an annual visitor. Amongst the Common Tern which stay to breed, Sandwich Tern and Little Gull are nowadays regarded as rare visitors. Large numbers of hirundines pass through on their way to the many other riverside gravel workings in the area.

As the frenetic activity of the spring passage abates, Dinton becomes the domain of 50 or so nesting species, notable records including the first Gadwall to breed in Berkshire. Common Tern nest on Sandford Lake alongside the Little Ringed Plover, and also on Lavell's. Local Kestrel have also raised young, and Sparrowhawk regularly hunt on the reserve. By midsummer, visiting warbler species have nested: Sedge and Reed Warblers near the car park, Whitethroat, Blackcap and Willow Warbler near Mungell's Pond. Bullfinch and Reed Bunting breed around Middle Marsh and Stock Dove near Lavell's Lake. Both Green and Great Spotted Woodpeckers breed occasionally; the Lesser Spotted species, although sometimes seen in the park, apparently nesting elsewhere. Amongst the more interesting recent visitors have been Little Egret, Honey Buzzard and Red-footed Falcon. Cetti's Warbler has not been recorded for some time but Grasshopper Warbler, Turtle Dove and Hobby have become end-of-century regulars, as has indeed Common Buzzard which has retaken Berkshire captive after many years of absence.

A nest box scheme has proven successful but attempts to attract Sand Martins to artificial nest holes in suitable sandy banks have, to date, failed. The Kingfisher, however, needs little encouragement to multiply within the confines of the park. Garganey, once rare, are now annual visitors, with up to five at one time. Increasing numbers of Chiffchaff call out their name throughout the complex, and Cuckoo has become more regular. The Nightingale too was uncommon but can be expected to enliven a highly recommended dawn chorus visit. As autumn approaches, the inevitable pull of the south takes its effect on summer visitors, their places taken by others paying a brief visit during their own journeys. More Green and Wood Sandpipers, or Greenshank may be encountered and, on the smaller side, Coal Tit and, occasionally, a dainty Firecrest. As the seasonal cycle completes itself, the more usual winter birds may be joined by Red-legged and Grey Partridges, Meadow Pipit and Brambling. A new phenomenon is a large concentration of gulls on an in-fill site at nearby Lea Farm, just a few hundred metres north-east of Sandford Lane. Observation from the roadside bank has revealed up to a dozen or so Yellow-legged Gull amongst huge numbers of commoner species, so who knows what else may crop up among them in whatever window of opportunity remains.

Regular winter flooding has effected both access and the species visiting Dinton and Lavell's. However, funding is being sought to raise the bunds, paths and hides, and to extend scrapes and reedbeds. Thus, Dinton Pastures will continue to be one of the foremost birdwatching sites in the county into this new millennium. A professional team of wardens plan a creative management programme, ensuring that its record will improve still further.

Calendar

Resident: Common wildfowl, Great Crested and Little Grebes (fewer of late), Grey Heron, Cormorant, Egyptian Geese, occasional Common Buzzard, Stock Dove, Skylark, Pied and Grey Wagtails, Kingfisher, Kestrel, Green Woodpecker, Reed Bunting, Bullfinch, Goldcrest.

December–February: Bittern almost annual. Pochard, Wigeon, Gadwall, Shoveler, other ducks in larger numbers, Siskin and Redpoll, occasional Yellowhammer, some winter thrushes, numerous Mute Swan, increased gull numbers, occasional Goldeneye and sawbills, Lapwing and Golden Plover flocks.

March–May: Passage migrants, including Wheatear, Nightingale and Yellow Wagtail, arrival of Willow Warbler and Chiffchaff, with Sedge Warbler, Whitethroat and Lesser Whitethroat soon after. Common Sandpiper, early Hobby.

June–July: Breeding period, Kestrel, Sparrowhawk and Cuckoo very active. Reed Warbler and Common Tern nesting, many nest boxes in use. Hirundines in large numbers, occasionally pursued by Hobby.

August–November: Late breeding Great Crested Grebe, large numbers of juveniles of many species, hirundines gathering for departure, winter thrushes arriving, Goldfinch, Siskin and Linnet flocking.

22 ENGLEMERE POND — OS ref. SU 905 687

Habitat

Originally Crown Estate, this 26-ha (65-acre) site of general mixed woodland was acquired by Bracknell District Council in the 70s, and subsequently designated a Local Nature Reserve. The tree-line to the north, adjacent to a golf driving range, is essentially deciduous with numerous Silver Birches but with conifers near the timber yard. South of the pond the woodland comprises Oak and Hornbeam, but mainly Scots Pine, with an area of heathland, partially replanted with Rowan and Cherry.

Nestling in the middle of the woodland is Englemere Pond, a SSSI and approximately 10 ha (25 acres) in size, surrounded on three sides by one of the largest reedbeds in East Berkshire. The water edge nearest the car park has a small patch of Alder carr. Work in 2000 has extended the boardwalks in what is a very muddy site at most times, opened up more of the heathland, and encroaching Rhododendron has been cut back.

Access

Englemere Pond is 500 m (546 yds) south of the A329, mid-way between Bracknell and Ascot. A 15-space car park is entered from the Swinley Road (B3017). There are pedestrian entrances near the railway bridge

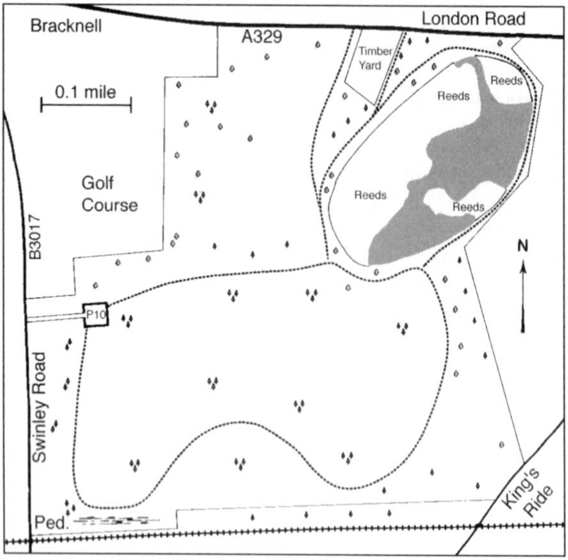

and on either side of the timber yard. A number of tracks criss-cross the woods and circle the pond, although this remains the boggiest part of the site. Golf balls are often found on the paths north-western sector, so beware!

Species

A walk around Englemere can be of interest at anytime of year, although spring and summer are best. The winter scene is dominated by small flocks of various tits, Goldcrest and Treecreeper moving through the conifer stands in the south, occasionally joined by Reed Bunting. The deciduous woods near the pond exhibit a similar spectacle but here mixed finch flocks predominate, often including Redpoll and Siskin. The adjacent driving range offers suitable roosts for Redwing and Mistle Thrush, but Fieldfare less frequently. Groups of Long-tailed Tit are particularly active, even after some have paired off for nesting in March. As spring approaches the resident Great Spotted Woodpecker begin hammering out courtship intentions, and Green Woodpecker may be seen on the golfing fairway or the deciduous stand, having been perhaps a little less obvious during the winter months. Tawny Owl may not be resident in these woods but are often encountered, being more vociferous at this time of year. Now the pond can be almost empty, save for a few Black-headed Gull or common duck species, but Water Rail are resident and being encouraged with an artificial nest scheme.

The pond edge, particularly the western carr and the southern tree-line, hosts Goldcrest throughout the year and with luck, the courtship routine of the Willow Tit can be observed, with high-pitched Nightjar-like 'churring' from the female and single piercing notes from the excited male. An early morning visit may be rewarded with a Grey Heron or occasional Pochard, but the water is not especially inspiring until the summer months when the chattering of breeding Reed Warbler is conducted by the metronome calls of Chiffchaff in bankside trees. The slightly different song of Sedge Warbler should also be listened for, the cream-coloured supercilium being the give-away if seen. At the height of summer the reedbed becomes an important roost for many House Martin, wagtails and the occasional Swallow. Pied Wagtail have nested in the timber yard, which also provides a haven for Wren and Robin to rear their offspring.

Sparrowhawk has bred in Englemere Wood though they are equally attracted to the similar habitat surrounding the site in the form of mature gardens and private copses. In fact, breeding passerines are more likely to be harassed by the local Jay than by the Sparrowhawk. As summer draws to a close numerous juveniles of a variety of species swell the woodland population. Speckled offspring of Reed Bunting may be found and there may even be the opportunity of seeing a young Cuckoo being urged on its way by its unsuspecting Reed Warbler foster parents. Many immature Blue and Long-tailed Tits will be active in both types of woodland, unaware that pitifully few of them will survive to maturity. Second broods of noisy Nuthatch will also be readily located. A more recent addition to the species list is Hobby, its breeding range extension ensuring regular over-flights, and Woodlark has ventured from more suitable habitat nearby.

The season's end might result in short visits of Crossbill and there is always the prospect of a Firecrest among the Goldcrest. The tall trees on all sides of the pool prevent flocks of roosting ducks and geese; however, occasional Shoveler and Gadwall may be seen in small numbers. As the nights draw in and the foliage falls from the Oaks and Birch in the northern area, it will certainly be worth keeping an eye open for an occasional Lesser Spotted Woodpecker as they move around a number of small treescapes in the area.

Despite being a somewhat diminutive locale, there is every prospect of seeing a reasonably wide range of woodland and wetland birds. The 100 Snipe flushed by a reedbed maintenance team recently will not often be repeated, but indicates the possibilities for this well-managed site.

Calendar

Resident: Little Grebe, Mallard, Sparrowhawk, Water Rail, Moorhen, Blue, Great, Long-tailed and Coal Tits, possible Willow Tit. Goldcrest, Reed Bunting, Chaffinch, occasional Bullfinch, Greenfinch, Nuthatch, Treecreeper, Pied Wagtail, Green and Great Spotted Woodpeckers.

December–February: Redpoll, Siskin, Crossbill (occasionally), winter thrushes, Black-headed Gull, Shoveler, occasional Jackdaw, infrequent Lesser Spotted Woodpecker.

March–May: Willow Warbler on passage, Chiffchaff, occasional Blackcap, Garden Warbler, possible Cuckoo.

June–July: Possible Spotted Flycatcher, occasional sightings of Hobby, hirundines in good numbers.

August–November: Small passage movement, gathering of mixed feeding flocks of finches and tits.

23 FREEMAN'S MARSH

OS ref. SU 334 687

Habitat

Set in between the busy A4 and the bustling town of Hungerford, this 40 ha (100 acres) of water-meadows, reedbeds and woodland is indeed a haven for wildlife, especially those creatures attracted to water-logged habitat. Registered a SSSI in the early nineties, this 2 km (1.25 mile) stretch of land runs alongside the Kennet and Avon Canal and also hosts the meandering River Dun. The carr forms rough grazing and includes bushes and some established trees such as willow and Alder. At the small BBOWT reserve, Hungerford Marsh, at the eastern end of the site, one is transported back to a pastoral England of yesteryear, rich in botanical delights from the billowing Hawthorn blossom in spring to the June showing of Marsh Orchid and the dazzling Yellow Iris of high summer. The area has a relaxing and open aspect and fishing is a popular pastime, particularly on the canal, where Water Voles can be seen. The railway embankment harbours Cowslips in spring and various chalkland species.

The northern perimeter is tree-lined, though not densely so, and beyond lie the vast arable Hopgrass Fields. To the south is the main railway line with arable land beyond. The marsh is well served with footpaths and footbridges across the canal, river, ditches and streams. The ditches created by successive generations of landowners for flooding the meadows still serve to ensure constant wetness of the site, so some parts can be exceptionally boggy after wet weather.

Two decades of observation and monitoring has resulted in records of over 300 species of trees, shrubs, grasses, sedge, rush, flowers and herbs, many of them uncommon in the region. Stoats may well be seen hunting along the river bank.

Access

The site is 5 km (3 miles) south of junction 14 on the M4 and the most popular approach on foot is along the canal footpath out of Hungerford Town, crossing at the swing bridge (known locally as Church Bridge) opposite the church. If parking in the town proves difficult, an alternative is to travel west from Hungerford along the A4 for approximately 1.5 km (1 mile) to a large lay-by beyond the pick-your-own centre, suitable for 20 vehicles, and adjacent to a small fruit farm. From here, access to the marsh is via Ford Gate, about 100 m back towards town. One may wander over the non-private sections of the marsh, but there is a footpath route around much of the perimeter. The canal may be crossed at any one of three locks or via Church Bridge. In any event it may prove worthwhile exiting at Ford Gate to view the large fields north of the marsh for flock activity, especially in autumn and winter.

Species

Over 130 species of bird have been known to use or visit the marsh and adjacent fields. Herds of Mute Swan accumulate on the canal where Moorhen also do well in the reed-lined sections. Species expected here are Grey Heron and Little Grebe, the latter with several breeding pairs, whilst Kingfisher is seen mainly along the overhanging vegetation of the

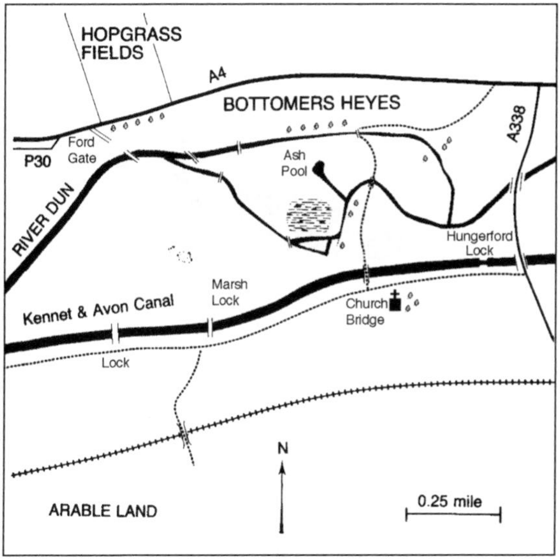

River Dun. The status of Water Rail is less certain, mainly regarded as a regular winter visitor, best seen during an early winter's morning when all is frozen. Teal are a regular winter visitor in small numbers, with larger groups of Mallard, Tufted Duck and Coot, and occasional Gadwall.

Local raptors make good use of the marsh for hunting, Kestrel being the most likely, and Sparrowhawk may swoop over from adjacent farmland. Hobby has been doing well in the county of late and sightings of this dashing falcon are a distinct possibility, perhaps in late summer. Common Buzzard too will be seen soaring in the area. Skylark embellish the sights and sounds of the marsh whilst Goldfinch and Linnet strip the plentiful thistles, twittering pleasantly as they do so. Occasionally, during winter, Golden Plover occur amongst the Lapwing but the only other regular wader is the Snipe, which has used the marsh as a breeding ground. In wintertime, vast numbers of gulls and corvids are often disturbed by helicopters flying low over nearby farmland, causing clouds of these birds to swirl over the marsh before settling again a few minutes later.

Numbers of hirundine vary from year to year, but quite sizeable roosts occur in the reedbeds and both Sand and House Martins will be 'pond dipping' for insects in summer, whilst Swallow breed in barns and outbuildings around the periphery. The resident thrushes all nest regularly, and in the early part of winter, before the Hawthorn bushes have been stripped, they are joined by groups of Fieldfare and Redwing. The short days of this season offer the observer swaying flocks of Starling, noisy hoards of Lapwing and parties of feeding House Sparrow from the neighbouring town. Pied, and Grey Wagtails frequent the waterside whilst small groups of Meadow Pipit, rising to incessant 'tseeps', express their annoyance at being flushed by the unwitting walker. Any groups of Chaffinch near the railway embankment should be checked for an occasional Brambling. The plaintive calls of Reed Bunting sharpen up as spring approaches and soon, the songs of Sedge

Little Grebe

and Willow Warblers change the ambience of the marsh for a few weeks. In denser vegetation, Lesser Whitethroat should be seen, possibly even more regularly than Whitethroat.

Blackcap and Chiffchaff also breed in the area but the Grasshopper Warbler is only an erratic visitor. Once any passage Yellow Wagtail have passed through, Spotted Flycatcher can be expected, particularly near the church and at Bottomers Heyes. The setting seems just right for Turtle Dove but sightings (or hearings) are far from guaranteed. Contact with Cuckoo, however, is more assured with many Dunnock and Meadow Pipit nests to be sought out. Snipe are probably present throughout the year, though how many might be lurking at any one time in the extensive network of ditches and swathes of meadow grasses is anyone's guess. Nonetheless, the marsh continues to attract a wide variety of species, and whilst visits of such birds as Wryneck, Red-backed Shrike, Dipper, Jack Snipe and Garganey may be something of the past, there is still much to intrigue field naturalists of all persuasions on this natural history haven.

Calendar

Resident: Mute Swan, Little Grebe, Tufted Duck, Kestrel, Sparrowhawk, Skylark, Snipe, Great Spotted Woodpecker, Reed Bunting, Pied and Grey Wagtails.

December–February: Water Rail (occasional), gulls and corvids, Jack Snipe (occasional), Meadow Pipit, winter thrushes, Siskin, sometimes accompanied by Redpoll.

March–May: Common warblers, Spotted Flycatcher, Grey and Yellow Wagtails, Turtle Dove (occasional), Cuckoo.

June–July: Rather quiet during breeding period, much disturbance from weekend visitors.

August–November: Flocks of Swallow, House and Sand Martins preparing for migration, early Redwing and Fieldfare, small numbers of winter-visiting duck arrive, mixed flocks of finches build up.

24 GREENHAM & CROOKHAM COMMONS

OS ref. SU 524 645

Habitat

Take a modern aerodrome, dig up some 95 ha (234 acres) of two-metre thick concrete, sow with heathland plants, wait a while and you get the 'new' Greenham Common. In fact, the site of this Royal and American Airforce base had always been common land before it had been built and, after 50 years, Berkshire's citizens got a millennium present when the whole site was handed back to the public. Together with the adjacent Crookham Common, this 500 ha (1,250 acre) piece of land is managed by West Berkshire Council under the Countryside Stewardship Scheme and already is registered as a SSSI.

The two commons make up the largest area of lowland heathland in Berkshire and are home to many rare and endangered plants and animals. Newly created ponds and areas of grass merge well with established sphagnum bogs, valley mire, ancient woodland and Alder-lined gullies. Areas of open gravel are being recolonised by heathland and grassland plants where mowing and grazing regimes maintain scrub and invasive undergrowth to a minimum. Strips of land which once bore the weight of massive B52s now just have to support the seedheads of mown grasslands, scattered to gradually transform these parts of the Common. Although the commons already attract a good range of hoped-for species, the passage of time will only make this important feature of the county's natural history better and better.

Access

The site is east of the A339(T) which passes through Newbury, south of junction 13 of the M4. For Crookham Common, the 25-space car park at SU 524 645 is best. Then, for Greenham Common, walk from this point or relocate the vehicle to the main car park off Burys Bank Road (SU 500 650), checking the closing time on the gate, or further west along this road at SU 484 654. Crookham Common has an obvious lattice of

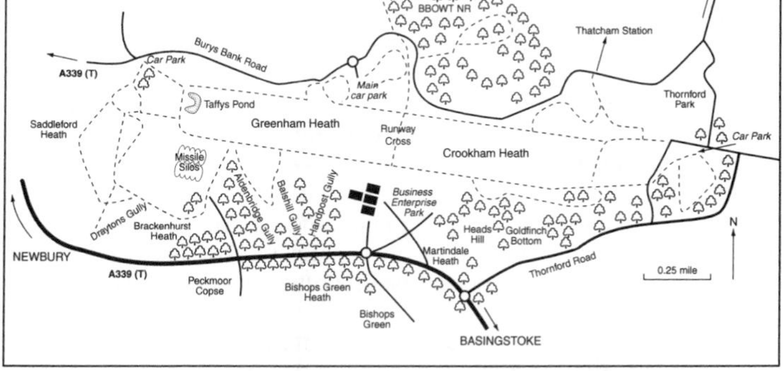

footpaths through the Birch coppice, whilst Crookham Heath and Greenham Heaths have fairly random access but it is planned to keep walkers to obvious tracks, enabling the heathland to re-establish and to help ground-nesting species from disturbance.

A number of circular walks are possible around the old airfield, including a lengthy one around the taxiways, and the gullies are also worth checking. To the north, and on the opposite side of Burys Bank Road, is a BBOWT reserve, part of which was once the base ammunition store, and is now reclaimed heath and woodland. In the southern sector of the former airfield, the 'cost' of this remarkable new natural facility is represented by a significant business park. The nearest railway stations at Newbury and Thatcham are both about 2.5 km (1.5 miles) away.

Species

Access has always been possible in Crookham Common and so a little more is known about the species here, comprising mainly all the common tits and finches, Green and Great Spotted Woodpeckers, Treecreeper and Nuthatch. Robin and Wren abound whilst Chiffchaff and large numbers of Willow Warbler warm the air with summer songs. Encroaching scrub seems to be encouraging more Song Thrush to the area but possibly at the cost of losing some of the Nightjar and Woodlark currently present. Nonetheless, an evening visit in May or June should be rewarded with churring or clapping Nightjar and roding Woodcock. Nightingale can be heard in any of the scrub areas with several pairs of Garden Warbler and Blackcap maintaining their own harmonies. Yellowhammer might be found all year round, mainly in the outskirts of the treescape, where Tree Pipit and Whitethroat will be encountered in summer. Tawny Owl are resident and 'eyeing the skies' is likely to result in seeing the local Sparrowhawk or an inquisitive Common Buzzard.

Emerging onto Greenham Common, a 'big sky' environment is immediately presented, with distant horizons tempting a spot of raptor hunting, especially over the hills to the south, a telescope of course being needed for such a pursuit. The most likely find will be distant Common Buzzard, but Red Kite is becoming a more and more likely companion. With that out of one's system, the huge area of Crookham and Greenham Heaths opens up to an extensive vista of heather and grass, with pools and gravel spoil piles. It does not take long to realise that this is a home for Stonechat, Skylark and Meadow Pipit, which are soon located on a lengthy stroll around the 6 km Taxiway Walk. Once the ear is attuned to the lark's song, the different melodies of Woodlark may well be discerned, several pairs of this increasing species being present. During passage, Wheatear will be found on areas of shorter grass. Lapwing have quickly taken up territories near the flashes and pools, whilst Little Ringed and Ringed Plovers and Redshank too, have seized upon the breeding facilities offered, and Snipe can be anticipated in most months. Even Shelduck have been noted near these wetter areas. Any outcrop of gorse should be checked for Dartford Warbler and Whitethroat, and if Meadow Pipit are nesting, Cuckoo may well take an interest. More pools in the north-eastern corner attract Little Grebe, Grey Wagtail and hawking hirundines.

By the time the western end of the Common is reached, around Sandleford Heath, denser scrub and woodland increases chances of find-

Tree Pipit

ing Tree Pipit and Redpoll. The fenced-off Silo area may host a few Pied Wagtail and the fence itself might attract a passage Whinchat. The various gullies and wooded clumps to the south of the site are home to tits and Chaffinch, Goldcrest, additional Green and Great Spotted Woodpeckers, and summer Chiffchaff. And a visit on a sultry spring or summer evening may well be rewarded with the scything flight of hunting Hobby, the haunting buzz of churring Nightjar and the circuit training of roding Woodcock. Once cloaked in controversy, this delightful setting is becoming clothed in a garment of wildflowers and birdsong, now available for everyone to experience.

Calendar

Resident: Little Grebe, Tufted Duck, Kestrel, Sparrowhawk, occasional Common Buzzard, Snipe, Woodcock, Tawny Owl, Green and Great Spotted Woodpeckers, Skylark, Woodlark, Meadow Pipit, Pied and Grey Wagtails, common tits and finches, Reed Bunting, Linnet, Stonechat.

December–February: Gulls and corvids, possible Jack Snipe, flocks of Meadow Pipit, Goldfinch and winter thrushes, Siskin, sometimes accompanied by Redpoll.

March–May: Common warblers, Spotted Flycatcher, Grey and Yellow Wagtails, Tree Pipit, Turtle Dove (occasional), Cuckoo, Redshank, Ringed and Little Ringed Plovers, Common Sandpiper. Hirundines and Hobby arrive, possible Dartford Warbler on passage.

June–July: Nightjar churring, Hobby hunting and Woodcock roding.

August–November: Flocks of Swallow, House and Sand Martins preparing for migration, early Redwing and Fieldfare, possible Whinchat.

25 JUBILEE RIVER

OS ref. SU 935 791

Habitat

In the latter half of the last century, much development occurred in what has been the traditional Thames floodplain. These developments have been subjected to an increase in flooding and, following extensive research of the Thames basin, a flood relief channel was designed and a £100m implementation scheme commenced in the summer of 2000. A new trench, now officially named the Jubilee River, was constructed from Cookham to Windsor and great attention has been paid to conservation issues in the design, with landscaping along the entire 12 km length of the river.

Particular attention has been paid at the site of the previous Slough Sewage Farm area, historically one of the birding hot spots of the region. Design of islands, wader scrapes, hides and plant selection has been carried out with the intention of attracting back many of the species present before construction, particularly waders. This will be a tall order but initial signs are good. In addition, some of the open beds are still viewable from the north of the complex and still attract good numbers of waders and gulls.

Access

Footpaths are being constructed along the entire length of the new river, and although they are often close to the river bank, there are sections where the path is diverted away from the River to enable vegetation and wildlife to become established. The main area of interest from a birdwatching point of view is the section near Eton where specific conservation measures have been taken.

Access to this location is off the B3026 between Dorney and Eton at SU 935 787, following the track north to the obvious parking area at the grid reference above. From here, footpaths and observation points are available to scan the scrapes, islands and banks.

Views over the main STW beds can be made from the track beyond the footbridge over the motorway at SU 938 797, which can be accessed having parked in Mercian Way at the north-east corner of the Recreation Ground. An adjacent site which is also proving to be good for birds is the recently-constructed rowing trench at Dorney, accessed at SU 936 777.

Species

Prior to the immense amount of work undertaken at this location, the site was one of the most significant for birds in the county. The original filtration beds attracted large numbers of waders, and good concentrations of Corn Bunting frequented the surrounding farmland and scrub. One of the last colonies of Tree Sparrow in Berkshire eked out a living here and amongst the more unusual visitors were Short-toed Lark and several Dartford Warbler.

Only time will tell if the conservation plan works but the amount of forethought that has gone into the design deserves success. Gravelled islands and banks have been created to encourage Little Ringed Plover to return to breed again and will hopefully lure back passage wader

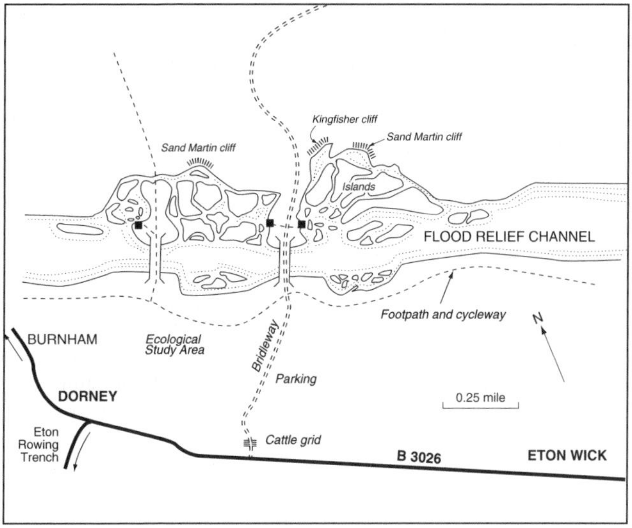

species such as Greenshank, Ruff, Jack Snipe, Green and Common Sandpipers, Curlew and Dunlin. Ringed Plover and Redshank already find these new scrapes to their liking and the various banks around the water complex should ensure Shelduck return to breed, as Lapwing already do. The gullies and ditches constructed as part of the bankside design afford many nooks and crannies for Teal and perhaps Garganey, and should also prove acceptable to Water Rail. The Spotted Crake that favoured the stream just outside the complex in 2001 might even return to see the finished work, and the unfinished trench has already attracted Wood Sandpiper and Little Egret.

Moorhen are also finding the new surroundings to their taste, up to 50 gathering together in winter, whilst Coot, Tufted Duck and Gadwall are also finding their way back. Kingfisher has always inhabited the site and large numbers of Pied Wagtail are guaranteed by the adjacent STW. Yellow Wagtail are a possibility on spring passage, while Wheatear are also an annual visitor on their way through. Passage Whinchat and resident Stonechat have been regular in the past and may well be so again, whilst the new features will continue to bring in large numbers of hirundines and Swift. Sand Martin in particular will enjoy the artificial nest bank, as breeding facilities were non-existent before.

The rough ground and farmland surrounding the site draw good numbers of Goldfinch, Linnet and Skylark, with Reed Bunting providing a supporting cast. Both Grey and Red-legged Partridges, and Pheasant wander around the cropped areas, and resident Lapwing may attract groups of Golden Plover in winter. Snipe at this time have accumulated in quite good numbers too. The reed beds along the stream have attracted good numbers of Reed and Sedge Warblers in the past and their numbers should be enhanced as new reed sections mature. Pieces of scrub and Hawthorn hedges around the paddocks and farmland ensure Blackcap, Chiffchaff, Whitethroat, and occasional Lesser Whitethroat in summertime, and 'tseeping' groups of Dunnock in the colder months. Little Owl has been present for many years and should continue to thrive, as will large numbers of overwintering Meadow Pipit.

Sparrowhawk and Kestrel hunt the area regularly and Hobby is another potential visitor in summer. Another regular spectacle overhead is small groups of Ring-necked Parakeet wandering through, to or from their roost in Esher, and many gulls pass over, particularly at dusk in winter, heading for their own roost on the west London reservoirs. In this same season, flocks of Redwing and Fieldfare forage amongst the scrub and open fields, where Short-eared Owl has been recorded previously.

More gulls loaf and feed on the STW sludge beds and these can be observed from the track across the motorway footbridge to the north of the complex. Black-headed Gull is the most common though Common Gull is also regular. Waders in season will include Snipe, plus Green and Common Sandpipers, though Wood Sandpiper call in briefly most years. Small numbers of Dunlin are possible whilst Little Stint is another expected visitor, sometimes in parties of double figures. Curlew Sandpiper has been recorded and Little Egret is beginning to become regular on these beds.

Small pools which existed prior to the new layout have attracted Slavonian Grebe, whilst the wilder scrubby areas have resulted in sightings of Tree, Water and Rock Pipits, a wandering Barn Owl and a Wryneck being sighted on one occasion. Both Redstart and Black Redstart have been noted and at least one Lapland Bunting found the location to its liking for a brief stay. In short, anything has been possible over the years and the new enhancements should ensure this excellent track record continues.

Calendar

Resident: Little and Great Crested Grebes, Grey Heron, Canada Goose, Tufted Duck, Sparrowhawk, Lapwing, Little Owl, Ring-necked Parakeet, Kingfisher, Skylark, Linnet, Reed Bunting, Yellowhammer. Pied and occasional Grey Wagtails, Stonechat and mixed corvids.

December–February: Cormorant, Shelduck, Gadwall, Teal, Pochard, Shoveler, occasional Goosander. Snipe, Redshank, Green Sandpiper, Lapwing, occasional Golden Plover, mixed gulls, with potential for rarer species at any time. Flocks of Meadow Pipit, Skylark, Linnet, Chaffinch and occasional Corn Bunting.

March–May: Passage of Yellow Wagtail and Whinchat, arrival of hirundines and Cuckoo, prospect of Turtle Dove. Many common warblers, especially Whitethroat.

June–July: Breeding Lapwing and Ringed Plover, Redshank and Little Ringed Plover present, Common Tern feeding, Sand Martin hopefully using artificial nest bank. Potential for Hobby. Early wader passage, possibly with Little Stint, and wandering Little Egret.

August–November: Shelduck depart for a while, Canada Goose numbers swell, Common, Green and possibly Wood Sandpipers on passage, with Ruff, Greenshank and godwit species possible. Snipe and erratic Jack Snipe. Winter thrushes and mixed gull flocks.

26 MOOR GREEN LAKES

OS ref. SU 805 627

Habitat

A series of well-established and recently worked out gravel pits, adjacent to arable farmland, alongside the River Blackwater, on the Berkshire/Hampshire border, and also known as Eversley Gravel Pits. The lake verges have matured greatly during the nineties in terms of vegetation, and attract a number of bankside species. Several islands, mostly gravel-topped, play host to waders, terns and ducks. Angling is restricted on some of the waters, to the benefit of the breeding species. Under the guidance of the Moor Green Lakes Group, reserve status has been achieved for the site and two excellent hides have been constructed. A new extraction site west of the car park, commenced in 2000, has already attracted waders.

Access

The lakes infill the area between the River Blackwater, which constitutes the county boundary, and the lane from Little Sandhurst to Finchampstead. The most convenient car parking is just 1 km (0.6 mile) east of the B3016, adjacent to Moor Green Farm, where some 10 cars can be accommodated. It is wise, however, not to leave valuables in the vehicle as the car would be out of sight for much of the walk.

A typical circuit would be to follow the footpath going south from the car park to the river, alongside Colebrook Lake North, with its six islands. Turning east, and following the footpath which runs parallel and north of the Blackwater, Grove Lake comes into view. Continue past the third lake, Horseshoe Lake, eventually exiting near Mill Farm, returning to the car park via the lane. This affords views of the opposite side of the islands and some mature Oaks in fields and gardens on the way.

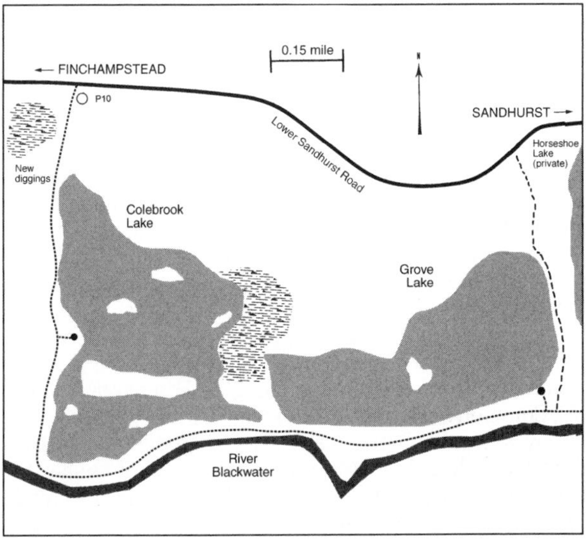

A longer walk can be created by continuing north to The Ridges at Finchampstead (see Additional Sites), where heathland species can be added to the day's list.

Species

This site is rapidly gaining a reputation for turning up the unusual, whilst also hosting a good variety of regular species. Sensitively restored with avian needs in mind, the complex offers excellent overwintering facilities for gulls and duck, good breeding features for common waders and terns and adjacent arable land accommodates typical farmland species. Consequently, the last few years have produced a very respectable 197 species, 60 of which breed regularly.

The tree-line west of the footpath leading from the car park is one of the regular haunts of Little Owl, and Lesser Spotted Woodpecker occurs in this area as well. Firecrest too has been seen among Goldcrest in this area. The fringes of the adjacent, most westerly, lake are good for breeding Lapwing, and prospective Redshank in summer, offering feeding grounds also for numerous Pied and occasional Yellow Wagtails. The islands viewed from this footpath attract passage Common and Black Terns, Ringed or Little Ringed Plovers and Ruff in summer, and good numbers of overwintering duck and Snipe in the colder months. The lake is overlooked by the main hide and many of the wader species and Water Rail can be seen within a few feet of the hide. Mandarin have bred around this water in recent times. The surrounding bushes provide nesting habitat for a number of species including Whitethroat and Reed Bunting whilst short-stay visitors have included Lapland Bunting and both Rock and Water Pipits. Even Great Grey Shrike and Hoopoe have been seen here, whilst perhaps the biggest surprise was a beautiful Shorelark in April 1998.

Having turned east where the footpath meets the river, the rough ground between the path and the lakes is worth checking for wintering Stonechat, whilst keeping an ear open for Kingfisher along the river. The bends on the river beyond the large bridge is another good place to look out for Water Rail. Alders here bring in Siskin and Redpoll occasionally, and Barn Owl have visited from across the river. The second lake, with its one island, is viewable from a new hide, and is particularly interesting to Goosander, usually arriving around the third week of November, and typical counts are around 80 birds, with a record high of 184. Another feature of this complex is the high numbers of feral Barnacle and Snow Geese which inhabit the site the year around, 225 and 20 respectively recorded at the end of 2001. These occasionally attract other wandering geese, such as White-front, Bar-headed or Greylag.

Recent visitors include Temminck's and Little Stints, Curlew Sandpiper, Whimbrel and Curlew, Spotted Redshank, Ruff, Black-tailed Godwit, Avocet and even Kentish Plover. Jack Snipe, Oystercatcher, Whimbrel and Wood Sandpiper could perhaps be expected annually. Passage raptors have been no less impressive including Honey Buzzard, Hen Harrier, Osprey and Peregrine, whilst Hobby can be expected daily during summer. Rarer ducks have included Ferruginous, Red-crested Pochard, Common Scoter, Scaup and Smew, whilst gulls have been represented by Kittiwake, Little, Glaucous and Mediterranean Gulls, and Little Tern has visited. It should not be expected, of course, to bump into these species regularly, but it does illustrate the rewards for well thought out restoration planning.

Little Owl

Calendar

Resident: Little and Great Crested Grebes, feral Barnacle and Snow Geese, Sparrowhawk, Lapwing, Little Owl, Kingfisher, potentially all three woodpeckers, Skylark, mixed corvids, Linnet, Reed Bunting, Yellowhammer. Pied and occasional Grey Wagtails, Stonechat and Goldcrest.

December–February: Gadwall, Teal, Pochard, Shoveler, occasional Goldeneye and Smew, high numbers of Goosander. Snipe, Redshank, Green Sandpiper, mixed gulls, with potential for rarer species at any time. Meadow Pipit, Siskin, large gatherings of feeding finches, including Redpoll and Brambling on occasions.

March–May: Arrival of Yellow Wagtail and Cuckoo, with prospect of Turtle Dove. Many common warblers.

June–July: Breeding Lapwing, Redshank, Common Tern, plus numerous passerine species.

August–November: Feral geese numbers swelled by juvenile Barnacle Geese, usually a fairly notable wader passage, good numbers of winter thrushes and mixed gull flocks.

27 NORTH COOKHAM

OS ref. SU 888 865

Habitat

There are many pleasant areas of Berkshire through which to walk and Cookham, although exhibiting a somewhat arable flavour, encompasses a varied habitat as it follows the River Thames by way of lowland marsh, chalk hills and mixed woodland, and as such provides interest for the birdwatcher. Cockmarsh comprises some 80 ha (200 acres) of National Trust land which is used for grazing for much of the year, and

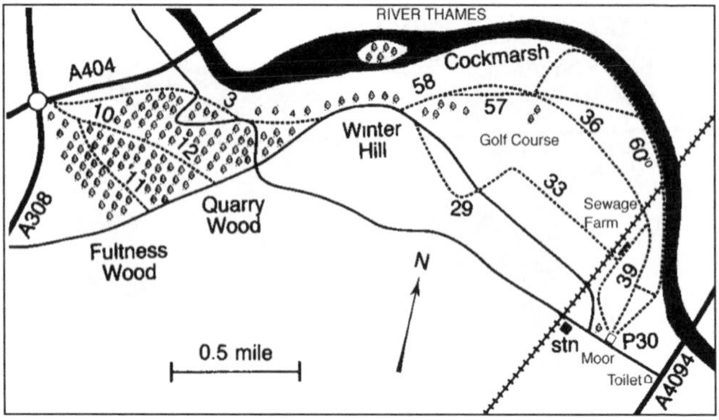

is suited to ground-nesting birds and waders. Parts of the marsh are flooded during the wetter periods of winter and indeed a small number of pools are present throughout the year. Nearby Winter Hill rises steeply to some 120 m (390 ft) above sea level and the chalky slopes suffer a little from erosion, but there is a liberal covering of Hawthorn and scrub. Further west is a series of deciduous woodlands, recently taken into the ownership of the Woodland Trust, including Quarry Wood, High Wood and Fultness Wood, which slope sharply downwards to the streams and meadows of Bisham below.

Access

Because of the Thames which bounds most of the walk to the north, and the lack of parking facilities on the A404 and Quarry Road, all access by car has to be along the southern parts of the walk. The National Trust car park at Cookham Moor, on the local bus route, caters for 30 vehicles and is approached through the picturesque village of Cookham from the A4094 Maidenhead–Bourne End road (the only toilets in the vicinity are at this junction). There are also parking spaces along Winter Hill Road and room for a small number of vehicles near the entrances to Quarry Wood. Most of the other lanes are too narrow to permit parking. A useful footpath map of the whole area is available from the Ramblers Association. (See Useful Addresses.)

(In the following text for this section, path numbers from the Ramblers Association map have been used. They also appear on the North Cookham map.)

Species

A convenient starting point would be the National Trust car park on Cookham Moor. Cross Marsh Meadow towards the river, looking for Kestrel, Little Owl, hawking hirundines and passage Yellow Wagtail on the way. On the river, there will most likely be Great Crested Grebe and possibly Kingfisher plus mandatory Mallard and Coot. In summer, Common Tern may be seen whilst in winter, small numbers of Pochard and Tufted Duck loaf against the far bank. Grey Heron are never far away and Little Egret has used this stretch in the past.

The riverbank leads to Cockmarsh, though in very wet spells it is preferable to use the path alongside the golf course, joining path 36, as this crosses the marsh on firmer ground. The copse near the railway bridge is popular for Goldcrest and Bullfinch and occasionally Whinchat, which favour the fence alongside the ditch. Follow the tree-line to the marsh, looking for Mistle Thrush, more Little Owl, and Whitethroat in summer.

On the marsh itself one might hope to see Lapwing, particularly in winter when quite large numbers will share the open space with flocks of Canada and Greylag Geese, often interspersed with Egyptian and Bar-headed varieties. Sizeable mixed flocks of winter thrushes may be present and only outnumbered by gatherings of Starling. Once a popular location for passage Snipe, Greenshank and even breeding Redshank, too much disturbance of late has spoiled that, but Lapwing will breed occasionally. The route to the top of Winter Hill will produce Linnet and Yellowhammer at most times and Whitethroat, Willow Warbler and Chiffchaff in summer. Blackcap and Garden Warbler breed among the bushes along the slope, and Cuckoo is another likely performer. From the 'peak' of Winter Hill, it is fascinating to watch hirundines and Swift from above as they make maximum use of the air currents fashioned by the slopes. And with Hobby breeding in the Thames Valley nowadays, up to 10 may be found hunting together towards the end of the season. But do take time to look along the escarpment to the north of Winter Hill as, on a good day, up to twelve Red Kite and half a dozen Common Buzzard should be seen in the distance. A telescope is most useful at this point.

The woods to the west of Winter Hill will guarantee Green Woodpecker 'yaffling' and, in summer, Chiffchaff singing. Countless Wren will disclose the observer's presence to every other species in the area in typical fashion. It is also a favourite courting place for Greater Spotted Woodpecker, the males vying for the attentions of indifferent females with much head bobbing and chattering. This first compartment, Quarry Wood, comprises mainly Beech, Oak, Sycamore, some Silver Birch and Rowan and approximately five per cent conifer. Storm damage in 1987 has opened up large areas for secondary growth, increasing prospects for Blackcap, Chiffchaff, and Willow Warbler to nest. All three species of woodpeckers are possible and the tit family is also well represented, including Marsh Tit. Numerous Tawny Owl boxes have been installed by the Hawk and Owl Trust and are monitored annually by the RSPB. Several have already been used by Tawnys and even Mandarin Duck have got in on the act.

Exploration of the woods against a backdrop of Bluebells is most pleasant, and returning via Fultness Wood will pass a small colony of Jackdaw and, with moderate good fortune, Sparrowhawk will be seen, dashing through the wood at low level with an uncanny ability to avoid collisions. Other species encountered will be Goldcrest, Mistle Thrush and Nuthatch, whilst wintertime sees large numbers of Fieldfare and Redwing, and flocks of Chaffinch should be checked for Brambling. When back on top of Winter Hill, one may return via the outgoing journey or traverse the golf course towards footpath 33. This will afford opportunities to find Green Woodpecker, all three wagtails (in season), Skylark and Meadow Pipit and possibly Grey Partridge. Keep an eye to the skies as both Red Kite and Hobby are possible. For the unsated, and perhaps after a break at the car park, the pathway leading south from that point leads via paddocks, farmland and Widbrook Common to pass near Summerleaze Gravel Pit some 2.5 km away. This walk may well turn up Yellowhammer, Linnet, Reed Bunting and Stonechat along the way, with Ring-necked Parakeet a distinct possibility as they often breed in the streamside poplars there. Many of the 30 Little Owl boxes

Grey Partridge

installed around adjacent fields have been utilised, so scanning of open trees and fence lines might be appropriately rewarded. Widbrook Common to the east of the trail often floods in winter and may host waders such as Redshank and Greenshank, most of the likely gulls and large numbers of winter thrushes. Access to the lake itself is not possible but adjacent pathways will allow views of breeding Common Tern and hundreds of Sand and House Martins, often harried by Hobby, with roosting Cormorant, hundreds of gulls and rafts of waterfowl in season. The lake has hosted Smew, Goldeneye, Goosander, breeding Little Ringed Plover and even Bittern, so anything is possible.

It is clear that several hours can be consumed in following a variety of routes, but the scenery and variety of species will warrant return visits to enable more time to be spent in particular areas.

Calendar

Resident: Kestrel, Sparrowhawk, Lapwing, Great Crested Grebe, Grey Heron, Kingfisher, Pied and Grey Wagtails, Mute Swan, all three woodpeckers, Ring-necked Parakeet, Marsh Tit, Skylark, Yellowhammer, Reed Bunting, Goldcrest, Little and Tawny Owls. Red Kite and Common Buzzard from Winter Hill.

December–February: Pochard, Tufted Duck, Snipe, winter thrushes, Meadow Pipit. Large Starling flocks, Siskin, occasional Redpoll and Teal. Overwintering Chiffchaff.

March–May: Whinchat, Cuckoo, hirundines, Blackcap, Willow and Garden Warblers, both species of spotted woodpecker. Wheatear, Redshank and Greenshank on passage.

June–July: Whitethroat, occasional Lesser Whitethroat (especially around the golf course), Spotted Flycatcher. Common Tern over the Thames, Hobby particularly active.

August–November: Family groups of Canada Geese, family parties of Hobby hunting over Widbrook Common, House Martin and numerous wagtails into October. Redwing and Fieldfare (often exceeding 200 of each species), large numbers of Black-headed and Common Gulls on flyway to London reservoirs.

28 OLD SLADE AREA

OS ref. TQ 040 780

Habitat

Consider the perfect birdwatching location, then consider this: a series of overgrown, unkempt and partially-abandoned pits in an area of landfill and 'wasteland', encapsulated in the constant roar of 'Decibel Valley', with traffic noise from two motorways, a low-flying 'plane every minute, and occasional firing from the adjacent gun club. Add massed ranks of silver power pylons, a few impassable tracks, destruction of the only hide and one of the busiest lorry parks and storage complexes in west London, and you have Old Slade. Yet birds seem not to mind, so why should we.

The restored Old Slade Lake with adjacent sewage treatment work, was at its best many years ago before being re-excavated for gravel when the M25 was built. It was under a BBOWT development plan for a while, but threats of yet further excavation if M25 widening occurs has resulted in the site becoming somewhat overgrown. Now that Terminal 5 at Heathrow has been given the go-ahead, the STW too will be modernised, potentially to the detriment of its avian value. To the west are paddocks and a significant area of rough pasture, while the River Colne separates this lake from the Orlitts fishing lakes to the south. Nearby is an occasional gull roost on farmland, and the relatively-new and better-maintained Thorney Park, comprising rough meadow and a sizeable reed-fringed lake.

Access

Hemmed in between the M4 and M25 north of Poyle, Old Slade Lake is accessed from Old Slade Lane, off the road between Richings Park and Langley (North Park Road). Park at the end of the lane and walk across the motorway bridge to avoid being locked in by a swing-gate operated by local horse riders. The Colne Valley Way passes the entrance of the lake. Footpaths are available to the west of the lake, and the open ground abutting the STW can be used to search for birds through the chain link fencing around it. The gull roost can be observed from North Park Way just west of Old Slade Lane, looking north at TQ 025 794, whilst Thorney Park is just two minutes away on the same road, east of Old Slade Lane and taking the first turning on the right having crossed the M25 motorway. Orlitts North and South lakes can only be accessed through the entrance to Lakeside Industrial Estate off the A4 at TQ 037 773.

Species

The gull roost is used by birds from nearby Queen Mother Reservoir and may contain up to 100 Great Black-backed Gull, numerous Herring and hundreds of Black-headed Gulls in season. Of course, the modern challenge is to seek out Yellow-legged, Caspian and Mediterranean Gulls, all of which have become more likely as these species establish themselves inland and birders get better at sorting them out. Old Slade Lake may infrequently hold overwintering Scaup and Goosander and occasional Shelduck, but in the main it is a scene of Pochard, Tufted Duck, Gadwall and several Little Grebe. The gentler sloping edges can attract

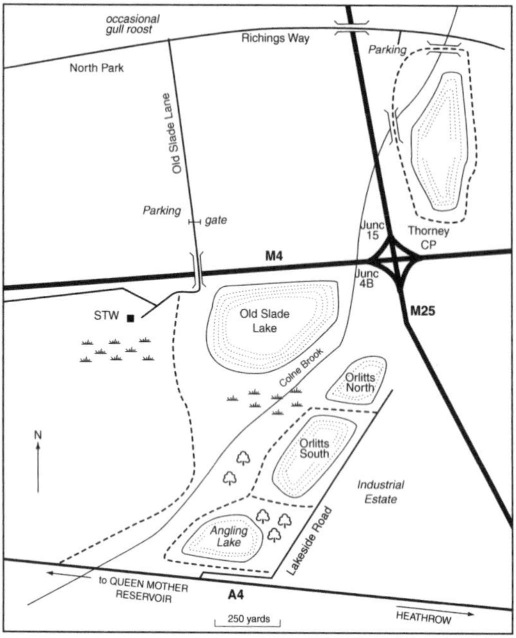

Common and Green Sandpipers, but the heady days of numerous wader species seem behind us. A single island near the entrance occasionally harbours Snipe, whilst the bushes and hedges around the pit host winter thrushes and mixed feeding flocks of Long-tailed, Blue and Great Tits, Goldcrest and Goldfinch in winter, with Blackcap and Whitethroat in summer. Bullfinch and groups of Greenfinch are regular and Song Thrush seem content here, with several pairs around. There are small reeded areas which attract Reed Warbler. The adjacent STW still depends on the old techniques and has several small pools and a good area of reed mace, encouraging Moorhen and possible Water Rail in winter, and Reed Bunting, Sedge and Reed Warblers in summer. For that reason, Cuckoo might be expected, and Pied Wagtail are always about. Rough pasture adjacent has produced Wheatear, and both Whinchat and Stonechat are regular prospects along with more Reed Bunting. The local Rook seem to have abandoned their rookery, as indeed the Tree Sparrow have forsaken the locality. The Common Tern raft has been withdrawn from use, but the birds still feed on the lake and carry morsels off to other breeding waters.

Orlitts North and South lakes comprise two medium-sized waters, used for angling and have been constantly under threat of development as the adjacent industrial estate has flexed its muscles for some years. However, they are still there and can attract a good variety of birds. They are probably best in winter when good numbers of duck use the site, including a few dozen Teal which have grown accustomed to people wandering about quite close. Small numbers of Gadwall and Pochard will be found, and both Goldeneye and Smew are real prospects. Cormorant use dead trees on the small islands to roost, and are worth checking in case a Shag decides to join in. Snipe also use these islands for roosting. The surrounding vegetation is home to groups of mixed passerines in winter, including Bullfinch, and Sedge Warbler try to shout loud enough to be heard above the summer travel madness around this busy location. There is a trail behind the lakes, but it is effectively impassable and access would only disturb the waterfowl, so it is best to observe from the banks near the Industrial Estate feeder road.

Thorney Country Park is a recent addition to the manicured Colne Valley Park scheme stretching through much of southern Bucks, and is in stark contrast to the areas mentioned above. Consisting of a good-sized lake, with beds of mature reeds, it is a typical country park, with a footpath all the way round the lake perimeter to guarantee the maximum disturbance to waterfowl, or to afford the best views of whatever is about, whichever viewpoint is preferred. In the event, however, fair numbers of duck and other waterfowl use the lake, and in winter that includes Goosander, Goldeneye and possible Smew. A tern raft is sometimes taken over by Heron and Cormorant, and Black-headed Gull bred here in 2001, the first breeding record for the county. The adjacent stream serves the local Kingfisher well. Carefully planned shrubbery and copses are maturing nicely, attracting summer migrants in addition to resident Grey Wagtail and common parkland species. Indeed, Chiffchaff have already adopted the site for overwintering. Not as yet a haven for rarities, but worth a look if visiting the other sites of Old Slade and Orlitts.

Calendar

Resident: Kestrel, Sparrowhawk, Lapwing, Little and Great Crested Grebes, common waterfowl, Grey Heron, Kingfisher, Pied and Grey Wagtails, Mute Swan, Green Woodpecker, common tits, Skylark, Bullfinch, occasional Yellowhammer and Meadow Pipit.

December–February: Cormorant roost, Pochard, Tufted Duck, Teal and possible Goldeneye. Snipe, winter thrushes, more Meadow Pipit. Starling flocks, Reed Bunting, possible Stonechat (also on adjacent golf course). Overwintering Chiffchaff. Numerous gulls on adjacent roost fields.

March–May: Whinchat, Cuckoo, hirundines, Blackcap, Chiffchaff, Willow Warbler, Great Spotted Woodpecker. Yellow Wagtail, Wheatear, Common Sandpiper and Redshank on passage.

June–July: Whitethroat, possible Reed Warbler, Common Tern.

August–November: Family groups of Canada Geese, House and Sand Martins feeding into October. Redwing and Fieldfare on paddocks (sometimes exceeding 200 of each species), large numbers of Black-headed and Common Gulls on flyway to London reservoirs.

29 QUEEN MOTHER RESERVOIR

OS ref. TQ 005 770

Habitat

Queen Mother Reservoir is a totally artificial, steep-sided body of water, 140 ha (350 acres) in size with concrete walls and no marginal vegetation. The water is very deep and this, together with its enormous size, ensures it does not freeze over even during the most insistent of frosts. The outer banks, which form the retaining walls, are grassed on the outside and grazed by sheep. A small stream surrounds the site. The reservoir is managed jointly by Datchet Watersports Ltd (01753 683990) and Thames Water, who provide a birdwatching permit for this and several other local reservoirs. (See Useful Addresses.)

Access

The site is south of junction 5 of the M4, the only entrance halfway along the Colnbrook–Horton road, the local bus route. Ascending the ramp, permit holders may park near the sailing club centre at water level. A telescope is essential to scan this enormous pond. The main gates are only open during sailing hours (from 09:00 hrs Tuesday to Sunday, closed Monday) and observations can only be made in the vicinity of the club building, walking around the periphery of the reservoir being not allowed. Presentation of one's Thames Water permit to the Club office will enable the necessary exit pass card to be obtained or a £5 parking charge may be applied.

Species

Perhaps as a result of being the most westerly of the London reservoirs, Queen Mother has a reputation for turning up the rarer species, as well as attracting typical birds of large water bodies. One of the main spectacles here is the enormous gull roost which is formed just prior to dusk. Streaming in from locations up to 24 km (15 miles) away during the last hour of daylight, past the stark outlines of Windsor Castle, the gulls descend noisily and argumentatively before alighting on the ever-reducing area of free water in the centre of the lake. Usually, Great Black-backs are amongst the throng which, in modern times, has been shown to include Yellow-legged and Caspian Gulls. Iceland, Glaucous and Mediterranean Gulls have all been detected, and the reservoir afforded the county's first record of Sabine's Gull and in March 2001 a Kumlien's Gull.

Duck movements are changing and Queen Mother rarely holds the four-figure rafts of Tufted Duck nowadays, but such groups as are present should be checked for Scaup. Great Crested Grebe may be plentiful but it is the more scarce grebes that steal the attention. Red-necked and Black-necked Grebes are regular visitors in ones or twos and Slavonian Grebe spend a few days here occasionally. Cormorant are regular visitors but it is as well to look twice at any distant bird as all three divers are possibilities during December to February, with occasions when Black-throated and Great Northern Divers have been seen together.

Wintertime occasionally produces a Brent Goose or two and Shelduck are more regular, one pair in fact producing young for possibly

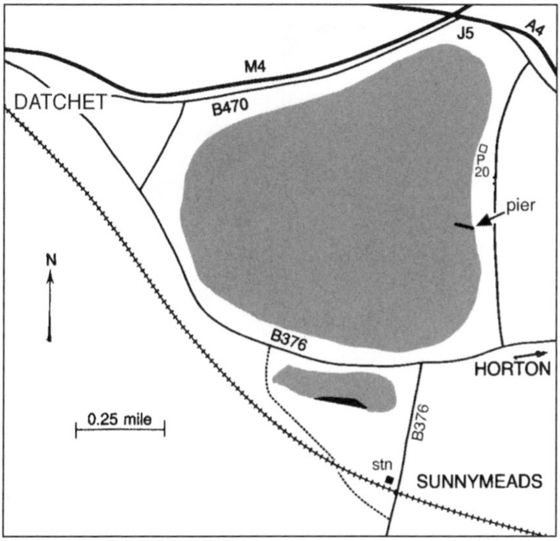

the first time here in 2000. Ducks are well represented with Mandarin beginning to visit occasionally, and reasonable numbers of Shoveler and Pochard. Common Scoter turn up almost annually. Goldeneye and Smew on the other hand, though occasionally present, seem to prefer Wraysbury gravel pits. Meanwhile, the small gravel pit near the railway station is likely to tempt several Goosander (usually redheads) and increased numbers of Canada Geese, though they are often disturbed by water-skiing. Red-breasted Merganser may be found there but the third sawbill, the Smew, seems to be seen in ever-reducing numbers of late. Back on the reservoir, bad weather in late autumn may well entice a Grey Phalarope, and any of the skuas may pass through. The grassed surrounds of the lake attract numbers of Meadow Pipit and Rock Pipit can be found in most months, whilst fields to the east occasionally hold Lapwing and Golden Plover. Kestrel hover hopefully and Sparrowhawk often frequent the area. A more recent feature has been the presence of two or three Peregrines in the area, increasing hopes of possible breeding in the county for the first time in may decades. The various towers and pylons should be checked for these magnificent birds. Of the more unusual passerines, Snow Bunting, and even Lapland Bunting, have been seen on the gravel path and sloping concrete walls.

From mid-March, the water's edge should be checked on every visit for passage waders. Common Sandpiper and Little Ringed Plover may be first through, followed by Ringed Plover, Sanderling, and Dunlin. Wheatear and Yellow Wagtail are recorded in most years. The spring passage usually involves spectacular numbers of Swift and any of the usual terns can be expected, the Black Tern perhaps looking the most attractive, unless of course White-winged Black Tern choose to visit, as occurred in May 2000. Check the bushes around the periphery for Whitethroat, Lesser Whitethroat and Blackcap and the fields opposite the gateway for gulls and wandering geese. The return passage commences in July with Oystercatcher, Redshank, Greenshank, Ruff, Curlew, Turnstone and Green Sandpiper the most likely participants,

Wheatear

and Common Sandpiper in double figures. Less regular visitors have included Bittern, Curlew Sandpiper, Little Stint, Long-tailed Duck and Eider, Pintail, and Little Gull. The sight of a dashing Leach's Petrel amongst very surprised gulls provided a spectacle in October 2000, to be followed by a dark-phase juvenile Arctic Skua chasing the same gulls the following month, reflecting a similar scene two years earlier with a Long-tailed Skua. A visit here on the way to or from Wraysbury gravel pits is therefore thoroughly recommended.

Calendar

Resident: Great Crested Grebe, Cormorant, Mute Swan, Canada Geese, occasional Shelduck, Mallard, Tufted Duck, Kestrel, Black-headed Gull, Kingfisher, Green Woodpecker, Jackdaw, Reed Bunting. Possible Peregrine.

December–February: Most active period. Spectacular gull roosts, numbers of common winter ducks. Possibly all three divers and five grebes, Shag, scoters, Scaup, all three sawbills, Ruddy Duck, Eider and Long-tailed Duck. Prospect of Merlin. Heavy weather may produce wrecks of auks or rarer gulls. Many Meadow Pipit, occasional Rock Pipit. Possibility of Black Redstart or Snow Bunting.

March–May: Much of the December–February scene overflows to March, gradually enhanced with spring movement. Occasional Kittiwake and Black Tern on the reservoir. Large numbers of Swift by April. Wheatear, Whinchat or any of the three wagtails on the walls or lower car park.

June–July: The quiet period.

August–November: Gradual build-up to winter scene. Winter ducks arriving from end of September by which time passage terns will have gone through. Meadow Pipit flock around the reservoir. Chance of late autumn pelagics.

30 SNELSMORE COMMON COUNTRY PARK

OS ref. SU 460 708

Habitat

Comprising some 100 ha (250 acres), Snelsmore Common represents the largest tract of lowland heath (one sixth of the total) remaining in Berkshire. Some of the heath has been overtaken by woodland, mainly Birch, Oak, Hazel and Crab Apple, to the west, but more coniferous in the east. The boundary between heath and woodland is fashioned by advancing Birch scrub, controlled by voluntary groups who are attempting to increase the area of Heather and moorgrass. Habitat variety is enhanced by valley bog with its particular flora, including Bog Bean, Bog Asphodel and sundew. The site, a SSSI, is excellent for butterflies, including White Admiral and Purple Emperor. Lizard and Grass Snake are common, and Adders are prevalent in some years. Mammal species on the common include Fox, Badger, Stoat, Weasel and occasional deer. Frogs and Newts too are plentiful in the various pools that have been formed.

Access

The common lies to the west of the B4494 Newbury to Wantage road, approximately 2 km (1.25 miles) north of Donnington. The area is reached from junction 13 of the M4 or via the A4 which runs through Newbury. There are ample parking facilities and toilets are available at the main entrance. Although not a rural common as such, the owners of the land permit visitors to roam freely. However, it is preferable to utilise the many footpaths and tracks to avoid damage to plants. A bridleway has been nominated around the periphery which, in wet weather, can be difficult to traverse but in summer provides a useful track for circumnavigation of the common.

Species

The winter scene on the common serves up a fairly typical menu of Blue, Great, Coal and Long-tailed Tits, in consortium with Goldcrest in woodland and shrubs near the car park, and foraging Song Thrush and Robin, with occasional Redwing. Nuthatch, Treecreeper and Great Spotted Woodpecker will be building up reserves with an eye to the coming breeding season and Tawny Owl will be heard calling. Lesser Spotted Woodpecker may be found, as will small numbers of Siskin and Redpoll working the Birch and Alder trees. Away from the woodland, the open heath attracts Meadow Pipit and small groups of Yellowhammer and an occasional Stonechat.

The nesting season attracts many species, such as Bullfinch, Greenfinch and Goldfinch, with Linnet occupying the heather where Whitethroat can also be expected. Willow Warbler seem to occupy every small Silver Birch, together with less numerous Chiffchaff. The edges of the open valley bogs and heather beds are likely places for Tree Pipit. Four or five pairs of this speckled bird are usually found here, observed either in full song-flight with pink legs dangling, sitting on a prominent perch, or moving about low down amongst marginal leaf-litter. During the passage period in April, numbers of this exorbitant songster may

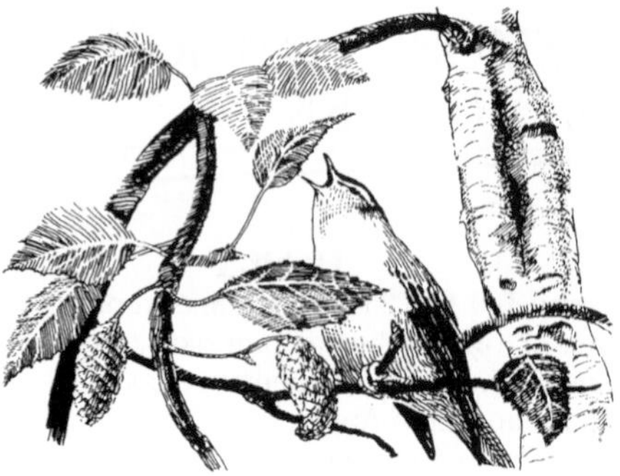

Wood Warbler

reach double figures. In the wooded area, all three woodpeckers can be seen, the two spotted species utilising existing holes in dead Silver Birch trees. Willow Tit, however, may have forsaken the common in recent years. Cuckoo exploit the area, as does the resident Sparrowhawk. Circling quite high or dashing past at low level, a Hobby may pay a visit, but regrettably sightings are not as regular as those of the expanding Common Buzzard population.

Of the specialty birds, Nightingale seem not to find favour with the common all that often and conditions are perhaps not ideal for Redstart. However, an evening visit between May and July could well be rewarded with the 'churring' of Nightjar. Numbers have never been high here and recently even fewer have turned up, but the prospect certainly remains. In any event, whilst waiting, 'roding' Woodcock are another possibility. While never numerous, Wood Warbler appear quite regularly, particularly in areas of deciduous woodland with a sparse understorey. In song the bird can be confiding, but if the single note alarm is given, withdraw to give the maximum chance of successful breeding.

Reed Bunting is present but Spotted Flycatcher are not recorded as often as one might expect and Garden Warbler will probably take some finding. Blackcap are, however, relatively common, breeding in the shrubbery in the deciduous woodland. During the autumn passage it will be difficult to separate those birds which had oversummered here from their relatives which may make fleeting visits during their return from northern breeding grounds. Adjacent farmland hosts Yellowhammer, Little Owl and there are often more Common Buzzard soaring over nearby Home Farm.

Threatened in modern times by the construction of the infamous Newbury by-pass across the southern tip, the common remains a place of solitude with a good range of species throughout the year.

Calendar

Resident: Sparrowhawk, Kestrel, soaring Common Buzzard, Woodcock, Stock and Collared Doves, Tawny Owl, Green, Great Spotted and Lesser Spotted Woodpeckers. Mistle Thrush, Goldcrest, Marsh Tit, Nuthatch, Treecreeper, occasional Jackdaw, common finches, Yellowhammer and Reed Bunting.

December–February: Small mixed feeding flocks of tits and Chaffinch, some Redwing, but few Fieldfare. Groups of Siskin and Redpoll.

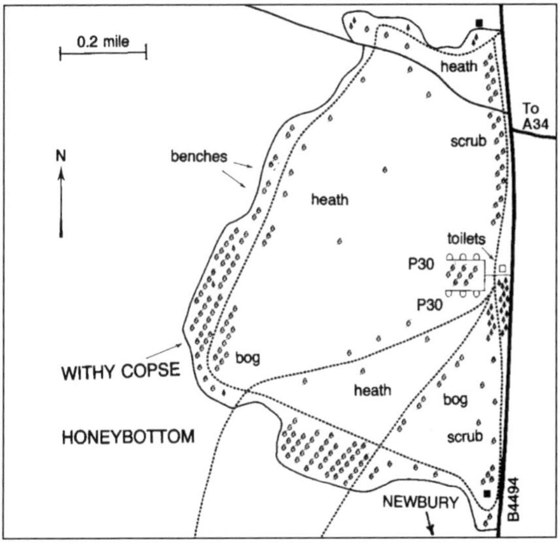

March–May: Arrival of breeding species, possibility of passage Hobby and Nightingale.

June–July: Breeding in progress. Possibility of Wood Warbler and Turtle Dove. Tree Pipit, Nightjar and 'roding' Woodcock.

August–November: Reverse migration during August and early September, though Willow Warbler seen almost to October, when winter thrushes arrive.

31 THATCHAM MOOR AREA **OS ref. SU 505 667**

Habitat

Straddling the A4, Thatcham rests in the umbrella of sprawling Newbury 3.2 km (2 miles) away, and is a little east of where the River Lambourn drains the Downs into the River Kennet. At Thatcham Moors, the River Kennet and the Kennet and Avon Canal combine with woodland, well served with footpaths, providing a varied habitat for birds. Pits formed by earlier gravel workings have been flooded and landscaped to the benefit of birds and anglers alike. The recently-constructed Discovery Centre has brought an important educational facility to this excellent reserve, and a new hide has been positioned opposite the STW. Further south is the canal and river complex, beyond which are the Race Course Gravel Pit used for trout fishing. Adjacent to these pools is the locally-renowned Lower Farm pit, recently equipped with an excellent hide courtesy of

Messrs Tarmac. Sculpted to attract birds of water, scrape and island, its species richness is increasing all the while, though there are plans for some of it to be made accessible for still more angling.

Further south lies the Baynes and Bowdown Reserve, a 50 ha (150 acre) wood comprising mixed deciduous trees and a large number of woodland plant species, BBOWT's largest Berkshire reserve. With the small area of heathland separating the two woods, the whole complex is a SSSI. The wood slopes down into the Kennet Valley and a matrix of small streams passes through the woodland glades, supporting Alder at these levels, in contrast to the Oak, Hazel, Birch and Rowan, plus some Cherry trees, on the higher reaches. Deer can be found in these woods together with a good cross-section of woodland birds. The area between the woods and waterways is taken up by the meadows, pastures and arable fields belonging to Lower Farm.

Access

Thatcham can be approached going west along the A4 from junction 12 of the M4, or from junction 13 via Newbury on the A34. Running parallel to, and south of, the A4 through the town is Lower Way (a local bus route) where there are three accesses points. Prince Hold Road, the most westerly, is an unmade track which can hold a few vehicles, but the official Discovery Centre car park, with capacity for more than 50 vehicles, is on the left along a track almost opposite Heron Way. Further down this track is a smaller reserve car park for about 20 vehicles, which is nearer to the 'wild side' of the reserve. If it is intended to walk the whole area referred to, including Baynes and Bowdown Woods, the Centre, which has toilet and catering facilities, is as good a starting place as any (telephone 01635 874381).

Bowdown Wood itself has parking facilities. Taking the A34 south from Newbury, turn left at the island at the end of the dual carriageway and follow this road through Bury's Bank. Passing the golf course on the left, there is a track, also on the left, which leads to Lower Farm, the trout pool, and the wood. The car park is 500 m (550 yds) along this track. BBOWT members wishing to visit the Baynes Reserve should continue along Bury's Bank Road to another track on the left down which a small car park will be found past Beggars Roost.

Lower Farm pit can be accessed from the BBOWT car park, continuing along the lane for 300 m, or can be approached by car from the Newbury direction, taking Hambridge Road off the A4 east of the town, and turning left at the first roundabout, taking care at the traffic lights under the railway bridge as construction traffic coming in the opposite direction often use them on a discretionary basis! A small car park is available at SU 499 663. If the hide is locked, views are easily obtained from the raised observation point at which an information board is positioned.

Species

Willows Lake (or Leisure Lake), immediately adjacent to the centre, hosts a collection of typical confiding waterfowl, but it is worth checking for Goldeneye, Pochard and other wild ducks. An artificial Sand Martin structure on the small island has been regularly used, and waders have used the banks of the island too, even Whimbrel on one occasion. South of this pool, a high hedge of Hawthorn and willow extends around the east end of Long Lake and attracts Whitethroat in summer and Yellowhammer and Bullfinch all year, in addition to more

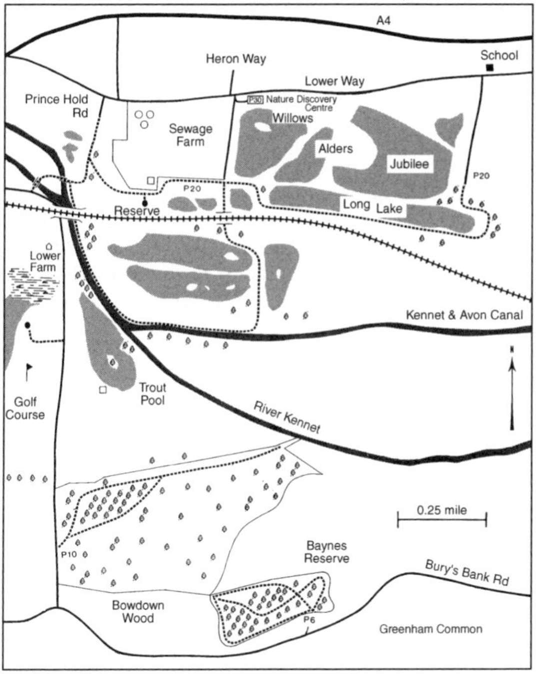

common hedgerow species. The lake itself is always likely to contain Great Crested Grebe and even held a Great Northern Diver on one occasion, whilst Osprey has used the lakes in passing. Beyond the ditch, and extending to the railway line some 50 m (55 yds) away is a large bed of Yellow Iris, nettles, docks and thistles, covered in pink Field Bindweed in summer. This patch is often host to Goldfinch, Linnet, Greenfinch, warblers and Reed Bunting.

West of Long Lake, there is a permitted crossing over the high-speed railway line. The scrub and reedbeds beyond here are host to Cetti's Warbler and other warblers in summer and the reedbed is being enlarged to attract Bittern and Bearded Tit to join the many Water Rail on the reserve. Ringing exercises here often result in dozens of adult and young Sedge and Reed Warblers getting manacled. There are further possibilities of Turtle Dove here and, throughout the reserve, Whitethroat and Lesser Whitethroat can be expected, with Grasshopper Warbler a definite prospect. Cuckoo are often busy enough for the females' bubbling calls to be heard clearly in response to excitable males. This track leads to the canal at the point of a renewed lock. A cautious approach plus a few patient minutes spent here will usually result in views of one or two Kingfisher, and almost certainly Grey Wagtail. Little Grebe favour this area too and small groups of five or so will gather in winter, diving in unison for food. Turning right to follow the canal bank, watch for Cuckoo in summer and Kestrel and Sparrowhawk all year round, and for Siskin in Alders on the opposite bank. Further along, the point is reached where the railway passes over the canal. Here, one can decide on a shorter circular walk by re-entering the reserve at its western edge, returning to the car park via the STW. If so, look out for

Reed and Sedge Warblers, and listen again for Turtle Dove, and with luck, more Cetti's and Grasshopper Warblers. Otherwise, use the small swing bridge to cross the canal, and the small footbridge opposite to cross the gravel chute, taking the footpath which approaches the railway embankment. The lane on the other side of the tracks leads to Lower Farm.

The first pools on the left beyond the railway line, known as Race Course Gravel Pit, attract warblers and occasional Water Rail. Great Crested and Little Grebes breed on these pools and Canada Goose is fairly common. In between fishing sessions, numbers of Coot, Pochard and Gadwall move freely about, whilst in surrounding shrubbery, Blackcap, Chiffchaff and occasional Lesser Whitethroat summer, replaced by mixed flocks of tits and finches in winter. The small islands on the pools often attract Cormorant and Black-headed Gull, and occasionally Redshank and other waders use the water's edge. Large flocks of Lapwing gather on the surrounding farmland and more Cetti's and Grasshopper Warblers have been recorded in the perimeter vegetation, though are more likely heard than seen. Access is strictly limited but views from the Lower Farm track suffice.

At this point there is a good view of the racecourse and, on non-racing days, there may well be sizeable flocks of Lapwing and Carrion Crow. In winter, these will be joined by 2,000 or more Golden Plover. Fieldfare and Redwing can be expected at this time of the year and Skylark and Meadow Pipit will almost certainly be seen.

Beyond the farm buildings, on the right-hand side, is Lower Farm gravel pit, which has quickly matured, encouraging waders such as Common and Green Sandpipers, Redshank, Greenshank, Ringed and Little Ringed Plovers, the latter two species breeding here. Snipe, feeding just outside the hide window, may reach 30 or more and can be accompanied by Jack Snipe. Rarer visitors have included Temminck's Stint, Curlew Sandpiper and Black-tailed Godwit. Ruddy Duck, Smew and Goldeneye, or even Garganey can be anticipated in season whilst the wasteland surrounding the site occasionally holds Stonechat, Whinchat and a few breeding Shelduck. Hirundines attract hunting Hobby to a backdrop of singing Lesser Whitethroat. Common Tern are present in summer followed by large numbers of Lapwing and Golden Plover, some of the latter obtaining their glorious breeding plumage before departing in April. Not a notable gull roost but Little Gull have visited whilst a pair of Black-necked Grebe called in during May 2000. Marsh Harrier visited later the same year, as did an Osprey and a Spoonbill, while Peregrine has been a regular visitor from nearby Theale.

A little further along the track is Bowdown Wood. At the entrance to the wood is a noticeboard indicating the routes of paths through the area. It is an interesting woodland, more open than most and contains a wide variety of plants so it is worth taking a suitable guide book. All three woodpeckers are present and there are numerous Wren, Robin and Dunnock territories. Nuthatch, Treecreeper and Marsh Tit may be few in number but all the woodland summer warblers can be anticipated and the owl-like hoots of the Stock Dove heard. Along the right-hand footpath a small and rudimentary shelter has been constructed from which tits, Goldcrest and finches may be watched in relative comfort or, in early morning, possibly Roe and Muntjac Deer. Be prepared for mosquitoes, especially at evening time if waiting for Nightingale, Tawny Owl or Woodcock. Butterfly species include Purple Emperor, Purple Hairstreak and Grayling. The adjacent Baynes Reserve has produced regular sightings of Tree Pipit.

Retracing one's footsteps over the farm lane, railway track and canal, rejoin the original footpath under the railway bridge. Continuing north, over the western edge of the marsh, may reveal Grey Heron and mixed gull flocks from a small pit on the left which has recently been landscaped. Cross the small footbridge at the far side of the marsh and turn right to the STW and visit the new hide. Several species may be seen here, including Nightingale. Grey Wagtail frequents this area too, until the local Sparrowhawk puts everything to flight. Further along this path is the smaller reserve car park which abuts a number of small pools on which Little Grebe and Reed Warbler breed. The overhead power cables are another favourite roosting place for purring Turtle Dove. Beyond the car park are Willows and Alders Lakes again and the return path to the Discovery Centre car park. Throughout the walk, Lesser Black-backed Gull and Common Tern may be seen and Black Tern has been recorded. Wintering duck species include Gadwall, Pochard, and Teal with occasional Shoveler, Goldeneye and sawbills.

Thatcham Moor has matured greatly in recent years and continues to draw in many species. Typical of such sites, almost anything might turn up and recent records include Curlew, Ringed and Little Ringed Plovers, even Oystercatcher, Osprey, Goshawk and Bittern. American Wigeon has been a recent addition as has Pintail and Spotted Crake, Whimbrel and Avocet. No doubt the 'list' for the area will increase with further observation in the future.

A dawn chorus at Bowdown, followed by a day's wandering around the pits and pools, ending up on Greenham Common for Nightjars at dusk; what better way to spend a spring or summers day.

Calendar

Resident: Little Grebe, Grey Heron, Mute Swan, Canada Goose, Shelduck, Kestrel, Sparrowhawk, Grey Partridge, Lapwing, Woodcock, Collared Dove, Tawny and Little Owls, Kingfisher, all three woodpeckers, Skylark, mixed corvids, Treecreeper, Linnet, Reed and Corn Buntings, Yellowhammer. Pied and Grey Wagtails, occasional Barn Owl.

December–February: Bewick's Swan (occasional), Gadwall, Teal, Shoveler, Pochard, Ruddy Duck, Goldeneye (occasional), Smew, Water Rail, good numbers of Golden Plover, Snipe, sizeable flocks of mixed gulls, Meadow Pipit, winter thrushes, Siskin and Brambling, overwintering Chiffchaff. Chance of rarer waders and waterfowl.

March–May: Peregrine, Turtle Dove, common warblers, Whinchat, Cuckoo, Common Sandpiper.

June–July: Breeding Ringed and Little Ringed Plovers, Hobby, Common Tern, Swift, hirundines, occasional Yellow Wagtail. Reed and Sedge Warblers, Nightingale. Chance of Cetti's Warbler.

August–November: Canada Geese start flocking, winter ducks arrive, many on passage, final broods of Great Crested Grebe, passage waders, large flocks of gull, especially Black-headed and Herring, and regular Yellow-legged Gull, hirundines massing for migration and winter thrushes arrive. Mixed flocks of finches gather from September. Irregular visits of Stonechat.

32 THEALE GRAVEL PITS

OS ref. SU 676 703

Habitat

This well-known site consists of a series of gravel pits, of varying sizes, most of the waters being fished regularly. Many are used for sailing and water-skiing; however, there are quiet corners where waterfowl and waders exist with less disturbance. In total, the complex includes some 50 ha (125 acres) of water surface, but this is changing continuously as extensive mineral extraction work continues and much was lost to the construction of a motorway service centre. Some pits have become landfill with eventual agricultural and light industrial use planned. Adjacent to the area, the A33 relief road and Green Park office development has been built on the original flood-meadows, destroying some valuable habitat. To assist the reader, the area has been divided into three complexes: Burghfield, Moatlands and Theale, with numbered references used on each map.

Burghfield (Map A) The two pools north of Smallmead Road (1 and 2) are less productive these days, and are heavily fished. Further north a former pit (3) is now a major landfill site and many gulls frequent the adjoining pits to wash and preen. The pools each side of Kirtons Farm (4 and 5) are becoming well grown with vegetation but the eastern one of the pair (adjacent to the Hanover Hotel) is used for water sports. The larger areas of water around Searles Farm Lane are the best for birds in this sector, pools 6 and 8 being the most productive, with annual Red-crested Pochard and Ferruginous Duck encountered in autumn. Pools 9 and 10 can be scanned from several locations, the latter having areas of short grass suitable for loafing. Pools between Burnthouse Lane and Pingewood Road South have been particularly good for waders in recent times.

Moatlands (Map B) Either side of Mill Road (7 and 3) are more recent workings, now all flooded with the exception of Field Farm (8).

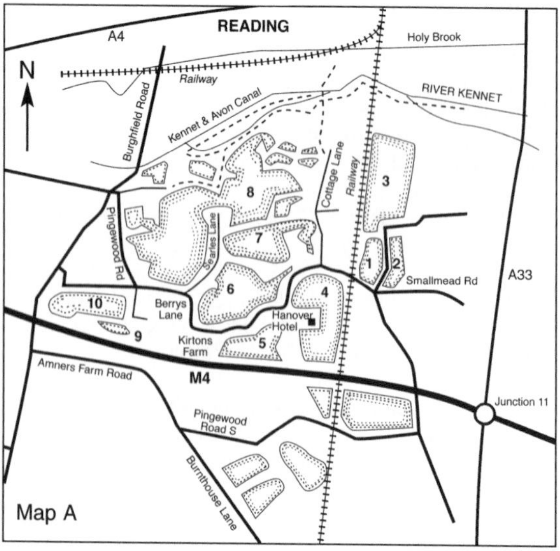

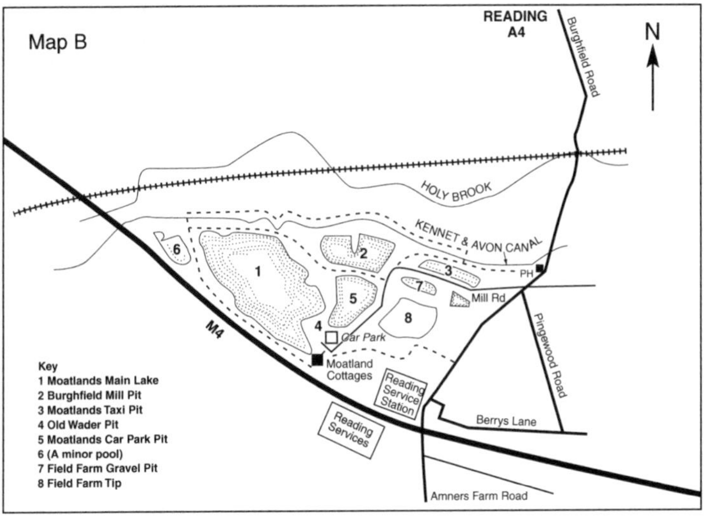

Burghfield Mill (2) and Moatlands Pits (1, 4 and 5) remain especially productive, number 1 with a sizeable island in the centre.

Theale (Map C) The lake immediately south of the motorway, Main Pit (10) is by far the largest in the area and is used by a busy sailing club. Despite this, it attracts a good range of unusual birds. The productive areas tend to be the islands near the south-west shore or beyond the islands adjacent to the motorway, and can be viewed from 'The Gardens', accessed via the pub car park. An area of continuously flooded grazing land at Bottom Lane, near Sheffield Bottom (1 and 2), can be very productive, especially for passage waders and Little Egret, whilst pits 6, 7 and 8 can be less productive, though the surrounding vegetation is good for tits and warblers. Hosehill (9) is now a Local Nature Reserve with artificial Sand Martin and Kingfisher banks and extensive reedbeds, all created by the Theale Area Bird Conservation Group (TABG). With

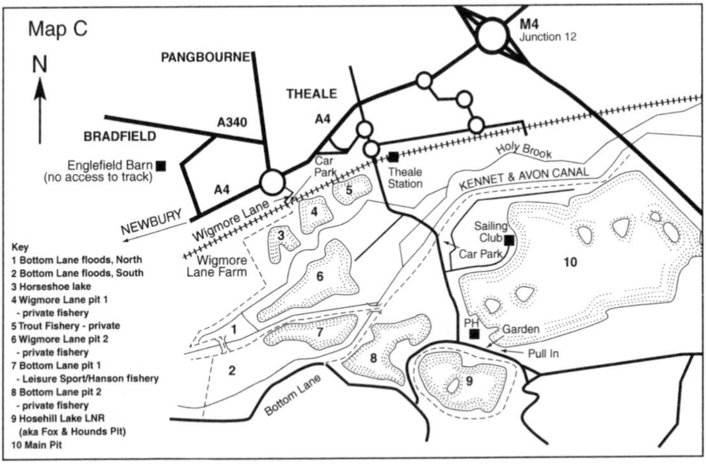

extensive islands and gravel bars, and tern Rafts, it is kept free of angling and water sports. Finally, the farmland at Englefield is under Country Stewardship and is sympathetically managed, being a favourite place for passage chats and Yellow Wagtail, together with resident Grey and Red-legged Partridges, plus some one hundred breeding Skylark.

Access

The general area lies either side of the M4 motorway between junctions 11 and 12. Few of the pools have specific access or parking facilities, save for permit holders of the various angling associations or sailing clubs. However, most of the lakes can be viewed from adjacent road-sides. Most of the lanes are narrow and twisting but the associated map indicates the more suitable places to leave a vehicle.

The area may be approached from the Southcote district of Reading, or via Theale with access from the first road on the left on the A4 south of junction 12, or via Three Mile Close off the A33 south of junction 11. Hosehill is close to the Fox and Hounds pub where parking will be possible with agreement of the landlord. A series of fishing lakes are accessible from Wigmore Lane off the main A4 and the footpath between them allows different views over the flood-meadows at Bottom Lane. Park at SU 689 692 for the footpath overlooking Pingewood Road wader pit.

Many of the waters are very deep and subject to leases granted for fishing or water sport clubs. Birdwatchers are therefore encouraged to remain outside the sites to observe. This in any case reduces disturbance and can still result in close views.

Species

Needless to say, most birds one might expect to see here are waterfowl, waders and gulls, the best time being between September and May. Prolonged frosts in winter produce interesting concentrations of ducks and gulls on pools that retain open water, such as Searle's Farm Lane (A8), Moatlands (B1) and Main Pit (C10). Kirtons Farm (A4) near the Hanover Hotel can be good for gulls and if Mediterranean Gull visit, as has happened in recent years, careful scanning of Black-headed Gull here may pay dividends. Ring-billed Gull was also recorded here in 2001. The Searle's Farm pools (A6, 7 and 8) are favoured by Pochard and Shoveler and is one area where occasional Smew can be anticipated, and both Scaup and a fine male Ferruginous Duck were present at the turn of the millennium. It is also a good spot for Kingfisher, whilst being one of several local waters that Bittern has visited. The frosty scene at Moatlands Lake (B1) will be dominated by 50 or more Cormorant on the main island but if the water is more open, there will be many Mute Swan, and reasonable numbers of Gadwall, Mallard and Teal, up to 100 Pochard and several Goldeneye. The island is again worth checking for passage waders. Wigeon favour the grassy banks of the renovated Burghfield Mill (B2) and Scaup is certainly a possibility, necessitating the checking of all available Tufted Duck. Both Merlin and Osprey have been recorded here and in October 2000 this lake hosted the surreal event of a Storm Petrel being taken by the local Sparrowhawk! Huge numbers of hirundines guarantee Hobby in summer, and a Red-rumped Swallow once hawked at the lake's edge.

A 'must' for visitors is Hosehill Lake (C9) opposite the Fox and Hounds pub. It is the southernmost pool in the complex where Teal may reach three figures and huge numbers of wintering Coot can be seen. Waders such as Redshank and Snipe are regular on this pool and Lapwing breed, but more luck is required to spot the one or two wintering Jack Snipe. An artificial Sand Martin bank and a tern nesting raft has been provided by the TABG, and both Reed and Sedge Warblers are present in summer. The adjacent Main Pit holds all the common duck species, Shelduck, lots of Cormorant and has attracted Red-breasted Merganser, Eider and Ruddy Duck. Everywhere the air is constantly full of gulls, and huge numbers roost here. Little Gull is a distinct possibility, whilst passage on any of the larger lakes should include Arctic and Black Terns, and occasionally Little Tern. The electricity pylons need checking for the frequent presence of Peregrine Falcon.

A springtime walk northwards along the towpath between Main Lake and the canal from Hosehill to Moatlands (passing under the motorway) will be rewarded with Grey Wagtail, Nightingale and Cetti's Warbler and more Kingfisher, whilst Siskin and Redpoll are more likely in winter. An easterly walk along the southern towpath from the small car park north of the Fox and Hounds (SU 647 704) to the Bottom Lane floods (C1 and 2) will lead to pools and scrapes where Redshank, Greenshank, Green Sandpiper, Snipe and even Curlew are possible in season, and where Little Egret has lingered previously. This area can also be viewed from the other side after walking from Wigmore Lane pits. The small woodland to the south of the scrapes host Treecreeper, Great Spotted and occasional Lesser Spotted Woodpeckers, possible Turtle Dove, all the common tits and is one of the few places in the county for both Marsh and Willow Tits.

The entire complex is very much a place to be during passage periods. Ringed Plover are noted from early in the year, the later arrivals staying on to breed, as do Little Ringed Plover. Redshank, seen in most months of the year, are more numerous in spring but Greenshank, seen at Bottom Lane, Field Farm or Pingewood, are more obvious during autumn migration. Golden Plover, often in small numbers at Burnthouse Lane or Pingewood, move out in March. Waders such as Grey Plover, Dunlin and Ruff might be seen at any of the pool edges as well as occasional Whimbrel or Sanderling. Snipe will be moving around everywhere, Kirtons Farm being perhaps as good a place as any to see them. Canada Geese winter at Burghfield Mill (B2) and move to Berrys Lane pits (A9 and 10) to breed.

The spring passage commences in March and April with large numbers of hirundines returning, an occasional fall of around 1,000 House Martin providing a wonderful spectacle, bringing with them the possibility of Hobby. This period is also the more notable for gulls and terns. Little Gull and Black Tern are found almost annually at Main Pit (C10). Common Sandpiper might be found, at Burghfield Mill lakes and Hosehill in particular. Breeding is soon underway with Little Ringed Plover and Common Tern on the island on Moatlands and Hosehill. Other breeding species at these locations include Reed Bunting, Sedge and Reed Warblers and occasionally Lesser Whitethroat, with the artificial Sand Martin bank at Hosehill being also well used. The whole Theale area south of the motorway, and the Searle's Lane sector to the north hold good numbers of Nightingale and are of national importance for this species.

By late summer, the earlier returning migrants such as Green Sandpiper put in an appearance. Greenshank are also seen more often at this time of year. Large numbers of noisy corvids will be dominated by Jackdaw and the size of the Coot rafts reveals another successful breeding season. The Goldeneye and Goosander that winter here gradually arrive and the seabird spectacle of the year begins to unravel; the annual roost of Lesser Black-backed and Black-headed Gulls, which reach almost biblical proportions, with some 10,000 individuals, means the chance of rarer species amongst them is ever present. As nights draw in, the overall scene is taken over by increasing numbers of these gulls, sometimes in such numbers that some smaller pools look almost white at dusk.

The Theale and Burghfield complex is therefore important at any time of the year. Rarer species that have featured recently include Great Northern Diver, Shag, Spoonbill, American Wigeon, Garganey, Blue-winged Teal, and several Ferruginous Ducks. Waders have included Wood Sandpiper, Whimbrel, Avocet, Temminck's Stint and Grey Phalarope, whilst raptors have been represented by Marsh Harrier, Honey Buzzard, Osprey and Black Kite. Both Ring-billed and Mediterranean Gulls continue to visit, whilst interesting passerines have been Firecrest, Cetti's Warbler, passage Pied Flycatcher, Waxwing, Hawfinch and Mealy Redpoll. With the added prospect of Bewick's Swan, Black-necked and Red-necked Grebes making their infrequent visitations, these pits beckon even more strongly to the many birdwatchers who brave the ravages of winter to ensure nothing is missed.

Calendar

Resident: Great Crested and Little Grebes, Cormorant (most months), Grey Heron, Mute Swan, Canada Goose (and regular feral Egyptian Geese), Mallard, Tufted Duck, Kestrel, Sparrowhawk, Peregrine, Water Rail, Moorhen, Coot, Dunlin and Redshank (most months). Black-headed Gull, Herring Gull, Snipe. Great Spotted Woodpecker, Pied and Grey Wagtails, common tits and finches.

December–February: Little Egret, chance of rare grebes and divers, occasional Bewick's Swan, large rafts of Coot, Tufted Duck, Pochard and Mallard. Fewer Wigeon, Shoveler and Teal. Occasional Pintail and scarce Scaup. Goldeneye regular, but sawbills not usually numerous. Huge gull flocks. Chance of Jack Snipe, Golden Plover.

March–May: Much wader activity. Redshank, Greenshank, Green and Common Sandpipers. Occasional Calidris waders. Good tern movement, including Little and Black Terns. Possible Little Gull. Singing Nightingale and Turtle Dove by late May.

June–July: Common Tern, Ringed and Little Ringed Plovers nesting on islands. Sand Martin colony of up to 100 pairs in artificial nesting bank.

August–November: Autumn passage commences by early August. Chance of Whimbrel and Little Stint. Greenshank regular, as is Green Sandpiper. Gull colonies established by November. Winter thrushes and ducks moving in. Possible Common Scoter. Whinchat likely.

33 TWYFORD & HURST GRAVEL PITS

OS ref. SU 785 755

Habitat

The site comprises a series of worked-out gravel pits in picturesque surrounds, rich in mature trees and vegetation but few reeds at present. The first lake to be restored was the 13.8 ha (34 acre) northern lake adjacent to Twyford Mill (quite near the railway station) and this is now the Loddon Reserve, managed by BBOWT. This lake possesses a number of small islands which offer sanctuary to breeding birds. South of the railway line are several more lakes, the largest one as yet with only sparse vegetation but with a substantial island at its centre. Further south still is another sizeable pool, Hurst Green Lake, and the recipient of many young trees recently planted by the gravel company. The River Loddon embellishes the scene as it passes through the site via the mill-race and provides even more 'footage' for the angler. There is no significant flora but the shrub layer is quite dense in places. Extraction was completed in 2000 when the whole complex south of the railway was put up for sale for 'leisure pursuits'. The affects on birdlife are awaited by birders across the region!

Access

The Mill and its lakes are to the south of the A3032 between Twyford and Charvil, the nearest main road being the A4, 1 km (0.6 mile) to the north. Some 100 ha (250 acres) of water are accessed by a number of public footpaths and anglers' tracks, though some of the fishermen's walkways are only available to permit holders.

A public car park, with room for some 30 cars and including toilet facilities, is available on the Twyford side of the railway bridge. Additional parking is available off Park Lane (anglers' car park) near the railway. The nearest railway station is Twyford only 250 m (270 yds) away from the Mill. The southern complex is approached from narrow lanes with few parking facilities.

Species

In common with other habitats of this nature, birds of the water predominate in winter, those of the scrub and hedgerow being more numerous in summer. Prolonged freezing affects most of the lakes but usually only the smallest become totally iced over. Charvil Lake is home to many Coot and Tufted Duck, with a few loafing Pochard and there is a small sand spit to the north of this lake, viewable from the footpath in the north-west, often having Grey Heron, Snipe or Redshank, with Green and Common Sandpipers also present during migration periods. The adjacent meadow floods quite often in winter and can be another location to find Snipe, together with Lapwing and Meadow Pipit. The scrub margin attracts many passerine species and some 70 species have been recorded in this area. The Loddon Reserve is where the main groups of Pochard, Wigeon and Tufted Duck seem to congregate, in so doing attracting varying numbers of Teal, Gadwall and Shoveler. Pintail occasionally show on this water but Goldeneye are not especially regular.

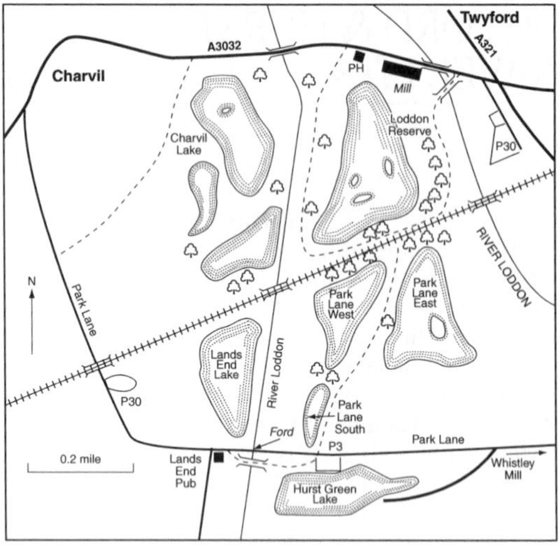

The small islands are used by Canada Geese and Teal, competing for space with Black-headed, and equally numerous Common Gulls, whilst the biggest island often has numerous Snipe in winter. Reed Buntings and overwintering Chiffchaff are evident and this area is also good for Bullfinch. Kingfisher are resident on the lakes and the Loddon and frequently encountered, as are Little Grebe, which occasionally outnumber Great Crested Grebe.

Beyond the arches of the railway bridge, which accommodate Kestrel and Pied Wagtail, lies another group of lakes, on the Hurst side. Those that flank the Loddon are not especially well blessed with winter visitors but Park Lane East is beginning to attract large numbers of common gull species, and occasional Goldeneye and Goosander. Smaller and newer pools to the south of this lake also hold common ducks, many Canada Geese and sometimes groups of Egyptian Geese, with Common Sandpiper and Greenshank around the shallow shores. This sector recently attracted a Pied Flycatcher on passage and a Great Northern Diver in January 2002.

Hurst Green Lake seems to attract most of the Gadwall, often with up to 25 pairs in situ and twice that number of Wigeon. Teal are also found here but the lack of a protective loafing island possibly deters larger numbers from accumulating. Cormorant seem happier on this pool though, and most of Twyford's Mute Swan use this particular water for much of their overwinter stay. Ruddy Duck and Smew might visit, Great Crested Grebe breed on the edges of the water and Common Tern feed here in summer. Perhaps the new owners will erect nesting rafts for subsequent seasons. Large groups of Sand and House Martins feed over this water whilst Whitethroat can be found in surrounding shrubbery. The substantial waste ground to the south of this lake holds hundreds of winter thrushes, flocks of geese and Lapwing and occasional waders in the colder months. Lands End Lake, opposite the pub of the same name, has seen good numbers of wintering Shoveler and is the site of the local heronry, where perhaps Berkshire's first nesting Little Egrets may arrive. More recent extraction has left another suitable wader habitat at Whistley Mill where Green Sandpiper, Ringed or Little Ringed Plovers can be expected, and Little Grebe breed alongside Lapwing and Common Tern. Passage Wheatear are another possibility here, with Stonechat on the adjacent waste ground, and it is one of the best local sites for Turtle Dove, but infill work has already commenced.

Overall, the site is worth walking around in most seasons. Such a walk in April 2000 provided a surprise Hoopoe for one local birder, some 1,000 visitors being thrilled with this confiding individual over the ensuing weeks. The lakeside shrubbery hosts numerous passerines, especially in summer when resident species are enhanced by Sedge and Willow Warblers, Blackcap and occasional Garden Warbler. Probably best visited during December to February and April to June, during which months in recent years Scaup, Common Scoter, Oystercatcher, Golden Plover, Curlew, Ruff, Lesser Spotted Woodpecker and Firecrest were all seen.

Calendar

Resident: Great Crested and Little Grebes, Grey Heron, Mute Swan, Canada and Egyptian Geese, Mallard, Tufted Duck. Sparrowhawk, Kestrel, Moorhen, Coot, Lapwing, Black-headed Gull, Stock Dove, Woodpigeon, Collared Dove, occasional Tawny and Little Owls. Kingfisher, Green and Great Spotted Woodpeckers, Grey and Pied Wagtails, Jay. Possible Chiffchaff. Long-tailed Tit, Treecreeper, Bullfinch, Greenfinch, Goldfinch, Linnet, Reed Bunting, occasional Yellowhammer.

December–February: Cormorant, good numbers of Gadwall, Wigeon, Teal and Shoveler. Prospect of Pintail and occasional Shelduck. Numerous Pochard. Goldeneye and Goosander regular in small numbers, Smew less frequent. Water Rail sometimes reported, Snipe frequently seen. Large rafts of mixed gulls. Possibility of Stonechat. Winter thrushes in small numbers, probability of Brambling, small parties of Siskin.

March–May: Chance of scarcer grebes on passage, Common and Green Sandpipers, Greenshank, Ringed Plover and Ruff passing through. Gulls dispersed by April. Cuckoo, early warblers mid-April, Sand Martin and Swallow even earlier. Spotted Flycatcher and Yellow Wagtail passing through.

June–July: Redshank and Common Tern holding territory. Sedge and possible Reed Warblers breeding.

August–November: Departure period for summer visitors, primarily in September, though House Martin still seen in October. Possibility of Whinchat, and some wader movements.

34 WALBURY & INKPEN HILLS

OS ref. SU 370 620

Habitat

Part of the North Wessex Downs Area of Outstanding Natural Beauty, a visit just for the view alone is worthwhile, looking down over a scene resembling a vast Constable painting, with the generously-wooded area surrounding Newbury to the east and the rising downland to the north. On a clear day, the military antics from Lyneham, played out by transport aircraft and helicopters, in the valley to the north, are back-dropped by those of the tanker aircraft at Brize Norton a full 43 km away! Appropriately, the base of the hills hosted the rehearsals for the famous Normandy Landing. At 297 m (975 ft) Walbury Hill is not only the highest point in Berkshire, but the highest chalk downs in England; an ideal place to get on top of one's birdwatching. The local flora includes Chalk Milkwort, Woolly Thistle and Dropwort. Inkpen Hill is grassed on both its steep and gentler slopes and has a thick hedge, whereas Walbury has a more arable flavour with stony fields on either side of the ridge. The southern slope is used for grazing but possesses scattered Gorse and Hawthorn shrubbery. A small conifer plantation complements a dense Hawthorn thicket, with a horseshoe-shaped line of mature Beech trees, and passage birds can be seen passing over the roadway between. The north-facing slope of Walbury is also partly tree-covered, affording good shelter for wandering birds. Hang-gliding is a popular pastime but does not appear to disturb the birdlife in the area.

Combe Wood is the most south-westerly part of Berks whilst West Woodhay Down, the eastern part of the rise, angles down through rolling farmland. The view to the south embraces a complex pattern of

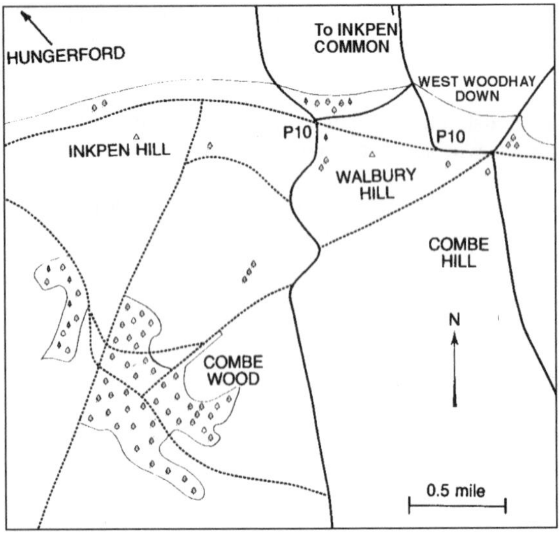

steeply-sloping fields and pasture, dotted with sheep, and compartments of woodland moulded to the valleys, and cuttings to the hills which fall sharply away from the highest view points. Don't forget to visit Inkpen Common whilst in the area.

Access

The Hills overlook a mosaic of country lanes which interlace the lowlands between the A343 running south from Newbury and the A338 running south from Hungerford. An Ordnance Survey map will be necessary to extricate oneself from this maze of picturesque roadways and to arrive at either of the two car parks situated on the top of the escarpment. These two parking spots are joined by a track but this is not always capable of taking a vehicle due to depth of mud or reduced ground clearance when tractors have made regular use of the link during periods of heavy conditions. One is free to walk the ridge itself and footpaths lead to various adjacent locations, including Combe Wood 1 km (0.6 mile) to the south. An information board outlines the terrain and the history of the grim Gibbet and a neolithic long barrow.

Species

This lofty perch has become more and more one of the major raptor watchpoints in the region. As Common Buzzard have spread their territory from adjacent counties towards the Chilterns, irregular sightings of previous years have given way to groups of five or more on a good raptor day. Just occasionally, a Peregrine might harry the Common Buzzard as it passes through the area. The opportunity often presents itself to view Kestrel, and sometimes Sparrowhawk, from above as they traverse the slopes at a lower elevation and one might possibly see a Red Kite from the Chiltern re-introduction programme. From Inkpen Hill, the antics of numerous corvids can be observed, especially Jackdaw which can gather in huge numbers, though even in such large flocks one can observe pair-bonding by early April. The site ought to attract Raven, but records are sparse to date. The stony fields around Walbury are worth checking for Pheasant and Grey Partridge (though Red-legged is becoming more common) and passerines such as Corn Bunting (much rarer nowadays), Yellowhammer and Meadow Pipit. Linnet and Goldfinch explore the hedges and field boundaries, whilst numerous Skylark provide a musical accompaniment to this airy place. Any scrub and woodland area is likely to attract Chiffchaff and Whitethroat in summer, and Greenfinch seem quite happy here.

During spring passage, one of the earliest visitors is the Wheatear, usually seen on the grassed southern slope of Inkpen Hill but usually just one or two at a time, and whilst Ring Ouzel are not regular, it is always worth hoping. Both Redstart and Black Redstart are possible, low bushes and hedgerows probably being the best places to look. Stonechat and Whinchat are other birds one might hope to come across. Larger birds too will be present on occasions with Hen Harrier recorded in most years, and Hobby is found both on passage and from time to time throughout the summer. Golden Plover have been reported at this level and many gulls move through the gap between the hills.

Owls too can be quite prominent up here, particularly between October and April when resident Little Owl on the Hills and the Tawny Owl of Combe Wood and Inkpen Hill are joined sporadically by Short-eared and more regularly by Barn Owl. Woodcock have been reported in the

Buzzard

same wood. In March, just prior to the main incoming movement, Fieldfare and Redwing gather in flocks of 200 or more of each species south of Walbury Hill. Chaffinch flocks should be checked for Brambling, up to 100 recorded around West Woodhay. For most of the other migrating passerines, however, one will have to spend time either in Combe Wood, where Black Redstart, Crossbill, Tree Pipit, Marsh and Willow Tits and Lesser Spotted Woodpecker have been recorded, or the scrub and thicket areas of Walbury where many of the common warblers, and possibly Cuckoo, are likely to be found, best hunted for in the morning. A check around the church in Combe may result in a Spotted Flycatcher or two, Treecreeper or Willow Tit. The small clump of woodland half a kilometre east of Walbury Hill has hosted both Marsh and Willow Tits, Bullfinch, Nuthatch, Treecreeper and Coal Tit, joined in summer by Spotted Flycatcher, Chiffchaff, Garden Warbler and Willow Warbler. Even at this height, with relatively sparse woodland, Roe Deer will be encountered. Autumn on West Woodhay Down will be a scene of southerly movements of Meadow Pipit, Skylark, House Martin and occasional Redstart, and incoming winter thrushes on a different trajectory, whilst a springtime or summer walk here may be rewarded with more Yellowhammer, Tree Pipit, Goldcrest and Lesser Whitethroat. A stroll over the undulating terrain of the Hills, and through Combe Wood can be invigorating in spring or autumn, to say the least, and anything might be possible during the migration seasons. A still, dry day in autumn or winter may be best for soaring raptors.

Calendar

Resident: Sparrowhawk, Common Buzzard, Kestrel, Pheasant. possible Grey Partridge. Woodcock and Tawny Owl at Combe Wood. Little Owl in the arable areas. Green and Great Spotted Woodpeckers. Possibly six tit species plus common finches, Yellowhammer numerous. Large numbers of Jackdaw.

December–February: Meadow Pipit, Yellowhammer and Skylark numerous. Possibility of Short-eared Owl, Merlin or Brambling. Flocks of Linnet and Woodpigeon. Crossbill possibly in Combe Wood.

March–May: Possibility of Hen Harrier and Barn Owl. Large flocks of winter thrushes and Chaffinch. Wheatear, Ring Ouzel and Turtle Dove on passage. Redstart and Black Redstart also moving through with common warblers. Likelihood of Tree Pipit.

June–July: Several species breeding in Combe Wood and in surrounding arable farmland, good chance of Hobby. Occasional Cuckoo.

August–November: Stonechat, Whinchat, Meadow Pipit. Winter thrushes arrive in November. Prospect of Merlin.

35 WISHMOOR & SWINLEY FOREST

OS ref. SU 877 662

Habitat

The huge area of woods and open heathland between Bracknell and Camberley is just part of remnant Windsor Forest, which once covered large parts of south Berkshire and north Surrey. Swinley Forest itself possess a rich mixture of deciduous and evergreen compartments, ensuring all the avian variety that such habitat might promise. In some areas, earlier felling and fires have resulted in valuable heathland sections equally rich in fauna and flora. Much of it lies within the domain of Crown Estate, but creative management has permitted large areas with public access and imaginative features for educational and recreational enjoyment of the huge woodland resource, recently made part of the Thames Basin SPA.

Wishmoor rolls into adjacent Old Dean Common on the Surrey border and lies quite near the Royal Military Academy at Sandhurst, which uses the heath for a variety of training exercises, but public areas are clearly marked. The large number of tracks and trails are, however, a little complex and daytime visits would be recommended to familiarise oneself with the site before attempting night-time visits for owls and Nightjar.

A good sized pool, Rapley Lake, exists on the east of the site, and although regularly attracting breeding Little Grebe and common waterfowl, it is mainly noted for the range of dragonfly it hosts.

Access

Excellent parking facilities exist at the Swinley Forest location off the B3430 at SU 877 662. A visitors centre and toilet facilities are available. Numerous colour-marked routes can be taken from the centre allowing short walks or an all-day roam across this capacious woodland. Maps of the various routes available can be collected at the centre which caters for group visits, family parties or, of course, the lone explorer. An Ordnance Survey map (sheet 175) is recommended for the all-day visitor.

Wishmoor can be approached by walking from the Swinley Forest

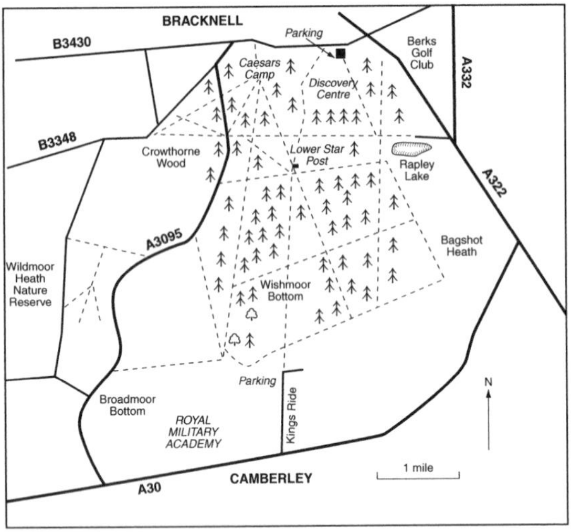

entrance (The Lookout Discover Centre), time permitting, but more direct access would be via the northern end of Kings Ride (SU 875 622), which in turn connects to the main A30 through nearby Camberley, from where trains between London and the west can be used. Remember to take a torch if waiting for crepuscular species at night.

Species

With such a large area involved, the site guarantees almost the full gamut of woodland and heathland species. Perhaps the main evacuees of recent times have unfortunately been Wood Warbler (although passage individuals are occasionally located in Caesars Camp and Rapley Lake areas most springs) and Hawfinch, but there is plenty to make up for these previous residents. Walking around the mosaic of differing stands of tree types, magical woodland sounds reflect the dominant tree species in each compartment. One minute the busy calls of Blue and Great Tits, excited to a frenzy by a chattering group of Long-taileds, the next the squeaks and rattles of delightful groups of Siskin and Redpoll. In summer, no sooner has the last Chiffchaff or Willow Warbler passed out of hearing, then the next two are in ear-shot. High-pitched trills of Treecreeper give way to piping Nuthatch whilst hunting packs of finches, often containing Brambling in winter, accede to chipping Crossbill, fluting Coal Tit and hissing Goldcrest. The visiting Crossbill have an enormous area in which to play, so contact with the species might take patience, but the song of the male, resplendent in his magnificent red plumage, and uttered at the top of a suitable tree, is a delight to hear.

Magpie and Jay spend the year squabbling noisily over nothing at all whilst all three woodpecker types can be expected. Recent surveys have revealed up to 50 pairs of Redstart breeding in the forest, especially in the areas west of Lower and Upper Star Points, and nest boxes have been provided to encourage them further. This is certainly the highest concentration of Redstarts in the region and the opportunity of the male's song being included in a dawn chorus here is just too good to miss. Plaintive yet melodic, the liquid notes have an echoic quality, totally suited to this locality. As with any woodland, an early morning walk will be best, a dawn visit in spring definitely something to experience. Caesars Camp to the north of the site is a good place to be at this hour, and encounters may include Woodlark and Dartford Warbler, accompanied by many of the summer warblers' songs. The more open areas will host good numbers of Tree Pipit, and Willow Warbler will abound.

Wishmoor to the south provides an opportunity to find all the expected heathland species, with Stonechat, Reed Bunting and Tree Pipit all present, and good prospects for Dartford Warbler which have benefited in the region from several mild winters. The summer of 2000 saw some of the highest numbers of this perky star of the furze throughout the Berkshire, Surrey and Hampshire heaths. Here at Wishmoor, the habitat is again suitable for Woodlark. Few songs can be more beautiful or distinctive, uttered from a flopping flight aloft, before a wandering descent to a perch or the ground itself. Again, this is a species making a comeback on commons and heathland in the area and it is worth a visit just in the hope of encountering this wonderful songster. The very same balmy, bright and sunny days that coax the Woodlark to perform will also entice Hobby to seek out dragonflies and other insects along the many rides and ditches that criss-cross the 16 km^2 of this landscape. For this reason, it is advisable to keep to the obvious tracks and pathways to avoid getting into difficulties in the many boggy areas. However, the self-same insects guarantee a good population of breeding Spotted Flycatcher. Although in recent years, a Great Grey Shrike has overwintered at Wishmoor, and a Wryneck spent several of May 2001's days here, rarities should not be anticipated.

However, there is more than enough to make up for that, as other specialists of this habitat reside here. As dusk falls (and the midges let you know they are about), roding Woodcock are soon circling overhead, usually first heard before hoving into view. At about the same time, the first Nightjar will belie their presence with their amazing churring calls, and the wing-clapping of the males may be observed with a little luck. Their aim, of course, is to make their white wing panels as obvious as possible to the females so it is worth trying the handkerchief stunt to tempt the males nearer, thinking they have competition. (i.e. putting one down on the ground or flapping it at arm's length). And as the

Redstart

midges win, and the satisfied birdwatcher departs guided by the essential torch and map, Tawny Owl will be calling across the great expanse of this significant piece of natural heritage in south Berkshire. Rapley Lake in the east, as mentioned, is excellent for dragonfly species and may also draw Mandarin and Gadwall.

Any yet to be sated by a good day's birdwatching in the verdant sprawl of the woods and heathland might want to visit Crowthorne Woods, to the north-west of the complex, and dissected from it by the A3095. Generally more coniferous, the undulating nature of the area, and its own open areas and heaths extend both breeding and overwintering facilities for many of the species mentioned earlier. Access is best by parking at Caesars Camp and walking across this busy road, or selecting one of the few pull-offs along this road, preferably at the highest point where it is safer to see traffic from both directions when departing. Still more heathland to explore, with further prospects of Dartford Warbler, Stonechat, Hobby and Tree Pipit is Wildmoor Heath further south along the A3095 at SU 842 627. Access here is safer from the small car park on the westward side of this small nature reserve off Crowthorne Road, but do not be too surprised at coming face-to-face with the resident Highland Cattle, munching their way through encroaching vegetation.

Calendar

Resident: Sparrowhawk, Kestrel, Stock Dove, Woodpigeon, Collared Dove, Tawny and occasional Little Owls. Green and Great Spotted Woodpeckers, Jay. All the common tits, Stonechat, Treecreeper, Bullfinch, Greenfinch, Goldfinch, Linnet, Reed Bunting, occasional Yellowhammer.

December–February: Possibility of Stonechat. Winter thrushes in small numbers. Probability of Brambling. Parties of Siskin and Redpoll. Crossbill, varying in numbers with availability of food sources. Great Grey Shrike has overwintered.

March–May: Cuckoo, Redstart and early warblers in position by mid-April. Spotted Flycatcher in good numbers, Woodlark, Skylark and Tree Pipit becoming more obvious.

June–July: Nightjar and Woodcock more obvious. Worth looking for Dartford Warbler. Hobby regular.

August–November: Departure of summer visitors, primarily in September. Possibility of Whinchat, in addition to winter thrush movements.

36 WRAYSBURY GRAVEL PITS

OS ref. TQ 005 743

Habitat

These lakes form part of the southernmost sector of the Colne Valley Park, a major scheme originated in the 1960s to improve and conserve the remnants of the Metropolitan Green Belt in a region extending over the 23 km (14 miles) from Rickmansworth to the Thames. Whereas much of the park is being restored to agricultural usage, most of the Wraysbury development has been water-based, providing some 16 km (10 miles) of bankside fishing and large sailing and powerboat recreation facilities. Part of the 180 ha (450 acre) complex forms one of only two nature reserves in the whole park scheme and SSSI status was granted to some of the site in the early nineties. More recently, in September 2000, Silverwings Lake and Village Lake were designated a Special Protection Area (SPA) and a Ramsar Site, primarily due to the numbers of overwintering Gadwall and Shoveler.

The northern part of this site is a wetland habitat of a rural nature situated between the Thames and the Colne Brook. Adjacent arable areas give this section a distinct rural visage. Streams with established reeded banks and mature trees interlace an area which has undergone extensive management and tree-planting. This section is quite rich in plant species and attracts good numbers of butterflies. Heathrow's incessant activity does not seem to disturb the birdlife.

Horton Lakes are used for angling and sailing, but have some uninterrupted corners favoured by birds, including the recently completed

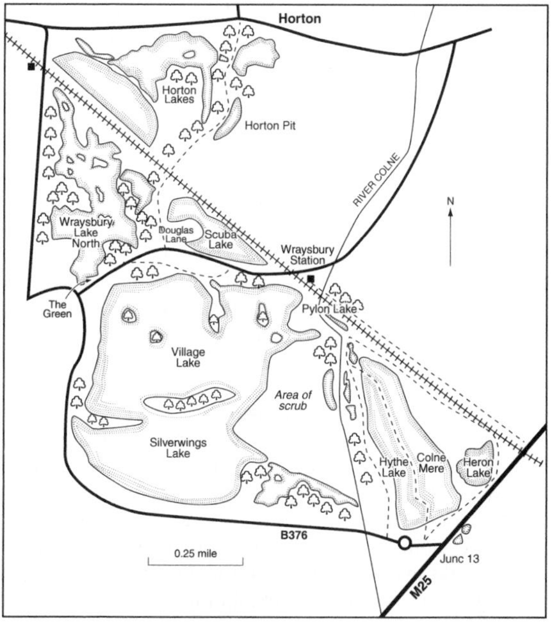

workings at Horton Pit, suited to waders. A footpath crosses the lake at its most narrow point via a bridge, beyond which extensive extraction continues. Wraysbury Lake North is a SSSI but is used for fishing and boating, particularly at weekends. Nonetheless it offers some suitable roosting and breeding facilities, especially for the less timid species. A new lake, Scuba Lake, was fashioned in 1991 to the east of Douglas Lane, with nicely graded banks suitable for waders but has been allowed to become overgrown. Village Lake, the nature reserve designated a SPA, is bounded by built-up areas, a busy road and the local railway line and is regularly fished. However, the numerous islands and small bays formed by its somewhat 'random' shaping has made it very suitable for waterfowl, and a roost for Cormorant and Heron. Much of the bank is steep-sided and unsuitable for waders.

Silverwings Lake is almost exclusively used for sailing on a regular basis and little habitat management has been carried out but it is excellent for rafts of winter duck, hence its SPA status. Colne Mere and Hythe Lagoon are reed-edged and also good for wintering waterfowl but the trail between them has become almost impassable in places. Heron Lake, nearest the motorway, is used for water-skiing but has perversely held some of the rarer visiting birds.

The River Colne runs alongside the lake, with mature trees over much of its length, and good numbers of established bushes interspersed along the land between these two waters.

Access

The site is served by rail from Waterloo. By road, the pits are south of junction 5 on the M4 and reached via the B470/B376. Alternatively, one may exit the M25 at junction 13 and travel west on the B376. Parking is difficult in all sections of the site, the main car park being at The Green, accommodating about 50 vehicles, and is the best for an all-day visit. A further 20 spaces exist in the station car park but are naturally utilised by commuters, and often visited by vandals! At the Horton end, limited parking is available in Park Lane near the access to the public footpath.

To some extent, public access to the pits is restricted. The Horton–Wraysbury footpath, although often a little overgrown, passes through the more rural areas, affords good views over much of the Horton waters and follows the route of Colne Brook for some of its length. Another short footpath known as the Worple Footpath passes beside the northern extremity of Village Lake, the nature reserve, and a third footpath runs south from the railway line to Hythe End between Colne Brook and Heron Lake. On the other hand, much of the water can be seen from various parts of the B376 or from the football pitch near The Green.

The new owners of the Silverwings/Heron Lake complex, North Surrey Water (01784 455464), are very supportive of ornithological activity on their property.

Species

The overall site supports a wide variety of species. Horton Lakes host many Great Crested Grebe and Grey Heron in winter, and numerous Cormorant (with occasional Shag), whilst summertime produces Common Tern, thousands of hirundines and possible breeding Shelduck. If Scaup are in the vicinity, this is the most likely lake on which to find them. Recent workings at Horton Pit to the east improve the chances of finding passage waders such as Redshank, Snipe, Green Sandpiper,

Smew

Ringed and Little Ringed Plovers at least. All the common summer warblers can be expected, and Spotted Flycatcher favour the dogs home at the Horton end.

On non-sailing days, Wraysbury Lake North can often host quite large numbers of dabbling and diving ducks, with Mallard, Gadwall and Tufted Duck all year and Teal and Wigeon in autumn. Goldeneye in small numbers are also fairly common early in the year together with occasional Pintail and Shoveler, but Smew, which were once a notable feature, are becoming more infrequent. However, even during sailing, the numerous small bays may still hold some duck and occasional waders such as Snipe and Common Sandpiper. It is always therefore worth looking at this lake, best viewed from the B376 or the footpath at Douglas Lane. The two resident grebes can be seen at any time and Water Rail has been recorded, but an early start will be necessary to find one. In summer, hirundine numbers may be less than at Horton but Common Tern can be expected, particularly late in the season when family groups move in from adjacent breeding sites. In winter, small flocks of Siskin, with occasional Redpoll, forage among the lakeside Alders.

Village Lake and Silverwings Lake are arguably the most productive waters in the complex. Although some of the bank is fished, Little and Great Crested Grebes find places to breed, often into October, and as many as 50 or more of the latter species can be seen towards the end of the year. Coot, Moorhen and Canada Goose do well here also, their winter numbers swelled by visitors from outside. A sizeable raft of Tufted Duck, Pochard and Shoveler builds up toward the end of the day for roosting but probably the most rewarding sights are afforded by several thousand Jackdaw, their early morning dispersal being a spectacle in its own right. Winter visitors include Smew (usually redheads), Goldeneye, Goosander and Teal whilst less regular visits may be made by Shelduck and Ruddy Duck. Slavonian, Red-necked and Black-necked Grebes have been seen by a lucky few as have Red- and Black-throated Divers.

In summer, although affording few breeding facilities, Common Tern will be seen, Arctic and Sandwich Terns having also been known to visit. One bird that will be seen at almost any time, however, is the Kingfisher which breeds in the vicinity and the lake appears able to support several birds, all of which seem particularly confiding, often flying low over the water between small islands and the bank in front of observers. Sometimes views are close enough to detect the red lower mandible of the female. Of the smaller birds, Reed Bunting, Bullfinch, Linnet and Goldcrest are regular residents whilst most of the more common warblers occur in summer, particularly in the areas of scrub between Silverwings and Pylon Lake and along the railway line, where Green

Woodpecker breed. This same area is also prominent for Stonechat, Grasshopper Warbler, Reed Bunting and occasional Nightingale in season, the rough grass area often hosting Snipe in winter.

Hythe Lagoon and Colne Mere are home to large numbers of Coot and Gadwall. Mute Swan breed in the reedbed to the south-east of the lake along with Reed and Sedge Warblers, whilst Goosander, Pochard and Goldeneye occur in winter. The tree-line abounding the Colne and the footpath is favoured by resident Treecreeper and Great Spotted Woodpecker, with Blackcap and Chiffchaff in summer, the latter often found amongst mixed feeding flocks in winter whilst flocks of up to 100 Fieldfare wander overhead. Small numbers of Siskin may also be encountered. Heron Lake actually does have Heron roosting in winter, but more interestingly has often held overwintering Bittern in reeds opposite the Water Ski club house, and is another possible location for Smew. The adjacent Wraysbury reservoir is an important gull roost and large numbers will be seen over the gravel pits on their way to and from the reservoir.

A circular walk from Horton to Hythe End via the footpaths, and returning along the B376 will result in a good number of species at any time of the year, although the Ring-necked Parakeet roost, now comprising some 3,000 individuals, has relocated to Esher Rugby ground.

Calendar

Resident: Great Crested and Little Grebes, Grey Heron, Mallard, Tufted Duck, Coot, Moorhen, Water Rail, some Pochard, Canada Goose, Kingfisher, groups of Ring-necked Parakeet, Reed Bunting, Yellowhammer, Linnet, common species of tit, Kestrel, Jackdaw.

December–February: Wigeon, Gadwall, more Pochard, Teal, Cormorant, increased numbers of common grebes, occasional Black-necked and Slavonian Grebes, irregular Pintail and Ruddy Duck, gull roost with even larger numbers overhead. Occasional Snipe and Redshank, regular Smew, Goldeneye and Goosander, possible Bittern, regular Siskin.

March–May: Reed and Sedge Warblers, Sylvia warblers, Spotted Flycatcher, possible Nightingale, Swift and hirundines.

June–July: Cuckoo, Turtle Dove, Grasshopper Warbler and riparian species breeding.

August–November: Canada Geese flocks, large numbers of House Martin and Swallow in August and September, passage waders, Fieldfare and Redwing begin to arrive in October.

ADDITIONAL SITES

Ambarrow Court Local Nature Reserve (OS ref. SU 824 628)

Originally the grounds of a private manor house, and subsequently used by the MOD, this small woodland of coppiced Birch, Willow and Hazel became a LNR in 1990. Tracks, some with wheelchair access, lead off in several directions from the small car park off the A321 north of Little Sandhurst. The deciduous woodland hosts Marsh Tit and summer warblers, whilst the more mixed areas with established evergreens include Goldcrest and Coal Tit. A few open clearings are good for Willow Warbler and Garden Warbler whilst all three woodpeckers are a possibility. Hobby may stray from adjacent heathland and Sparrowhawks are resident.

Ashley Hill Woods (OS ref. SU 830 810)

Ashley is some 80 ha (200 acres) in size and comprises a significant mixed deciduous section, with conifer and Larch compartments, surrounded by arable land and managed by the Forestry Commission. Access is either on the A4 at SU 829 802 where up to ten cars may park, or SU 832 805 with room for three vehicles on the A404. Other access points can be found on the side roads at SU 824 815.

The mixture of woodlands permits a comparison of the favoured habitats of a number of species of bird. The conifer stands are utilised by many of the tit family for food, particularly Coal Tit with its slightly longer bill. However, Blue and Great Tits will probably nest only in the adjacent deciduous wood, where Marsh Tit also reside. Blackcap and Garden Warbler rarely stray into the conifers but Siskin can be found in both, with up to 50 at one time. Woodcock is regular and Lesser Spotted Woodpecker occasional. Chiffchaff is a regular visitor, especially near the picnic facility halfway down the western side. Jay are common, their calls easily confused with those of squirrels to the untrained ear. There is always the possibility of wandering Crossbill but the woodland is now too mature for two previous occupants: Nightjar and Tree Pipit. The northern edge abuts the grounds of the Burchetts Green College of Agriculture, and footpaths lead from the wood into the grounds, where winter reveals magnificent numbers of corvids, with up to 500 Rook the noisiest element. Huge numbers of gulls are to be found in the vicinity of the piggery. Collared Dove, Stock Dove and Starling too can reach impressive numbers. Little Owl breeds here and a new feature has been Common Buzzard often soaring overhead.

Bowsey Hill Wood (OS ref. SU 810 800)

Just a short distance from Ashley Hill, and equally varied in tree-scape, this much larger piece of woodland can also be rewarding to visit. Despite being temporarily disturbed by a huge in-fill site in the very centre of the wood, large tracts of Beech, Oak and coniferous plantations, much of it very mature, attracts the expected range of species. Easiest access is by parking in the lay-by near the Seven Stars public house at SU 822 794, just off the A4 west of Maidenhead. The two main tracks which go up into the wood are both just west of the pub, the left hand one passing a small pool, with an uncertain future, that can hold Little Grebe and Teal amongst common duck species. The woodland is excellent for Nuthatch, Marsh Tit and Treecreeper, with Tawny Owl calling during the day from February to April. A popular haunt for Sparrowhawk, and both Common Buzzard and Red Kite can be anticipated overhead. Exposed banks attract breeding Sand Martin. A new mixed plantation on the top of the hill may prove attractive to Whitethroat, Tree Pipit and Nightjar, though the much larger plantation scheduled when the pit is filled is even more likely to achieve this. The woodland butterfly population has been disturbed by the work mentioned, but Marbled White can be found along the woodland edge, also a favourite location for the many Muntjac Deer that frequent the site.

Bucklebury Common (OS ref. SU 555 692)

This site, and parts of Upper Common (overgrown) to the west, comprises dense, young Birch thicket, more open woodland sections with Oak, and areas of heathland, mainly in the eastern section, where some 12 ha (29 acres) of clearing has been achieved by local volunteers. The two locations are to the north of the road between Cold Ash and Chapel Row and car parking is at the above grid reference and also 500 m east. By contrast, Carbins Wood to the south is mainly an established deciduous wood with Beech, Whitebeam and Sweet Chestnut and some evergreen stands.

Resident birds on the commons include Green and Great Spotted Woodpeckers (with the prospect of Lesser Spotted Woodpecker), Woodcock, Marsh Tit, Linnet and Goldfinch. Redstart and Whinchat are potential passage visitors but species which might be found in summer include occasional Tree Pipit and Lesser Whitethroat, with Spotted Flycatcher frequenting the nearby churchyard. Nightjar and Whitethroat are present in summer, Kestrel and Sparrowhawk readily seen, but Hobby requires more good fortune. Bullfinch are plentiful in the scrub areas. Carbins Wood tends to attract Tawny Owl, Jay, Nuthatch, Chiffchaff and Garden Warbler, Coal Tit, Goldcrest and more Woodcock. A worthwhile site at any time, but probably best from March to June.

Similar habitat is found in nearby Ashampstead Common (SU 565 745) whilst the mainly coniferous woodland north of Yattendon (SU 560 750) adds variety to a visit to the area.

California Country Park (OS ref. SU 786 649)

Lying to the east of Arborfield Garrison is an area of mixed woodland, nowadays nominated as a Country Park, with a caravan and tenting facility. It can therefore be a 'popular' area in summer, but is much quieter for the remainder of the year. There is ample pay-and-display parking within the site itself. The large amenity pool in the centre is not particularly productive for birdwatchers but an extensive boardwalk leads through areas of bog and heathland, giving variety to the park and its bird species.

A good general range of woodland birds exists including all three woodpeckers, the common tits, finches and numerous Jay. Stock and Collared Doves are common, and occasionally Jackdaw roost. Winter visitors include small flocks of Redwing, Siskin (Redpoll take a little more finding) and occasionally Brambling near the pool. Summer birds are Blackcap, Chiffchaff and occasional Willow Warbler. Adjacent arable fields, viewable from a peripheral track, are excellent for gulls, Mistle Thrush, Fieldfare and mixed corvids in winter. Goldcrest are always numerous and soaring Common Buzzard is possible. The bog area and the streamsides are of botanical interest. Best visited midweek.

Child Beale Wildlife Trust (OS ref. SU 620 780)

Situated at the A329 Pangbourne to Oxford road, this Thames-side site is the headquarters of the World Pheasant Association and contains a collection of wildfowl, pheasants and owls in a parkland setting including several lakes. Whilst not everyone is in favour of collections, they can afford the opportunity for birdwatching beginners to become familiar with more unusual visitors to British shores such as Red-breasted Goose, Garganey and Pink-footed Goose. There are over 120 species in the collection spread over the 40 ha (100 acre) site, but the overhanging Beechwoods to the west and the widening Thames in the east have also created an attractive habitat for wild birds. Over 134 such species have been recorded here since the sanctuary was created, including Bittern, Mandarin, Osprey and Peregrine, Barn Owl, Wryneck and Hawfinch. Of course, one will not see such species on every visit but the centre is of educational value to the younger birdwatcher (although an entrance fee is levied).

Hamstead Park (OS ref. SU 425 660)

Situated to the west of Newbury, this attractive parkland site is bounded by the Kennet and Avon Canal to the north and open countryside to the south, with imposing views of Combe and Walbury Hills in the same direction. A lay-by to the railway crossing at Marsh Benham in the north-west or another along the Enborne Road in the south-east hold a small number of vehicles. The tree-lined avenues and open parkland hold Green and Great Spotted Woodpeckers together with Jay, Mistle Thrush and numerous corvids. Redwing and Fieldfare vie for morsels under the bare trees in winter, whilst any flocks of tits may include Coal and Marsh species. Spotted Flycatcher can be anticipated and Nightingale has been encountered near the Enborne Road. Scanning the high escarpment linking Berks., Hants. and Wilts. 5 km away may well reveal soaring Common Buzzard or other roaming raptors. From the area around the main house on top of the hill, the park slopes down to a group of small lakes to the north, popular with common waterfowl, summer hirundines and resident Pied Wagtail. The woodland sector near the north gate hosts Treecreeper and further tit flocks and Tawny Owl which may be heard during a summer evening dalliance with dusk, which is worth considering to experience Woodcock as they rode the park in traditional style. An enjoyable walk is guaranteed through established parkland set amidst impressive Berkshire scenery, and stepping out along the adjacent canal would add such species as Sedge Warbler, Reed Bunting and Grey Wagtail.

Heathlake Park (OS ref. SU 828 653)

Designated a SSSI due to the presence of plants such as Six Stamened Waterwort and Shoreweed, the site is north-west of Crowthorne off the B3430 Devils Highway, where a car park exists close to Ravenswood school. An early morning visit is recommended for a walk amongst our commoner birds in pleasant surroundings.

The lake holds common resident waterfowl such as Mute Swan, Coot and Moorhen, and Great Crested Grebe nest here. Late summer and early autumn are the times to expect Common Sandpiper, whilst in winter, Pochard, Shoveler and Gadwall move in with Tufted Duck, and Goosander can be seen quite close on this small pool. More unusual visitors have included Mandarin, Pintail and Goldeneye. Egyptian Geese may also visit in this season. Kingfisher is always a prospect along with Grey Heron and Grey Wagtail. The surrounding trees and vegetation hold resident Nuthatch, Treecreeper, Goldcrest and Coal Tit, together with Great Spotted and Green Woodpeckers, and Lesser Spotted Woodpecker has also been noted, especially in winter when they are a bit easier to see. Siskin, and occasional Redpoll, feed in the conifer stands in January and February whilst Redwing exploit the grassy fringes. The summer scene in the woodland is the familiar one of singing Chiffchaff, Blackcap and Willow Warbler, whilst Swift and hirundines hawk over the water.

Hungerford Common (OS ref. SU 345 680)

Somewhat underwatched and comprising about 50 ha (125 acres) of dry pasture and peripheral woodland, this parkland habitat is adjacent to the Kennet and Avon Canal, and the River Kennet, south of the A4 at Hungerford. A quiet corner of the county, with picturesque views of nearby Inkpen Hill, the site attracts a good range of parkland and woodland species. A pleasant walk eastwards along the towpath passes reedbeds and water-meadows, and the STW, where Pied, Grey and Yellow Wagtails can be seen in season and Water Rail are a prospect all year. A westerly walk passes a Trout Farm on the way to Hungerford Town. Best in summer, when riparian warblers are numerous. Look out for Hobby and keep an ear open for Grasshopper Warbler and Nightingale.

On the common itself, Jackdaw and other corvids are numerous throughout the year, and Green Woodpecker feed on the open grass areas. Passage Wheatears are possible and Turtle Dove frequent the more open-wooded areas in summer. The tree-lined fringes are host to Garden Warbler, Blackcap, Chiffchaff, Marsh Tit, Spotted Flycatcher and all the common woodland species, whilst clouds of hirundines hawk overhead. In winter, it may prove profitable to scan the arable land beyond the waterways for Golden Plover amongst the Lapwing.

Inkpen Common (OS ref. SU 382 643)

Settled in the valley below the impressive slopes of Inkpen Hill, this remnant piece of heathland, managed by BBOWT, comprises 10.4 ha (26 acres) of boggy heath and woodland, with a small pool, Ashton's Pool, named after the first secretary and financier of the Common, Jack Ashton. Parking is available at a couple of locations in Great Common Road and whilst there are two main footpaths through the Common, a number of side-tracks and trails enable deeper exploration of the thickets and copses around the periphery. A summetime walk to the tune of Gorse seeds cracking in the heat of the sun is likely to reveal typical heathland species such as Yellowhammer, Linnet, Chiffchaff and Willow Warbler, with the possibility of Tree Pipit and Whitethroat. Probably not a large enough area to support Hobby, but Common Buzzard soaring overhead is a distinct possibility.

The denser Oak and Birch tree-scape hosts Goldcrest, Treecreeper, Blackcap and Bullfinch, with Marsh Tit quite prominent and Willow Tit a fair prospect, as are Siskin in winter. The small pool attracts several species of dragonfly and White Admiral butterflies can be seen in July.

Maidenhead Thicket (OS ref. SU 855 807)

The Thicket comprises 70 ha (175 acres) of dense Hawthorn, Blackthorn and other shrubbery in the east and mature mixed deciduous woodland with some conifer stands and heath-like areas to the west. Situated astride the A404(M) road to Henley, it is managed by the National Trust. Parking for 25 vehicles is in Pinkneys Drive.

A good site for general woodland birds, the dense portion around the car park being attractive to all common tits, Treecreeper, Great Spotted Woodpecker and Bullfinch all year round, plus Blackcap, Garden Warbler, Willow Warbler and Chiffchaff in summer. Lesser Whitethroat are regular passage visitors to this sector and large groups of Redwing and Fieldfare roost in winter. The more open and mature woodland on the western side of the main road hosts all three woodpeckers, numerous Jay and occasional Tawny Owl. Treecreeper and Nuthatch are quite abundant and both Collared and Stock Doves are present, the former preyed upon regularly by Sparrowhawk. Spotted Flycatcher are quite regular, especially around the edges of the wood. The mammal life of the Thicket includes Fox and occasional Muntjac Deer, and several species of bats are prolific in summer.

Simon's Wood & Finchampstead Ridges (OS ref. SU 813 635)
These two sites which straddle the B3348, Wellingtonia Avenue, between Finchampstead and Crowthorne, are managed by the National Trust, with a car park for 30 vehicles at the grid reference given. Comprising some 24 ha (60 acres) of Oak, Birch, chestnut and Scots Pine woodland, Simon's Wood on the north side of the road is excellent for general woodland birds, whilst a naturally acid pond, Heath Pool, to the north has a few Moorhen, Coot, Mallard and Canada Geese. A heathland restoration project was completed in 1999, which Stonechat and Willow Warbler have been quick to exploit. These open areas may in time attract Tree Pipit and even Nightjar. Hobby are possible overhead.

Finchampstead Ridges to the south of the road is a much denser woodland, sloping down to a boggy region at the lowest point, with Marsh Tit and Treecreeper in evidence. Sparrowhawk breed here and Tawny Owl is present. Crossbill, Siskin and Redpoll are found in winter as they wander between larger plantations nearby.

Summerleaze Gravel Pit (OS ref. SU 895 827)
A sizeable pit to the north-east of Maidenhead with several planted islands for breeding ducks and geese. There are also some flat gravel spits used by Common Tern and Little Ringed Plover for breeding, and a gravel-filled floating raft provided by the local RSPB group. In winter the water is very busy with mixed gull roosts of several hundreds of birds, providing a challenge to find the Yellow-legged Gull amongst them, and significant numbers of Coot, Tufted Duck and Canada Geese. Quite a few Pochard overwinter and there are always small numbers of Goldeneye and Wigeon, occasional Ruddy Duck, Goosander and Smew. Winter and passage waders have included Greenshank, Ruff, Redshank, Snipe, Dunlin and Common Sandpiper and occasional Ringed Plover, but much depends on water levels, which have been too high for waders in recent years. Kingfisher are resident and Sand Martin breed in the area. Surrounded by farmland, Yellowhammer, Skylark, Reed Bunting and Little Owl are frequently encountered and Meadow Pipit are numerous in winter. Hobby hunt over the lake from mid-summer, up to 10 being possible over adjacent Widbrook Common in August, and Ring-necked Parakeet are regular visitors.

Set-aside areas to the north have encouraged occasional Stonechat and the reed-lined stream in the vicinity has nesting Reed and Sedge Warblers. Though good for general birdwatching all year, access is restricted to views over the lake from public footpaths to the west and north of the pool. However, there is a prospect of a hide being constructed in the near future.

The Downs (OS ref. SU 430 800)
The extensive area of the Downs where north-west Berkshire collides with Oxfordshire via the Vale of White Horse is wonderful habitat for birds. This is the world of huge flocks of quarrelsome corvids, rattling Corn Bunting and wheezing Yellowhammer, with vast tracts of rolling

Corn Bunting

pasture and stony arable fields, in an almost treeless landscape. Viewing from one of the highest spots, such as the Devil's Punchbowl southwest of Wantage or the steeper rises at Thurle Down near Streatley, offers not only stunning scenery, but the chance to watch the movement of birds over wide areas, and improves the prospects for spotting wandering raptors. The Ridgeway runs along the north of the Downs, providing a walk from which the species encountered typify the surroundings, with birds of the fields such as Carrion Crow and Rook, Skylark and Meadow Pipit, Pheasant and Grey Partridge and, in winter, Fieldfare. Wherever pig farms are found, groups of Lesser Black-backed Gull will be present. The Downs are the only area in the county where one might chance across a Stone Curlew, which has a tenuous and threatened grip. Small numbers still attempt to breed, with uncertain success. One may stand a better chance of seeing them during spring passage. The Quail too may be expected in small numbers, around Compton and Thurle and over in the Lambourn Downs.

The vast open prairie-like field system also appeals to Britain's larger raptors. The Compton and Blewbury area seems the most productive and Hen Harrier are recorded in most years, East Garston Downs, the Compton area and Sheepdrove sector seeming to be favoured. Marsh Harrier are less frequent, but Common Buzzard are regular visitors and breed in the Lambourn area. Hobby are attracted by the hirundine flocks that sweep the pastures for insects, and the number of Merlin overwintering on the Downs is almost certainly under-estimated. Short-eared Owl put in regular appearances at the Thurle end, and Barn Owl is another, though scarcer prospect. The River Lambourn, in the south-west corner of the Downs, provides a more varied habitat in which Snipe and Kingfisher thrive. In winter, Brambling are a likely find, though never numerous and Great Grey Shrike has been a notable December bird in some years. Wheatear could be found almost anywhere in ones and twos during April and May, and some Yellow Wagtail stay throughout the summer. Wherever there are outbreaks of scrub and woodland, Whitethroat, Lesser Whitethroat, Garden Warbler and Great Spotted Woodpecker will be encountered, such as at Seven Barrows NR north of Lambourn (SU 329 827) which is also excellent for butterflies. After very wet winters, flooding between East Ilsley and Compton draws a variety of waders and waterfowl, and Curlew breed in one or two places.

In summary, a huge area which one could spend a lifetime becoming familiar with. There is the possibility of some really good species being found but only through regular and detailed prospecting.

Windsor Great Park (OS ref. SU 962 723)

At some 2,000 ha (4,800 acres), the Great Park is aptly named. Stretching away from the Royal Castle, the park comprises deciduous woodlands of Oak, Beech and Hornbeam, open deer parkland, farmland, and three bodies of water, including Virginia Water which, at 3 km (2 miles) from end to end, is by far the largest and rests partially in Surrey. Vehicles are not permitted in the park but there is ample parking on the A332 to the west and several car parks at Blacknest Gate, Virginia Water in the south, and Bishops Gate in the east. Fees are charged at some of these. The farmland attracts species which typify such habitat, including winter flocks of mixed corvids, with Jackdaw the most numerous. Green Woodpecker frequents the open parkland whilst both other woodpecker species can be found throughout the woodlands and near 'The Village' at the centre of the park. Smiths Lawn, the polo grounds, sometimes attracts passage Wheatear and surrounding Birch scrub will host the first Chiffchaff and Willow Warbler. The more open woodlands contain many hole-nesting birds including Lesser Spotted Woodpecker, Nuthatch, Stock Dove and Willow Tit. The local Hawfinch only occur infrequently these days, but Spotted Flycatcher, Treecreeper and Goldcrest are plentiful and Firecrest always possible in such a large suitable area.

Great Meadow Pond is not available to the public but its resident flock of Canada Geese, together with the local group of Barnacle and Bar-headed Geese, will be seen flying in to roost at dusk. The once large colony of Mandarin Duck, which breed successfully here, has now distributed itself county-wide but their high-pitched call, seemingly inappropriate for a bird of this size, can still be heard as they too arrive to roost. A major loss to twenty-first century birdlife has been the clouds of thousands of Starling that used to gather at the park. They are still plentiful, but no longer in dramatic numbers. With the main areas of water containing Cormorant, Little Grebe and Gadwall in winter, and most of the common summering species in the wooded areas, a visit at most times of the year can be worthwhile. Midweek days between October and July might be best, but allow plenty of time.

It is a long time since Long-eared Owl bred here regularly, but Common Buzzard are breeding once more after a long gap and Barn Owl have been seen again. The park will doubtless see many more changes, but the site could be ideal for introducing Lady Amherst's or Golden Pheasant, and the nearby flock of 3,000 Ring-necked Parakeet at Esher may, in due course, establish a colony at the park.

Wood End (OS ref. SU 938 695)

A pleasant walk through paddocks, pasture and private parkland with a sizeable lake in the centre. Parking is near the entrance, off the lane between Cheapside and Ascot; a footpath runs north along the private drive. Approximately 100 m (109 yds) along, another footpath leads off left into a small woodland and emerges near the lake. This path follows a tree-lined lane to Wood End from where one may retrace one's steps or follow the B383 to the northern end of the estate taking the southerly footpath to complete a circular walk.

The deciduous woodland is inhabited by Great Spotted Woodpecker and Marsh Tit, whilst the trees to the west of the lake form a substantial Jackdaw roost and the northern coniferous area hosts Treecreeper, Goldcrest and Coal Tit. A sizeable poplar plantation attracts Mistle Thrush and quite probably, Lesser Spotted Woodpecker. The Lake

Dartford Warbler

forms a significant roost for winter gulls and Pochard whilst Great Crested Grebe and Mandarin are present in the breeding season. The paddocks are favoured by Green Woodpecker, Goldfinch and winter thrushes and the tree-lines around adjacent fields are good for Little Owl. Kestrel and Sparrowhawk are resident. A further, smaller lake in Silwood Park, 360 m (400 yds) south of the starting point, has additional pairs of Mandarin, and Kingfisher is present.

Woolhampton Gravel Pits (OS ref. SU 573 665)

Turning south off the A4 at the Angel pub, a series of pools and scrapes will be seen south of the Kennet and Avon Canal, accessible from the car park of the Rowbarge Public House (letting the publican know you are using his car park) at the above grid reference. A permissive footpath runs west from here to other pools and pits at nearby Midgham, and connects to others heading to Shalford Lakes. Details of permissive path networks in the area together with permit information can be obtained from the Estate Manager at Wasing Estates, 0118 971 4140.

Depending on water levels, waders or waterfowl or both will be found on the various waters and gravel mounds viewable from the footpath. Passage waders include Redshank, Common and Green Sandpipers, Ringed and Little Ringed Plovers, whilst Snipe overwinter. Shelduck and common duck species can be expected, including Wigeon in winter, and Ruddy Duck summer here, having bred on at least one occasion. Rarer visitors have included Red-crested Pochard and Red-necked Grebe. A walk along the canal or River Kennet may produce Water Rail and Grey Wagtail, and Cuckoo will be busy seeking out suitable nests to parasitise, whilst Lesser Spotted Woodpecker has been recorded near the lock in recent times. Blackcap, Willow Warbler and Chiffchaff abound along this walk, with Garden Warbler and Spotted Flycatcher worth looking for, and Nightingale worth listening for. Yellow Wagtail may pass through and a check above may be rewarded with a soaring Common Buzzard or hawking Hobby. Winter thrushes, Siskin and groups of Goldcrest and Long-tailed Tit accompany the wellington'd walker during the shorter days when floodwaters invade the footpath and nearby Little Owl may be heard 'kowing', especially in the vicinity of the STW near the Rowbarge.

Willow Tit and Great Grey Shrike have both been recorded, the former species ranking alongside the latter in rarity status these days regrettably.

BUCKINGHAMSHIRE

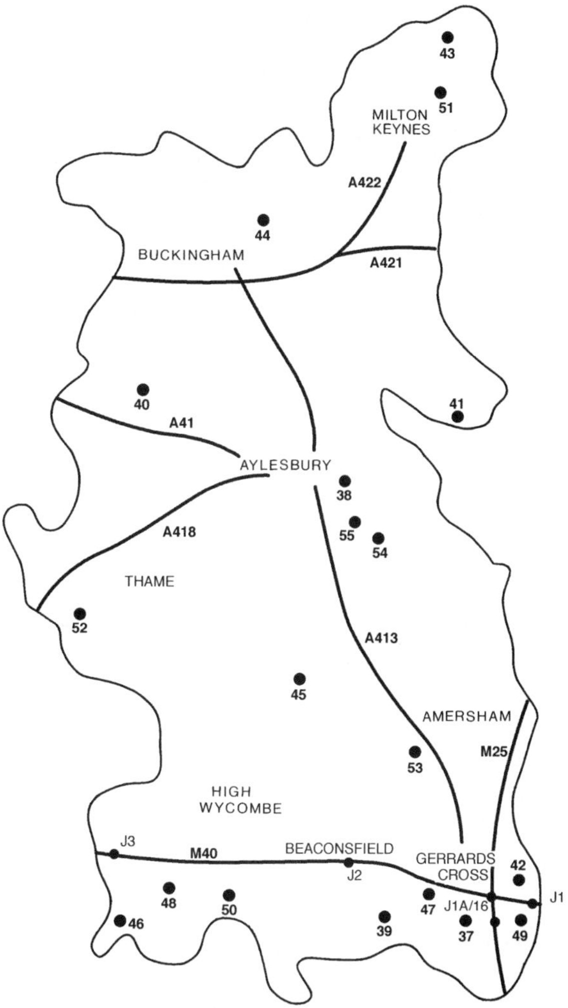

37 BLACK PARK & LANGLEY PARK

OS ref. TQ 010 825

Habitat

These two adjacent locations were once part of the Langley Marish Estate, but were purchased by Buckinghamshire County Council in the 1940s and are now classified as country parks. They are still regarded as being in the green belt and as such form the western extremity of the Colne Valley Park stretching from Staines to Rickmansworth. Black Park covers 220 ha (550 acres) and got this name around 1880 from its plantations of black-barked Corsican Pine. This species covers some 30 per cent of the planted area, but nowadays there exists a greater variety of trees, with Larch and Scots Pine in the conifer stands, in subtle diffusion with deciduous woods which cover about half of the estate with Oak, Beech, Sweet Chestnut, Hemlock, Birch and a few Rowan. Large areas were replanted after the Second World War and were thinned 20 years later, with more deciduous plantations than previously.

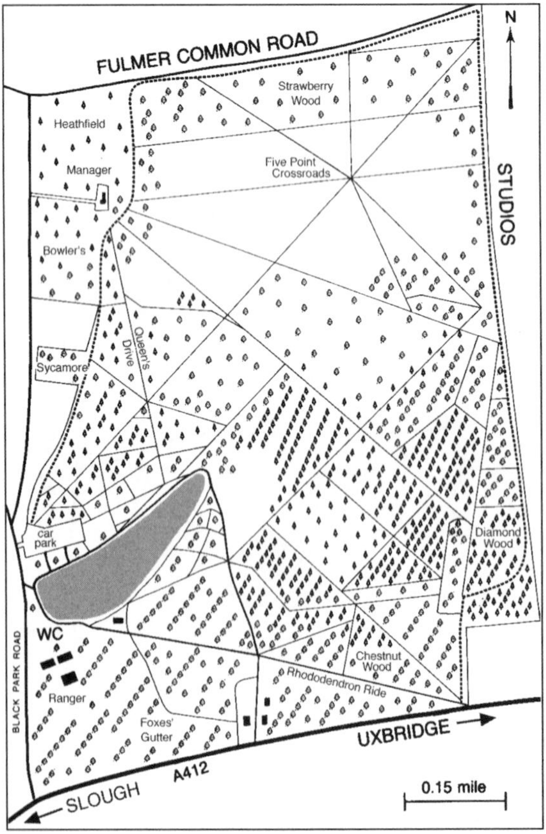

Black Park

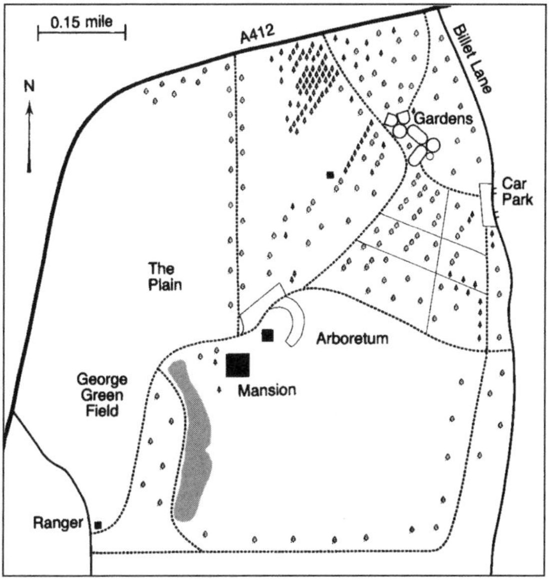

Langley Park

Different habitat again exists at the Five Points Crossroads where, during the drought of 1976, nearly 20 ha (50 acres) were lost to fire. This area was sparsely planted with conifers but has since reverted to scrub, Heather, Gorse and Broom, providing a lower vegetation level than elsewhere in the park, and was registered a SSSI in 1990. The lake itself is 5 ha (12.5 acres) in area and, for many years, was quite deep. Recent work has created a shallow section and small islands to attract waterfowl. A successful nest box scheme with some 125 boxes has run for several years.

Langley Park is classified as parkland, rather than woodland, although a proportion of its 55 ha (135 acres) is committed to mature Oak stands. At its centre is the Ashlar-faced Langley Mansion, recently converted to offices, but the grounds have been maintained and include a small lake, a significant arboretum with some 40 species of tree, and a large expanse of Rhododendrons and Azaleas. The remainder is open grassland with a small farmed area and adjacent orchards.

Access

The two parks straddle the A412 between Uxbridge and Slough and the nearest trunk road connections are junction 1 on the M40 and junction 5 on the M4. The nearest main line station is at Slough. Access to Black Park is along Black Park Road, turning into the pay and display car park which has space for some 400 vehicles and is surrounded with picnic sites. Beyond the lake are refreshment and first-aid facilities, toilets, changing huts and the ranger's office. Special note should be made on arrival of any information on closing times. The park has a peripheral footpath and the many accessible tracks through the woods are indicated on the map. More detailed maps are available on arrival. The area north of the lake is a small marsh and, although a boardwalk is present, wellingtons are recommended here and along the main footpath by the side of the Pinewood Film Studios. About 20 car parking spaces are available in Fulmer Common Road.

Access to Langley Park is from Billet Lane, turning into the car park which can accommodate 100 or so vehicles, also now a pay and display facility. No transfers are permitted with paid-for car park permits between the two locations; a compromise if you intend visiting both in the same day is to park in one of the lay-bys on the A412. Toilets are provided between the formal gardens and the open area. The park has a clearly arranged path scheme and the private area surrounding the mansion has public footpaths around the periphery. Several pedestrian entrances are available.

Species

Black Park is large and varied enough to cater even for birdwatchers who prefer to avoid 'formal' parkland. Winter can be an excellent time to visit whilst there is little vegetation in the shrub areas or on the trees. Discovering all three species of woodpecker, particularly in Strawberry Wood, can be satisfying, whilst Nuthatch and Treecreeper are also easier to locate at this time. Roving groups of Goldcrest, Long-tailed, Blue and Coal Tits are especially prominent as are the boisterous Jay and Magpie. Small parties of Redpoll can be found throughout the park and, at the periphery, Redwing and Grey Partridge can be regularly seen. The car park can be a good place to find Brambling, the male still looking magnificent even in his winter plumage. An evening visit could well be rewarded with Tawny Owl or even occasional Woodcock. This same compartment is one of the more usual sites to find Crossbill. The pool at this time of year is not likely to be too productive as the adjacent heronry was abandoned some 20 years ago.

Meanwhile, the winter scene at Langley Park is slightly different, the more open parkland and less enclosed pool attracting additional species. Little Owl in particular is far more abundant than in Black Park. The pool, though smaller and more prone to freezing over than its neighbours, is generally better populated, with Pochard, a few Shoveler and the occasional Wigeon usually present. A pair or two of Gadwall might well be passing through and Teal could be present whilst Cormorant are also likely, on one occasion in December 2000 accompanied by a solitary Shag. Grey and Pied Wagtails can be found whilst Kingfisher may be a little more shy. Gulls are also more numerous here though usually restricted to Common and Black-headed species. Redwing are joined by slate-headed Fieldfares in and around the orchard to the east of the park and at the formal garden area which is often visited by a few Brambling. The woods, being generally less mature than Black Park in many places, possess fewer birds, but the list of species is similar including all three woodpeckers. The farmland in the meantime attracts the usual flocks of corvids, sometimes numbering near 1,000, with gulls and Lapwing. They are often joined by large numbers of Starling just before nightfall, first wheeling casually into the general area and then finally descending to the ground rapidly, almost violently, like heavy rain. A dozen or two Ring-necked Parakeet may be found roosting in the boundary hedgerows.

The approach of spring at Langley Park sees the gulls moving off and the winter ducks bequeath the pool to breeding Mute Swan. Sightings of Meadow Pipit diminish, and Reed Bunting set up their own nesting territories. Small flocks of Yellowhammer disperse in pairs as the spring

Spotted Flycatcher

passage unwraps its annual surprises. A pair or two of Gadwall may stop over and Pintail have been noted. The arboretum has produced Pied Flycatcher at this time of year and once the migration floodgates are fully open, Chiffchaff, Willow Warbler and Blackcap are soon in evidence. The formal gardens attract Song Thrush, Blackbird and Collared Dove. The first Nuthatch broods will be piping amongst the deciduous parts of the woods while less discernible calls of countless other young birds seem to emanate from every bush and tree hole. In fact a suitable tree hole was clearly sought out by a pair of Egyptian Geese which produced six goslings in summer 2001! It will be worth looking for Spotted Flycatcher near the mansion outbuildings.

Black Park will also be changing its scenery and, perhaps being more recognised as an amenity than Langley Park, numbers of visitors will be increasing and the pool will be utilised for paddling and boating, becoming almost devoid of birds save for the few breeding Coot and Mallard at the reserve end of the lake. Here again, family groups of Nuthatch make themselves most obvious and the majority of the 120 or so nest boxes provided will have been utilised by something, even if it is Wood Mice. Kestrels also breed on the site and on rare occasions can be seen posturing with Sparrowhawk for hunting rights. Hobby have been an exciting addition to the breeding species in recent years, seen over the woodland and especially the heathland section.

Without doubt, this latter habitat, situated at Five Point Crossroads, is the single most important sector of Black Park in summer from the birdwatcher's point of view. Since the fire, the area has attained a dense covering of mature Heather, Gorse and Broom, interspersed with young conifers and emerging Birch scrub. Ongoing management of Gorse and Birch has created an area large enough for a number of heathland species. A warm summer's morning, ideally at 06:30 hrs or so, is the best time to visit this corner of the park. Stepping out into the sunshine from the wooded approaches, one is first likely to be greeted with the plaintive calls of Willow Warbler and the equally distinctive sound of Yellowhammer. Several pairs of Linnet will be busily collecting food in the bushes and trees, pausing only occasionally for song before disappearing into a dense nest site. A small number of Reed Bunting have found this to be a suitable breeding area and several pairs of Bullfinch also indulge. Garden Warbler also afford ample opportunity for the birder to become familiar with the sight and sound of this drab-looking but cheerful bird in comparison with the similar-sounding Blackcap. Green Woodpecker move between the few mature trees that survived the ravages of the fire. These same trees, mainly Oaks, are used as songposts by two birds that very much specialise in this sort of terrain: the Tree Pipit and the Whitethroat. Several pairs of each are usually present and it is interesting to compare the 'parachute' song-flights of the pipit with the falls and hoverings of the Whitethroat.

Long-tailed Tit also inhabit this new plantation, building their domed nests in Gorse bushes. Much less regularly, but doubtless with even greater pleasure, one might be fortunate enough to come across a Grasshopper Warbler reeling from within the denser vegetation. Surrounded by these ornithological delights one may well overlook the Muntjac Deer that occasionally stroll out of the plantation onto the pathways. Small though it may be this section of the estate is of great significance given that there is little similar habitat for quite some distance. It may only be a question of time before Nightjar and Dartford Warbler set up home here. Recent SSSI registration should secure the future of this sector. In the meantime these parks will continue to offer good opportunities to study a wide range of woodland bird species.

Calendar

Resident: Cormorant, Mute Swan, Mallard, Tufted Duck, Sparrowhawk, Kestrel, Ring-necked Parakeet, Pheasant, possible Snipe and Woodcock, Woodpigeon, Stock and Collared Doves, Little and Tawny Owls, all three woodpeckers, Skylark, Meadow Pipit, Pied Wagtail, common corvids, Goldcrest, Marsh Tit, possibly Willow Tit, Nuthatch, Treecreeper, Bullfinch, Goldfinch, Linnet, Redpoll, Reed Bunting, Yellowhammer.

December–February: Occasional Little Grebe and Wigeon. Teal, Shoveler, Pochard. Red-legged Partridge irregular, large flocks of Lapwing. Most of the more common gulls in small numbers. Occasional Grey Wagtail, numerous Redwing and Fieldfare. Mixed flocks of feeding tits and Goldcrest. Possibility of Brambling, Crossbill, Siskin and groups of Redpoll.

March–May: Winter thrushes and mixed feeding flocks persist through March. Passage birds include Wheatear, Whinchat and prospect of Redstart. Cuckoo and early passage warblers by early April. Prospect of migrant Turtle Dove in May by which time Tree Pipit, and the common Sylvia and leaf warblers have arrived. Spotted Flycatcher by mid-May.

June–July: Breeding residents and summer visitors, nest boxes in use for second broods of several species.

August–November: Adult Cuckoo depart in August. October passage not particularly marked. Winter thrushes return and gull numbers increase in November.

38 BROUGHTON POOLS

OS ref. SP 843 142

Habitat

The Broughton Pools comprise two adjacent wetland areas on the banks of the Grand Union Canal, surrounded by farmland. Trout Pools were created in 1994 but abandoned as a commercial enterprise shortly afterwards, leaving an area of shallow water, ditches and marsh that has attracted an increasing number of species. In wet seasons, other pools form attracting transient visitors. Mature willows and other hedgerow trees outline pastures and farmland. Unfortunately, there is a footpath through the middle of the site which, though only infrequently used, can cause disturbance. The Flood Alleviation Area abuts a nearby housing estate and comprises small pools, a narrow stream (Bear Brook), and shallow marshy sections with dense tussocky plants and bulrushes, ideal for waders. Despite the proximity of the estate, and a footpath along one edge, normally timid species seem to have grown accustomed to human activity to a degree.

Access

The site is just 2 km east of Aylesbury along the Grand Union Canal. The small car park for about 10 vehicles is located on the south-eastern corner of Broughton Lock Bridge at the map reference mentioned above. Nearest main roads are the A41 Aylesbury–Tring road and the A418 from Aylesbury to Wing. The Trout Pools can be viewed from the towpath accessed from the car park, looking due north, and a little height can be gained by viewing from the first bridge encountered when walking east. In fact the towpath continues east to the nature reserve north of Tring, some 6 km distance, and can make for an enjoyable walk. The Flood Alleviation pools are approached by walking west from the car park and viewing from the raised bank, although in winter and early mornings, the sun is poorly positioned for this. A footpath between the housing estate and the pools affords good views not only of ducks,

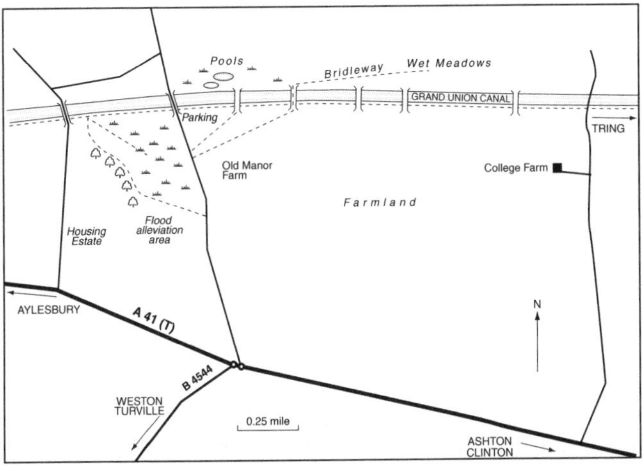

grebes and gulls on the water, but any waders and Teal lurking in the marshy undergrowth. Bushes and shrubs along this route are maturing nicely and ideal for common finches, tits and sparrows. The far end of this path then links back to the car park by turning left on the road at the end of the pools.

Species

Dedicated observation by local birdwatchers over the last five years or so has amassed over 140 species. Indeed, the ornithological record obtained has been used in evidence to combat plans for a further housing development in the area. The avian picture here is constantly changing season by season, with summer and autumn migrants, and other birds which dominate in winter. The Trout Pools in the colder months will often be surrounded with several dozen Snipe, and Jack Snipe can occasionally be found. Up to a dozen Grey Heron may laze around. When the ground is hardened by frost, the Snipe range into more open areas to feed and can be more easily seen. Teal, Gadwall, Shoveler and Wigeon may be joined by less usual species such as Cormorant, Pintail, Shelduck, Goosander and Scaup, but being enclosed and shallow, the pools quickly freeze in cold weather, pushing duck species off to larger and more open waters elsewhere. Separated from the stronghold of mid- to east Berkshire by quite a few miles, any Mandarin Duck seen here are likely to be escapes. All sorts of ornamental ducks appear on the canal; Black Swan are penned not 200 m from the car park and a nearby aviary has held such species as Golden Oriole, so beware of the unusual. Large numbers of winter thrushes will occupy adjacent meadows and Golden Plover may be found amongst Lapwing in fields beyond the first bridge or two. Quite large flocks of Goldfinch and Greenfinch can occur, and Meadow Pipit, Yellowhammer and Reed Bunting will be in the vicinity in various numbers. Spring passage, and more exposed mud, draws a variety of wader species onto or over the Trout Pool site, typical amongst these being Greenshank and Whimbrel, whilst Redshank can occur more generally. Dunlin, Ruff, Little Ringed Plover and Common Sandpiper may well be found and visits have been made by Spotted Redshank, Little Stint, Oystercatcher, Curlew, Green Sandpiper and Black-tailed Godwit. Wheatear and Whinchat have been seen passing through, especially on fences and fields east of the first and second bridges. Yellow Wagtail too find this area to their fancy, perhaps though being seen in greater numbers in the reverse movement during autumn. One field north of Bridge 13 often has a noticeboard listing the fauna and flora to be found there.

As spring turns to summer, resident Water Rail, Kingfisher, Grey Wagtail and Little Owl find attention turned from them to feeding Common Tern, and a variety of summer warblers, including good numbers of Lesser Whitethroat. More unusual holidaymakers have included Redstart and Ring Ouzel. Corvids, Skylark and Green Woodpecker breed in the area, but as in so many similar areas, Lapwing seem to have forsaken the locale for nesting. However, Sedge and Reed Warblers are now breeding in greater numbers to partly make up for this. Both Spotted and Pied Flycatchers have been noted.

The Flood Alleviation sector also reflects the changing seasons, largely dependent on water levels in both pools and marshy areas. Any waders and skulking duck species amongst the tussocks can be viewed from the raised bank, but this might accentuate any disturbance, so viewing from the lower footpath around the housing estate may be best, an early visit ensuring less activity from the residents. In addition to the resident Mallard, Coot and Moorhen, Little Grebe can be viewed at close quarters. In fact, the narrowness of the site enables close views of species often only seen at greater distances, such as Snipe, Jack Snipe, Teal and gulls. Similar passage waders have been seen here, plus Spotted Redshank and Bar-tailed Godwit, and Garganey provided wonderful viewing opportunities on one occasion. Brambling are rather rare, but Wheatear, Whinchat, Black Redstart, Stonechat and even Waxwing have all added to the variety, plus Turtle Dove.

The whole area is one of those places where anything might turn up, and the range of feathered foodstuffs have attracted such raptors as Peregrine (even a displaying pair seen on one occasion recently), Merlin, Goshawk and Hobby, with the extending range of Red Kite guaranteeing visits from this dramatic bird of prey too. Barn, Long-eared and Short-eared Owls have all been encountered over the years whilst the site's first Hen Harrier, and a possible Montagu's Harrier both appeared in the same month during 1999. Lesser Spotted Woodpecker has been noted repeatedly as have Redpoll. Adjacent meadows were a magnet to two Common Cranes in April '99 whilst an Osprey evaluated the area fleetingly two months later. Little Egret appeared inevitably in September 2000. At the beginning of the new century, the Bucks. species list stood at 278. Will perhaps Broughton rate amongst the sites that might supply number 279?

Calendar

Resident: Little Grebe, Grey Heron, Mute Swan, common duck, Kestrel, Sparrowhawk, Water Rail, Little Owl, Collared Dove, Kingfisher, all three woodpeckers, Skylark, Meadow Pipit, Grey and Pied Wagtails, Greenfinch and Goldfinch in good numbers, Yellowhammer.

December–February: Cormorant, Shelduck, Wigeon, Gadwall, Teal and Shoveler. Occasional Pintail and Goosander, Golden Plover on adjacent fields, many Snipe and regular Jack Snipe. Large flocks of winter thrushes. Corvids, occasional Brambling, Siskin and Redpoll.

March–May: Passage waders including Little Ringed and Ringed Plovers, godwits, and Curlew, with occasional Dunlin, Whimbrel and Green Sandpiper, Greenshank and Redshank. Cuckoo, arrival of common warblers, passage Yellow Wagtail, Whinchat and Wheatear, thinning out of finch flocks

June–July: Breeding Little Grebe and Tufted Duck, Spotted Flycatcher possible, good numbers of Lesser Whitethroat, feeding Common Tern, all the common tits and finches breeding, hirundines and Swift hawking for insects, perhaps in the company of Hobby. If disturbance could be controlled, good prospect of breeding Snipe.

August–November: Passage migrants move through with departing warblers and returning Yellow Wagtail. Good variety of waders and Lapwing numbers build up, joined by Golden Plover later. Resident bird numbers greatly enhanced, numbers of Starling and corvids increase.

39 BURNHAM BEECHES

OS ref. SU 950 850

Habitat

If you like ancient woodland, the 220 ha (540 acres) of Burnham Beeches is the place for you. The wood once stretched from Taplow to Burnham and as far as the Thames, and some of the Beech specimens are between 600 and 800 years old. In addition to stands of mature Oak and Beech, with little secondary undergrowth, there are areas of Hazel coppice, pasture woodland, and a new development to open up some original heathland. There are sizeable areas of scrub and bracken and also small conifer plantations. Burnham Common occupies the centre ground, with open grassland, heathland, bushes and bramble. Rhododendron is fairly common but being managed, particularly in the north-western sector, where moss-covered mounds and a more prolific herbaceous layer exists. The undulate nature of the woods enhances the atmosphere and facilitates a number of streams leading into a series of pools of varying size. Reflecting both the careful management traditions in place, and the importance of such woodland, the site has been declared a National Nature Reserve and is a Candidate Special Area of Conservation.

Over a century ago, locals appealed to Queen Victoria to purchase this woodland for the people, as it fell just inside the 25-mile London boundary. However, her purse strings were stretched with Empire matters. And so it was left to the Lord Mayor of London to purchase this sub-boreal grade 2 wood on behalf of the Corporation of London who have, since 1879, provided roads and pathways. Whilst many of the ancient trees are left untouched other than pruning for safety, management policy for younger trees follows a felling programme of approximately 80-year cycles. There is evidence of the earlier pollarding of Beech for charcoal. White Helleborine and Bird's-Nest Orchid are just two of the woodland flowers that can be found and work continues to encourage sundew to flourish again. Grey Squirrel have colonised the woods whilst Fox and Muntjac can be seen around the periphery.

From the northern sector of Burnham Beeches, one can step into the 160 ha (400 acres) of Egypt Wood, part of the Portman Burtley Estate. The treescape here is more coniferous and whilst adding this extra dimension, also almost doubles the overall size of the woodland area and therefore has an important overall effect on birdlife. There are two public footpaths through this additional area, which is believed to have got its name from an early gypsy encampment. Alternate stands of Larch, Birch and evergreen specimens lend character to the scenery. It is a much quieter area, so Roe and Muntjac Deer may be seen regularly.

Access

Burnham Beeches is north of Slough and on the western side of the A355, which runs between junction 2 of the M40 and junction 6 of the M4. There are several points of entry from the A355 itself and also from Hawthorn Lane and Pumpkin Hill to the south, and Park Lane to the west. There is a small network of metalled roads through the wood, a number of them joining at Victory Cross near the centre, where the main car park and refreshment area is located. However, many are now closed to create car-free zones and the main Lord Mayor's Drive is only

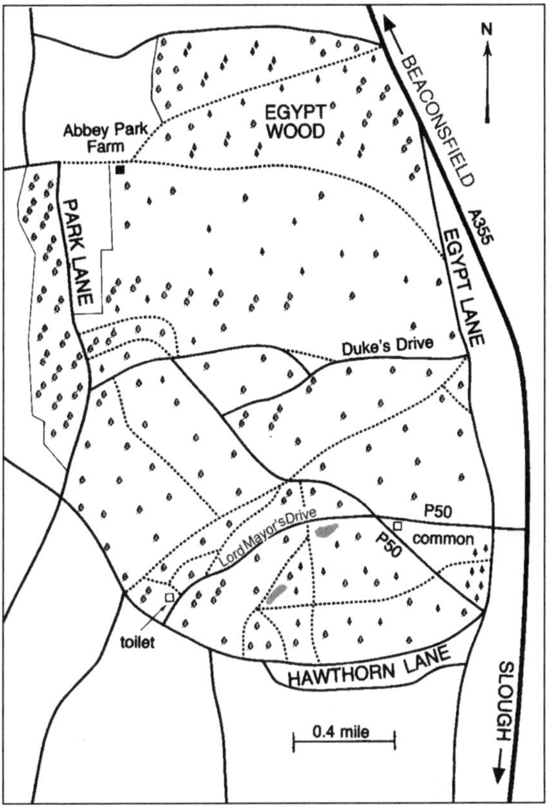

open from 08:00 hrs to dusk. Subsidiary car parks and other pull-offs combine to accommodate up to 1,500 cars (an indication of how busy it can get at this popular site). Toilets and a café have been provided at the southern end of Lord Mayor's Drive, and a seasonal refreshment booth can be found at the main car park. Egypt Wood is not so well blessed for parking with just one or two places near Abbey Park Farm or in Egypt Lane on the opposite side. The nearest main line railway station is at Slough, which is served from Paddington.

Species

There are few places which afford the distinctive scenery of ancient woodland and even without birds, a walk here would be a sheer delight. A clear frosty morning in January can portray a wood in all its avian glory almost as well as on a warm spring day. There may be fewer species but the resident birds are more active, and the absence of dense foliage makes observation all the easier. So what better time is there to practise one's skill of identification by sound? The winter orchestra is somewhat less confusing but nonetheless challenging, as courting calls and territorial outbursts start early in the year. Probably the most prominent species is the Great Spotted Woodpecker, calling and drumming in every sector.

Mixed feeding flocks of tits, Treecreeper and Goldcrest in winter give way in summer to family groups of the same species but added to by Nuthatch fledglings clamouring noisily for morsels. Jackdaw, raucous and rowdy in their year's-end gatherings, split up to raise young in the larger trees, often contesting potential breeding territories with Mistle Thrush which have similar intentions. The striking colours of the male Bullfinch may prove difficult to find when the woods are in full foliage, and the same is true of the Lesser Spotted Woodpecker, which at best is infrequent.

The scrub around Crabtree Heath and the bushes on East Burnham Common are likely areas for Blackcap and a singing male can be quite captivating. However, the mature treescape forbids sufficient understorey bushes to encourage summer warblers to stay for breeding, so Garden and Willow Warblers may be absent. Regrettably, Nightingale and Wood Warbler have forsaken even these perfect conditions but it is hoped that the heathland regeneration scheme may attract passage Tree Pipit, Redstart and Stonechat. However, these losses are somewhat ameliorated by the recent addition of breeding Mandarin (up to four pairs) and regular Ring-necked Parakeet. Chiffchaff are numerous.

As with any reasonably large expanse of trees, Burnham Beeches is a refuge for Woodpigeon, Collared Dove and also Stock Dove, and quite large numbers roost in the area. The size of the woods also makes it an ideal location for owls and whilst it is many years since the Long-eared species nested here, the more common Tawny Owl is being encouraged by a significant nest box scheme, in conjunction with the Hawk and Owl Trust. Little Owl and Kestrel boxes have also been installed and Hobby baskets are being experimented with. A reintroduction scheme for Dormice is also in progress. Beechwoods produce leaf-litter in prodigious quantities, anything up to 4,000 kg (3.9 tons) per hectare in a year, furnishing ground foraging birds with good feeding, particularly in winter when the leaves shelter insects and maintain soil warmth and moistness. Blackbird, Song Thrush and Robin can be heard searching noisily and occasionally Green Woodpecker, or Yaffingale as it is sometimes called, may join in this feeding technique. Chaffinch flocks should be scrutinised for occasional Brambling. Meanwhile in the northern parts of Egypt Woods, small numbers of Redpoll and Siskin will be moving amongst the Silver Birches. In early spring, the wood is filled with tapping sounds as woodpeckers search for food, Nuthatch hammer open small nuts, Great Tit tap inquisitively and, with luck, a Willow Tit may be found excavating a nest hole, thereby providing one of the more distinct ways of discerning this species from neighbouring Marsh Tit. The pools, in addition to hosting the Mandarin Duck, will have Moorhen and Mallard, whilst Swilly Pool just outside the southern entrance may have Tufted Duck and roaming Bullfinch.

As for raptors, Sparrowhawk is regular with both Common Buzzard and Red Kite now putting in appearances. Some 150 years ago Honey Buzzard nested in these woods; those days are gone but if any of their many passage descendants in October 2000 had alighted here, they would have affirmed the special atmosphere of woodland birdwatching which is still readily available on this site in any season.

Calendar

Resident: All three woodpeckers, Nuthatch, Treecreeper, Jay, Kestrel, Sparrowhawk, Tawny Owl, Marsh, Coal and perhaps Willow Tits, Goldcrest.

December–February: Siskin, Redpoll, winter thrushes, Woodpigeon and Stock Dove flocks, small groups of Bullfinch, occasional Brambling and Crossbill, flocks of mixed tits, Pheasant, Woodcock possible in south-east corner, Mandarin.

March–May: Turtle Dove rarely, Garden Warbler, and possible Wood Warbler all on passage. Chiffchaff, Blackcap, Whitethroat, Cuckoo.

June–July: Quieter period with breeding in progress, including Mandarin. Raptors particularly busy.

August–November: Passage migrants move through with departing warblers. Resident bird numbers greatly enhanced, large numbers of Starling gather.

40 CALVERT JUBILEE **OS ref. SP 683 250**

Habitat

Calvert Jubilee is a nature reserve of some 38 ha (95 acres), managed by BBOWT on a lease from the London Brick Company, by whom it was previously used as a clay pit. The resulting lake is about 20 ha (50 acres) in area and, being very deep at the centre, acts as a refuge for numerous species of waterfowl. The northern area of the reserve was used as a municipal refuse dump but is now covered with fine-grained clay. This soil supports relatively little plant life but specialist grasses and mosses are present and some Bee and Common Spotted Orchids thrive along with Cowslips. There are extensive patches of dense and thorny scrub making ideal nesting and roosting sites. Many of these bushes can be looked down upon from the raised embankment formed by a disused railway line in the north-east. There is a narrow strip of land around the remainder of the lake with further scrub, areas of open tall grass, favoured by Great Spotted and Green Woodpeckers, and a row of mature trees to the south.

Threats of the site being used for infill have reduced but a nearby housing development, to the south, could have an indirect impact in the form of an increase in visitors from the likes of dog-walkers. However, until such a fate befalls Jubilee, it will continue to be a quiet refuge for many species. The adjacent Grebe lake is private, although it can be partially viewed from the road.

Access

Calvert Jubilee Nature Reserve is situated 2 km (1.5 miles) north of Edgcott along the road to Gawcott. The nearest main road is the A41 between Aylesbury and Bicester, to the south. There are no public transport facilities. A small car park for three vehicles is available at the main entrance to the reserve, nearly opposite the access point for Grebe

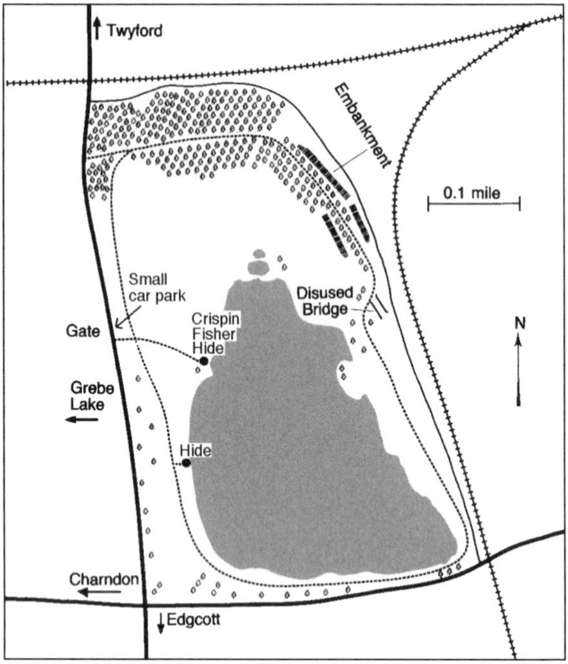

Lake. The site has two hides, one (Crispin Fisher hide) is well positioned and with good facilities for the disabled, while the second is only accessible for the able-bodied and ideal for studying the gull roost.

A peripheral footpath exists, although this involves negotiating a fairly steep bank by the old railway bridge and removing a lift-off fence on the bank, opposite the hides, to facilitate a full circumnavigation. Mature vegetation screens the birder from the lake causing little, if any, disturbance.

Species

'The Jubilee' is most noted for its wintering wildfowl and gull roost and is an excellent site to study both groups of birds from the well-positioned hides in relative peace and tranquillity. The winter scene consists primarily of rafts of Coot and Pochard, the latter spending most of the daylight hours loafing in the sheltered southern bay. Wigeon arrive, in some numbers, a little later and depart earlier than the Pochard, but Tufted Duck are omnipresent with several pairs staying on to breed. Lesser numbers of Teal, Shoveler and Gadwall are dwarfed by several hundred Mallard. Goldeneye, more often 'redheads', than males, regularly overwinter while Goosander and Smew are noted more irregularly, but just about annually. Great Crested Grebe are numerous and the occasional Little Grebe remains to breed with its larger congener. The non-breeding Cormorant and Grey Heron can be seen at any time of year with the former preferring Grebe Lake opposite.

Calvert has a habit of turning up the odd rare waterbird during the winter months, typically ducks like Pintail, Red Crested Pochard, Scaup and Red-breasted Merganser. Occasionally a long-staying Red-necked

Grebe occurs, or rarer still a diver such as Great Northern or the Black-throated in 1998 and once a Ferruginous Duck. Wild swans have been recorded in recent years, as have Shag and Little Egret.

By late March wildfowl numbers generally diminish by the time Shelduck appear on their spring passage. The optimistic birder should be prepared for glimpses of Black-necked Grebe and Garganey on the move in early spring, and Common Scoter in April. Common Terns pass through with several pairs nesting on the prepared raft and later on, during May, Black Terns may briefly put in an appearance during their overland migrations. Although not a wader-friendly site, Common Sandpiper are typically noted feeding along the brick rubble margins and flitting across the water on bow-wings, with occasional visits from Little Ringed Plover and Redshank.

By April, passage Meadow Pipit and Pied Wagtail will be paying short-stay visits on the open ground in the north, with a couple of pairs of pipits remaining to breed most years. The last of the winter thrushes will have left the hawthorn scrub, soon to be colonised by resident Yellowhammer, Bullfinch, Goldfinch and Linnet, and migrant Willow Warbler, Garden Warbler and Whitethroat. The declining Turtle Dove also favours these areas and still breeds in small numbers, as does Cuckoo. The open grassy areas are favoured by Green Woodpecker, whilst adjacent farmland should be checked from the embankment for Skylark, Lapwing, Grey Partridge and other farmland species. Corn Bunting and Tree Sparrow have occasionally been noted near Calvert and are worthwhile looking out for, particularly in mixed passerine flocks outside the breeding season.

The reedbed in front of the main hide holds Sedge and Reed Warblers with the adjacent scrub attractive to Reed Bunting and Nightingale, which can be heard singing from late April; Calvert is a reliable site for this spectacular songster which has declined significantly in the Chilterns region in recent years. Although the terrain is not ideal, leaf warblers such as Willow and Chiffchaff can be found breeding, along with the four common Sylvia warblers. Kingfisher is resident while hirundines or emerging mayflies may entice a Hobby to hunt over the water.

Over 40 species of birds regularly breed at Calvert Jubilee, including all six species of tits, although Willow is now difficult to find, and Kestrel and Tawny Owl have taken advantage of purpose-built boxes, along with Stock Dove and Jackdaw.

As autumn advances, waterfowl numbers gradually increase and the last of the warblers desert the scrub and reedbeds. Southward-moving martins and Swallow swoop over the water building up reserves and the small secondary pools to the north should be checked for passing Snipe, or even Jack Snipe and Water Rail by October. By November the hawthorn scrub and other berry-bearing bushes attract large numbers of Redwing and small groups of Mistle Thrush. Goldcrest join together with tit flocks, and maybe a late Chiffchaff, while a migrant Woodcock may be flushed from cover. The tall poplars host large roosts of Woodpigeon and corvids and the surrounding scrub, thrushes and variable numbers of Starling. Patrolling raptors have included Common Buzzard and Peregrine as well as the more expected Sparrowhawk and Kestrel.

From October to March Calvert Jubilee attracts a substantial gull roost on the open water. Many are prevented from roosting on Grebe Lake, due to sailing activities, making the southern hide on Jubilee Lake an ideal

Whitethroat

position from which to study the incoming gulls. An hour or two before dusk, thousands of Black-headed, Common and Lesser Black-backed Gulls rain in with smaller numbers of Herring and Great Black-backed Gulls. For the gull aficionado, Iceland, Glaucous and Mediterranean Gulls have all been recorded among the throng, along with individuals of the debatable Yellow-legged Gull tribe. Kittiwake are noted most autumns and in 1997 a Sabine's Gull was recorded. For this spectacle alone, the site is probably best visited from December to February.

In summary Calvert Jubilee offers a good variety of species throughout the year and is worth a visit in the winter for wildfowl and gulls, and again in late spring when Nightingale and other summer migrants arrive. As the site is well away from human habitation it is underwatched and consequently, more often than not, the visiting birder has the site to his or her self.

Calendar

Resident: Great Crested and Little Grebes, Grey Heron, Cormorant, Canada Goose, Mallard, Tufted Duck, Sparrowhawk, Kestrel, Moorhen, Coot, Stock Dove, Tawny Owl, Kingfisher, Green and Great Spotted Woodpeckers, Mistle Thrush, six species of tit, Tree Sparrow possible, Bullfinch and Reed Bunting.

December–February: Possible rare grebes, Gadwall, Wigeon, Teal, Shoveler, Pochard, occasional Smew, Scaup, Red-breasted Merganser and Pintail, Goldeneye and Goosander in small numbers, large gull roost with prospect of rarer species such as Iceland or Glaucous. Water Rail, Skylark, Meadow Pipit, Redwing, Fieldfare, groups of Yellowhammer.

March-May: Gulls and wildfowl numbers dwindle, chance of Common Scoter, Garganey or Black-necked Grebe, Common Sandpiper, passage terns, Hobby, Turtle Dove, Cuckoo, Swift, hirundines, Nightingale, Chiffchaff, Willow Warbler and Blackcap, followed by Whitethroat, Garden Warbler, Lesser Whitethroat, Sedge and Reed Warblers.

June-July: Main breeding period, chiefly for wildfowl and warblers, chance of Hobby pursuing hirundines. Occasional non-breeding Common Tern over the water.

August-November: Warblers depart from late August, occasional passage terns before winter thrushes arrive, Water Rail, Snipe, increase in waterfowl, gulls return, roosting pigeons and passerines, Goldcrest.

41 COLLEGE LAKE

OS ref. SP 925 155

Habitat

In 1985, following completion of mineral excavation, a combined project by Castle Cement Ltd and BBOWT successfully created a site of varied habitat for birds and other wildlife. As the site name suggests the main feature is an 11 ha (28 acre) lake complete with two small islands and a tern raft. The north-west bank of the lake features a very steep wall of chalk, its grey tones contrasting with the more natural colours around the site. Deciduous woodland surrounds this sector of the site and a sizeable new plantation has been created south of the main lake. There is a stretch of marsh, a wet meadow and ponds near the entrance that is stock-grazed and overlooked by hides and a viewpoint. This is the main birding area and is ideal for waders and dabbling duck. The site also houses an arable weed centre, where cornfield flowers are cultivated by traditional methods, a flower meadow and an area of chalk grassland behind the main lake. A chalk cliff to the north has been designated a SSSI on geological grounds.

College Lake is a well-planned nature reserve with excellent facilities for observers. It is a perfect example of how local industry (Castle Cement) and conservationists (BBOWT) can work in partnership for the benefit of wildlife and the environment. In October 2000, the company handed over a further 45 ha (110 acres) to the Trust's management. It

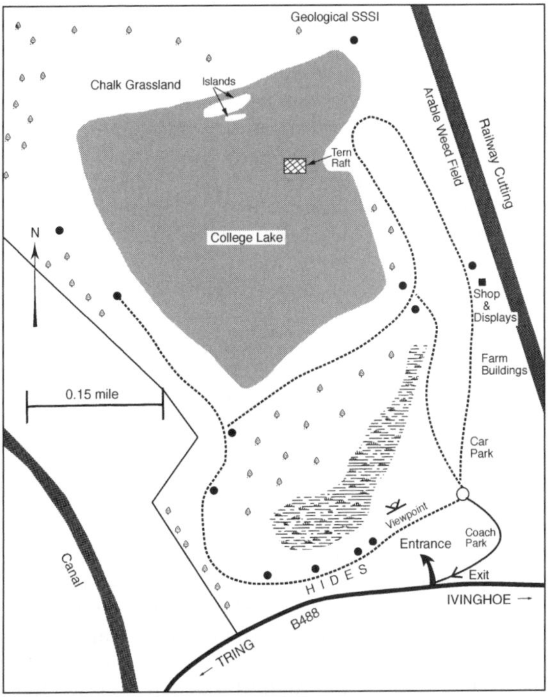

would be churlish not to single out the massive contribution made by the warden at College Lake, Graham Atkins, a former Castle employee. The reserve's success is due in no small part to his dedication and Graham was subsequently awarded the MBE for services to nature conservation.

Access

College Lake is north of the B488, approximately halfway between Tring and Ivinghoe. The main entrance is about 100 m west of the railway line which bisects this road. The site is open daily from 10:00 to 17:00 hrs with ample car and coach parking available. A collection of huts includes an information centre, tearoom and toilet. All visitors must have a permit which can be bought for a small fee at the Warden's Office or at the car park entrance. BBOWT members can visit at any time with a free annual permit obtained from the Trust headquarters (please include a stamped addressed envelope). Only Guide Dogs are allowed on the reserve.

A string of hides have been provided along the ridge near the entrance looking down over the complex and it is good to find hides designed for telescope users. Several are glazed and doors are full height. Special thought has been given to wheelchair users around the site with concrete paths leading from the car park to the hides overlooking the wetlands. Several more hides overlook the main lake but the majority of the northern section of the site is only accessible to BBOWT members or 'Friends of College Lake'.

Species

Over the years, an impressive range of species has taken to College Lake, whatever the season. The lake itself is home to varying numbers of common ducks during the year. Wintering Wigeon reach treble figures and Gadwall and Teal might also exceed 100 at peak times making this site one of the most important in the county for dabbling ducks. Shoveler on the other hand are less abundant. Tufted Duck and Pochard are also well represented among the common diving duck. Short-stay visitors in wintertime and early spring can include Shelduck, Pintail, Goldeneye and Goosander. Ruddy Shelduck and Mandarin have been recorded and the site is near enough to attract any of the rarer species from the more established Tring Reservoirs. Bewick's and Whooper Swans have been noted but relatively few geese use the site apart from feral Canadas. Lapwing are nearly always present, possibly several hundred, and in winter they can induce Golden Plover to join them. Grey Heron can be plentiful. Raptors will often be represented by Kestrel and Sparrowhawk, although Peregrine and Merlin are increasingly noted, along with Common Buzzard drifting over from the nearby Chiltern Hills. Listen out for Water Rail in the reedbeds and Little Owl calling from the chalk cliff to the north.

Waders expected at College Lake include breeding Lapwing, Snipe and Redshank, while Dunlin, Common and Green Sandpipers are regular on passage. In spring and summer, Ringed and Little Ringed Plovers will be encountered, and on occasions have stayed to nest, with passage Curlew and Oystercatcher most likely of the larger waders. At this time of year, Common Tern pass through, with variable numbers remaining to seek out nesting territories on the islands or tern raft. When weather conditions are suitable (normally, easterly winds and rain) occasional visits from Sandwich, Black and Arctic Terns may be expected.

Pied Wagtail

Spring passage commences with early Sand Martin and Swallow over the lake, Wheatear and Meadow Pipit on the chalk grassland and Chiffchaff and Blackcap in the plantations. All the common warblers pass through, along with Yellow and Pied Wagtails, plus small and ever decreasing numbers of Cuckoo, Turtle Dove and Whinchat. Most years Ring Ouzel are noted in the scrub or on the chalk cliff, sometimes in small groups. Swift, hirundines or large flying insects, such as dragonflies, feeding over the lake in summer, will often bring in a hunting Hobby or two, while occasional Grasshopper Warbler and Nightingale are noted singing from deep cover.

The quickly-maturing plantations, open scrub and surrounding bushes are already a lure for many resident species including Linnet, Bullfinch, Goldfinch, Reed Bunting and Yellowhammer. Long-tailed Tit occur alongside summering Willow and Garden Warblers and Whitethroat, with Reed and Sedge Warblers nesting in and around the reedbeds. Skylark and Meadow Pipit both breed on the chalk grassland, where Green Woodpecker often feed. Corn Bunting breed on the nearby chalk hills and occasionally stray onto the reserve, more so during the winter months.

A typical midsummer scene over the marsh would include cattle wading in the water amongst flocks of post breeding Lapwing, along with numerous common wildfowl ducklings, Coot, Moorhen and Mute Swan. Ruddy Duck occasionally breed and Little Grebe regularly do so. A Kingfisher may zip by and Pied Wagtail seem to be everywhere. A Little Egret spent a number of weeks on site in July 2001 and rare inland passage waders such as Grey Plover, Knot and Black-tailed Godwit are not unknown.

During late summer, duck numbers begin to increase, particularly Shoveler, and Common Tern busily feed their chicks in preparation for the long journey ahead. The site burgeons with juvenile warblers, tits and common passerines. Kingfisher and Grey Wagtail are more noticeable in August and September as the young disperse from their natal sites. Flocks of finches feed on the weed seeds and may be joined by a passage Stonechat or Whinchat. Hirundines mass over the water, particularly during cool weather, attracting the attention of Hobby. Osprey have appeared in the past during the autumn and a return wader passage is noted involving mainly sandpipers, Snipe and Greenshank.

With winter approaching and the wildfowl having moulted out of eclipse plumage, winter thrushes are joined by continental Blackbird and Song Thrush in search of berries. Check the scrub for tit flocks, which may contain Goldcrest or a late warbler, and be prepared for the chance of a Firecrest. As the Alder trees mature Goldfinch, Redpoll and Siskin may become more regular winter visitors

Calendar

Resident: Little and Great Crested Grebes, Grey Heron, Coot, Moorhen, Kestrel, Sparrowhawk, Lapwing, Little Owl, Kingfisher, Green and Great Spotted Woodpeckers, Skylark, Meadow Pipit, Pied Wagtail, common tits and finches, Yellowhammer, Reed Bunting.

December–February: Cormorant, Canada Goose, Wigeon, Teal, Shoveler, Pochard, Tufted Duck, occasional Shelduck, Ruddy Duck, Goldeneye, Goosander and Pintail, Green Sandpiper, Snipe, possible Jack Snipe, prospect of Golden Plover, Water Rail, winter thrushes, roosting finches and buntings.

March–May: Shelduck, Green and Common Sandpipers, Dunlin, Redshank, Ringed and Little Ringed Plovers, Common Tern, occasional Black or Arctic Terns, Hobby, Cuckoo, Turtle Dove, Swift, Meadow Pipit, hirundines, Wheatear, Whinchat and Stonechat, chance of Ring Ouzel, Grasshopper Warbler and Nightingale, common warbler passage.

June–July: Breeding resident finches, tits and thrushes, Common Tern, Lapwing, Redshank, Ruddy Duck, Snipe, Common and Green Sandpipers, Swift and hirundines over the water, Hobby, warblers breeding.

August–November: Duck numbers increase particularly Shoveler, wader passage with chance of rarity, possible Peregrine, Osprey or harrier, passage of pipits, chats, thrushes and finches, Grey Wagtail, Goldcrest.

42 DENHAM COUNTRY PARK & LAKES

OS ref. TQ 055 865

Habitat

Nestling between the Grand Union Canal and the River Colne, Denham Country Park comprises 28 ha (70 acres) of damp meadows and wet woodlands, stretching over a 3.2-km (2-mile) strip of land, recently allocated the accolade of Local Nature Reserve status. A mixture of mature tree-lines and new plantations, a small golf course and an area of rough pasture are the main features of this new park, only opened to the public in the early 1990s as part of the extensive Colne Valley Park scheme. The Colne Valley Park Centre has been located on the site, incorporating an information office, café and toilet facilities. Small reedbeds and areas of scrub occupy the region between the two linear waterways. Beyond the canal, to the east, are the four waters which comprise the 73 ha (180 acres) of Denham Quarry Lakes. These established waters suit a wide range of species, and they too have recently been redesignated as a LNR, under the name of 'Frays Valley'. Thus the overall area facilitates wetland, meadowland and woodland birds on a well-thought-out management scheme, likely to be of significant importance to the county's ornithological picture as it becomes better recorded. Mammals present include Weasel, Muntjac Deer and a declining population of Water Voles.

Access

The site is 1 km (0.6 mile) north-east of junction 1 of the M40, and is signposted where it meets with the A40. Taking the A40 northwards, turn right down the lane to Denham Court off the Denham Roundabout, following the signposted directions to the park. A small car park is on the right, but more secure parking is available at the centre itself on the opposite side of the road, costing £2 per day. Denham station on the Marylebone to High Wycombe line is a short walk away from the northern end of the park. The only other way in is by barge! There is a circular walk around the park itself but the more adventurous can occupy several hours by taking the canal towpath and crossing to the Quarry Lakes all the way to Harefield, crossing over the canal to come back via the Park footpath.

Species

Much of the area has established habitat that has held typical woodland and farmland species for some time. At the Colne Valley Park Centre car park, the trees and bushes surrounding the buildings attract Goldfinch, Linnet, Greenfinch, Nuthatch and Treecreeper. The same location is worth checking for Lesser Spotted Woodpecker, as well as this bird's bigger relative. Kestrel and Sparrowhawk haunt this end of the complex too. In summer, Chiffchaff, Willow Warbler and Spotted Flycatcher occupy this section whilst the golf course will have Green Woodpecker at any time, an early morning visit catching Grey Partridge checking their handicap. In winter, huge numbers of Fieldfare and Redwing sprawl all over the fairways and passage Wheatear have to be a possibility. Corvids are much in evidence and large numbers of Woodpigeon move around in the winter months, Stock Dove mixed in with them. A recent addition has been Ring-necked Parakeet extending their area of influence, and Woodcock has been noted on at least one occasion.

The adjacent Misbourne Meadow is cut just once per year for hay to maintain species-richness. Feeding Canada Geese here are worth checking for other species amongst them and there is a possibility of Snipe overwintering. Skylark and Meadow Pipit are numerous, and a wandering Little Egret used the Meadow briefly in December 2000. The tracks between the river and canal are coppiced or thicketed and a quiet, slow stroll through this section may reveal all six tits, more Nuthatch and Treecreeper, Goldcrest, Bullfinch, Song Thrush and numerous Wren. The summer scene is one of Blackcap, Willow Warbler, Chiffchaff and, to the discerning ear, Garden Warbler. The most northerly feature of the complex is known as Flagmore Scrape. Its name is a little misleading as it is essentially an overgrown reeded area, but is nonetheless distinctive compared to its surroundings. Hosting Reed and Sedge Warblers, Whitethroat and Reed Bunting, it is one section where Water Rail is a real prospect.

Flagmore Pasture is a different perspective again, with rough pastureland, beyond which is a line of mostly dead trees. In this region one

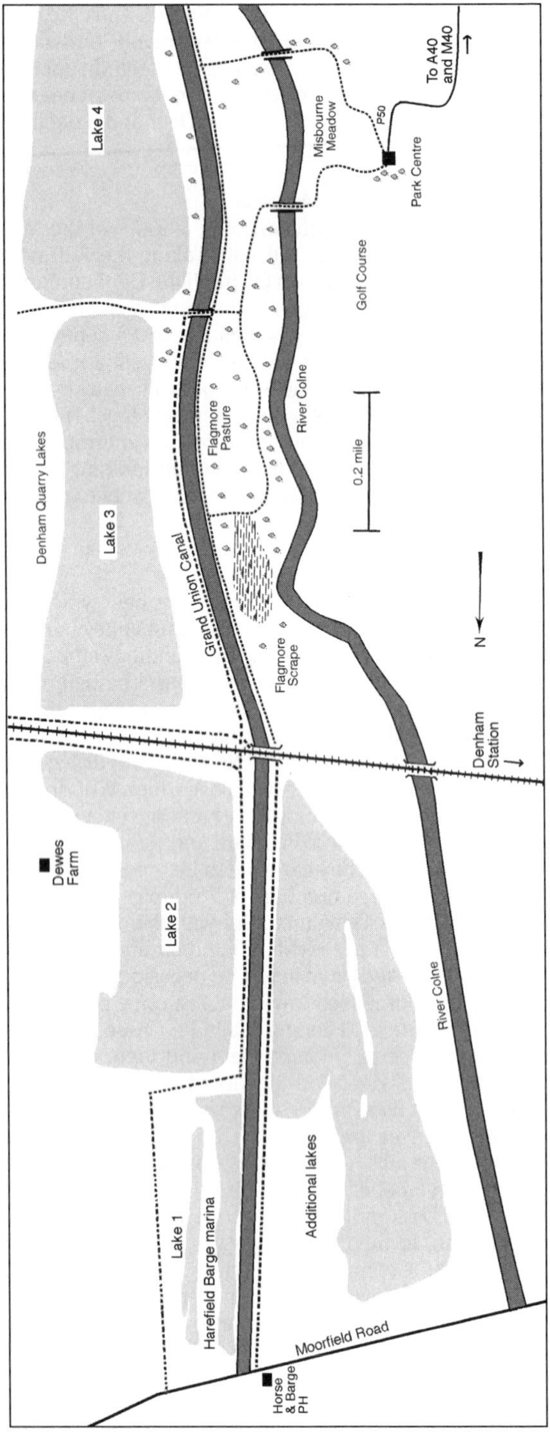
To A40
and M40
P50
Misbourne
Meadow
Park Centre
Lake 4
Golf Course
River Colne
Flagmore
Pasture
0.2 mile
Denham Quarry Lakes
Lake 3
Grand Union Canal
Flagmore
Scrape
N
Denham
Station
Dewes
Farm
Lake 2
River Colne
Additional lakes
Lake 1
Harefield Barge marina
Moorfield Road
Horse
& Barge
PH

can expect Grey Heron, on the ground or in the trees, the prospect of all three woodpeckers and perhaps several Spotted Flycatcher launching themselves repeatedly for their lunch from the same branch. Jay, Linnet, Redpoll and Siskin operate in this locality and, in winter, more Fieldfare and Redwing will be seen here.

The eastern pathway follows the canal, along which Kingfisher cruise, their brilliant blue backs contrasting with the grey/brown waters. Ripples along the canal often denote a Dabchick or two trying to find cover, which proves difficult as much of the canal is metal-lined. The shrubbery on either side is favoured by still more Willow Warbler, Blackcap and Whitethroat and it is worth keeping an ear open for Turtle Dove in appropriate months. Grey Wagtail might also be seen here. Check canal-side Alders for Siskin and Redpoll. Crossing over the bridge which leads to Ickenham brings the intrepid birder to Lakes 3 and 4 of the Denham Quarry Lakes. These are regularly fished and stocks are such that Cormorant and Great Crested Grebe find the site to their satisfaction. All three sawbills are prospects on these waters, especially Goosander, and Pochard, Tufted Duck, Shoveler and occasional Shelduck are possible during winter. Ruddy Duck have been recorded and Goldeneye will pop in occasionally. In summer, Common Tern can be expected and Hobby may be seen pursuing a hirundine supper. Turning north to follow the lakeside path leads to Lakes 1 and 2 with similar expectations, passing the Harefield marina, with it's picturesque scene of some 100 colourful barges.

On encountering the main road, turn left to cross back over the canal and walk south on the opposite bank, scanning the additional mature lakes to the west for more seasonal waterfowl, including Goosander and Goldeneye. Eventually, one re-enters the country park at Flagmore Scrape to return to the centre via a woodland track. An extremely pleasant walk can be had around this new facility, with some good quality birding at almost any time of the year.

Calendar

Resident: Grebes and common ducks on the lakes, Grey Heron, Grey Partridge, Pheasant on pastureland, all the common woodland species, Collared Dove, Kestrel, Sparrowhawk, three woodpeckers, Skylark, Song and Mistle Thrushes, Kingfisher, Reed Bunting, Yellowhammer.

December–February: Fieldfare and Redwing, Siskin more abundant, grazing geese, Goldeneye, Goosander, Ruddy Duck and possibility of Smew.

March–May: A period of change with flocks of Starling and winter thrushes giving way to Sand Martin, Sylvia warblers and mixed finch feeding flocks breaking up to breed. Chance of passage Snipe or Redshank on wet meadows.

June–July: An opportunity to swot up on warbler calls, although thicker vegetation hinders viewing. Spotted Flycatcher, Common Tern, possible Turtle Dove and Hobby.

August–November: Woodlands bursting with immature passerines, late Swallow and House Martin hawking over pastureland before departure, juvenile Grey Heron on Flagmore Pasture, a quieter time on the lakes.

43 EMBERTON COUNTRY PARK

OS ref. SP 885 505

Habitat

This 70 ha (174 acre) site, opened in 1965, is situated alongside the River Great Ouse and consists of several lakes with mature willow trees and swards of close-cropped lawns for picnickers. A conservation area is sandwiched between the two main waters, but consists of little more than an overgrown island, woodland and a few ponds. The farmland north of the river is of interest, as is the Ouse itself, which can be viewed at several points east of Heron Water.

It needs to be said straightaway that Emberton is a fairly typical country park in that it caters for a wide range of activities such as sailing, camping, caravanning, fishing and even climbing, and as such may not be every birders cup of tea (although having said that, there is a welcome tearoom on site!). As such, a car parking charge is levied, although pedestrian access is free. However, as a consequence of creating these facilities, habitats suited to a range of bird species can be found. There are four main waters: Otter and Snipe Pools have no boating, Heron Water and Grebe Lake being reserved for such pastimes.

Access

The park rests between the River Great Ouse and the A509 Olney–Newport Pagnell Road, just 1 km (0.6 mile) south of Olney. The car park entrance is at SP 887 501 and vehicles may use formal parking facilities or the grass aside the peripheral roadway (which does not actually go all the way round!). One thousand vehicles can be accommodated. Drivers are typically charged £2.60 in summer and £1.70 in winter. For more details on opening times and charges (too numerous to list here) contact Emberton Park on 01234 711575.

For free access park in the large lay-by, just north of the main entrance, and follow the bridlepath between Otter Pool and Heron Water towards the river.

Species

Common thrushes, finches, tits, Treecreeper, Goldcrest and other familiar resident species are all present, while Tawny Owl inhabit the large stand of trees in the conservation area. Stock Dove and Jackdaw are typical parkland species found here and both Green and Great Spotted Woodpeckers visit the area. The site appears to have a great attraction for a wide variety of feral geese, probably because they are regularly fed by visitors. Snow, White-fronted and Bar-headed Geese can be expected, along with several hundred Greylag and Canada Geese. A flock of around 60 resident Barnacle Geese is worryingly self-sustaining.

In winter small rafts of Pochard and Tufted Duck can be found amongst the common Mallard and Coot with occasional visits from Goldeneye, Goosander, Shelduck and Teal. Cormorant occur and Great Crested Grebe are resident with a few pairs breeding. Slavonian Grebe has been recorded during this period. Pied Wagtail are plentiful in all seasons and the weir to the north of the site often attracts Grey Wagtail. The willow scrub holds Reed Bunting and Bullfinch all year round and

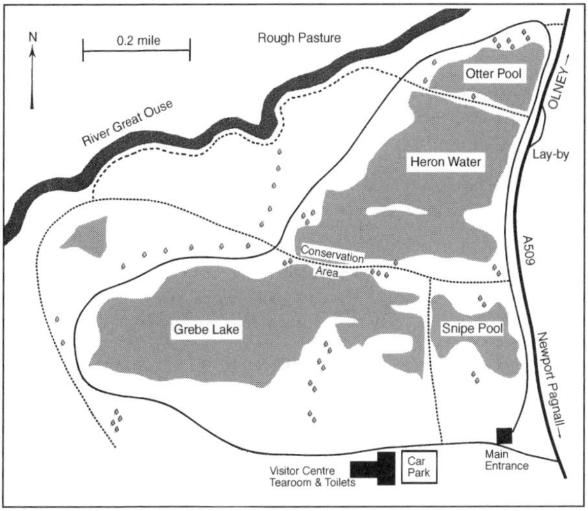

the cover around Otter Pool looks good for roosting birds. Siskin and Redpoll are a possibility in the mature Alders.

During the spring and summer reasonable numbers of Sedge and Reed Warblers, Whitethroat, Willow Warbler and Chiffchaff can be found and Spotted Flycatcher nest in the Ivy-covered trees by the lay-by. The lakes attract Common Tern to fish, Great Crested Grebe to breed and Hobby are noted feeding on hirundines and dragonflies.

The rougher ground beyond the river attracts the odd Yellow Wagtail in summer and the sheep netting should be checked for a passage Whinchat. Meadow Pipit and Skylark nest here and Grey Heron can be seen loafing at the field margins. Little and Barn Owls are resident and several pole nest boxes have been installed to encourage the latter species to breed. The same locale is probably the most likely area to produce an occasional Snipe and Redshank, while the river forms a natural flyway for Kingfisher and Grey Wagtail.

Allowing for the nature of the site, an early morning visit in winter or spring might be advisable, using the lay-by on the A509 for access. Emberton Country Park is underwatched and regular recording is required to upgrade the status of many species.

Calendar

Resident: Great Crested Grebe, Grey Heron, Mute Swan, feral geese, Coot, Moorhen, Tawny, Little and Barn Owls, Jackdaw, Stock Dove, Kingfisher, Green and Great Spotted Woodpeckers, Skylark, Pied and Grey Wagtails, common tits, thrushes, finches, Reed Bunting and Yellowhammer.

December–February: Increased numbers of geese, Pochard, Tufted Duck, prospect of Shelduck, Goldeneye and Goosander, Lapwing, Snipe, chance of Siskin and Redpoll.

March–May: Common Tern, Redshank, Cuckoo, Hobby, Meadow Pipit, passage hirundines and warblers.

June–July: Yellow Wagtail, Reed and Sedge Warblers, with the commoner Sylvia warblers, Spotted Flycatcher.

August–November: Pre-migration gatherings of hirundines, duck and goose numbers increase, winter thrushes, roosting passerines.

44 FOXCOTE & HYDELANE WATERS

OS ref. SP 715 364 and OS ref. SP 725 348

Habitat

Foxcote Reservoir was formed in 1956 by flooding about 24 ha (60 acres) of farmland along a river valley feeding the Great Ouse. Since the early 1960s, the site has been a reserve of BBOWT, subject to an arrangement with Anglian Water. The reserve, now a SSSI, comprises a large lake and a narrow strip of land around the periphery, partly planted with willows and Alder. To the north of the lake is a small private deciduous wood with a public footpath skirting the eastern boundary, while the remaining adjacent farmland is mainly arable. There is some fishing, but this is restricted, and crucially does not occur in winter.

Hydelane Lake is a little smaller than Foxcote Reservoir but is quite different in shape. The water is nowhere very wide, and it is very heavily fished; as a result the variety and numbers of wildfowl at Hydelane are restricted. The site's main interest lies in its habitat variety with mature woodland, wetlands and adjacent farmland bordering the nearby River Great Ouse. On the south-east side of the water is a BBOWT reserve comprising a narrow strip of land between a public footpath and the lake, which was part of the (now defunct) Buckingham canal. It was obtained by the Trust to protect aquatic fauna in the remnant pools of the canal and is bounded by ancient hedgerows and mature willows.

Access

Foxcote Reservoir lies 1.6 km (1 mile) north of the A422 Buckingham to Northampton road on a lane between Maids Moreton and Leckhampstead. There is a recently constructed hide near the south-west corner of the lake, providing good views over much of the water, but its use is restricted to members of BBOWT. For non-members, most of the water can be viewed from the road just east of the dam at SP 715 353, but a telescope is essential. Further views across the water can be gained from the public footpath to Foxcote Wood that runs parallel to the east bank. It's worth bearing in mind that when the sun is out viewing from the east can be poor from late afternoon onwards due to reflected light. There is no formal parking, but there is usually no problem in pulling up on the roadside verge.

Hydelane Lake is accessed south of the A422 opposite the entrance

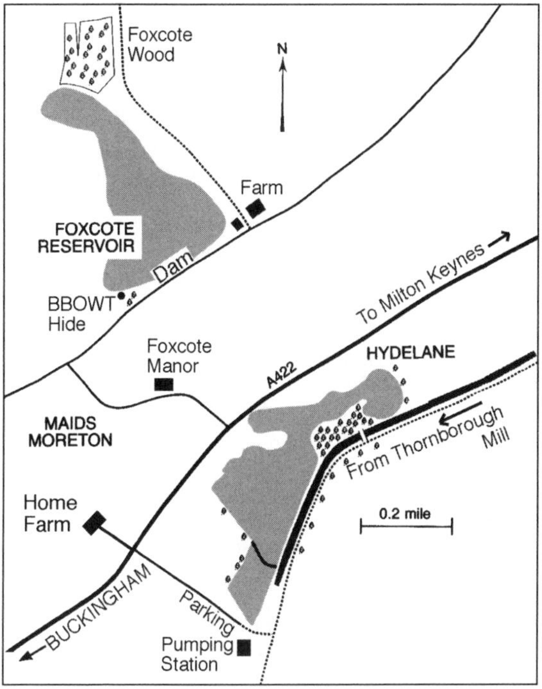

into Home Farm. There is room for one or two cars to park at the end of the rough track by a water pumping station, at the southernmost tip of the lake. Access to the two car parks is restricted to fishermen and the gates are liable to be locked if used. A public footpath borders the south-eastern flank of the water passing through the BBOWT reserve, and beside a tributary of the Ouse. Alternatively, park along the lane leading south off the A422, at Thornborough Mill (SP 738 354), and follow the public footpath past the mill, westwards, along the Ouse to the site.

Species

It is in winter that Foxcote is most prominent. The reservoir is currently the best site for Wigeon in the county, with regular counts of over 400 from October to December. There are usually good numbers of Goldeneye (20 is typical) and often of Goosander, though this species may spend the day feeding on the other local waters, so counts tend to be largest early morning and evening. Except in midsummer, this is one of the more reliable sites for Ruddy Duck, but only in small numbers, and they tend to be rather shy. Winter counts of Coot and Gadwall can be as high as any site in the county, and good numbers of Great Crested Grebe, Mallard, Tufted Duck and Pochard can be expected. Teal are found in lesser numbers, while Shoveler are rather scarce and Pintail irregular. Early winter, and late hard weather movements, may produce rare species such as wild swans, Smew, Slavonian Grebe, Red-breasted Merganser or Scaup. There is a small gull roost at Foxcote that is less prone to produce the rarer gulls, although Sabine's Gull and Great Skua have been recorded together! Black-headed Gull are joined by good numbers of Lesser Black-backs in autumn and later by Common and a few Herring Gulls.

Foxcote retains interest during passage periods, with the focus still on waterbirds. There is virtually no edge habitat for waders, although Common and Green Sandpipers will use the dam wall. Other species do occur, such as Dunlin and Greenshank, but are usually seen flying around looking for somewhere to land. A variety of wildfowl have been recorded on migration, such as Garganey, Common Scoter and Black-necked Grebe, as well as Black Tern and Wheatear.

Foxcote is not a great site for a wide range of species but at any time of year it is worth looking out for Kingfisher and Grey Wagtail. Common Buzzard are increasingly seen over the wood and in summer Hobby is fairly regular, as are Common Tern. Both Sedge and Reed Warblers breed, along with Reed Bunting and common wildfowl. The surrounding farmland holds Little Owl, and Tree Sparrow are sometimes noted amongst the House Sparrow around the farm. The reedbed in front of the hide attracts Water Rail in late autumn and winter.

Nearby Hydelane has nothing like the variety or number of winter wildfowl, but if there is a herd of Mute Swan feeding in the fields it is worth checking to see if any wild swans have joined the throng. The farmland between the two sites sometimes attracts Golden Plover and the general area still retains a few breeding Corn Bunting; try the minor road to Thornborough in the spring. In winter Hydelane may produce Water Rail or Kingfisher, but the woodland holds as much interest, with Redpoll and Siskin often present and an outside chance of Lesser Spotted Woodpecker. Bittern have been recorded more than once but the site is too much disturbed by fishing activity to retain the species for any length of time. Resident species include Great Spotted Woodpecker, Marsh Tit, Treecreeper and Tawny Owl.

In spring and summer the BBOWT reserve along the canal walk is at its best, with Hawthorn and willow in full flush, and a variety of woodland species in song. One could hope to see or hear eight species of warbler with the two Whitethroats more likely at the south-eastern end, Reed and Sedge by the lake, with Chiffchaff, Blackcap, Willow and Garden Warblers in the trees and bushes. Nearby the fields bordering the Ouse adjacent to the Thornborough Road, can hold large flocks of winter thrushes and may have the occasional migrant Yellow Wagtail. The river by the mill can be good for Grey Wagtail and Kingfisher.

Because access is rather awkward, and the emphasis is on woodland species, Hydelane is only worth visiting if one can spend a few hours or more there. Foxcote though might reward the birder with only a short time to spare, and is unlikely to be without interest, particularly between September and May. When moving between the two waters the parkland either side of the gated road at Foxcote Manor is worthy of attention for thrushes in winter and the large House Martin colony in summer.

Calendar

Resident: Great Crested and Little Grebes, Cormorant, Grey Heron, Mute Swan, Canada Goose, Gadwall, Tufted Duck, Coot, Sparrowhawk, Kingfisher, Little and Tawny Owls, Green and Great Spotted Woodpeckers, Pied and Grey Wagtails, Marsh Tit, Treecreeper, Jay, Yellowhammer, Reed Bunting.

December–February: Winter ducks, particularly Wigeon, Goldeneye, Goosander, prospect of rare grebe or duck at Foxcote, and wild swans at Hydelane, Lapwing and Golden Plover, gull roost, Water Rail, winter thrushes, Siskin, Redpoll.

March–May: Gull and wildfowl decline, Shelduck, Ruddy Duck, Common and Black Terns, Hobby, Common Sandpiper, Swift, Cuckoo, Wheatear, hirundines, Yellow Wagtail, warblers, Corn Bunting.

June–July: Breeding Great Crested and Little Grebes, common ducks, Common Tern, Spotted Flycatcher at Hydelane, nesting warblers, tits and finches.

August–November: Pre-migration gatherings of hirundines, Hobby, Common and Green Sandpipers, chance of Common Scoter or Black-necked Grebe, Water Rail, duck numbers increase, gull roost forms, winter thrushes arrive.

45 GRANGELANDS & PULPIT HILL

OS ref. SP 827 049

Habitat

Occupying part of the Chiltern ridge, this 20 ha (50 acre) site comprises ancient chalk downland and Beech woodland. The National Trust wooded area, known as Pulpit Hill, is 248 m (800 ft) high and, in addition to Beech, many Whitebeams are present, representing the natural succession to the rose, Hawthorn and Elder scrub evident on the slopes of Grangelands below. Unfortunately, these slopes had to be ploughed during the Second World War and are only slowly restoring themselves to their previous status. Juniper is another feature of the area, which was created a SSSI in 1972. The surrounding grassland is being encouraged by scrub control and a wide range of plants and butterflies are found. The wood is not particularly dense and includes areas of coniferous trees. A new plantation has been created to the north-west.

Part of the associated area was once a rifle range which has been left gradually to emulate Grangelands, both areas being reserved for BBOWT members. The wood, however, has full public access. To the north of the site lies the well-known Box-wood belonging to the Chequers Estate, much of which is also a BBOWT reserve.

Access

The Pulpit Hill car park is approximately 1 km (0.6 mile) to the east of the A4010 Princes Risborough to Aylesbury road, along the lane from Askett to Great Missenden. The car park accommodates 12 to 15 vehicles. There are several footpaths and tracks through both the woodland and downland sectors, some of these meeting the Ridgeway footpath to the north.

Species

The birds of Grangelands and Pulpit Hill are perhaps typical of those encountered on the pleasing grassy slopes and wooded peaks of the Chiltern escarpment. A winter visit will reveal most activity on the woodland edge and in the areas of scrub. Mistle Thrush ferry between the open feeding areas and the protection of the tree-line, often accompanied by Fieldfare and Redwing. Fair numbers of Chaffinch, with occasional Brambling among them, may be found on the wider pathways, and parties of Yellowhammer work the Hawthorn bushes on the slopes. Green Woodpecker forage on the grassy banks before 'yaffling' their way back to the wood and Kestrel hover over any of the downland areas. The conifer compartments, particularly the one at the base of the hill, host flocks of Siskin and Redpoll, especially where Silver Birch is present, and the Goldcrest amongst the mixed feeding flocks in the main woodland should be examined carefully for a Firecrest or two paying a visit from neighbouring, and more traditional, sites. Another rare visitor during the nineties was a Great Grey Shrike.

The farmland edge to the west is found inviting by Meadow Pipit and the same area may produce Stonechat at this time of year. Huge numbers of corvids on these fields can be quite dramatic and the Rook in particular may be seen collecting acorns from caches prepared when food was more plentiful. Towards a wintertime dusk, many of the more mature trees will find themselves be-decked with hordes of plump Woodpigeon, facing into the setting sun, their bright chests reflecting an orange glow. On the periphery of Pulpit Wood, Marsh Tit can be found busily removing tufts from teasels and taking them to a nearby branch for a vigorous attack upon them to extract edible elements. Within the wood itself Long-tailed and Coal Tits stick together in noisy protective groups in their search for a meagre meal, ever watchful for the resident Tawny Owl.

The advent of spring brings the annual movement of migratory birds and, as with any reasonably high point, the possibility of a variety of

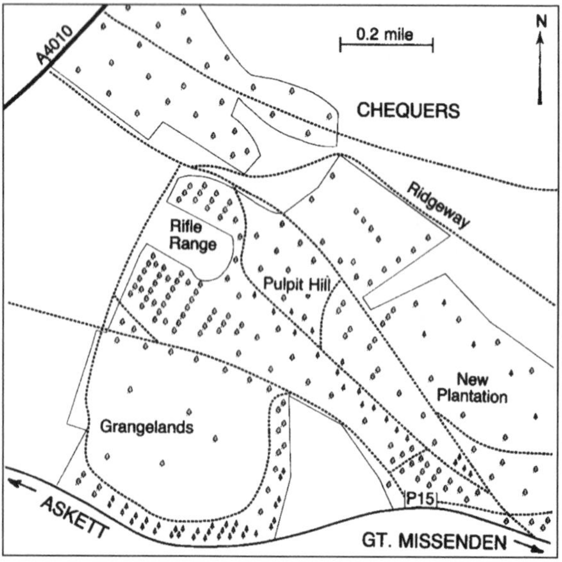

Meadow Pipit

passage birds stopping off briefly. Any 'Blackbird' seen should be checked to ensure it is not a Ring Ouzel, easily recognised when face-on by its white crescent-shaped bib, but more difficult to discern from other angles. Of the larger birds moving around at this time of year, the Short-eared Owl may occur for the fortunate observer, hunting over the chalkland slopes briefly, but far more likely, any sizeable raptor seen will be Common Buzzard or Red Kite, meandering from nearby strongholds. The first sounds of summer are, as may be expected, generated by the Chiffchaff, one or two of which will have overwintered in the area, and by late March, Yellowhammer are singing about their 'little bit of bread and no cheese'. This last species was once accompanied by Corn Bunting issuing their territorial jangling, a sound all too rare in south Bucks. these days. A little later, Whitethroat will be seen (or more probably heard) and it will be difficult to determine passage birds from those intent on staying. The Lesser Whitethroat is a less regular visitor, as is Tree Pipit, but Blackcap and Willow Warbler abound in the scattered bushes of Grangelands and those of the Ridgeway Path at the top of the slope. As the general movement of birds becomes less frantic, the late arrivals such as Spotted Flycatcher and occasional Turtle Dove settle down for their summer residence. Cuckoos, which will have arrived up to a month earlier, will be quite active looking for the nests of unsuspecting Dunnock, particularly to the north of the site from which impressive views of the lowland Vale of Aylesbury can be seen stretching into the distance. Sparrowhawk on the other hand may be seen at any point either soaring above Grangelands or charging through the wood itself.

The early summer flora of Grangelands can be quite a spectacle and a pleasant time can be had sitting on the top of the slope looking at birds from above against a backdrop of yellow Cowslips and Primroses. Equally colourful are the Bullfinch which breed here, although once again, at the height of summer with the foliage most dense, it will be the somewhat mournful single note call that will betray its presence. In the woodland, Nuthatch, Treecreeper and Great Spotted Woodpecker breed, but Pheasant which roam the forest floor sifting through tree-litter are probably disturbed too often to make breeding attempts worthwhile. The same disturbance probably deters Woodcock from using the site often but the bracken-filled and less dense woodland to the north is a likely place for them, at the appropriate time of day. The ubiquitous Blue and Great Tits colonise open and enclosed areas alike whereas Goldfinch and Linnet are more likely to be found on the slopes of Grangelands. Swift and hirundines over these slopes may attract a Hobby, sightings of which have increased in the region in recent years.

Before winter visitors rejoin the resident species there is a brief period during which the crop of juveniles that have survived thus far swell the numbers of birds noticeably. Tawny Owl become a little more prominent, often active during the day and adult passerines which have struggled through the breeding spell can forget marauding Jay, Magpie and squirrels for another season. This part of the year challenges springtime for being the best time to visit Grangelands and Pulpit Hill. The area should be avoided on a dull, wet winter's day but a visit on a crisp, sunny morning during a cold snap provides a good start to the day for a birdwatcher heading for Weston Turville or Tring Reservoirs.

Calendar

Resident: Kestrel, Sparrowhawk, Pheasant, possible Woodcock. Stock and Collared Doves, Tawny Owl, Green and Great Spotted and occasional Lesser Spotted Woodpeckers. Skylark, occasional Pied Wagtail, common corvids, Goldcrest, infrequent Stonechat, the six common tits, Nuthatch and Treecreeper. Possibility of Hawfinch. Goldfinch, Linnet, Redpoll, Reed Bunting and Yellowhammer.

December–February: Large flocks of Woodpigeon, Meadow Pipit more evident, other birds of the field in greater numbers. Redwing and Fieldfare, Siskin, additional Redpoll.

March–May: Occasional Common Buzzard. Cuckoo, Swift, passage Tree Pipit, Sand Martin and Swallow, occasional Yellow Wagtail, Garden Warbler and Blackcap following Willow Warbler and Chiffchaff. Whitethroat regular, Lesser Whitethroat less so. Chance of passage Wood Warbler. Wheatear on passage, chance of Whinchat on the Ridgeway, possible Corn Bunting.

June–July: Spotted Flycatcher well ensconced. Likelihood of Turtle Dove, though not guaranteed. Chance of Hobby, especially in the evening.

August–November: Warblers gradually disappear, though one or two Chiffchaff may stay over. Any Cuckoo sighted likely to be juvenile, parents long since departed.

46 GREAT WOOD

OS ref. SU 775 858

Habitat

Driving from Marlow to Henley, one eventually notices an imposing piece of woodland laid on the sloping countryside to the north of the road, sculptured to create many pockets of different treescapes and open areas. This is part of a huge area of scattered woodlands and meadowlands spreading eastwards and northwards from the nearby bend in Old Father Thames. And this particular sector of it is known as Great Wood.

A huge expanse of mixed deciduous and evergreen woodland, the two halves of Great Wood are separated by Gussetts and Henleyhill

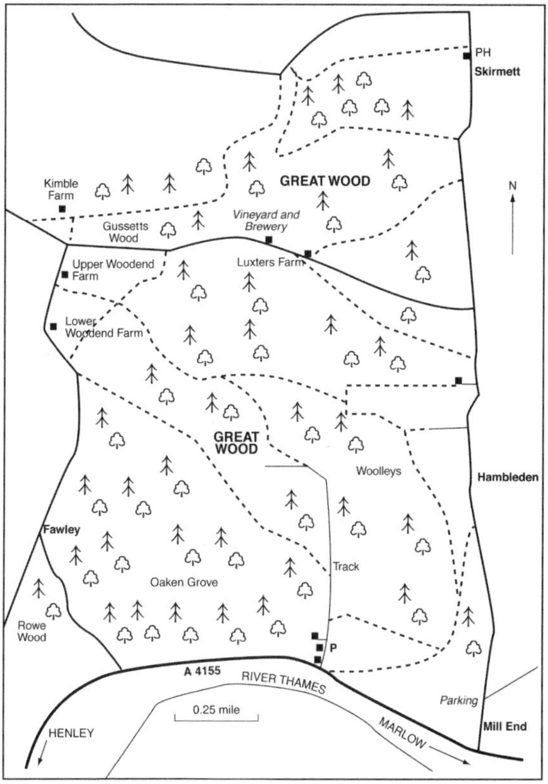

Woods, all having generally a similar habitat of mature and new stands of trees, relatively little understorey, and good areas of open meadow and pasture. The overall area covered not only extends some 5 km laterally, but also over 200 m vertically so good exercise is guaranteed to accompany good birdwatching. There are numerous Pheasant rearing and feeding sites, and clearly marked areas where the public is not allowed for very good safety reasons!

Access

The southern half of Great Wood can be explored by parking halfway along the track going north off the Marlow-to-Henley A4155 at SU 775 858, just west of Mill End. Walk up the track until encountering and taking the bridleway to the left, keeping to the right-leading track as it climbs up the face of the woodland. Beyond the wood at the very top, a small and timely bench can be found from which a relaxing scan of the valley looking back over the route followed this far will afford views across to Swinley Forest and Wishmoor near Camberley, over 25 km away. On a clear day, raptors soaring in valleys viewable from this vantage point will give many minutes entertainment. This track exits the wood at its highest point on the small road from Fawley to Turville Heath. Turning right on this road, the footpath can be recaptured a few metres further on the right, where it turns up towards Lower Woodend Farm. Passing through the gate straight ahead at the end of the track leads to a stile after which a left turn takes the visitor to Upper Woodend Farm. Lingering in this field at the elevation it occupies gives views to the north and west for further raptor hunting. Continue across the field, turning right at the field exit to take the first track on the right back down into Great Wood. This path joins onto the main (private) vehicle track at the bottom of the valley, which leads back to the starting point.

The more northerly part of great Wood is best explored by driving up to Skirmett and taking the footpath on the left into the wood just prior to the public house. As mentioned, to explore the entire complex in one go necessitates a few hours being allocated, but will be rewarding nonetheless.

Species

It might be said that the list of species found in one Chiltern Woodland is much like any other, and there is an element of truth in that. But there is something about finding familiar and favourite birds in a new location that brings out the explorer in all birdwatchers, so time at Great Wood will be all the more enjoyable for the first-time visitor.

The tracks through the various sectors of the woods give an alternating impression of dense tree-lines one moment, then tempting glimpses of open countryside the next. All the commoner species are found in most of the compartments, though the denser coniferous areas are usually restricted to impressive numbers of Coal Tit, accompanied by Goldcrest, belying their presence with their high-pitched 'tsipps' which can be difficult to locate even when close. They are often lower than they sound so a search of the lower-level vegetation may give success. One of the most predominant species here is Robin, if one ignores the numerous Pheasant scurrying along the woodland floor as if having premonitions as to why they have been placed there! Wintertime can be somewhat quiet in the middle of the woods, though the deciduous areas will ensure mixed feeding flocks of tits and finches. Perhaps one of the specialty birds here is the Marsh Tit, regularly encountered throughout the complex. Usually heard before being seen, an opportunity is presented to separate this delightful brown tit from its companions, especially by call. The one or two explosive 'pichoo' calls are likely only to be confused with the more repetitive and higher-pitched 'tsiu tsiu tsiu' calls of Coal Tit, the latter more often singing from a loftier perch than the Marsh Tit. But only experience and patience, watching a mixed flock of tits whilst noting the subtle differences in contact calls, warning notes and phrases of song, will help in picking out the various individuals as they move through the woodland. Then, some way further on, another mixed group is encountered which immediately confounds us because we have forgotten the distinguishing sounds already. But that is all part of the fun. Regrettably, the chance of separating Marsh from Willow Tit is diminishing year on year as the latter relative continues to decline.

Spring is of course an excellent time to visit a Chiltern woodland, with the prospect of passage Wood Warbler and Nightingale, which might just linger a few days prior to moving onwards north and west. Their places will be taken by Chiffchaff and Blackcap, in those areas where shrubbery and lower bushes have not been shaded out by the treescape. The edge of the woods will be worth checking for Willow Warbler and possibly Whitethroat. Numbers of Woodpigeon vary through the seasons from relatively few to potentially thousands, whereas Stock Dove move around in smaller groups, or will be heard individually uttering their deep hoot-like calls to breeding partners. More appropriate hooting sounds will come from the fairly healthy population of Tawny Owl, but Little Owl are less frequently encountered, as one might expect. Woodcock are present but with the accompanying difficulty of seeing this secretive species other than during the roding season. Lesser Spotted Woodpecker seem more likely in the northern parts of the wood.

It is perhaps within the surrounding open pastures and farmland that much of the entertainment will come, in most seasons of the year. Good-sized flocks of winter thrushes scour these open areas and large numbers of corvids gather on any ploughed or grazed surface, in winter usually accompanied by flocks of up to 100 Common Gulls. It is worth checking even distant groups on the ground, as there will often be a Red Kite or two, or a Common Buzzard, down on the ground amongst them. Skylark will be singing above these idyllic scenes whilst the 'chacks' of argumentative Jackdaw and yaffles of restless Green Woodpecker echo across the valley. And always, the sky above is likely to be interspersed with still more Red Kite and Common Buzzard, though between October and March, careful checks will be necessary for the higher soaring birds as this location is a popular play area for Herring and Lesser Black-backed Gulls which like to take to the thermals themselves, often at the same elevations as the raptors. Smaller soaring shapes need to be checked for Kestrel or Sparrowhawk, and whilst by no means an assured sighting, medium-sized silhouettes might be worth checking for Goshawk or Raven, both of these species being reported more frequently in the Chilterns these days.

But without doubt, the star turns at this location will be the Red Kite and Common Buzzard already mentioned, and from the little bench at the top of the first track, or the open field between Lower and Upper Woodend Farms, up to 15 or 20 kites and perhaps 6 to 10 Common Buzzard may be encountered at any one time on a good day. This is a site where so many hours may pass by watching these two fascinating species, little time is left for anything else!

Calendar

Resident: Red Kite, Common Buzzard, Woodcock, Jay, Magpie, Marsh and Coal Tits, Pheasant, Green and Great Spotted Woodpecker, Nuthatch, Treecreeper, Goldcrest, Sparrowhawk, Tawny and Little Owls, Bullfinch.

December–February: Siskin, Redpoll, occasional Yellowhammer, roosting Woodpigeon, Stock Dove and Jackdaw.

March–May: Willow Warbler, Chiffchaff, Blackcap, chance of Redstart or passage warblers and flycatchers.

June–July: Spotted Flycatcher, Swift, Skylark in surrounding fields, occasional Cuckoo and Woodcock more obvious.

August–November: Large numbers of young Pheasant wander through the woods, mixed flocks of tits and Goldcrest, and still more Red Kite and Common Buzzard.

47 HEDGERLEY AREA

OS ref. SU 972 872

Habitat

An interesting and varied day's birdwatching can be had by visiting a number of sites south-west of Gerrards Cross. The recommended locations comprise open farmland used as a significant roost by gulls from a nearby landfill site, a small mixed woodland called Church Wood, managed by the RSPB, a nearby piece of heathland, Stoke Common, close to Stoke Poges, and a small but significant pool with flashes near Fulmer.

Church Wood is a deciduous woodland of about 13 ha (34 acres) comprising mature Oak and Beech with Ash, Alder, Birch and Hazel interspersed widely over the area. It is the only RSPB reserve in the county and local members' groups carry out coppicing and clearing to encourage improved secondary growth. Areas of grasses and bracken are encouraged by streams which flow down the gently sloping ground from the denser parts in the northern sector.

Botanically, some 200 species of plant have been identified and certain of these attract numerous butterflies in summer, including Purple Hairstreak, White Admiral and Common Blue. Foxes make regular use of the wood and Muntjac Deer can be seen regularly in the early morning. A nest box scheme is operated, and the site is surrounded by pastureland and small meadows, the tree-line of the edge of the wood forming a sanctuary for birds of the fields between bouts of feeding.

Stoke Common is an area of 100 ha (250 acres) of traditional common land, with heath and coniferous outcrops. Following an extensive fire some years ago, the site is just beginning to resemble its previous best again.

Fulmer Mere is an artificial lake on farmland, with a good adjacent area of smaller pools, scrapes, and rough, boggy ground alongside a

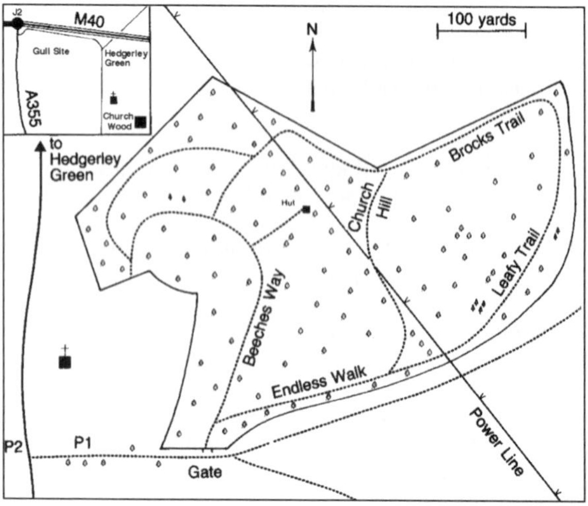

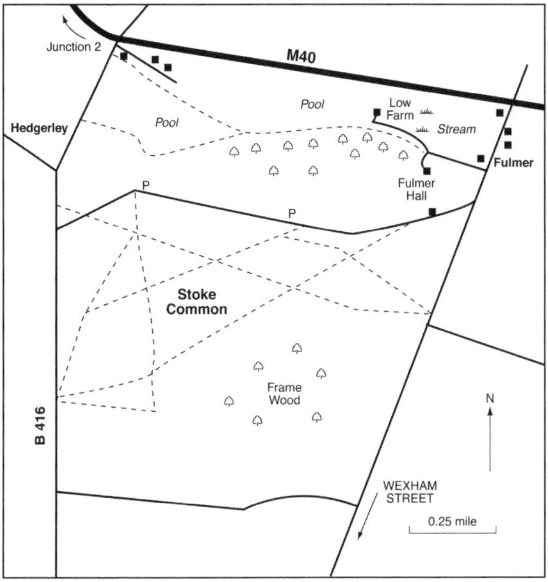

stream. Once considered as a possible BBOWT reserve, a change of ownership caused the site to deteriorate for a while, but it remains good for ducks and waders.

Access

Whilst the landfill site itself at Hyde Farm (SU 960 895) cannot be viewed effectively, fields to the south of the M40 attract varying numbers of gulls to roost on a daily basis, at approximately SU 965 885, accessed along the lane parallel to the motorway, east of junction 2.

Church Wood lies behind the church in Hedgerley (SU 972 872). The nearest main road routes would include junction 2 of the M40, from which the first road on the left along the southerly A355 reaches the village at the second turning on the right. Alternatively, the B416 from Gerrards Cross to Stoke Poges can be used to approach Hedgerley from the south via other local roads. There may be space for one or two vehicles along the lane leading to the wood south of the church but cars left beyond the white-topped post on the left will incur the wrath of the local landowner wishing to gain access to his fields. There is also a stile along the bridleway to the north of the church. The paths essentially follow the perimeter but there are tracks through the centre of the reserve.

Stoke Common is situated to the east of the B416 between Gerrards Cross and Stoke Poges, with parking at one of several obvious pull-offs along the lane (SU 985 857).

Fulmer Mere at Low Farm is best approached by the east-going public footpath from the B416 Slough–Gerrards Cross Road at SU 986 868.

Species

The Hedgerley gull roost has risen to fame in recent years as more gulls have used it and more birders have watched it. Varying numbers of mixed gulls fly over the motorway at different times of day, either for a scheduled roost and preening time, or because of disturbance on the landfill site opposite (often occasioned by a mischievous Sparrowhawk). Amongst the huge numbers of Black-headed, Common and Herring Gulls, there is always the anticipation of something rarer to get one's ID teeth into. Mediterranean Gull are being found but more are probably being overlooked and for those local birdwatchers who have taken the trouble to swot up on the matter, more and more Yellow-legged Gull are being discerned. Caspian Gull too has been found on several occasions and both Glaucous and Iceland Gulls have not infrequently joined the foray. Several hundred Great Black-backed Gull may impose their presence on the scene. Surrounding farmland will host many Lapwing, groups of Meadow Pipit and Skylark, and Stonechat has been noted, but the main attraction will be the gulls, especially when the entire ensemble rises in one spectacular mass of whites, greys and blacks against a winter sky.

The compact nature of Church Wood attracts a surprising variety of birds and can be a delightful place to visit in any season. In winter, with the trees bare and undergrowth less dense, a slow stroll will be rewarded by close views of all the common tits, including Marsh Tit, especially along Leafy Trail and Endless Walk. The dried-off bracken in this area is also where one might be lucky enough to see Woodcock roaming unobtrusively amongst the undergrowth during the daytime if there is no obvious disturbance. The southern sector, being adjacent to farmland, is favoured by both Tawny and Little Owls, and all three species of woodpecker can be anticipated. The middle of the wood often attracts parties of Redpoll, joined by a few Siskin, feeding fervently on the Silver Birch seeds. Usually seen only in silhouette, it is worth trying to position oneself in such a way that an evergreen tree or large bole is immediately behind the feeding group, so as to appreciate the delicate markings of the Redpoll and the varying degrees of pink on the chests of the males. Towards the end of February, Nuthatch become more vociferous and other resident species become territorial.

Early spring is heralded with the songs of Blackcap, Chiffchaff and Willow Warbler, joined later by Spotted Flycatcher and Turtle Dove, the latter possibly seen sharing the power line perch with a Kestrel, totally unconcerned. By summertime many of these species, together with Garden Warbler, are quietly breeding and during this time the more open feeding areas such as Endless Walk and the open ride beneath the pylon route may be the most productive birdwatching location. As autumn approaches, the enlarged population prefers the protection afforded by the denser foliage around Brock's Trail for the main feeding forays, as they build up fat reserves for their imminent migration, shortly leaving the expiring vegetation to the resident birds. This exclusive ownership lasts just a few weeks before overwintering finches return to complete the cycle.

This small area thus provides an ideal opportunity to monitor the seasonality of birdlife in mixed woodland, and a dawn visit during spring can be exhilarating and rewarding.

Stoke Common's gradual reparation ensures a good representative species list for this type of habitat can be expected. Best in spring and summer, when Tree Pipit, Willow Warbler, Chiffchaff, Whitethroat, Reed Bunting and Yellowhammer will be found, Cuckoo, Turtle Dove and Woodcock are all possible. Good prospect of Hobby, Stonechat breeds, and even Dartford Warbler has sampled the site. Winter visitors

Gull Roost

include Brambling, roaming Crossbill, Redpoll, Siskin, and most years, Snipe and Jack Snipe. Resident species include Sparrowhawk, Linnet and Great Spotted Woodpecker with Lesser Spotted Woodpecker making occasional visits.

Having sampled gull roosts, woodland species, and birds of open heathland, it is time for some waterside birds, and whilst not being a Willen Lake or Little Marlow, Fulmer Mere has its moments. The main lake varies in size throughout the seasons, and usually has Mallard, Coot, breeding Tufted Duck and Gadwall, Grey Heron, one or two pairs of Dabchick and numerous Canada Geese at any time, with Wigeon, Ruddy Duck, Shoveler and Shelduck adding occasional variety. Moorhen are plentiful and Water Rail doubtless present, but rarely seen in the dense and rich undergrowth. Teal may approach three figure numbers in midwinter and even a Little Egret has transited the site. Little Owl and Marsh Tit occupy surrounding tree-lines and wader species noted include Little Ringed Plover, Jack Snipe, Snipe (sometimes in impressive numbers), Redshank, Green and Common Sandpipers, Greenshank, and Black-tailed Godwit, but don't expect them all at once!

Calendar

Resident: Overall area: Red Kite, Common Buzzard, Pheasant, corvids. Woods: Green and Great Spotted Woodpeckers, Woodcock, Jay, Magpie, Marsh and Coal Tits, Nuthatch, Treecreeper, Goldcrest, Sparrowhawk, Tawny and Little Owls, Bullfinch. Mere: Canada Goose, Coot, Moorhen, Tufted Duck, Gadwall, Grey Heron, possible Water Rail. Grey Wagtail. Common: Stonechat, Woodcock, possible Lesser Spotted Woodpecker, Reed Bunting.

December–February: Woods: Siskin, Redpoll, Stock Dove and Jackdaw. Fields: partridges, Lapwing, Yellow-legged, Caspian, Iceland, Glaucous and Mediterranean Gulls possible. Common: Jack Snipe, possible Crossbill. Mere: wandering geese, Wigeon, Teal, Pochard and Shoveler. Many Black-headed Gull and Snipe.

March–May: Mere: light wader passage, breeding Little Grebe, Tufted Duck and Gadwall. Sedge and Reed Warblers, possible Lesser Whitethroat. Woods: Garden Warbler, Blackcap, early Spotted Flycatcher. Common: passage Tree Pipit, some stay. Whitethroat, Hobby.

June–July: Fields quiet, woods, mere and common active, especially in June.

August–November: Fields: huge gull and corvid flocks here and on infill site opposite. Common: Jack Snipe, passage Whinchat. Mere: hirundines gathering for departure. Winter thrushes on all sites.

48 HOMEFIELD WOOD

OS ref. SU 815 866

Habitat

From the air, Homefield Wood probably looks like any of the other woodland stands that dot the southernmost undulations of the Chiltern Hills. Part of the Chiltern Forest and comprising 100 ha (250 acres) of mixed Forestry Commission woodland, it is a fairly 'young' wood with the majority of trees less than 50 years old. Many stands are well blessed with a range of primitive evergreens including Scots Pine and Douglas Fir, together with Corsican Pine, European and Japanese Larch. The scene is enhanced by small numbers of Noble Fir, Western Hemlock and Lawson Cypress. There are, however, a good number of broadleaved species, primarily Beech, but also Silver Birch and a few Oak. This is not immediately apparent due to the imaginative way the species are mixed in the various stands. Holywick Wood is the least dense of the three main sectors, whilst Heath Wood rises to 120 m (390 ft) and is the highest sector.

BBOWT manages a small area of chalkland meadow of much botanical interest and butterflies abound in summer, including such species as Marbled White, Dark Green Fritillary and White Admiral. From the point

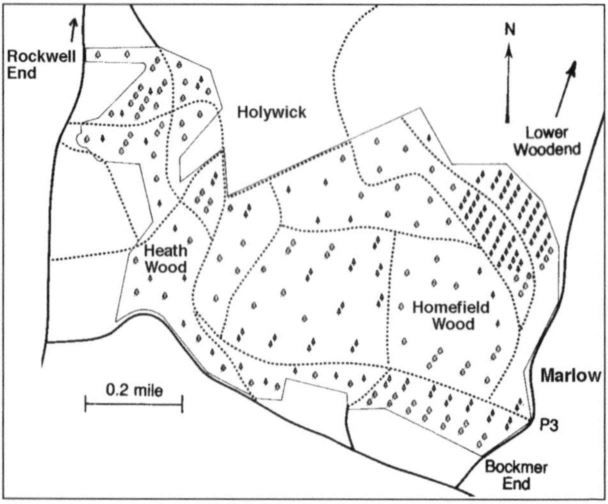

of view of birds, it is perhaps best visited in spring and summer. The rides and firebreaks provide grazing for Muntjac Deer which can be seen or heard barking from the denser parts of the wood. Roe Deer occur occasionally, encouraged by the fact that sporting rights are reserved.

Access

Homefield Wood is 3.2 km (2 miles) west of Marlow and is best approached from the lane between Bockmer End and Lower Woodend, the main entrance facilitating four or five cars, and from where the Chiltern Way passes through the middle of the woods. Other parking and access points exist around the perimeter, particularly near Heath Wood and Holywick. Clear-felling in this latter wood has created areas that might suit such species as Tree Pipit and Stonechat in due course. There are many wide tracks through the woods and a number of more intimate pathways that penetrate most of the woodland. After rain, conditions under foot are quite difficult, but few of the main tracks are on particularly steep slopes. Some of the paths are numbered at various points on the sides of prominent trees.

Species

Although some of the blocks of trees in Homefield Wood are too dense for species such as woodpeckers and Nuthatch, even the more tightly packed areas provide a territory for various tits including the Willow Tit, whose presence is becoming more infrequent. Goldcrest are far more numerous in the confines of the close-knit stands, usually searching for food at the height where the brown lower bracts of conifers meet the greener growth of the upper tree. By August, mixed hunting groups of Coal, Blue and Long-tailed Tits, and the two species mentioned previously, work their way noisily through the woods. Where the trees are more thinly spread, such as in Holywick Wood, these groups are joined by Treecreeper, and these areas do attract woodpeckers. The shorter days of the year are dominated by argumentative Jay and Magpie and the hoarse protestations of Pheasant as they browse amongst the pine needles. Tawny Owl call from these, and surrounding woods and Little Owl can be seen feeding young in trees abutting the fields of Woodend Farm where rattling Mistle Thrush patrol the same area. Parties of Yellowhammer decorate the barren hedgerows which radiate from the northern extremities, whilst Siskin and Redpoll feast on the Silver Birch which are scattered throughout the wood.

In summer, resident species referred to are joined by various much-travelled visitors, temporarily at first as passage warblers move through, but by late spring the flower-edged rides and tracks echo to the songs of Chiffchaff, Willow Warbler and Blackcap, birds which seem not to mind the relative lack of significant understorey. The absence of such secondary growth does however mean that Whitethroat and Garden Warbler are less likely to be seen. Any Robin-like movement seen at this time of the year will be worth verifying as there is always the possibility of Redstart, their chestnut tails quite distinctive even in the darker parts of the wood which they seem to favour.

A warm summer's day will tempt clouds of insects into the pine-scented air to be eagerly consumed by hordes of Swift whilst an occasional Swallow will hawk the wider pathways. Spotted Flycatcher favour the more open areas such as the Beech stand near Homefield Hall to the south and the mixed Beech and Oak at the centre of the main wood. The later part of summer brings the newer sounds of breeding Tawny Owl, Red Kite and Common Buzzard into the area, their young uttering a range of calls, sometimes confused with those of juvenile Green Woodpecker or, in the northern sector, the persistent squeaks of young reared Pheasant. Hobby is seen from time to time and Sparrowhawk breed here too. Bullfinch may be much in evidence at this stage, the lifelong pairs having moved away from the small winter groups to fashion their own breeding territory, especially in the areas north of Heath Wood where Greenfinch also reside. Flocks of Goldfinch haunt the woodland edge and adjacent farmland, with Skylark and Meadow Pipit in good numbers, and, as night approaches, a 'roding' Woodcock may be encountered on its lap of honour. Then, as autumn turns to winter, and the foliage falls, chances of seeing Lesser Spotted Woodpecker increase again.

Homefield Wood is not an especially large area and does not possess the bird density of more open deciduous woodland; however, with a rich flora, numerous butterflies, and resident Dormice, it does have its own character and offers a tranquillity not often found in this busy part of the county.

Calendar

Resident: Jay, Magpie, Willow and Coal Tits, Pheasant, Green, Lesser Spotted and Great Spotted Woodpeckers, Nuthatch, Treecreeper, Goldcrest, Sparrowhawk, Red Kite, Common Buzzard, Tawny and Little Owls, Bullfinch.

December–February: Siskin, Redpoll, Yellowhammer, flocks of Linnet, roosting Woodpigeon and Jackdaw.

March–May: Willow Warbler, Chiffchaff, Blackcap, chance of Redstart.

June–July: Spotted Flycatcher, Swift, Skylark, occasional Hobby, Cuckoo and Woodcock.

August–November: Large numbers of young Pheasant wander through Holywick Wood, mixed flocks of tits and Goldcrest.

49 LITTLE BRITAIN COUNTRY PARK

OS ref. TQ 050 810

Habitat

Little Britain Country Park is situated to the west of Uxbridge and is a part of the Colne Valley linear park. The river meanders through a region of industrial estates, abandoned factories, derelict buildings and scrapyards making for a somewhat unkempt appearance. Surrounded by busy roads, motorways and the sounds of Heathrow Airport, it is not a tranquil place to birdwatch, but does manage to harbour a wide

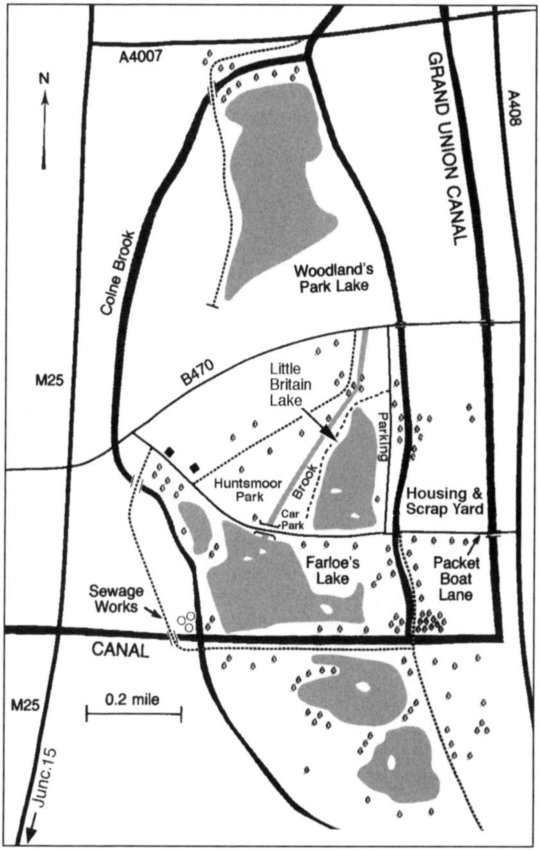

range of resident species amongst the scattering of lakes and wasteland.

There are three main elements to this site. South of the Grand Union Canal are two pits, one of which is fished and surrounded by mature bushes. Adjacent is an abandoned factory estate where most of the buildings have been demolished and the remaining area has been taken over by scrub and mature Buddleia. North of the canal is the large Farloe's Lake, restored for angling and yachting, with the creation of many small tree-covered islands. On one side of the lake is a small thicket, whilst on the other is a sewage works. Further north is the private parkland of Huntsmoor Park and Little Britain Lake itself, a small lake with established vegetation which is popular for walking and fishing.

Still further north is Woodland's Park Lake, which is used for angling and yachting. The River Colne and the Grand Union Canal provide a further habitat with many mature willows and Alder bordering the watercourses.

Access

The site lies to the west of the A408 West Drayton to Uxbridge road. The nearest main road connections are junction 4 of the M4 and junction 1 of the M40. Woodland's Park Lake can be accessed from the A4007 (where a small number of riverside parking spaces exist), prior to crossing the bridge in a westerly direction. A few parking places also exist on the B470 near Huntsmoor Park and there is always room along the lane south of the park. However, the most convenient places are around the edge of Little Britain Lake, which is accessed via Packet Boat Lane from the A408.

From this location one can circumnavigate the lake, at the western side following a narrow footpath between the pond and the Colne River which forms the county boundary at this point. A small footbridge over the river at the end of Packet Boat Lane enables one to cross to Farloe's Lake. Further along this lane a public footpath leads through Huntsmoor Park with its mature Limes, Sweet Chestnuts and Copper Beeches. This path exits on the B470 just north of a small weir and a circular walk can be completed via the canal-side lane which in turn rejoins Packet Boat Lane. South of this lane, a circular route is possible via the pathway south alongside the M25, viewing the STW along the way.

Species

This is not a site for the aspiring rarity-hunter, although Merlin and Ferruginous Duck have been recorded here, but for those who want a local patch throughout the year in somewhat unusual surroundings. In winter, when it is not completely frozen over, it hosts small numbers of Common and Black-headed Gulls, with occasional visits by Herring and Lesser Black-backed. The resident Mallard, Coot, Moorhen and Great Crested Grebe are joined by Little Grebe, particularly on the adjacent Colne, plus Pochard, Tufted Duck, Gadwall, Teal, small numbers of Goldeneye and the occasional Smew and Goosander. Kingfisher and Grey Wagtail can be seen more often at this time of year and both are resident, nesting along the river or canal. Grey Heron are always present and Cormorant are more numerous during the colder months.

The trees around, and in the vicinity of the pond, are inhabited by Nuthatch, Treecreeper, common finches and tits (with the exception of Marsh Tit) and all three woodpeckers; although, as is now the norm, Willow Tit and Lesser Spotted Woodpecker are in decline and difficult to find. Redwing and Fieldfare frequent the open parkland with increasing sightings of Ring-necked Parakeet, while Redpoll and Siskin can be expected in the riverside trees. Water Rail are sometimes encountered on the island at Little Britain Lake, or near the sewage farm where rough grasses attract Meadow Pipit, Skylark and the occasional Stonechat. Black Redstart is a possibility, wintering around the derelict factories or in the scrapyards. Tit flocks should be checked for Goldcrest and wintering Chiffchaff. Thrushes, Starling and finches roost in the available scrub.

Spring passage entices Common Tern to fish whilst moving along the valley and they are usually present until September. Hirundines, Swift and all the common warblers filter through on migration. In summer all three species of wagtails, the Yellow now mainly on passage, can be expected and both Kestrel and Sparrowhawk breed in Huntsmoor Park, where Little Owl is occasionally heard. Farloe's Lake at this time of year has breeding Great Crested Grebe, Sedge and Reed Warblers, while Bullfinch and Reed Bunting can be found just about anywhere. A few Turtle Dove and Cuckoo visit the area on passage and sometimes remain to breed.

Ring-necked Parakeet

Autumn may turn up a passage Black-necked Grebe from nearby Staines Reservoir and Hobby are noted over the lakes, tracking the assembled hirundines. Large finch flocks form on the masses of weed seeds on waste ground including many Goldfinch.

Considering the area as a whole it can be seen that an unexpected range of species can be found amongst the ramshackle and desolate surroundings. Ring-necked Parakeet is the one site specialty and there is always the chance of an unusual winter visitor.

Calendar

Resident: Little and Great Crested Grebes, Grey Heron, Canada Goose, Mallard, Tufted Duck, Sparrowhawk, Kestrel, Moorhen, Coot, Stock Dove, Little Owl, Ring-necked Parakeet, Kingfisher, all three woodpeckers, Grey and Pied Wagtails, Goldcrest, Willow Tit and Long-tailed Tit, Nuthatch, Treecreeper, Bullfinch, Goldfinch, Linnet, Reed Bunting, Yellowhammer.

December–February: Cormorant, Water Rail, Gadwall, Wigeon, Teal, Shoveler, infrequent Shelduck, Pochard, Goldeneye, chance of Smew and Goosander, gulls, Meadow Pipit, occasional Black Redstart and Stonechat, Redwing, Fieldfare, Siskin, Redpoll.

March–May: Common Sandpiper, Common Tern, Swift, hirundines, Yellow Wagtail, Sedge, Reed and Garden Warblers, Blackcap, Whitethroat, Willow Warbler, Chiffchaff.

June–July: Breeding activity, chance of Cuckoo and Turtle Dove.

August–November: Passage terns, Black-necked Grebe, hirundines, Hobby, finch flocks, winter thrushes arrive in November.

50 LITTLE MARLOW GRAVEL PIT

OS ref. SU 876 876

Habitat

This 20 ha (50 acre) Thames-side site has been, and continues to be restored as, a sallow-lined lake, though still being worked for minerals in places. Peripheral vegetation has matured greatly in recent years, proving useful for nesting warblers. A small overgrown island is used for nesting by Grey Heron and waterfowl. An extensive area of exposed sand in shallow water is favoured by gulls and waders, whilst perching birds are accommodated by stands of Beech and poplar on the approach road and an avenue of Oak and Hawthorn which leads to the river. Adjacent waters host a variety of sports leaving the subject site free of disturbance save for anglers. An adjacent STW has undergone significant building and extension work during the nineties and has lost some of its attraction to birds, but there are patches of grasses, willowherb and nettle, adding some variety to the range of bird species which can be expected. A small stream runs parallel to the northern bank and a look over the farmland and woods beyond needs to be included in any visit.

Access

The gravel pits are to the south of the A4155 road between Bourne End and Marlow, the nearest main road being the A404 which joins the M40 at junction 4. Access is via the public footpath that runs along the western edge of the lake; park in Church Road and walk past The Cottage on the right. Adequate views are available from this footpath, which runs between the lake and the sewage works. One may cross the railway line at the end of the path and follow the Thames eastwards to another crossing at Coldmoorholme Lane, passing a useful car park before taking the westerly footpath which rejoins the original route at Church Road. Views from the eastern side of the lake are made difficult by evening sunshine. Alternatively, park in the Coldmoorholme car park, walking north to the north-east corner of the pit and walk anticlockwise around the lake back to the car park.

Species

As one of the birding hot spots in the vicinity, the site can be a good place to visit at any time, the lake being probably more productive for the winter birdwatcher, whilst the surrounding woodland and sewage works are very active in spring and mid-year.

The year starts with good numbers of Starling and Pied Wagtail attracted by the shelter and food source offered by the STW, their morning chorus quickly silenced by Sparrowhawk which frequently traverse the site, causing the Starling to swirl silently in open squadrons or simply cower in adjacent tree-tops. During the day, substantial flocks of Black-headed and Common Gulls use the exposed sand flat on the gravel pit for bathing and loafing, often being disturbed by nothing in particular, towering over the lake before swinging back to land in a grey-and-white procession, usually accompanied by even more skittish Lapwing. These gull flocks have been a source of challenge in recent times as Yellow-legged Gull have been detected amongst the few Herring and Lesser Black-backs present. Mediterranean and Ring-billed Gulls have also been spotted. It takes a lot of cold weather to completely freeze this lake, so the winter scene will always be accompanied by such ducks as Gadwall, Wigeon, Shoveler and Teal, but more numerous will be Pochard and Tufted Duck. Smew and Goldeneye put in irregular appearances. Scaup has become an almost annual occurrence, with Ruddy Duck, Pintail, Goosander and Red-breasted Merganser not infrequently encountered.

The resident flock of Canada Geese has recently had to endure an even bigger gathering of Greylag Geese, up to 100, whilst over 20 Egyptian Geese have also taken up residence of late and feral Bar-headed Geese have bred recently. Less frequent visitors will include Brent Geese whilst the home Mute Swan have entertained Bewick's and wandering Black Swans. Grey Heron successfully breed, with up to 20 nests in a good year. A large Cormorant roost of up to 80 birds exists on the site and Shag is also becoming a more common, if elusive visitor. Not so, however, with the resident Kingfisher which can be surprisingly confiding and easier to see at this time of year. A significant feature of the wintertime here is the nightly roost of several hundred Jackdaw, accompanied by dozens of Magpie and some 150 Stock Dove. Several dozen Long-tailed Tit may also be seen hurrying in the direction of the roost site at dusk. Flocks of Meadow Pipit and small numbers of Siskin and Redpoll feed on the scrub area around the sewage works, which is an area favoured by overwintering Chiffchaff which associate with the tits and Goldfinch.

The gulls, and most of the Starling, disperse with the onset of spring and the small woodlands, previously occupied by mixed feeding parties of tits, resident Nuthatch, Goldcrest and Treecreeper, are soon colonised by Reed Warbler, Blackcap and Chiffchaff and, quite often, Willow Warbler too. The lake will be more empty but passage waders

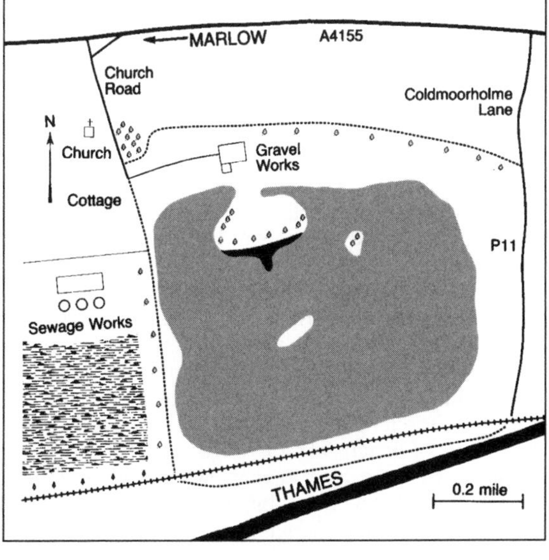

such as Oystercatcher, Redshank, Snipe, Little Stint, Green and Common Sandpipers may be seen along with the more regular Redshank, whilst Garganey has traversed on occasions. The resident Reed Bunting will be seeking out nesting places as early Swallow arrive and, by the time Swift and Spotted Flycatcher have appeared, many species will already be breeding. Local birders have installed nesting rafts which were quickly taken up by Common Tern. With so many waters to choose from in the vicinity, wandering Osprey may only by chance investigate this particular lake but more than one observer has chanced to be there on such an occasion.

The sewage works meanwhile will have released its hordes of gulls and been taken over by passage Yellow Wagtail, Goldfinch and Sedge Warbler, and occasionally Grasshopper Warbler are attracted to the quieter corners of the site. Lesser Whitethroat have nested in the confines of the works. Linnet occupy the southern hedgerow throughout the summer. The summer scene is enhanced by occasional Turtle Dove, hordes of feeding hirundines and hunting Hobby. Lesser Spotted Woodpecker are regularly seen. Less usual visitors have included Water Pipit and Yellow-browed Warbler.

Lesser Spotted Woodpecker

The autumn passage tends to be less obvious than that of spring but it is always worthwhile checking the lake's shallows for Ringed and Little Ringed Plovers and occasional Ruff before the pool becomes the domain of Lapwing and wintering gulls once more. But one spectacle is assured as returning gulls may build up to 1,500 Lesser Black-backs, usually hiding a number of Yellow-legged cousins amongst them. There follows a short period of relative calm before Shoveler lead the winter ducks back and the contact calls of Fieldfare and Redwing can be heard once again amongst the clamouring of mixed finch flocks in perimeter hedges. The lengthening nights are preceded once again by the roosting rituals of dozens of Woodpigeon and Jackdaw, occasionally accompanied by the calls of Tawny Owl and Water Rail.

A visit to Little Marlow must include some time scanning the treescape to the north of the site with Red Kite and Common Buzzard generally a daily occurrence, often with Sparrowhawk and Kestrel in view simultaneously, and not infrequently, Peregrine and Hobby, whilst both Goshawk and Merlin have also been noted. The large market garden crops between these woods and the observer have themselves produced Water Pipit, Redstart and Black Redstart. With notable accounts of late including 27 Whimbrel overflying, visiting Little Egret, Pied Flycatcher, Osprey, Mediterranean Gull and a Roseate Tern (in June 2000), the overall location should guarantee a good day's birding at any season.

Calendar

Resident: Great Crested Grebe, Water Rail, Cormorant (most months), Tufted Duck, Mallard, Coot, Moorhen, Kestrel, Sparrowhawk, Lapwing, Snipe, Grey Heron, Stock Dove, Kingfisher, Great Spotted, Lesser Spotted and Green Woodpeckers, Pied Wagtail, Reed Bunting, Meadow Pipit, Treecreeper, Linnet. Red Kite and Common Buzzard observed over woodland to the north.

December–February: Mute Swan (numbers vary year-to-year), Canada Geese more numerous and alternate with nearby Summerleaze pits, dabbling ducks such as Gadwall, Teal, Wigeon and Shoveler, diving ducks such as Pochard. Scaup rare. Smew and Goldeneye infrequent. Occasional Dunlin. Large gull roost with prospect of rarer species. Redpoll, Siskin and Grey Wagtail.

March–May: Hobby on passage, Wheatear on adjacent meadow, occasional Whinchat. Common Sandpiper and other wader species. Arctic and Common Terns in April, with Sylvia warblers returning. Cuckoo arrives early April. Barn Owl has been noted.

June–July: Large numbers of hirundines, Spotted Flycatcher, occasional Turtle Dove, Common Tern nesting.

August–November: Mixed groups of juvenile wagtails, late broods of Great Crested Grebe, many House Martin leave by early October, some stay on until end of the month. Starling roost, winter thrushes and ducks arrive. Occasional Stonechat.

51 MILTON KEYNES AREA

Birdwatchers living in and around the new city of Milton Keynes are fortunate enough to have one of the region's top wetland sites on offer, at Willen Lake, plus a good supporting cast that includes Great Linford Reserve and Caldecotte Lakes. While it could be argued that most of the wetlands around the city were more productive for waders 20 years ago, when in the early stages of excavation, at least the main three waters now have varying degrees of protection from further development.

Milton Keynes Parks Trust have stewardship of Willen and Caldecotte Lakes, plus a variety of other sites, and while they have a wide brief on

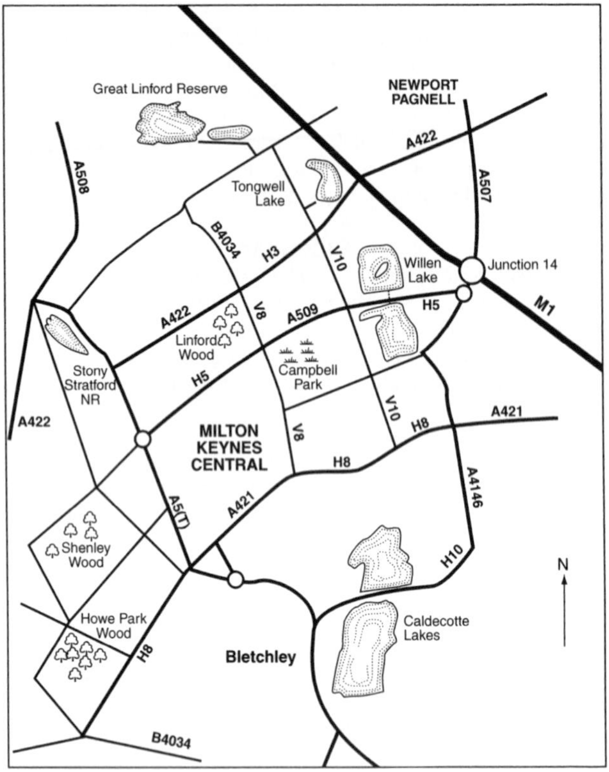

managing sites for the public good, conservation of wildlife features strongly in their mission statement. For further details the Trust can be contacted on 01908 233600, (or e-mail, info@mkparks.co.uk). Great Linford is managed by the Council in partnership with the Hanson group and incorporates an environmental study centre with a variety of wetland habitats solely for wildlife. The North Bucks Birders (see Useful Addresses for details) are an active recording group within the area and well worth contacting for further information, as are the local RSPB group who have produced an informative booklet entitled, Birds Around Milton Keynes.

In this section we will look at the three main birdwatching sites in Milton Keynes followed by several other Additional Sites. If birding the Milton Keynes area regularly, a good tip is to buy an A–Z street map which should help with navigating the myriad grid roads and roundabouts.

CALDECOTTE LAKES

OS ref. SP 893 355

Habitat

The twin waters at Caldecotte were originally built as storm water balancing lakes for flood control on the River Ouzel, which subsequently has been diverted along a new channel. The H10 road, Bletcham Way, bisects the two lakes, on the former causeway, with wide grass verges and trees. Milton Keynes Parks Trust manage the peripheral parkland and have a number of information boards scattered around the lake.

The smaller north basin is quite open with grassy banks and parkland shrubberies on the western side, but is dominated by a pub (Caldecotte Arms) and hotel complex, complete with full-size mock-windmill! The eastern shoreline has several reedbeds, more bushes and abuts a small mature woodland, Walton Park.

The larger, south basin, which is generally more productive, has a small conservation area at the southern tip of the lake with reedbeds and a small hide, while the north-eastern corner has a mixture of shrubs, maturing willows, ponds and islands. The western edges resemble sloping grassed parkland with extensive patches of trees and shrubs, whereas the eastern side is now largely closed in by housing development.

Caldecotte has an excellent past record for bird species (it featured heavily in bird reports of the 1980s), but has declined recently due to building encroachment and water sports on both lakes.

Access

Caldecotte is located in semi-rural south-east Milton Keynes and the lake occupies the area between the A5 trunk road and Brickhill Street (V10). The nearest motorway link is junction 14 of the M1, 4.8 km (3 miles) to the north, bridged by the A5130. From the Northfield roundabout take the A509 (H6) south onto Tongwell Street (V11) which eventually leads on to Bletcham Way (H10). The nearest railway station is at Brickhill, 400 m (0.25 mile) to the south, which is within easy walking distance of the lakes.

There are ample parking facilities at three car parks. For the north basin, if using the Caldecotte Arms public house for refreshments, park by the 'windmill', and for the south basin there are two small car parks signposted off Monellan Grove. Both lakes have tarmaced perimeter footpaths suitable for wheelchair users and bicycles.

Species

The loose stone walling constructed in the nineties has taken its toll on the wader species previously associated with this site. Whereas Green or Common Sandpipers may still visit, the graded mud slopes favoured by other waders have, in the main, disappeared. The sailing activity on the southern lake also deters shorebirds but a few Lapwing and Snipe can be found in the conservation area, mainly during late autumn and winter. Rarer passage waders are now a bonus at Caldecotte Lakes.

What habitat has been lost around the edges has not affected wintering wildfowl as much. Groups of Mute Swan, Greylag Geese, Wigeon, Pochard and Tufted Duck can be seen and Great Crested Grebe and Coot are resident. Pintail are not infrequent winter visitors, along with Scaup and Ruddy Duck, while Common Scoter can occur on passage. A few Goldeneye winter and Goosander are regular most years, sometimes in good numbers. Smew are rare and Red-breasted Merganser are occasionally noted. Red-necked and Slavonian Grebes have both wintered in the past and can stay for long periods, although this is less likely now. Black-necked Grebe are more infrequent passage migrants, normally staying for only a few hours. Divers have previously visited the lake, and a Great Northern Diver in the winter of 1997/98 proved popular with many local birders. The maturing Alders can attract groups of Redpoll and Siskin to feed on the seeds.

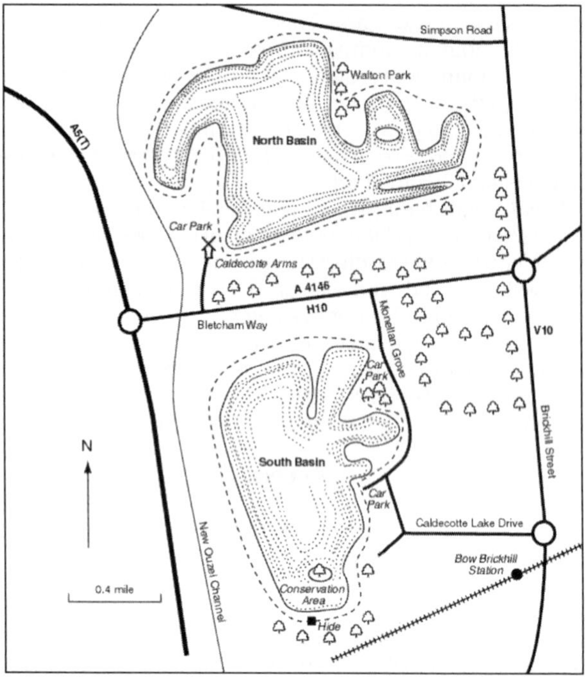

The open grassy banks are as good a place as anywhere locally to find the first spring Wheatear or Yellow Wagtail, along with Skylark, Pied Wagtail and Meadow Pipit, and maybe something rarer such as a Rock Pipit and White or Blue-headed Wagtails. Early hirundines, usually Sand Martin, flit over the lake and are joined by Swift in May and the occasional Hobby. Surrounding scrub attracts the commoner passage warblers along with resident finches and Reed Bunting, while Green and Great Spotted Woodpeckers are more often heard than seen in the maturing trees.

Common Tern are omnipresent from mid-April with the rarer Black, Sandwich and Arctic Terns more likely a month later, if at all. Kittiwake and Little Gull are also occasionally noted but like the rarer terns mostly only stay for a few hours. Early May is probably the best time of year for variety of species and the chance of finding an unusual passage migrant.

Summer is a quiet period and features mainly breeding wildfowl and warblers with Common Tern fishing over the lake or resting on boats. Skylark and Meadow Pipit just about breed annually in the long grasses. In cold wet weather the lake can be swarming with Swift and hirundines feeding low down on insects over the water. Finch flocks develop by late summer, particularly Goldfinch, while Kingfisher and Grey Wagtail become more obvious.

Autumn holds the prospect of the odd Whinchat, Wheatear or Stonechat amongst the returning migrants and the scrub should be checked for warblers and later on Goldcrest. By October winter thrushes can be in evidence and an overhead passage of larks, pipits, finches and buntings is noted. Short-eared Owl have turned up at Caldecotte previously with November onwards the best time of year.

Calendar

Resident: Great Crested Grebe, Cormorant, Grey Heron, Greylag Goose, Tufted Duck, Sparrowhawk, Kestrel, Coot, Stock Dove, Kingfisher, Green and Great Spotted Woodpeckers, Skylark, Meadow Pipit, Grey and Pied Wagtails, Bullfinch, Goldfinch, Reed Bunting.

December–February: Chance of rarer grebes, Little Grebe, Cormorant roost, increase in wildfowl, Greylag flocks, Gadwall, Wigeon, Pochard and Tufted Duck, small numbers of Teal, Goldeneye, Goosander, occasional Pintail, Shoveler, Ruddy Duck, Smew and Red-breasted Merganser. Snipe, Lapwing, gull roost, Skylark, Meadow Pipit, winter thrushes, occasional Siskin and Redpoll.

March–May: Shelduck, wader passage such as Little Ringed Plover, Green and Common Sandpipers, Common Tern, chance of rare terns or Little Gull, Hobby, Cuckoo, Swift, early hirundines, Yellow Wagtail, Sedge Warbler, Whitethroat, Willow Warbler, Chiffchaff and Blackcap.

June–July: A fairly quiet period. Common waterfowl breeding, plus warblers and finches, non-breeding Common Tern.

August–November: Duck numbers increase, chance of Black-necked Grebe, chats possible, finch flocks, gull numbers increase, passerines overhead, winter thrushes arrive, Goldcrest.

GREAT LINFORD RESERVE & HANSON STUDY CENTRE

OS ref. SP 840 430

Habitat

Great Linford Pit is one of a string of old gravel workings along the Ouse Valley, north of Milton Keynes, formerly owned by Amey Roadstone Corporation. When extraction ceased it housed a research facility (jointly funded by ARC and the Game Conservancy) with a particular focus on creating wildlife habitats from disused gravel extraction sites. This project is now finished and since 1996 the site has been leased by its current owners, Hanson Aggregates, to Milton Keynes Council who maintain it as a nature reserve with a modern study centre, used mainly for environmental education. However, it remains one of the most important wildlife sites in the county. As well as the birds (with over 200 species recorded), there is a colony of Bee Orchids, while 19 species of dragonflies and 25 species of butterflies are regularly noted. Fox and Mink are often seen and it is hoped that Otters will once again recolonise this section of the Ouse, as numbers increase across the region.

The main lake within the 40 ha (100 acre) reserve is divided by a mud and gravel bund suitable for wildfowl and waders and, in summer, breeding birds. The reserve includes many smaller pools and 'finger' lakes with wooded surrounds of native trees, predominantly willow, some of which are fairly mature. It is hoped to reinstate a programme of rotational coppicing to increase the variety of woodland habitat.

The reserve is close to the River Ouse where grazing land forms a buffer zone down to the river. There are a number of other lakes in the vicinity but all are used for fishing and/or boating and are, as a result, less productive for birds.

Access

Great Linford reserve is reached from the A422 road between Newport Pagnell and New Bradwell, access to the site being just east of the Proud Perch public house. Turn north from this road (currently signposted to 'Hanson Study Centre') and then, after a few metres turn left to the Hanson Centre, not straight on to the Marle Inn. Along the access road Blackhorse Lake can be seen on the right but is not part of the reserve, being used for fishing, and a large sheep-grazed field to the left is of interest. After 400 m or so one reaches the reserve proper, which has a 30-space car park and can accommodate coaches. The main reserve building is well equipped with a substantial room suitable for lectures and meetings, or for school parties to work in, and with toilet facilities (often closed). From trunk roads one can access the area either from the A5 to the west, by travelling east from Stoney Stratford, on the H3 Monks Way and then north on the V7 Saxon Street, or from junction 14 of the M1 to the east, heading west on the H5 Portway then north on the V10 Brickhill Street.

Access to the reserve is by annual permit only, obtained from the reserve centre on 01908 604810, and a key is required to access the hides. The two main hides (Near and Far Hides!) enable viewing across the lake and bund from different angles, while a smaller woodland hide overlooks a feeding station and pool. The footpath to the hides is well screened throughout. Day permits are not available, but parties (including schools) can visit by prior arrangement and the centre can be booked for appropriate evening meetings. For those without permits, take the small metalled road beside the Grand Union Canal, opposite the Proud Perch pub and follow the waymarked footpath through a gate and across a field, towards a derelict church, from where most of the reserve lake can be partially viewed. This road is only open to cars accessing the canal houseboats. Parking is available across the road in a car park opposite a cemetery.

Species

One of the main features of Linford reserve is the variety of species that can be expected in a small area. This is due to the expertise employed in habitat development since its creation in the 1970s. At any time of year woodland species such as Green and Great Spotted Woodpeckers can be encountered, although Lesser Spotted Woodpecker, while present, is much scarcer. Resident Long-tailed Tit, Bullfinch, Goldcrest and Treecreeper can be found alongside the expected Little and Great Crested Grebes and Grey Heron. Kingfisher are regular on the reserve (but the Ouse itself is more reliable) while the surrounding farmland holds Little and Tawny Owls. Barn Owl have recently bred in the purpose-built nest boxes on site.

The large flock of feral Greylag and Canada Geese resident in the area is regularly joined by other more obvious exotics such as Bar-headed, Pink-foot and Snow Goose and up to 40 Barnacles from nearby Emberton. Winter sightings of White-fronted or Brent Geese may turn out to be genuine wild birds.

The winter scene is dominated by waterfowl with good numbers of Wigeon joined by an increase in Pochard, Gadwall, Tufted Duck, Mallard and Teal with a few Shoveler and Goldeneye. Goosander appear regularly, and Pintail sporadically, while Ruddy Duck and Shelduck may be seen at any time but most often during the spring. Smew

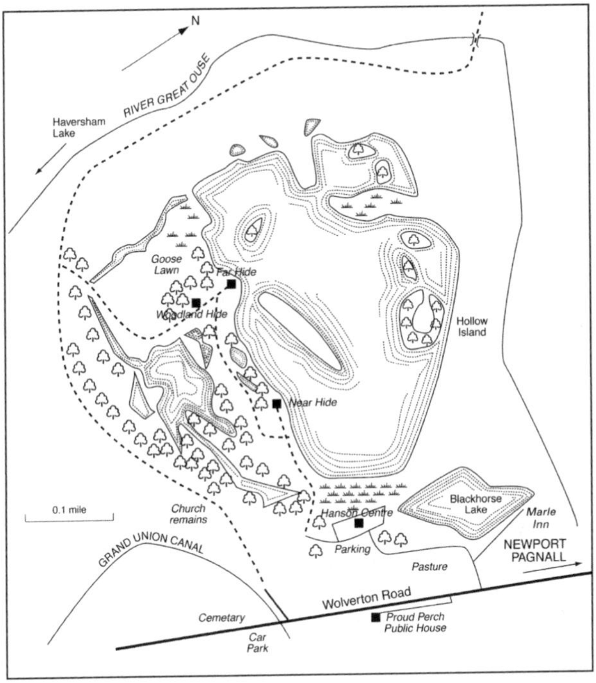

occur erratically but when they do arrive tend to stay for the season.

On winter visits the passerines should not be ignored. Small parties of Goldfinch, Siskin and Redpoll are regular, as is Grey Wagtail, and tit flocks may well be accompanied by a wintering Chiffchaff. From the reserve centre car park watch for Stonechat in the reedbeds and rough grass around Blackhorse Lake. At this time of year one can expect to see five species of thrush, and to hear Water Rail. Snipe and Lapwing might be joined by Golden Plover or Green Sandpiper and a roost of Long-eared Owl is sometimes discovered in the willows. Bittern has occurred while Scaup, Slavonian Grebe and Bewick's Swan put in an appearance most years. Of the more unusual species, both Firecrest and Cetti's Warbler have wintered on the reserve.

One of the birding highlights at Linford is the concentration of Hobby each spring. A May evening can often bring counts of double figures, with birds flying close to the hide as they hawk for flying insects over the water. The reserve is a delight in spring, as waves of newly arrived warblers compete for territories in full song, many staying on to breed. Passage visitors include regular Wheatear, irregular Whinchat and occasional Redstart, with Ring Ouzel and Black Redstart unusual but possible.

One or two smart male Garganey can be expected each spring, when Black Tern is regular, and other tern species such as Arctic, Sandwich and Little Terns may appear, although are more likely at Willen Lake. Little Gull has also been recorded. Osprey is being noted increasingly often on passage but an immature bird was a regular visitor for a couple of weeks during the summer of 2000. Wader passage covers a similar range of species as described for Willen, with Common and

Green Sandpipers, Dunlin, Turnstone and Greenshank the most regular visitors. Evenings are the best time for scarce waders such as Curlew, Whimbrel or a godwit, which never stay long, and Temminck's Stint has appeared several times during the spring.

The only reliable breeding ducks are Mallard and Tufted Duck, with Gadwall and Ruddy Duck occasionally nesting, but many other species are often found summering on site. There is a small heronry and Common Tern sometimes nest on the raft. Also present are breeding Redshank, Lapwing and Ringed Plover, though productivity is poor, while the odd pair of displaying Little Ringed Plover are quickly driven off by their larger relations. Oystercatcher attempted to breed in 1999 and have now suddenly become a regular part of the summer scene. Seven species of warbler regularly breed on the reserve, though they are more easily located in spring, and Turtle Dove can be heard 'purring' in the woodland depths. Cuckoo, Lesser Whitethroat, Yellow Wagtail and Spotted Flycatcher may also breed, but are more reliably seen on passage.

Just about anything can turn up during the protracted autumn passage period as wildfowl numbers increase and waders move through. Scan the eclipse ducks for Garganey. Sandpipers, Greenshank and Snipe are more numerous and there is another good chance of an Osprey. Water Rail typically return in September when the tern passage finishes. Linford is a good location for Whinchat, Stonechat and Wheatear, often noted together on the rough field near Blackhorse Lake.

It can be difficult to visit all the wetland sites in Milton Keynes in a single day, but if a choice has to be made then Linford may well come out on top. In summer a good variety of breeding birds, lack of crowds and the variety of wildlife interest make this a more attractive place than Willen, which for the rest of the year might just win if you are looking for something unusual. Linford has managed several genuine rarities itself, though: Great White Egret in 1994, River Warbler in 1997 and Caspian Tern in 2001.

Calendar

Resident: Little and Great Crested Grebes, Cormorant, Grey Heron, Canada and Greylag Geese, Mute Swan, Mallard, Gadwall, Tufted Duck, Sparrowhawk, Kestrel, Moorhen, Coot, Lapwing, Stock Dove, Little and Tawny Owls, Kingfisher, Green and Great Spotted Woodpeckers, Pied Wagtail, Goldcrest, tits, Treecreeper, Bullfinch and Reed Bunting.

December–February: Occasional Bittern, chance of Bewick's Swan, White-fronted and Pink-footed Geese, Slavonian Grebe, Smew and Goosander. Teal, Wigeon, Shoveler, Pochard, Goldeneye, chance of Pintail and Ruddy Duck, Golden Plover and Long-eared Owl irregular, Water Rail, Snipe, Meadow Pipit, Grey Wagtail, Stonechat, Chiffchaff, Siskin and Redpoll.

March–May: Shelduck, occasional Garganey, Osprey and Common Buzzard, Hobby, passage waders include Little Ringed and Ringed Plovers, Redshank, Greenshank, Common and Green Sandpipers, Dunlin and Curlew. Less frequently Turnstone, Sanderling and Ruff, Whimbrel, Curlew and godwit, Common and Black Terns, chance of Little or Sandwich Terns, Turtle Dove, Cuckoo, Swift, hirundines, Lesser Whitethroat,

Golden Plover

common warblers, Wheatear, Spotted Flycatcher, chance of Redstart, Whinchat or Ring Ouzel.

June–July: Many species breeding including Hobby, return wader passage commences, Common Tern, Ringed Plover, Redshank, Oystercatcher, Turtle Dove, Cuckoo, warblers and buntings.

August–November: Wildfowl numbers increase, passage waders, including chance of Little Stint and Curlew Sandpiper, chance of Little Egret, Osprey and other rarities, hirundines present until late October, passage of Goldcrest, wagtails, chats, thrushes and finches.

WILLEN LAKE

OS ref. SP 878 404

Habitat

One of the first lakes to be created out of the birth of the new Milton Keynes, this site is now over 25 years old. The lake is divided into two basins, by the H5 grid road, and is heavily used for general recreation, particularly during the summer when most activity is around the south basin. Water sports are confined to the south basin causing some disturbance, and generally holds fewer birds than the north, but should not be ignored by the birder. Both basins have peripheral parkland shrubberies, bushes and trees, complete with large areas of grass, some uncut, particularly in front of the Pagoda. The lake margins also have a few small reedbeds and the Ouzel forms a river boundary on the eastern flank.

The north basin has a large island, mostly overgrown with scrub and trees, plus an area of mud and gravel in the south-east corner. On the opposite bank is a hide, with a secondary scrape in front. Neither of these areas is very large and the attraction for passage waders is limited. However, on the shallow western side of north basin the water level is sufficiently low enough on occasions (mostly during late summer) for an extensive area of wader-friendly habitat.

In recent years, water quality at Willen has deteriorated with adverse effects on aquatic plant ecology resulting in a reduction of winter duck numbers. Since 1999, bales of barley straw have been moored in the north basin to reduce pollutants, and improvements have already been seen, with less algae and an increase in duck numbers. The site is managed by Milton Keynes Parks Trust who have a number of interpretive boards scattered around the perimeter footpath.

Access

Willen Lake is immediately adjacent to junction 14 of the M1 and is approached initially on the A509 (H5) to Milton Keynes. Turn north along V10 (Brickhill Street), at the Pagoda roundabout, and then right into the car park. A second car park can be accessed further down Brickhill Street, turning east along the H4 Danstead Way and right down Hooper Gate, while a third car park off the Pineham roundabout is ideal for a quick 'scope-view across the basin from the east. The north basin has an open hide, overlooking the scrape and island, which is wheelchair-friendly. The best view of the wader scrape is from the area in the vicinity of the weir between the two bodies of water.

The main water sports car park serving the south basin is signposted off the Lakeside roundabout on Brickhill Street (opposite the entrance to Gullivers Land theme park), where space for 30 or so cars will be found, plus picnic facilities, toilets and a tearoom open at weekends from Easter to October. A tarmac footpath circles both lakes enabling good access for the disabled. Willen Lake is within easy walking distance of Milton Keynes Coach Station, by junction 14 of the M1, and local buses stop near the Pagoda roundabout on H5. The city's red cycle paths also pass through the site.

Species

Willen Lake provides enough habitat variety and undisturbed areas to ensure that there is always something of interest throughout the birding year. In winter, wildfowl are the main focus of attention, some of which remain to breed in summer, when they are joined by a large and noisy colony of Common Tern. Spring and autumn offer the opportunity to find passage migrants, particularly waders, not usually seen in the area and as a result the site boasts a species list of over 200. Despite some reduction in species due to nearby housing development, the site continues to attract a wide range of birds and retains an ability to produce the unexpected, typified by the extraordinary record of a Great Shearwater in December 1999.

In periods of severe cold Willen freezes over rather rapidly. However, a winter visit should produce good numbers of Great Crested Grebe, Coot, Wigeon, Teal, Gadwall and Shoveler, variable numbers of Cormorant, Goldeneye and Goosander, and large numbers of Canada and Greylag Geese. Pintail, Ruddy Duck and Shelduck are possible and Water Rail are usually noted (mainly heard) near the hide. Lapwing and Snipe are omnipresent and may be joined by groups of Golden Plover, or a solitary Green Sandpiper, but there is little remaining habitat suitable for Jack Snipe, which formerly was a regular visitor. Kingfisher and Grey Wagtail are resident but easier to see during the winter and the occasional Stonechat can be found.

In winter, hard weather movements are more likely to produce something unusual. Smew is likely, with a chance of Red-necked and

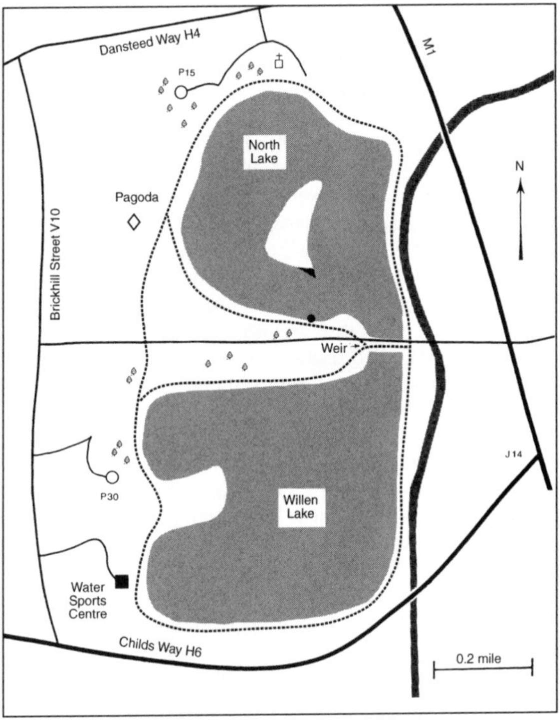

Slavonian Grebes and Red-breasted Merganser. If a freeze-up is underway do not ignore the deeper south basin, which retains open water for longer; and ices from the sides, thereby excluding boats from the lake. A party of Velvet Scoter in a gap in the ice in January 1982 provides an example of what can occur if you are lucky.

A large winter gull roost may initially gather on the north lake but the main roost is on the south basin, where it often has to compete with yachts and windsurfers. The roost sometimes contains a Mediterranean Gull (locating it is another matter) and, the much rarer, Iceland and Glaucous Gulls have both occurred. Although Kittiwake and Little Gull have been discovered in the winter roost, both species are more likely seen during passage periods, particularly in the spring.

This is one of the top sites in the region for numbers and variety of terns on spring passage. Black and Arctic Terns may appear in large numbers, while Little and Sandwich, although rarer, are still annual; even Roseate, Whiskered and Caspian Terns have occurred in spring. Passage terns often prefer the south basin to the north, and on a sunny day in May (preferably with an easterly airflow) don't be deterred by the hordes of ice-cream eating kids feeding the feral wildfowl, from checking through the Common Tern and windsurfers for a priceless rarity! Little Gull also favour similar April weather conditions to the terns, normally in ones or twos but sometimes in good-size flocks of ten or more. Most springs witness brief visits by migrant Common Scoter, and Black-necked Grebe is also annual, though more often seen in autumn, while Garganey also usually stay for extended periods on return passage.

Wader passage at Willen is unpredictable but at times can be excellent when water levels are low enough to expose mud and shingle on the west side of the north basin. Even in poor years Redshank and Ringed Plover are summer residents; Little Ringed Plover is more erratic. Common Sandpiper are common on migration, when Greenshank and Ruff are no surprise, and both Green Sandpiper and Dunlin can occur at any season. Black-tailed Godwit are annual and most coastal species turn up more-or-less every year, most often in spring, with Oystercatcher, Sanderling and Turnstone the more common. Late spring is the best time to seek out the easily overlooked Temminck's Stint. The site boasts some surprising wader counts, such as 18 Whimbrel, 11 Knot and 13 Little Stint. When water levels are low Spotted Redshank and Wood Sandpiper are likely in either passage season, but Little Stint and Curlew Sandpiper favour the autumn, usually in September. Many of the site's more unusual wader records coincide with periods of low water levels, and include Red-necked Phalarope, Pectoral Sandpiper, and a pair of Black-winged Stilt that stayed for a couple of weeks in 1988, and showed signs of breeding activity.

Wheatear is a typical spring passage passerine seen on the field by the Pagoda together with Meadow Pipit, Pied and, possibly, White Wagtails. Yellow Wagtail, while still a feature of spring migration, appear in much reduced numbers than in former years. Hirundines and Swift move over the water in large numbers and Reed Bunting can be expected at any season. Most years Nightingale, Whinchat, Redstart and Ring Ouzel briefly occur. Hobby are most noticeable from May until September, and Osprey regularly visit the site to and from their northern breeding grounds. Trans-Saharan migrants such as Turtle Dove and Cuckoo are today in short supply but all the common warblers pass through the site with, typically, Whitethroat, Sedge, Reed and Willow Warblers staying to nest.

Summer is a time of breeding warblers, finches, ducks and Common Tern with the return wader passage commencing from June onwards, with the arrival of Green Sandpiper and flocks of Lapwing. By late summer, moulting wildfowl begin to flock together and the gull roost steadily assembles; recent studies have discovered Yellow-legged Gull. Pipits should be carefully checked for any vagrant Rock or Water Pipits on the rocky edges and tit flocks searched for Firecrest. The bushes around the lake attract winter thrushes and tit flocks and most autumns a rarity of some description is recorded. By December Siskin and Redpoll can be found feeding on the lakeside Alders.

In summary Willen Lake is one of the top birding sites in the region, particularly when the water level is low and most attractive to waders. The spring passage of terns can be sensational and there is always something of interest among the wildfowl during the winter months. The trick is to read the weather patterns and visit accordingly.

To list the birds recorded here over the years would give an entirely misleading impression of a site teeming with rarities – but they do indicate why the site is hard to ignore, as testified by the likes of Fulmar, Leach's Petrel, Night Heron, Grey Phalarope, Spotted Crake, Franklin's, Ring-billed and Sabine's Gulls, Little Auk, Lapland and Snow Buntings.

Calendar

Resident: Little and Great Crested Grebes, Cormorant, Grey Heron, Greylag and Barnacle Geese, Gadwall, Mallard, Shoveler, Tufted Duck, possible rare grebe or duck, Sparrowhawk, Kestrel, Lapwing, Stock Dove, Green and Great Spotted Woodpeckers, Kingfisher, Skylark, Meadow Pipit, Pied and Grey Wagtails, common tits and finches, Reed Bunting.

December–February: Winter wildfowl including Wigeon, Pochard, Goldeneye, Goosander, chance of Ruddy Duck, Teal, Shelduck, Smew and Pintail, Snipe, Lapwing, Golden Plover, Green Sandpiper, gull roost, Water Rail, winter thrushes, Siskin, Redpoll.

March–May: Potentially the most exciting period, rare ducks such as Garganey and Common Scoter, waders such as Redshank, Greenshank, Little Ringed and Ringed Plovers, Common Sandpiper, Dunlin, chance of Wood Sandpiper, Oystercatcher or Temminck's Stint, tern passage, Cuckoo, wagtails, pipits, hirundines, Wheatear, chats, common warblers.

June–July: Breeding waterfowl, passage Lapwing, breeding Redshank, Ringed Plover and Common Tern, Hobby, Swift and hirundines plentiful, Reed, Sedge and Willow Warblers.

August–November: Black-necked Grebe, late autumn pelagics such as Shag or Grey Phalarope, ducks increase with chance of rarity such as Pintail, Long-tailed Duck, or Red-breasted Merganser, terns and Little Gull, wader passage with chance of godwits, Little Stint, Ruff, Whimbrel, Green Sandpiper numerous, gull roost may include Yellow-legged or Mediterranean Gulls, chance of Rock or Water Pipits, overhead passage of Skylark, finches, winter thrushes, Goldcrest.

MILTON KEYNES ADDITIONAL SITES

Campbell Park (OS ref. SP 865 395)

A typical town park situated close to the city centre with large areas of cut grass and shrubbery. Accessible off the V8 Marlborough Street. An early morning visit is essential as it is well used by the public.

Has a good track record for Wheatear and early warblers in the spring. Local rarities such as Nightingale, Redstart, Ring Ouzel, Firecrest and Grasshopper Warbler have all been found on passage.

Howe Park Wood (OS ref. SP 830 343) Linford Wood (OS ref. SP 847 407) & Shenley Wood (OS ref. SP 823 358)

All three of these small deciduous woods are managed by the Parks Trust and are fully accessible to wheelchair users with car parks at each. Howe Park Wood is in the south-east of the city and has a car park off the H7 in Chaffron Way, while nearby Shenley Wood can be accessed off the V2 Tattenhoe Street, opposite HM Prison. Linford Wood is completely surrounded by development just north of the city centre and has two car parks off the V7 Saxon Street.

The usual range of common woodland species exists across the sites, including Tawny Owl, Green and Great Spotted Woodpeckers, Nuthatch, Treecreeper, Jay, Goldcrest and Marsh Tit. Lesser Spotted Woodpecker and Willow Tit have been recorded but are now difficult to detect and may be extinct. Spring brings the common warblers, an occasional Spotted Flycatcher, and Nightingale have been heard in all three woods.

Stony Stratford (OS ref. SP 786 413)

This nature reserve is managed by BBOWT in conjunction with Milton Keynes Parks Trust. The reserve lies between the A5 and Queen Eleanor Street just north of Stony Stratford. There is good public access from a car park off Queen Eleanor Street towards a public hide which overlooks the meadow, a marsh and reedbed. BBOWT have two more hides, accessible to members only, on the southern side of the reserve, which overlook an overgrown wader scrape. Also included are several small lakes and ponds, a wet meadow and peripheral woodland.

A few passage waders occur and both Redshank and Ringed Plover breed. Lapwing, Snipe, Common Sandpiper and Greenshank are typical migrants in small numbers and Common Tern are regular. Reed and Sedge Warblers breed in the reedbeds, while Chiffchaff and Blackcap are typical of the woodland areas. Check out the Alders for Siskin and Redpoll in the winter and Grey Wagtail and Kingfisher along the river at any time.

Tongwell Lake (OS ref. SP 868 423)

A small sailing lake in the north of the city situated between the M1 motorway and a business park. Take the V10 Brickhill Street north, turning right down Yeomans Drive to the small car park by the lake.

Has small numbers of wintering wildfowl but is mainly noted for its Corn Bunting roost in one of several reedbeds. Water Rail are regular and Bittern have been recorded. In the summer Reed and Sedge Warblers nest along with Reed Bunting. Kingfisher, Grey Wagtail, Siskin and Redpoll also occur from time to time.

52 SHABBINGTON & WATERPERRY WOODS

OS ref. SP 620 110

Habitat

Forming a remote outbreak of woodland in a heavily-farmed area, these two woods form part of the Bernwood Forest Nature Reserve and are managed by Forest Enterprise. Shabbington Wood is the larger of the two at 287 ha (717 acres) and also more meandering in character. The majority of stands are between 25 and 50 years of age and the most numerous species is Norway Spruce, covering some 40 ha (100 acres). Shabbington actually comprises several woods, Oakley Wood being perhaps inappropriately named as most of its area is planted with Norway Spruce monoculture. However, there is a substantial area of Oak and Birch to the north. The Shabbington sector to the east has many mixed stands with Oaks variously paired with Spruce, Lawson

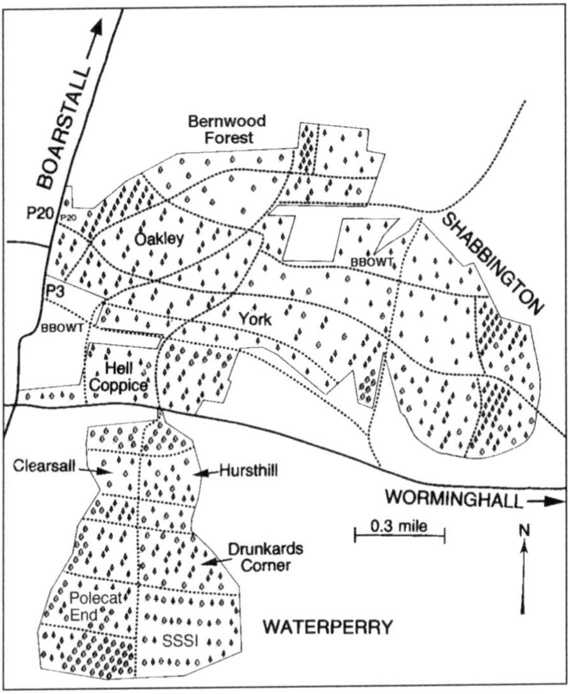

Cypress, Red Cedar and, in a 2-ha (5-acre) area in the north, with Beech. York Wood possesses similar mixed stands but in addition there are plantations of younger trees, especially Western Hemlock, Sweet Chestnut and a few Grand Firs. Hell Coppice is, in the main, densely planted Norway Spruce, mixed with Ash and Oak in places. A stream to the east of the wood attracts waders to adjacent wet meadows.

On the other side of the road to the south lies Waterperry Wood with an area of 136 ha (340 acres) and differing from Shabbington in character in that all the stands are mixed and generally more densely planted. Oak and Norway Spruce is the most common mix, but Clearsall has a sizeable area of Birch and Oak, whilst Hursthill has a 3.5-ha (9-acre) plot of Birch and a new plantation of Spruce and Oak at shrub level only. However, the size of this plot is unlikely to attract any specialist birds. Polecat End has a variety of small plots with Scots Pine, Lawson Cypress, Western Hemlock and some miscellaneous mixed deciduous trees. Drunkard's Corner has a large area of Oak and Birch but also a significant 8-ha (20-acre) sector which consists of a veritable patchwork of small 0.4-ha (1-acre) plots of such species as Scots Pine, Grand Fir, hybrid Larch, Corsican Pine and deciduous scrub. This particular section is classified as a SSSI. Elsewhere are a number of small glades and clearings which add variety to the general scene.

Adjacent to the two woodland areas is a small BBOWT reserve, Bernwood Meadows, which is well-known for its plant species, including 23 grasses, and its ancient hedgerows. The whole area is somewhat underwatched, so opportunity exists to make new discoveries.

Mammal species include numerous Grey Squirrel, small groups of half a dozen or so Fallow Deer and occasional Muntjac Deer. Both woods, and the BBOWT reserve referred to are particularly renowned for their butterfly populations, the open rides and meadows speckled with fluttering colour as many species wander from plant to plant.

Access

The site is north-east of Oxford, near the village of Holton. The Forest Enterprise car park at Bernwood Forest is on the road between Boarstall and Stanton St John with room for 20 vehicles. From here, trails are laid out for plant and butterfly hunting. There is no car park for Waterperry Wood but there is a small lay-by for a single car just beyond an entrance track. Parking in the management entrances to both woods is deterred to ensure rapid access of fire appliances if needed at any time. The BBOWT reserve has a small car park for three or four vehicles but the entrance is quite near a dangerous 'S' bend and caution should be exercised.

The system of pathways in Shabbington is extensive and, like all managed woodland, subject to change. The map for this site indicates the main tracks only and many of the offshoot tracks only go to the woodland boundary. There is no perimeter path. If it is intended to explore as far as the eastern extremity it should be noted that this involves a round trip of over 2 km (1.3 miles).

The path layout at Waterperry Wood is more straightforward and essentially on a square grid arrangement. Once again there is no perimeter track as such although some lateral paths do join adjacent parallel tracks at the periphery. However, the full character of the wood cannot be fully appreciated without exploring some of these side paths, especially in the south-east and north-east where there are open deciduous stands. There is no access into the SSSI in the south-west.

Due to the movement of heavy forestry machinery and permitted horse riding, the main tracks in particular can be muddy at any time of the year.

Species

Woodland management is similar to long-term farming. Crops are grown and eventually harvested, annually on farmland but only after many years in the case of timber. Accordingly the habitat change in woodland is gradual and bird species move in and out of the treescape over the decades that the trees take to mature. Then, almost overnight, the entire habitat will have disappeared after felling. If a small woodland is completely felled in one go the effect could be dramatic. If, however, only small portions are felled at one time the effect will be less noticeable. On the other hand, constant felling and planting work will cause disturbance to birds in adjacent stands. Size of woodland is therefore as important as management technique and the area encompassed by these neighbouring woods is adequate to ensure plenty of undisturbed land at any one time. This helps to maintain a stable community of bird species and the mixed nature of the tree types that exist here also maximises the range of varieties of birds present.

Like many woods of any nature, Shabbington and Waterperry have less bird activity in winter. The numerous conifer stands attract flocks of Treecreeper, Goldcrest, Blue, Long-tailed and Great Tits up to 50 or more in number. However, much of Bernwood Forest is undergoing a plan to gradually remove conifers from mixed stands and replace them with broadleaved species. This will doubtless have an effect on species such as Redpoll and Siskin which both may be seen currently. The same situation faces Crossbill which may also visit from time to time. Coal Tit are common, particularly near or on Larch trees and it is still possible to find both Marsh and Willow Tits, in the less dense evergreens, where Great Spotted Woodpecker can also be found. Pheasant, together with many Blackbird and Song Thrush, rummage amongst the field layer looking for prey, whilst the rides of both woodlands are occupied by numerous Jay and Magpie and some of the Goldfinch that stay to overwinter are found in perimeter trees. Another active area is the land east of the wood where a spruce plantation failed leaving a boggy sector which attracts dozens of Snipe in winter and occasional Curlew. Reed Bunting and Reed Warbler also use the streamside vegetation.

The deciduous and mixed stands exhibit several additional species, hole-nesting varieties being more free to roam outside the breeding season. Nuthatch and Treecreeper are abundant and all three woodpeckers are present. Ubiquitous Wren and Chaffinch are probably the most vocal at this time, apart from Jackdaw which also spend much time in the woods. Bullfinch too will be found, perhaps two or three pairs together near the BBOWT reserve, and Linnet should be looked for. It might also be worth keeping an eye open for remnant Tree Sparrow. Mistle Thrush and Redwing are usually located around the woodland edge. The most productive tracts of deciduous nature are to be found in the northern parts of Shabbington and in Clearsall and Polecat End at Waterperry, which often resound to the calls of Tawny Owl which frequent these sectors. Of other larger birds, Woodcock are present, Common Buzzard and Sparrowhawk are now regular, Red Kite are occasional and Goshawk are being seen increasingly.

Spring and summertime really cause the woods to wake up, many of the species mentioned staying to breed but joined by hordes of Willow Warbler, Chiffchaff, Blackcap and Garden Warbler. Spotted Flycatcher should be seen and Grasshopper Warbler has been encountered in Waterperry. A few Whitethroat can be expected, with Lesser Whitethroat around the hedgerows where the woodland edge abuts adjacent farmland, and where good numbers of Skylark and Yellowhammer can be anticipated. The numerous Dunnock territories around the woodland edge naturally attract Cuckoo. The extent to which other woodland specialties visit these sites is dependent upon the felling and replanting programme. Tree Pipit and Nightjar of course prefer fairly extensive areas of recently planted conifers, interspersed with Heather and small Birches. At the present time there are perhaps too few such sections in these woods to attract either species on a regular basis. There is one such patch on the eastern side of the Waterperry main path and odd clearings in Shabbington but it may be some years before any major felling, followed by a period of 'rehabilitation', creates the right environment for these two birds. In terms of species richness therefore, the two woods fare quite well and a visit would rarely be in vain. A winter visit guarantees little competition with other people but even in summer the place does not get crowded. The most popular pursuit apart from walking and horse riding is butterfly spotting and with several of the fritillaries, blues and skippers in residence during the warmer months it is advisable to go equipped with an appropriate guidebook.

Calendar

Resident: Sparrowhawk, Kestrel, Pheasant, Woodcock, Stock Dove, Woodpigeon, Collared Dove, occasional Little Owl, Tawny Owl, Green, Great Spotted and Lesser Spotted Woodpeckers, Goldcrest, Song and Mistle Thrushes, Long-tailed, Coal, Great, Blue, Marsh and Willow Tits, Nuthatch, Treecreeper, Skylark, Yellowhammer.

December–February: Mixed feeding flocks, Redwing, possibility of Crossbill. Siskin and Redpoll more obvious. Occasional Fieldfare. Lots of Snipe.

March–May: Winter thrushes depart in March. Early breeding of residents in April, summer warblers arrive. Chance of singing Nightingale. Hammering of woodpeckers.

June–July: Blackcap, Willow Warbler, Chiffchaff, Whitethroat, Lesser Whitethroat and Garden Warbler breeding. Occasional Cuckoo and Turtle Dove.

August–November: A quiet period though numbers increased by successful breeding. Warblers leave by September, winter thrushes arrive in November.

53 SHARDELOES

OS ref. SU 947 977

Habitat

Shardeloes House stands in its grounds of 100 ha (250 acres) consisting of arable and pasture farmland, open parkland and mixed woodland. The grand house looks out over a significant lake which has engulfed numerous bushes and small trees, providing many nesting opportunities for waterfowl. The lake has islands affording a roosting and breeding haven for geese and ducks. The treescape in the immediate vicinity of the house is mainly one of mature deciduous trees including Oak and Lime whilst the wood to the south-west is chiefly coniferous. In the area of Mop End, and surrounding an electrical sub-station, are more open areas recently created which have begun succession to Birch and Hawthorn scrub. This somewhat heath-like scene has been augmented by a small arboretum adjacent to a maturing stand of Larch.

Access

Shardeloes House and estate lies 2.5 km (1.5 miles) west of Amersham along the A413 to Great Missenden and Aylesbury. A small lay-by outside the lodge gates accommodates ten cars, and vehicles are not permitted inside the grounds. For a short visit the most favourable footpath is the recently-named 'South Bucks Way', which runs along the south bank of the lake and rejoins the A413, 1 km (0.6 mile) from the car park.

However, the main road is not too inspiring from a birder's point of view so retracing one's footsteps is preferable.

A longer walk is possible by way of the footpath to Mop End with a return route down the sloping pathway on the western side and following the lakeside path to the main entrance. This entails a round trip of some 4.8 km (3 miles) but is likely to be worth it as the path skirts both conifer and mixed woodland and the emerging scrubland in the vicinity of the sub-station. Alternatively one may pull off the A404 at Beamond End to approach the estate from the higher ground and perhaps visit the adjacent Penn Wood.

The nearest main line railway station is at Amersham, which is also served by the Metropolitan Line of the London Underground.

Species

If the owner of this estate were to keep a record of his 'garden' birds, a most impressive chronicle it would be. Birds of one species or another are active throughout the year, each day commencing with morning assembly in the Jackdaw roost adjacent to the main house, although in the months of winter the gathered ensemble are soon off to the arable fields for a day of feeding. These fields will often attract flocks of Meadow Pipit and Skylark, offering the opportunity of comparing the markings and behaviour of these two farmland birds. Other birds of the winter field such as Pheasant, Lapwing and Black-headed Gull are much in evidence, whilst the rolling lawns and pastures will accommodate creeping carpets of Redwings and Fieldfare in good numbers. Mistle Thrush are choosy about where they gather in any numbers and fortunately Shardeloes is one such place, with up to 30 or more most winters. The grassy banks of the lake and the cricket pitch feature Pied Wagtail stepping daintily between noisy Canada Geese and numerous Moorhen, and Little Owl has bred at this corner.

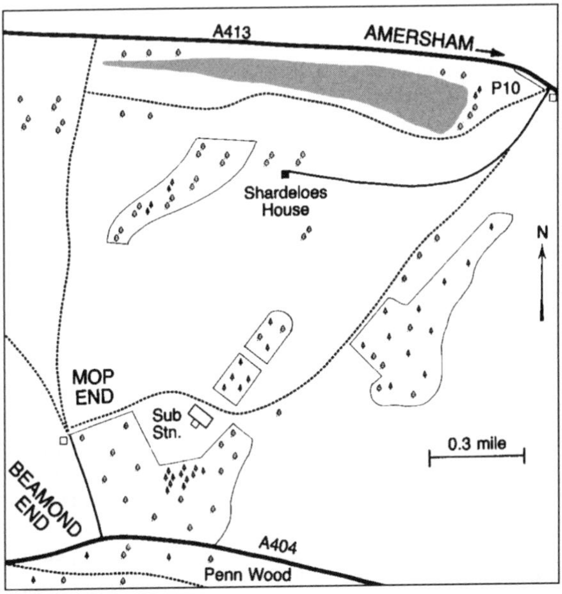

Sparrowhawk is frequently encountered, especially in the Mop End sector.

The water at this time of year provides an important refuge for a dozen or two whinnying Dabchick, two or three Water Rail, a few Canada Geese, Mallard and Gadwall, all of which have bred here. Shoveler pay irregular visits at this time of year, though not in large enough numbers to show off their tandem feeding technique, but any Pochard spotted may well stay on to breed. Snipe will also take up this locale in the event of inclement conditions affecting their more usual territory, and Woodcock may frequent the rough ground near the Lodge. Other waders tend to shun the site as there is little suitable structure to the water's edge. Nonetheless, two very fine Wood Sandpiper visited one notable springtime. The water area is not large enough to attract large numbers of gull, most being seen above heading roost-ward at evening time, but Kingfisher and Reed Bunting can be seen around the pool, the latter moving up to the field sectors to party the winter away. The woodland sectors can be rather quiet at this time of year though more flocks of Fieldfare and Redwing can be found near Mop End, which is another likely spot for Little Owl. The conifer stands, some of which grow in a conservation area, hold small mixed feeding groups of Goldcrest and tits, especially Coal Tit, and are an area of protection for flocks of Linnet which roam the surrounding district.

The spring passage is much in evidence with Wheatear likely to be found at Mop End whilst the first Sand Martin will stop fleetingly near the lake which is also the first place where the Chiffchaff may be heard. Wheatears also visit the fields to the west of the lake or sometimes the cricket pitch which they will share with Pied and early Yellow Wagtails. Redstart has been noted here too, later in the spring. Brambling, though not being a regular winter visitor, may well be seen up to April as parties of up to 60 move northwards with the newly-arrived summer species. The fence-line adjacent to the lake is worth checking for Whinchat and the water itself for traversing Garganey, one of this dramatically-plumaged species choosing to return this way in October 2000.

By early May, the breeding period already well underway for resident birds, the visiting migrants will also succumb to this seasonal urge and the lakeside is probably where this activity is most obvious. Dozens of Coot and Moorhen and several pairs of Little Grebe will be feeding young whilst Reed Bunting forage amongst the reeds on behalf of their offspring, accompanied by Sedge and Reed Warblers most years. In the meantime there is continuous aerial activity as Swallow and House Martin hawk for insects to the cackling accompaniment of unruly Rook. Predatory Crow cause more disturbance than do the Kestrel which breed on the site. The tree-line and gardens of the Lodge can produce singing Blackcap whilst the less intruded area of Mop End may well be favoured by the attractive Tree Pipit, whose slightly sibilant song can be thoughtlessly interrupted by the strident protests of the Mistle Thrush protecting their nests from marauding Jay and Magpie. Woodcock are often seen roding at this time of year and Tawny Owl will be particularly vociferous. Both Grey Partridge and Lapwing have a tenuous breeding toe-hold here but Spotted Flycatcher do far better and late summer sees up to a dozen or more busily feeding as family groups.

During summer, visitations from two other specialties of nearby waters are quite possible, whilst not frequent. One or two pairs of Ruddy Duck have bred in recent years and the occasional Mandarin might pay a visit. This perching duck may have the edge over the stiff-tailed Ruddy Duck in the plumage stakes, at least as far as the males are concerned, but both are striking additions to the Shardeloes scene when present. Even more so was a passing Wood Duck in April 1999, doubtless an abscondee from some collection.

The advance of colder, damper weather brings about the gradual departure of migrant birds to their winter quarters, including Sedge Warbler and Whitethroat. The Garden Warbler vacate the woodland at Mop End leaving its periphery free to increasing numbers of roosting Woodpigeon, whilst the reeded area of the lake becomes almost devoid of passerines for a while. The chance of a glimpse of roaming Crossbill in the conifer compartment is enhanced slightly and early Siskin return. Any Redpoll that may have stayed during the summer, though unlikely to have bred, will be joined by several others and the resulting group moves between various woodlands in the area, especially nearby Penn Wood, now in the hands of the Woodland Trust. Woodpigeon assemble in enormous numbers, doubtless to the consternation of the landowner. Birds of prey have traditionally included Hobby in summer, and the local Barn Owl may well include Shardeloes in their hunting territory, although one became a traffic victim on the dual carriageway recently. A significant end-of-century development, as in much of the Chilterns, has been the regular appearances of Common Buzzard, exploring from their home base in Weedonhill Woods on the opposite side of the valley.

Rarities are rare here; Little Bittern, Great Grey Shrike and Black-bellied Dipper are shadowy memories from past decades, but the nineties have contributed Osprey, Scandinavian Rock Pipit and Cetti's Warbler, whilst the 'noughties' have contributed Little Egret and Shag. A summer's 'bat and ball' evening watching the cricket and the feeding Noctule Bats, between visits to the club-house bar, is an added attraction. Thus it can be seen that something avian is happening continuously at Shardeloes, albeit not always on a grand scale, and therefore a visit at any time can be fulfilling. Perhaps on balance April/May and October/November are best.

Calendar

Resident: Little Grebe, Mute Swan, Canada Goose, Mallard, Tufted Duck, Kestrel, visiting Sparrowhawk, Water Rail, Pheasant, Coot, Moorhen, Little and Tawny Owls, Green and Great Spotted Woodpeckers, Skylark, Pied Wagtail, all six tits, Nuthatch and Treecreeper, Goldfinch, Yellowhammer, Reed Bunting, Rook, Jackdaw.

December–February: Great Crested Grebe in small numbers, winter gulls also in small flocks, occasional Wigeon, Teal and Shoveler, possibility of Goldeneye, Grey Partridge more prominent, Water Rail more obvious, Snipe, Meadow Pipit, Grey Wagtail.

March–May: Possible Hobby and Common Buzzard. Cuckoo, Swallow and House Martin, Yellow Wagtail on passage, Reed and Sylvia warblers in small numbers. Spotted Flycatcher, Whinchat and Wheatear. Tree Pipit.

June–July: Breeding passerines, some on second brood, Turtle Dove now infrequent, Swift.

August–November: Prospect of Common Sandpiper on passage, larger numbers of hirundines around the lake prior to departure, Redwing and Fieldfare arrive, Woodpigeon and Stock Dove numbers increase.

54 WENDOVER WOODS **OS ref. SP 890 085**

Habitat

At 325 ha (769 acres) Wendover Woods is one of the largest mixed woodlands on the Chiltern Hills and commands spectacular views across the Vale of Aylesbury. Owned by the Forestry Commission and managed by Forest Enterprise, an executive agency of the Commission, it was created for recreation, conservation and timber production, a good example of how to provide visitors with a variety of activities and environments to suit all tastes.

Much of Halton Wood is coniferous, but down the western slope to Halton Camp and Boddington Hill a good deal of scrub remains. On the eastern side are patches of Birch and Hawthorn thickets adjacent to large blocks of broadleaf woodland. The most important stand of trees, at the heart of the complex, is the mature Norway Spruce plantation, famous for its breeding Firecrests. To the south a large clearing affords spectacular views down a coombe to the tree-clad Boddington Hill and across a wide canopy suitable for raptor watching. Many of the rides are bordered with ancient Beeches and Limes, and are ablaze with Bluebells in the spring, and a number of ponds have been dug along the Firecrest Trail. As a working wood, rotational plantations regularly inject light and variety into the canopy.

The Firecrest has drastically altered the planned management of Wendover Woods. Tree felling is now programmed such that there are always mature spruce trees available, with the felled area replanted with conifers to ensure continuity of habitat.

Access

The woods are situated between Wendover and Tring, east of the B4009, where there are excellent access arrangements for visitors. Follow the directional signs south, off the B4009, towards St Leonard's and Chesham, turning right into the main entrance (SP 887 105), which is the only vehicular access point. The one-way road leads uphill, via a ticket machine, through the woods to a large car parking area with an information centre, toilets, barbecue and picnic facilities. The parking complex is only open between 08:00 and 17:00 hrs and is a pay and display with a £1.50 fee for weekdays and £2 at weekends. Long-term parking permits are available from the Forest Office (see below). The exit point is further along the lane leading to St Leonard's. For the early morning birder, park on the verge, or one of several lay-bys, along the St Leonard's lane and follow the tracks into the woods by the site exit.

Wendover Woods has a maze of waymarked footpaths, including a

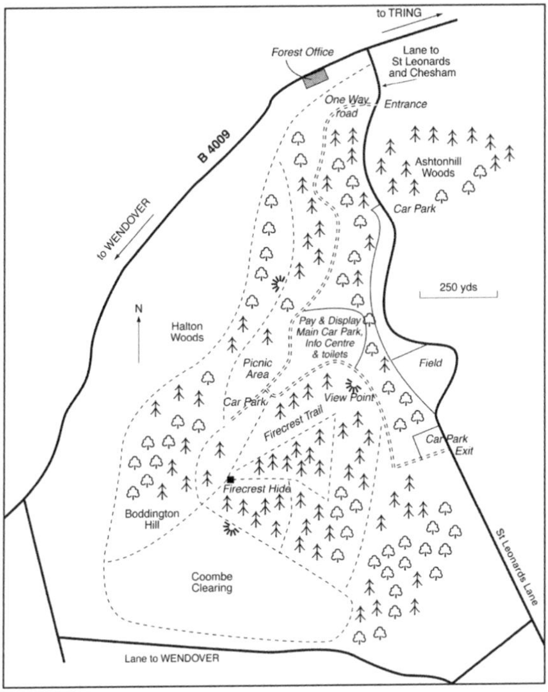

surfaced trail close to the main parking area suitable for the disabled. There are horse trails and cycle routes, and the well-publicised Firecrest Trail is signposted off the main parking area. It is 3.5 km (2 miles) in length, with information boards en-route to a secluded hide set high amongst the trees. Allow four hours to walk the full trail, which is thoroughly recommended as it passes through all the main woodland habitats and takes in the open coombe. The shortened route takes about two hours and still includes the hide.

A detailed site leaflet is freely available in the main car park and there are many interpretive boards scattered across the complex. Rangers are also available to lead school parties (contact the Forest Office on 01296 625825). One of the highest points of the Chiltern Hills can also be found within the woodland complex and is another good raptor lookout point. Aston Hill Wood, east of the St Leonard's lane is used by sport and mountain bikers, but is worth a visit early morning.

Species

Wendover Woods is nationally famous for its breeding Firecrests, which is one of the region's few genuine rare breeding birds, and is worth a springtime visit for this alone. The initial colonising pairs were recorded back in 1971, with an incredible peak of 46 singing males four years later in 1975, since when numbers have levelled off to less than ten pairs. The birds breed in a mature Norway Spruce plantation which was planted in the early twentieth century, a part of which was storm damaged in 1990. The tops of the 'Christmas trees', with their dense crowns, provide ideal nesting sites for the Firecrest, and the commoner Goldcrest, to build their delicate breeding structures. Although Firecrests can be present throughout the year the best time to visit is in April and early May when the adults are in full song, and before September when a post-breeding dispersal occurs and the birds fall silent. Follow the 'Firecrest Trail' and listen for the distinctive song amongst the spruce canopy, either from the hide or the trail itself.

In early spring, on a fine sunny morning, scanning from the view-points across the woodland should reveal soaring Sparrowhawk and Kestrel with a good chance of Common Buzzard, which now breed locally. Goshawk are also resident at Wendover, and increasingly Red Kite are noted as they disperse from their main release site further south-west along the Chilterns. Woodpeckers are best searched for now, before full leaf cover and while 'drumming' is at a peak, with the car park area as good as any for Lesser Spotted Woodpecker. Hawfinch were once regularly recorded here, but today are a rarity, early spring being a good time to listen for their distinctive 'tpik' contact call. Check out the coombe plantation for a passage Woodlark in March.

Migrant Chiffchaff are soon joined by Blackcap and Willow Warbler in the mature timber and Whitethroat and Garden Warbler in the scrub and plantations. All five species breed, along with a few pairs of Lesser Whitethroat on the periphery of the wood. Late April into May is a good time to check for any passage Nightingale, Wood Warbler and Redstart that may briefly visit the wood, and for the one or two remaining pairs of Tree Pipit and Grasshopper Warbler in the open plantations below Halton Wood. Spotted Flycatcher are last to arrive and a few pairs nest in the mature trees throughout the wood and around the main car parks.

Once the warblers have arrived a dawn chorus visit should yield around 50 species, with fly-overs such as 'roding' Woodcock or passage gulls and hirundines. All the usual woodland residents are on site although Nuthatch can be difficult to detect at times. In the mature woodland Marsh Tit outnumber Willow Tit, which should be looked for amongst the scrub on the western slope. The more open aspect can encourage Reed Bunting, Yellowhammer, Bullfinch and Linnet to nest when the trees are young, and below 3 m in height, and it is here that Turtle Dove and Cuckoo are most likely to be encountered. Crossbill, Redpoll and Siskin occasionally breed at Wendover but are more likely as winter visitors.

The summer period can be quiet as the day wears on, particularly at weekends when the site is busy with walkers and picnickers. An evening visit is worthwhile for more Woodcock and owl activity. The woods have a good population of Tawny Owl, but there must be a reasonable chance of Long-eared Owl nesting in the coniferous sections, a bird easier to detect when the young are calling in June and July. By late August the breeding season has just about finished and the woods fall silent as many species moult and prepare for migration or the coming winter. Large flocks of tits and finches can be encountered and warbler numbers increase as passage birds move along the downland ridge.

The woods are well used by roosting passerines, pigeons and corvids during the winter period, particularly in the thick and mature spruce plantation. Brambling may turn up in the finch flocks to feed on fallen beechmast while the conifers should be checked out for Crossbill, particularly in an irruption year. Roving tit flocks should be checked for Goldcrest and the occasional Firecrest or wintering Chiffchaff. The woods are far less populated by people, and birds, from November to February but are still worth a visit for the solitude alone and the bonus of a Woodcock flushed from a woodland ride.

Wendover Woods should be at the top of any birdwatchers list of must-visit sites, every springtime, to experience the 'Firecrest Trail', while the Forestry Commission should be applauded for the way they have reacted, with both habitat creation and informed public awareness, to ensure that this fabulous gem of a bird, the Firecrest, remains breeding in our region.

Firecrest

Calendar

Resident: Sparrowhawk, Goshawk, Common Buzzard, Kestrel, Woodcock, Stock Dove, Tawny Owl, Green, Great Spotted and Lesser Spotted Woodpeckers, Mistle and Song Thrushes, Goldcrest, Firecrest, Long-tailed, Marsh, Willow and Coal Tits, Nuthatch, Treecreeper, Jay, Goldfinch, Bullfinch, Hawfinch (rare), Crossbill, Redpoll, Yellowhammer.

December–February: Roving tit flocks, roosting pigeons, corvids, thrushes, Brambling, Siskin, Redpoll.

March–May: Best chance of Firecrest, raptor watching, Cuckoo, Tree Pipit, Woodlark on passage, Grasshopper Warbler, Lesser Whitethroat, Whitethroat, Garden Warbler, Blackcap, Chiffchaff, Willow Warbler, chance of passage Nightingale, Redstart and Wood Warbler, Reed Bunting.

June–July: Owl activity, chance of Long-eared, Woodcock, Turtle Dove, Spotted Flycatcher, breeding activity.

August–November: Chance of Crossbill irruption, resident species moult, warblers move off, finch and tit flocks assemble, Woodcock increase, Tawny Owl active, roosting thrushes.

55 WESTON TURVILLE RESERVOIR

OS ref. SP 859 096

Habitat

The reservoir at Weston Turville is owned by the British Waterways Board and was constructed in 1795 to supply water to an arm of the Grand Union Canal. The 5-ha (12-acre) lake is used for angling and sailing, and has extensive reedbeds on three sides. On the southern flank the surrounding area comprises marshy fen, dense shrubs and established hedges, whilst to the north there is a small area of woodland with a variety of deciduous trees and Hawthorn bushes. The site abuts arable farmland and overlooks an interesting grazing field near the main entrance. The land immediately adjacent to the water's edge is managed by BBOWT, on behalf of the waterways board, who have the shooting rights reserved. Management entails keeping the marsh area from becoming overgrown and containing the reedbed from encroaching into the sailing area. The bank to the north-east is raised and totally exposed but affords a good observation point from which to view the water. The site was classified a SSSI in 1976.

Access

Weston Turville Reservoir lies just north of the A413 between Aylesbury and Wendover, off the B4009. There is a large lay-by in World`s End Lane which can accommodate up to 30 vehicles, from where the main entrance can be accessed via a kissing gate. There is a perimeter footpath with full public access enabling a circuit to be completed, but the track is rough on the southern side where it passes an old open screen-type hide looking over the water. The Susan Cowdy hide, situated in the reedbed on the northern flank, has a wheelchair ramp, and for the disabled is best approached from the footpath off Halton Lane. Parking is also available in Grenville Avenue off Halton Lane.

Species

Although not a large area of water, the reservoir nonetheless provides a safe haven for a small number of overwintering waterfowl and as such is probably best visited in the winter months. The site's main asset is the large reedbed, which is a hive of activity throughout the year and holds a resident population of Water Rail. Numbers are at their highest in late autumn, as migrants arrive, and it is then that they are easier to see when the water level in the reedbed is low. Weston Turville is their county stronghold and their shrill voices can be heard from the reedbed hide at most times of the year. It is no surprise that Bittern are regularly recorded in the reedbed and a winter bunting roost attracts small numbers of Corn Bunting amongst the more numerous Reed Bunting. Little Grebe and Ruddy Duck haunt the reeds and both breed.

During the winter, whilst wildfowl numbers are not normally high, such species as Great Crested Grebe, Shoveler, Pochard, Wigeon, Gadwall and Teal will be found amongst Coot, Tufted Duck and Mallard. The exposed western shore, often fished, usually causes most of the

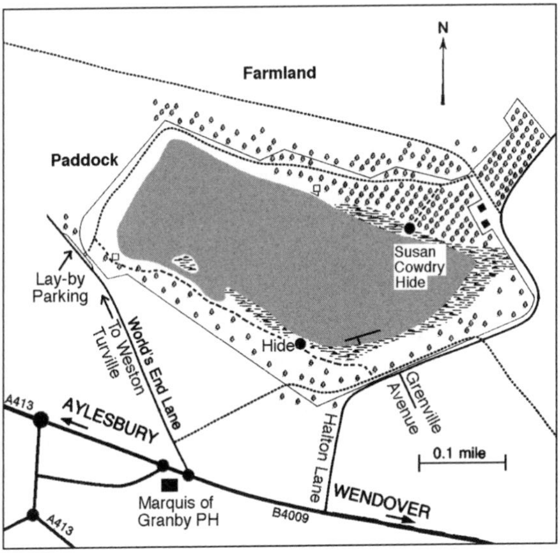

birds to collect near the reedbed at the far end and when sailing is also taking place, those that remain often retreat well into the reedbed itself. However, the location of the lake is such that a variety of visiting species may be expected including Grey Heron, Cormorant and small numbers of feral geese. Although perhaps more attracted to the larger waters of the nearby Tring complex, both Smew and Goosander may well be seen at Weston, while past records of Red-throated Diver, Slavonian Grebe and Scaup hint at what can turn up on occasions.

The surrounding tree-line caters for occasional small parties of Redpoll and Siskin to accompany the resident tits and finches, while the paddock should be checked for winter thrushes, sparrows and buntings. The arable fields sometimes attract partridge, pigeons, Skylark and Meadow Pipit.

The first passage of the year brings increased numbers of winter ducks for a short period but, as quantities begin to dwindle, Shelduck may call in for a few days and Garganey has been recorded. The paddock field may produce an early Wheatear, among the restless winter thrushes, while mixed flocks of Lapwing and Black-headed Gull begin to disperse; be on the lookout for wagtails and pipits. Of the warbler tribe, Chiffchaff and Blackcap are normally first to arrive followed by Willow Warbler, Whitethroat, Sedge and Reed Warblers, all of which breed on site. The small number of resident Ruddy Duck make fewer visits to other waters nearby and prepare for breeding with much head-bobbing and tails erect. Swift and hirundines appear over the water and a rare raptor such as Osprey or Marsh Harrier may pay a visit.

By midsummer, the reedbed is vibrant with chattering Reed Bunting, Reed and Sedge Warblers and as such is a major attraction to Cuckoo which can be seen perched in prominent lakeside trees scanning for a suitable host for their eggs. Their woodpecker-like feet are especially adapted for working through dense reedbeds with two toes forward and two back. Despite this predation, however, the warblers do succeed in raising young of their own. Another predator particularly active at this time of year is the resident Sparrowhawk, the male in particular making several sorties a day to collect prey for the much larger female to feed to her brood. Throughout the warmest months hirundines, often in huge numbers, billow over the water, accompanied by many Swift which, as evening advances, can be seen soaring upwards higher and higher until out of sight, spending the night on the wing. Another welcome visitor in summer, and on passage, is the Common Tern, although there are no nesting facilities available at this site. Kingfisher are more likely to be seen in late summer as juveniles disperse far and wide, and Barn Owl have recently bred nearby and have been noted hunting over the reedbed.

Being a small site the autumn passage may not be too evident, but as wildfowl numbers increase they may be joined by a passage Black-necked Grebe or an unusual duck; Long-tailed and Eider have been recorded in late autumn, as have storm blown pelagics, such as Manx Shearwater and Grey Phalarope. Whinchat often occur on the fence line of the adjacent paddock and Common Buzzard can be seen soaring over the nearby Chilterns.

Weston Turville Reservoir is worth a visit any time of year for reedbed birds and is an ideal springtime complement to the nearby Wendover Woods.

Calendar

Resident: Great Crested and Little Grebes, Coot, Moorhen, Mallard, Tufted Duck, Ruddy Duck, Sparrowhawk, Kestrel, Water Rail, Kingfisher, Barn Owl, Green and Great Spotted Woodpeckers, Treecreeper, winter thrushes, Long-tailed and Marsh Tits, Bullfinch, Reed Bunting, Yellowhammer.

December–February: Wildfowl including Pochard, Shoveler, Gadwall, occasional Goldeneye and Wigeon, chance of rare grebe or duck. Gull roost, Redpoll, Siskin, bunting roost.

March–May: Shelduck, chance of Garganey, Common Tern, Hobby, passage Osprey or Marsh Harrier, Cuckoo, Swift, hirundines, Wheatear, Chiffchaff, Blackcap, Willow Warbler, Whitethroat, Sedge and Reed Warblers.

June–July: Breeding waterfowl, hirundines, Common Tern, reedbed activity – Little Grebe, Ruddy Duck, Water Rail, Cuckoo and warblers.

August–November: Ducks and gulls increase, possible Black-necked Grebe, roosting hirundines, Hobby, migrant Water Rail, late autumn seabirds.

ADDITIONAL SITES

Chess Valley (OS ref. SU 995 985)

Between Chesham and Chenies is a scenic streamside walk which takes in trout farms, cress beds, farmland and deciduous woods. At the Chesham trout farm Water Rail and Grey Wagtail are always likely, together with Reed Bunting. The sewage works slightly to the east often has all three wagtails in summer, whilst the farmland around Blackwell Hall usually has Corn Bunting and Little Owl. The small pond west of Bois Mill has resident Little Grebe and Tufted Duck, which are joined by Gadwall and Pochard in winter. Frith Wood, in the centre of the walk, is privately owned but good for Tawny Owl and Jay. Woodcock are a prospect but regular shooting here may deter them. The fields to the north of the footpath usually have Grey Partridge and Skylark. The weir and wider waters at Latimer House are excellent for Grey Wagtail and breeding Dabchick, and Spotted Flycatcher are present in summer. The fairly extensive woodland south of the road, Lane Wood, is a mixed deciduous wood with shrubbery containing the usual common woodland species, with passage Nightingale a good prospect.

Beyond Chenies, the footpath north of the river passes through boggy pastures which often contain Snipe in winter. In summertime, the dense bushes around these paddocks provide nesting sites for Whitethroat and Bullfinch. The small Bluebell wood beyond is most aromatic in summer and also hosts Great Spotted Woodpecker, Willow Tit and Treecreeper. Valley Farm has its own feral Guineafowl but the river attracts large numbers of House Martin and occasionally Water Rail in winter. The cress beds are again an area where all three wagtails can be found, the Yellow mainly on passage. Each end of this walk has mature woodland to explore. Mount Wood to the east is excellent for the three woodpeckers, Garden Warbler, Turtle Dove and Chiffchaff whilst a similar wood at Chesham Bois was a past haunt for Hawfinch. Barn Owl are now regularly recorded hunting along the valley bottom, over the wet meadows, and are often seen from the adjacent lane.

Coombe Hill (OS ref. SP 847 066)

Situated south of the B4009 which runs between Wendover and Little Kimble, this significant pimple on the Buckinghamshire landscape rises some 262 m (850 ft) above the surrounding countryside to look down somewhat onto Wendover Woods 4 km (2.5 miles) away. It thus forms the highest point on the Chiltern escarpment and has been in the hands of the National Trust since 1918. Grazing has been introduced and Gorse that keeps appearing is mown off annually. An area of clear grassed hilltop with Heather has thus been formed but adjacent is a natural mixed woodland of Oak, Hornbeam, Birch, Rowan, Hazel and Hawthorn.

Such a site in such a place is ideal for visiting during migration, and regular passage visitors here include Redstart, Common Buzzard and numerous hirundines. Ring Ouzel regularly pass through as do occasional Wood Warbler and there is always the prospect of Hawfinch. The spring passage is more prominent than the autumn migration. Access is via the lane to Dunsmore. At the top of the hill where the lane swings sharply to the right there is space for parking vehicles.

Eton Rowing Trench (OS ref. SU 920 785)

Sculpted out of agriculture and wasteland, this 1,500 m-long water feature near Dorney has brought not only a new facility for this Olympics-invigorated sport, but the potential for a haven for birdlife. Whilst the long entrance road has been landscaped more for appearances than conservation, the grassy banks and clumps of trees and bushes will nonetheless develop as a base for summer warblers and resident finches, with Great Spotted and Green Woodpeckers already in evidence.

Stonechat

The more mature trees near the entrance have retained the Tawny and Little Owls which endured the disruption of construction and the adjacent meadows will continue to draw overwintering Lapwing and winter thrushes in good numbers. Although the water itself offers no breeding facilities, Tufted Duck and Pochard find it worthwhile spending time here, but more interest arises from the gravelly banks of both sides of the trench which regularly attract Common and Green Sandpipers, Redshank, Dunlin and both Ringed and Little Ringed Plovers. Common Tern ply between here and the adjacent river, though it is unlikely they will catch much in the rowing trench itself.

Of particular interest is the rough ground on the Thames-side of the trench which is scheduled to be managed as a reserve for wildlife, and it is hoped this will include the retention of extensive natural vegetation currently home to several pairs of Corn and Reed Buntings, and numerous Whitethroat. The soothing songs of numerous Skylark contrast with the rasping calls of over-flying Ring-necked Parakeet whilst flocks of Linnet, Goldfinch and Greenfinch feed on the wild flower seeds in winter. Flashes and small shelf-lined pools provide suitable features for more waders and wintering duck such as Teal or passage Garganey, and the mounds of surplus sand and gravel bring in breeding Sand Martin. Mandarin are already breeding here and a huge Jackdaw roost exists, with over 2,000 to be seen from late summer. Turtle Dove summer here and both Pied and Grey Wagtails are present.

Long Herdon Meadow (OS ref. SP 648 204)

An area of some 4 ha (10 acres) of wet meadows, remnants of unimproved ancient meadowland, set in the River Ray valley, north of the A41 trunk road between Bicester and Aylesbury. Take the road to Marsh Gibbon, parking near Grange Farm. This is a BBOWT reserve, with open public access, from a footpath south of Grange Farm. The main attraction is overwintering waders in the flooded areas, including Lapwing, Golden Plover, Snipe and possible Jack Snipe. Breeding species include Skylark, Reed Bunting, Yellowhammer and Linnet. Passage birds may well include Greenshank and Redshank.

A small area of adjacent flood-meadow was purchased by the Trust in 1998 and is open to visitors between July and September. For access walk back down the lane from the farm and enter the reserve near the A41 by a bridge.

Moor Common (OS ref. SU 803 906)

A delightful undulating, mixed deciduous woodland set either side of Church Road between Lane End and Frieth. With Oak and Birch stands plus scrub thicket to the west of the road, and dominant Beech amongst conifer and Oak/Hawthorn thicket compartments to the east, all the common resident birds are present including Nuthatch, Treecreeper, Stock Dove and Tawny Owl. The song of Willow Warbler, Garden Warbler, Blackcap and Chiffchaff bring extra magic in spring and summer and there is obvious potential for passage Nightingale or Wood Warbler. An extended walk is possible to the south-east by following the footpath into Moor Woods adjacent.

Philipshill Wood (OS ref. TQ 010 945)

Together with the adjacent Newland Park, the site represents some 100 ha (250 acres) of mixed woodland and open parkland. The scene is more deciduous to the west and the north. Access is off the B4442 road to Little Chalfont and parking is along the road to the park, or in the park itself. A good site for general woodland birds with Common Buzzard and Firecrest regularly encountered. Tree Pipit and Wood Warbler may visit on passage and a few Hawfinch are probably still resident. Good numbers of thrushes winter in the park.

Pitstone Fen (OS ref. SU 941 142)

This is a relatively tiny location which is perhaps of more interest to botanists than ornithologists but the extent of the flora and the protected nature of the reserve attracts a good number of birds and, in summer, there is a substantial community of breeding resident species and warblers. The 3.5-ha (9-acre) site consists of a strip of land adjacent to a railway line and possesses reedbeds, a copse of Scots Pine near the entrance and the Fen itself at the face of the old chalk quarry workings. Access is strictly by permit only, details of which are available from BBOWT. Best for summer warblers and Corn Bunting, which breed in the general area. Quiet at other times of the year. The reserve lies to the north of the B488 to the north-east of Tring and can be combined with a visit to adjacent College Lake (see main sites).

Rushbeds Wood (OS ref. SP 670 158)

A 40 ha (100 acre) long-neglected woodland adjacent to a railway embankment beyond which is the private parkland and lake of Wotton House. The site is some 5 km (3 miles) south of the A41(T) Aylesbury to Bicester road and parking is available where the 'T' junction of the lanes abuts the railway line. Another good site for woodland birds including all six tits, Nuthatch and Treecreeper. Great Spotted Woodpecker are regularly seen but Lesser Spotted Woodpecker less often, Tittershall Wood to the north being preferred. Passage birds seen are Tree Pipit and Nightingale. Tawny Owl is resident. Adjacent pastures host Lapwing, occasional Snipe and numerous winter thrushes. The lake, which can be viewed from the lane to the north-west, hosts Little and Great Crested Grebes, occasional Kingfisher and flocks of Canada Geese, with occasional feral Greylag. Sparrowhawk is a regular visitor in the general area and may breed in Tittershall Wood.

Salcey Forest (OS ref. SP 810 505)

The forests of Salcey, Whittlewood and Rockingham once provided hunting for monarchs but only part of the Salcey remains. Whilst it is the largest ancient forest in Northamptonshire, a goodly portion, containing a conservation area and a 14-ha (35-acre) reserve, lies on the Buckinghamshire side of the county border. It has been Forestry Commission land since 1924 and has been declared a SSSI. Many of the Oaks are 150 years old and there are a variety of other deciduous species of tree including Ash and Hazel, and large blocks of conifers. A usual range of woodland warblers exists, plus Nightingale, Grasshopper Warbler and the occasional Wood Warbler and Tree Pipit. All three woodpeckers are present, as are Woodcock and Common Buzzard.

HERTFORDSHIRE

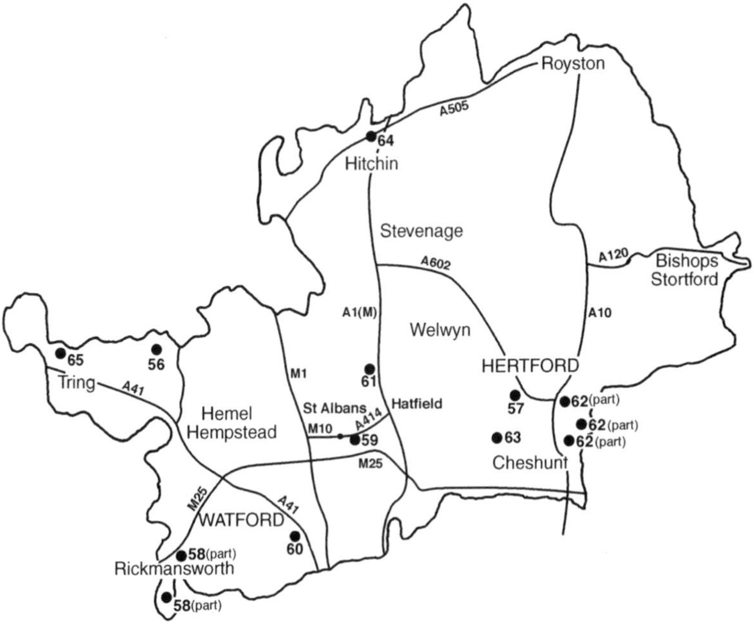

56 ASHRIDGE ESTATE

OS ref. SP 980 130

Habitat

From Ivinghoe Beacon in the north to Frithsden Copse in the south the Ashridge Estate covers an area of over 1,700 ha (4,500 acres), most of which is open to the public. It is a place of immense atmosphere and feeling, essentially Chilterns in flavour and, thankfully, in the safe hands of the National Trust.

Although the majority of the estate is in Hertfordshire the best examples of chalk downland can be found in Buckinghamshire at Ivinghoe Beacon, Incombe Hole, Steps and Pitstone Hills. In places sheep still graze these ancient pastures, close cropping the sward to ensure a rich downland flora, but the majority is smothered in Hawthorn scrub. Extending along the scarp slope to the north and south of The Monument is a fine Beech hanger with many Whitebeam growing along the periphery.

The woodlands of the plateau are varied in both age and content. Native trees such as Oak, Ash, Birch and Hornbeam predominate with a scrub layer of mainly Hazel, Elder and Dogwood. Ponds are found here, notably around The Monument, and are an obvious attraction for wildlife during dry weather. Conifer plantations are scattered widely but are still in the minority.

The commons are difficult to identify as many have been completely overgrown by trees. Northchurch Common is the most open with much bracken and gorse forming the semblance of a heath. Patches of heather exist on Ivinghoe Common while Ringshall Coppice is worth a springtime visit alone for the carpets of Bluebells. Arable land is mercifully at a minimum but the meadow adjacent to the visitors centre can be good for watching deer early in the morning.

With such a mosaic of habitats a wide range of wildlife takes safe refuge on the estate. Deer include a herd of over 400 Fallow and many Muntjac. Badger inhabit the chalk slopes and Fox are common. The squirrel-like Edible Dormouse, or Glis, is only found within a 24-km (15-mile) radius of Ashridge and is thought to have been introduced by Lord Rothschild around 1902. About 37 species of butterfly and 300 species of moth have been recorded, many of the former attracted to the calcareous plants of the open downland.

Access

The estate is situated in the west of the county on the border with Buckinghamshire and Bedfordshire. The B4506 bisects Ashridge north to south between the A4146 at Dagnall and the A4251 at Northchurch, west of Berkhamsted. There are many lay-bys and car parks with even more bridleways and public footpaths, all well marked, affording good public access.

For further details of nature trails and general information, apply to the National Trust shop and visitors centre at the end of Monument Drive. For the downland sites drive to the car parks at Ivinghoe (SP 962 160) or Pitstone (SP 955 150) Hills and explore along the Ridgeway footpath. Try to avoid the busy Sunday afternoons and Bank Holiday periods. Coming south onto the commons, Ivinghoe Common (popular with picnickers in the summer) is served with a car park making it ideal for exploring the surrounding mature deciduous woodland and conifer

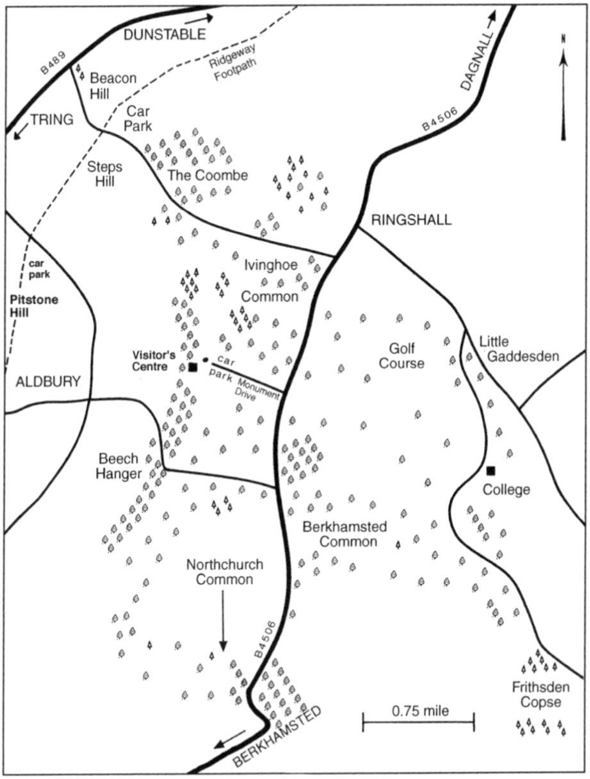

plantations. Aldbury and Pitstone Commons can be worked from Monument Drive, as can the Beech hanger. Northchurch and Berkhamsted Commons both have roadside pull-ins along the B4506.

Species

The estate may seem quiet in the winter without the hustle and bustle of the summer visitors but several areas merit attention. The open chalk slopes at Ivinghoe and Steps Hills attract small flocks of Linnet, Greenfinch, Yellowhammer and Corn Bunting, while the scrub gives good cover for Bullfinch. Ever shifting groups of Meadow Pipit and Skylark can be found on the open slopes or passing overhead along with winter thrushes and corvids; the downs are now thickly populated by Magpies with several large communal roosts. At dusk, gulls can be seen moving west along the ridge towards their roosts on Tring Reservoirs.

Further south in the Beech hanger, Chaffinch and Brambling forage in the leaf-litter for mast, their numbers fluctuating annually according to the amount available; some years the latter species is not recorded at all. Roving flocks of tits, including Marsh but rarely Willow, can be seen almost anywhere, most of them sporting shiny 'leg irons' applied by the local ringing group. All three woodpeckers are resident with Green Woodpecker the most obvious. Sparrowhawk and Kestrel can be encountered anywhere on the estate, as can the recently established Common Buzzard which now breeds locally. Hen Harrier rarely occur along the downs but increasing sightings of Red Kite and Goshawk are recorded as both expand their range eastwards.

Wheatear are the first spring visitors on the downs with Chiffchaff paving the way in the woods. Very soon the commons are alive with song as Willow Warbler and Blackcap pour onto the estate. The other common Sylvia warblers arrive with Lesser Whitethroat being most numerous along the chalk ridge; Grasshopper Warbler is now only a scarce migrant. Tree Pipit arrive during the second half of April and, although numbers in the county generally are declining the estate still holds a small population in the more open glades and along the downs beside Meadow Pipit and Skylark. Hirundines filter along the slopes and a passage of Whinchat and less obviously Ring Ouzel occurs, although numbers are minimal. Cuckoo favour the scrub and call continuously on arrival with occasionally a small group of four or five within earshot at any one time. A few Spotted Flycatcher arrive in late spring to breed but, as with many sub-Saharan migrants, numbers have dramatically declined in recent years. However, a dawn chorus visit in early May should still yield around 50 species.

Ashridge was formerly the county stronghold for breeding Wood Warbler and Redstart, but today both are all but extinct as breeding species, along with the fast-declining resident Hawfinch and Tree Sparrow. However, Firecrest is a recent coloniser and sometimes breeds in the coniferous plantations. Jay and Jackdaw are both abundant; the Jackdaw competing with Stock Dove and Tawny Owl for nest holes. Daylight sightings of the owl are rare but the Beech hanger can be a good spot to see them, perched close to the bole of a tree. An evening visit to any of the open commons in June should yield a 'roding' Woodcock. Hobby hunt the downland pastures for flying beetles and a few pairs of Turtle Dove breed in the scrub alongside the warblers and finches.

Autumn migration is usually evident on the downs with Steps Hill receiving a steady flow of warblers, hirundines and the occasional Redstart, Whinchat and Ring Ouzel. Meadow Pipit, finches and Skylark are on the move now as winter thrushes filter through with large numbers of Blackbird and Song Thrush. Migrating Goldcrest ceaselessly feed amongst the scrub with sometimes a Firecrest within their ranks. Increased birder activity at the downland sites has led to a number of local rarities being discovered, e.g. Dartford Warbler, Raven, Osprey and Richard's Pipit; while Pitstone Hill became locally famous for the unprecedented passage of Honey Buzzards in the autumn of 2000.

Calendar

Resident: Sparrowhawk, Kestrel, Common Buzzard, Red-legged and Grey Partridges, Woodcock (increase in winter), Stock Dove, Tawny Owl, Green, Great and Lesser Spotted Woodpeckers, Skylark, Mistle Thrush, Goldcrest, Marsh Tit, Nuthatch, Treecreeper, Jay, Jackdaw, finches on downs, Yellowhammer, Corn Bunting (declining).

December–February: Resident passerines, tit flocks, winter thrushes, Brambling (occasionally).

March–May: Lapwing, Turtle Dove, Cuckoo, hirundines, Meadow and Tree Pipits, Wheatear, Ring Ouzel, Whinchat, Redstart and Wood Warbler (rare), Blackcap, Sylvia warblers, Grasshopper Warbler (rare), Willow Warbler, Chiffchaff, Spotted Flycatcher (scarce).

June–July: Breeding passerines, Hobby on downs, chance of Firecrest.

August–November: Passage on downs, warblers, chats, Redstart, thrushes, Ring Ouzel, hirundines, Skylark, pipits, finches and buntings.

57 BROXBOURNE WOODS **OS ref. TL 340 080**

Habitat

Broxbourne Woods is a collective name for a number of woods that form the largest block of mixed woodland in the county, stretching approximately 5 miles (8 km) from Box Wood in the north (just off the map), to Derry's Wood in the south.

Wormley Wood and Hoddesdonpark Wood, both now in the safe hands of the Woodland Trust, are the most interesting, consisting mainly of Oak and Hornbeam; the former representing a classic piece of ancient woodland. Broxbourne, Cowheath and Highfield Woods are mainly blanketed with alien conifers but manage to support a few specialised species, particularly where the plantations are in their early stages of growth. Here the light encourages bramble and nettle patches to spring up allowing ideal conditions for scrub warblers to temporarily colonise during the summer. Streams dissect the entire complex making for interesting herbaceous growth and drinking sites even in the hottest summers.

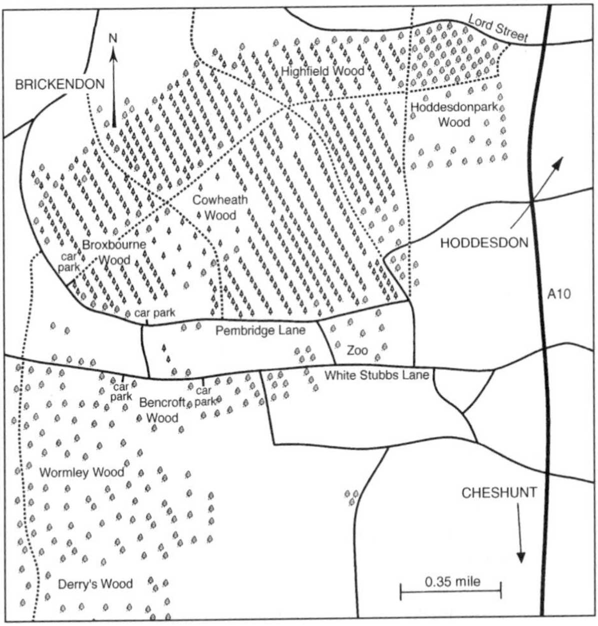

Hawfinch

Access

Situated west of Hoddesdon and south of Hertford, two lanes, Pembridge and White Stubbs, cross the centre of the woodland complex, east to west. Two small car parks are located north of Pembridge Lane at Broxbourne Wood and two south off White Stubbs Lane at Bencroft Wood. Marked tracks lead into the woods giving access north and south. The Woodland Trust area at Wormley can be reached from the Bencroft Wood west car park while Hoddesdonpark Wood can be visited by careful and considerate parking along Lord Street. Alternatively, park at either of the Broxbourne car parks and hike north and east until clear of the firs, entering Hoddesdonpark Wood from the west.

The Salisbury Estate owns the majority of the plantations around the centre of the complex and here birdwatchers should be particularly careful to keep strictly to the waymarked tracks. The pub at Brickendon is ideal for refreshments following a long morning's dawn chorus watch or prior to an evening conifer visit in the summer for crepuscular specialists.

Species

Winter is a fairly dull season with the usual roving tit and Goldcrest flocks, visiting parties of Redpoll and Siskin and an influx of wintering Woodcock. Tawny Owl are resident and become increasingly more vocal towards the winter's end, especially in the deciduous woodland. Small numbers of Hawfinch are still resident across the complex but are never easy to find. Declining in numbers, winter is the best time to seek them out, as they feed amongst the leaf-litter on the seeds of Hornbeam, Lime and Wild Cherry. Listen out for their distinctive 'tpik' contact call.

In early spring Wormley Wood reverberates to the sound of numerous Great Spotted Woodpeckers drumming and Green 'laughing'. The tiny Lesser Spotted is also present but is much harder to find within the canopy. Nuthatch, Treecreeper and all six common species of tit breed in varying degrees of abundance with Willow Tit the scarcest. Large hole-nesting species, such as Jackdaw and Stock Dove, breed amongst the Oak on the Woodland Trust holdings.

Warblers arrive throughout April with Chiffchaff, Blackcap and Willow Warbler first, closely followed by Whitethroat, Garden Warbler and Lesser Whitethroat. Wood Warbler and Redstart are all but extinct and the best one could hope for is a stray bird singing on passage. The plantations formerly attracted Grasshopper Warbler and Nightingale and are worth checking in the early stages of growth after tree felling for the occasional Tree Pipit too. Reed Bunting and Yellowhammer may also briefly colonise these plantations when young, and seem totally out of place surrounded by dense woodland. Watch out for Cuckoo and Turtle Dove flying between stands and, in early spring, soaring Sparrowhawk and Common Buzzard. The last migrant to arrive, the Spotted Flycatcher, is present from mid-May onwards and occurs in limited numbers amongst mature timber.

Formerly, an evening visit in summer for Nightjar would have paid dividends; sadly today it no longer breeds regularly in Hertfordshire; however, 'roding' Woodcock are almost guaranteed displaying above the woodland canopy and Long-eared Owl may breed again in the future.

Although some of the edge-of-range summer migrants, such as Wood Warbler and Redstart, are no longer present, around 50 species should be noted during a spring dawn chorus visit, particularly at Wormley Wood. Site rarities include Waxwing and Arctic Redpoll.

Calendar

Resident: Sparrowhawk, Kestrel, Common Buzzard, Woodcock, Stock Dove, Tawny Owl, three species of woodpecker, Mistle Thrush, Goldcrest, six species of tits, Nuthatch, Treecreeper, Jay, Jackdaw, Hawfinch, Redpoll.

December–February: Passerine flocks, Siskin and Redpoll, Hawfinch easier to find.

March–May: Woodpeckers drumming, Cuckoo, Turtle Dove (scarce), warblers.

June–July: Woodcock 'roding'. Spotted Flycatcher, breeding activity at its peak.

August–November: Quiet period with moulting taking place, roosting pigeons, thrushes and corvids, Crossbill in invasion years, roving passerine flocks.

58 COLNE VALLEY PITS – LOWER

The Hertfordshire section of the Colne Valley under discussion here consists of the watercourse from West Hyde to Rickmansworth, including Springwell Lake which, although in Middlesex, forms an integral part of the valley. In past years extensive gravel excavation has taken place leaving behind a chain of flooded pits, the majority of which are used for recreational purposes, such as fishing and water sports. As the pits are worked out banks become vegetated with willows, Alder and a typical lush summer undergrowth of water-loving plants. Most pits have fairly overgrown islands that are ideal for breeding wildfowl but less so

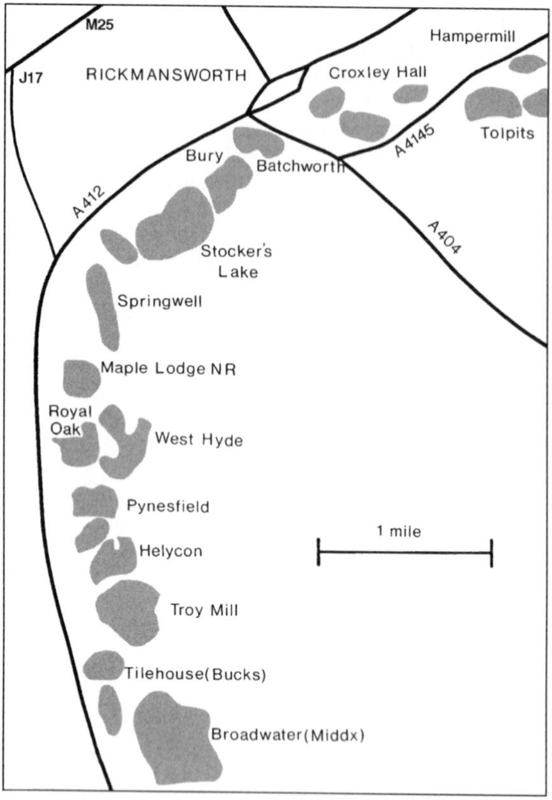

for passage waders, a feature that is sadly lacking in the valley. Flowing water is provided by the River Colne with numerous small creeks and springs. The adjacent Grand Union Canal is also of interest, having an accessible towpath. Damp meadows are in short supply, the best being at Stocker's Farm and Batchworth.

An interesting feature of the Lower Colne Valley in years past for the birdwatcher was its watercress beds. Now mainly infilled or derelict these bird-rich habitats are still worth seeking out for the occasional wintering Water Pipit. Relict cress beds survive at West Hyde but the best accessible examples are at Cassiobury Park on the River Gade (see Additional Sites) or along the adjoining Chess Valley at Croxley Hall (very private, best avoided). Reed swamp and marsh can be found on the old sewage farm site at Maple Cross with other patches scattered along the valley. The open fields west of the A412 at West Hyde and Maple Cross are worth checking in the winter for geese, Golden Plover, Lapwing and gulls, with the occasional raptor passing through; in May 1992 a party of eight Cattle Egrets briefly visited fields at Woodoaks Farm, Maple Cross and several other sites along the valley.

With this variety of habitats, it is not surprising that the area around Maple Cross proved to be the richest for breeding birds during the first Atlas recording period in Hertfordshire. Encouragingly the main site, at Maple Lodge, is now an established nature reserve, as is Stocker's Lake.

The scope of this book does not allow us to look at all of the Colne Valley sites. So, we shall select two only here, Maple Lodge Nature Reserve and Stocker's Lake, for further investigation with Batchworth and West Hyde Gravel Pits briefly described at the end of this section.

MAPLE LODGE NATURE RESERVE
(OS ref. TQ 036 925)

Habitat

Owned by Thames Water, Maple Lodge Nature Reserve comprises an area of 16 ha (40 acres) of prime wetland habitat. The Maple Lodge Conservation Society was formed in 1982 and manages the site on a day-to-day basis under a licence granted by Thames Water.

The reserve is a relic of the sewage farm days when sludge was disposed of into an old gravel pit, forming the main lake and some very unstable boggy areas. As pumping ceased, the shallow lake was in danger of drying out and becoming overgrown. However, manipulation of the water level and coppicing of willows have combined to create optimum feeding conditions for wading birds and wildfowl alike. Stony islands still survive and are kept clear of vegetation to entice passage waders to pause on their migration. Scattered timber grows on the larger island and around the periphery of the lake with an adjacent plantation of mainly native hardwoods. The west and north sides are bordered by mature willows and poplars respectively. Tangles of encroaching sallows grow vigorously around the western side and need to be constantly managed by the Society. An old, predominantly Hawthorn, hedgerow, known as Long Hedge, skirts the lake to the south and includes a particularly fine patch of Spindle, discernible in autumn by its unusual pink fruit. A small reedbed, a stream and marshes combine to make this a near perfect wetland site.

The smaller tree-fringed lake to the north is of minimal interest but, being deeper, attracts Great Crested Grebe, Cormorant and Grey Heron. Other areas that can be viewed from the footpaths whilst on site are the fields and lake at Lynsters Farm.

A number of hides and seats are strategically positioned around the lake and a feeding station is maintained in the winter outside the clubhouse information centre, attracting flocks of passerines. A hide has been constructed with facilities for the disabled and similarly wheelchair viewing is on offer from the hide in the information centre. Every conceivable type of nest box has been tried and tested over the years and many are visible from the nature trail.

An abundance of invertebrate fauna proliferates with many types of aquatic insects, moths and butterflies. Over 170 different species of wildflowers have been identified on the reserve and the Buddleia bank attracts large numbers of butterflies. Also present are 20 species of tree and what must be the largest and most hostile Stinging Nettle beds anywhere. At dusk, mammals as diverse as Fox and bats may be seen.

Access

Maple Lodge is to the east of the village of Maple Cross and can be reached along the A412 Rickmansworth to Denham road or from junction 17 of the M25. If approached from the motorway turn left at the traffic lights opposite The Cross public house. Drive down Maple Lodge

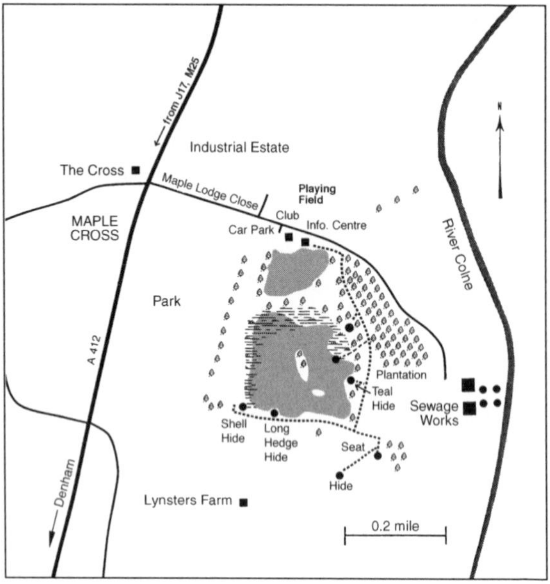

Close, parking at the bottom of the road near the clubhouse and the reserve entrance. By public transport there is a regular bus service from Watford, and Rickmansworth underground station.

Access onto the site is restricted to members of The Maple Lodge Conservation Society but visits by non-members and groups can be arranged by contacting the society in advance. For details of joining the Society or visiting the reserve contact Gwyneth Bellis, Chairman of the conservation society on 01923 230277 or Thames Water (see Useful Addresses).

Entrance to the reserve is via coded locks; code numbers are issued to new members following a guided tour given by a committee member. Toilet and washing facilities are available in the information centre. A footpath takes in all the hides and seats, although the western side of the lake is out of bounds in an effort to reduce disturbance. Please keep to the footpaths as parts of the reserve are treacherously boggy. When returning to the information centre do not forget to fill in the logbook of latest sightings.

Species

A good cross-section of wildfowl can be seen throughout the year with Mallard, Pochard, Gadwall, Shoveler, Teal and Tufted Duck present most months. Numbers increase in late autumn and winter when the occasional Goldeneye may appear. Cormorant peak at this time on both lakes and feral Greylag and Canada Geese can be seen in surrounding fields. Grey Heron stalk the shallows and Snipe can be seen in the more overgrown patches. The recently created marshy area can be a good place for Water Rail; be on the look-out for Bittern, as this fabulous heron has been recorded here in the past. A motley selection of gulls, mainly Black-headed, feed on the surface of the lake along with good numbers of Coot and Moorhen. Check the fields near Lynsters Farm for finches, and the occasional Yellowhammer, Meadow Pipit or Skylark. The feeding site, viewed from the hide at the information centre, attracts the usual common finches such as Greenfinch and Chaffinch as well as the odd Brambling, plus Great Spotted Woodpecker, tits and thrushes. A small Siskin flock, which has reached 100 plus, Goldfinch and Redpoll can usually be found feeding on Alder cones around the reserve. In winter, many passerines take advantage of the cover to roost, the most obvious being Starling and thrushes including Redwing and Fieldfare. Buntings roost in the reedbed and Pied Wagtail form sub-roosts before finally settling for the night on the sewage works buildings. This is a good time to see a hunting Sparrowhawk taking any stragglers.

Early spring Chiffchaff may not be migrants at all as a few winter along the valley, surviving in all but the harshest conditions. Willow Warbler and the common scrub warblers soon move through the reserve in good numbers, with some individuals of each remaining to breed. Whitethroat usually haunt the brambles at the car park and along the southern footpath, while Garden Warbler and Blackcap prefer the more wooded parts of the site. Sedge and Reed Warblers both breed in small numbers, the latter arriving latest. Yellow Wagtail sometimes alight on the playing field opposite the clubhouse, as does the occasional Wheatear. Hirundines filter over the lake and Cuckoo call from the reedbeds.

The spring and autumn wader passage can produce Common, Green and occasionally Wood Sandpipers along with groups of Snipe. Redshank and Little Ringed Plover occur only intermittently. Common Tern pass noisily through Maple Lodge (several pairs breed elsewhere in the valley) and can be seen fishing over the Clubhouse lake. Resident passerines are well represented with all three species of woodpecker breeding on the reserve; the spotted woodpeckers have plenty of dead trees left aside for them to find suitable nest sites. Black-capped tits will almost certainly turn out to be Willow Tit, while Treecreeper can be heard and seen amongst the mature timber. The declining Spotted Flycatcher nests in the Ivy-covered trees and is often noted along the Long Hedge.

A typical summer scene from any of the hides overlooking the main lake is of many ducklings foraging beside their moulting parents; check thoroughly as Ruddy Duck have recently bred. A Kingfisher may appear on a perch to fish and pose for the camera and warblers continually ferry insects to their nestlings. Swifts and hirundines hawk for winged insects over the lake and a Hobby may race overhead, sending them skywards. Tawny Owl regularly nest in a box close to the reserve entrance; occasionally the adults may be glimpsed during daylight hours.

Autumn passage commences in late July with returning sandpipers, Snipe and perhaps a Greenshank or Redshank. Grey Wagtail become evident with one or two wintering and a passage of Goldcrest is noted. Flocks of Siskin, Redpoll and Goldfinch haunt the Alder canopy feeding on seeds.

Calendar

Resident: Little and Great Crested Grebes, Grey Heron, Canada and Greylag Geese, Mute Swan, Mallard, Gadwall, Shoveler, Pochard, Tufted and Ruddy Ducks, Sparrowhawk and Kestrel, Moorhen, Coot, Tawny Owl, Kingfisher, three woodpeckers, Pied Wagtail, Mistle Thrush, Willow and Long-tailed Tits, Treecreeper, Jay, corvids, common finches and buntings.

December–February: Chance of Bittern, Goldeneye, Cormorant, Teal, Lapwing, Water Rail, gulls, Stock Dove, Siskin, Goldfinch, Redpoll, Brambling (rare), roosting buntings finches and thrushes.

March–May: Sandpipers, Snipe, Little Ringed Plover and Redshank irregular, Common Tern, Cuckoo, hirundines, Yellow Wagtail and Wheatear on fields, Chiffchaff, Willow Warbler, Blackcap, Garden Warbler, Whitethroat, Sedge and Reed Warblers, Spotted Flycatcher.

June–July: Breeding riparian birds, possible Hobby, Swift.

August–November: Wader passage, warblers, duck numbers increase, winter thrushes arrive, Goldcrest, mixed tit and finch flocks.

STOCKER'S LAKE
(OS ref. TQ 048 935)

Habitat

Stocker's Lake is a large mature gravel pit with well vegetated islands, just south of Rickmansworth. The main lake consists of deep water with, in later summer, a few shallows around some of the stony islands. Willows and Alders have colonised most of the islands and along the bank on the canal side, where a small damp wood has developed. A marshy patch has evolved nearby that becomes quickly overgrown during the summer with willowherb and sedge. The causeway and meadows between Stocker's and Bury Lakes are in places rank and overgrown and in the winter become quite boggy. The River Colne is of interest, along with the scrub-invaded fields towards the A412. Although strictly speaking not a part of the reserve the wet meadow and fields near Stocker's Farm are always worthwhile checking.

At 38 ha (93 acres) Stocker's Lake has Local Nature Reserve status and is also designated a SSSI. The lake is owned by Three Valleys Water Company and managed under a lease by the Hertfordshire & Middlesex Wildlife Trust.

Access

From Rickmansworth take the A412 south-west and turn left after 1.5 km (1 mile) down Springwell Lane at Drayton Ford. At the bottom of the lane park in either of two car parks alongside Springwell Lake, but not in the access road to the reserve entrance. Alternatively, park in the Aquadrome car park, off Harefield Road, which has toilet facilities, and walk alongside Bury Lake to reach the reserve. Check the car park closing times, particularly at the Aquadrome, as cars are often locked in overnight.

Stocker's Lake is a 15-minute walk, via the Aquadrome, from Rickmansworth station on the Metropolitan line of the London Underground.

Species

Annually well over 100 species can be expected at Stocker's Lake, with some 80 recorded breeding. Along with Maple Lodge NR it is one of the best sites in the Colne Valley and has been known to turn up a number of rarities, e.g. Night Heron, Cattle Egret, Blue-winged Teal and Red-necked Phalarope.

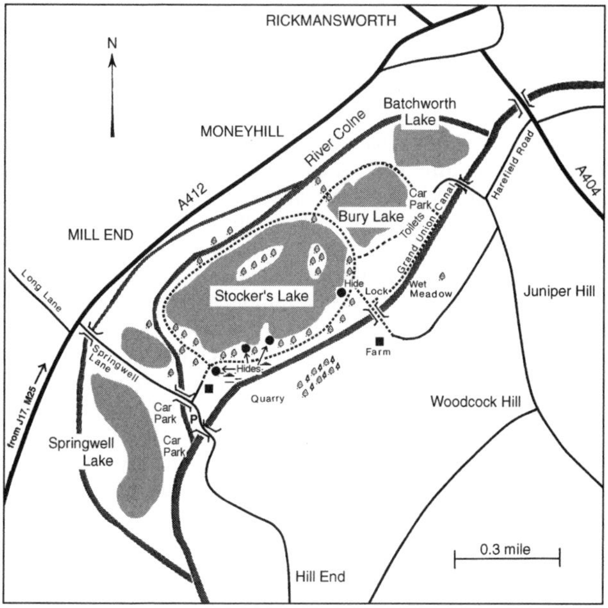

Winter is the best time of year to scour the large collection of wildfowl scattered across the open water, consisting predominantly of several hundred Coot, Pochard, Tufted Duck and Mallard; lesser numbers of Teal, Shoveler, Wigeon and Gadwall are always present. It is a particularly good site for Goldeneye and Goosander whilst most winters small parties of Smew appear. A Stocker's Lake speciality is the Red-crested Pochard with one or two usually arriving in autumn or winter. Typical local rarities at this time of year have included Shag, Ring-necked Duck, Scaup, Bittern and Bearded Tit. Good numbers of the commoner two species of grebe mingle among the ducks with several pairs of each staying to breed. Large numbers of gulls rest on the islands while Cormorant perch in the bushes drying their plumage. Grey Heron are ever-present as a large heronry with up to 50 nests has been established. The adults start nest building as early as February. The wet meadow near the farm attracts a motley array of feral Canada and Greylag Geese as well as small numbers of Teal and Snipe. Lapwing also pause here, and there is usually a flock of winter thrushes feeding on the drier parts. The small Alder wood can attract a mixed flock of wintering Siskin, Redpoll and Goldfinch, and Treecreeper are normally evident, perhaps within a tit flock. All three species of woodpecker are recorded with the scarce Lesser Spotted best looked for in early spring when 'drumming'. Check the nearby marsh for Water Rail and the paddock for finches.

The first signs of spring are heralded by Lapwing and Meadow Pipit moving overhead, with perhaps a couple of Shelduck on the open water, which in recent years have bred. They are soon joined by the true summer migrants such as Chiffchaff and Sand Martin, although several of the former sometimes winter along the valley. The sheep-grazed slopes near the farm attract a few Wheatear, as the main arrival of common warblers stream onto the reserve – Blackcap, Willow Warbler,

Whitethroat and Sedge Warbler. Wagtails feeding along the causeway, among the cattle, consist primarily of Pied and Yellow, with the occasional continental White and Blue-headed Wagtails in their midst.

A spring wader passage is not obvious, due to the lack of a suitable scrape; however, Common Sandpiper do regularly occur on the main lake, hugging the shingle islands. The wet meadow, by the lock, is the most likely spot to lure down a Little Ringed Plover or Redshank. Garganey have occurred in the past making it worthwhile scrutinising all small ducks during passage periods. A steady stream of Common Tern are noted over the lake with, most years, up to 20 pairs remaining to nest on the purpose-built tern rafts. Black Tern are only rarely noted in the Colne Valley, usually in small numbers at the end of the spring passage period and never for long.

Displaying Goldeneye linger on sometimes into May, along with a pair or two each of breeding Gadwall and Shoveler and occasionally a Pochard. The quarry wood across the canal normally harbours a pair of Sparrowhawk, while Kestrel prefer the more open quarry in which to breed. Kingfisher zip along the canal and across the lake performing their intricate breeding ritual at high speed, while Tawny Owl haunt the old Ivy-covered willows. Little Owl can sometimes be found on the buildings at Stocker's Farm and the track that leads behind the farm is worth a look for finches and sparrows. Reed and Sedge Warblers nest among the Phragmites, with the Cuckoo in close attendance, and all the common warbler species breed. Spotted Flycatcher and Turtle Dove are now in steep decline and more often noted on passage than in the breeding season.

In summer Stocker's Lake is best visited as early as possible when nesting species are most active and there are fewer people about; Bury Lake and the canal side are particularly busy later in the day. Hirundines and Swift swarm over the lake attracting the attention of hunting Hobby which breed along the valley. Look out for Grey Wagtail nesting at the lock gates or along the river race.

Early autumn brings a few more waders than spring, with the chance of small numbers of Greenshank and Green Sandpiper attracted to the stony islands. Wood Sandpiper have occurred in the past on the meadow, especially if it is damp. Whinchat are noted flicking along fence lines on open ground, their numbers made up mainly of drab immature birds. Grey Wagtail numbers increase and Goldcrest filter through the scrub with tits and finches. Meadow Pipit flocks are worthy of attention and could yield a larger dark-legged Water Pipit. Wildfowl numbers increase on the open water with the likelihood of a Pintail for a day or two and the rarer Ferruginous Duck has occurred at this time of year. Little Egret are on the increase and Stocker's Lake, with its large mature willows, has proved to be an ideal roost site.

Calendar

Resident: Great Crested Grebe, Grey Heron, Cormorant, feral geese, Mallard, Tufted Duck, Sparrowhawk, Kestrel, Moorhen, Coot, Tawny and Little Owls, Kingfisher, Green, Great and Lesser Spotted Woodpeckers, Grey Wagtail, Treecreeper, tits, finches, Reed Bunting.

December–February: Little Grebe, chance of Red-necked or Slavonian Grebes, Bittern possible, Water Rail, Wigeon, Gadwall, Teal, Shoveler, Pochard, Ruddy Duck, Goosander, Goldeneye, Smew (rare), Lapwing, Snipe, gulls, winter thrushes, Siskin, Redpoll.

Shoveler

March–May: Shelduck, Garganey possible, Little Ringed Plover, Common Sandpiper, Common Tern, Cuckoo, Turtle Dove, hirundines including Sand Martin, pipits and wagtails, Wheatear, Chiffchaff, Sylvia warblers, Sedge and Reed Warblers

June–July: Breeding birds, wildfowl and Common Tern, Swift, Hobby, Spotted Flycatcher, waders in late July.

August–November: Ducks increase with chance of Red-crested Pochard and Pintail, Greenshank, sandpipers, Yellow Wagtail, Whinchat, Goldcrest, finch and tit flocks.

BATCHWORTH
(OS ref. TQ 070 943)

An interesting wetland site at the confluence of the Rivers Colne, Chess and Gade. The rivers aside, there are several small gravel pits, the Grand Union Canal and one of the best remaining wet meadows in the valley to enjoy. Much of the complex can be viewed from the public footpath that runs atop an old railway embankment, commencing by Batchworth roundabout. For views across the eastern end of the meadow, park considerately along Tolpits Lane at TQ 078 941 at the entrance to the gravel works. The pits are private but it is worthwhile applying to the Thames Water offices for a permit, as permission is seldom refused to bona fide birdwatchers (see Useful Addresses).

Although the pits have attracted Cetti's Warbler in the past, the main focus of attention is the large cattle-grazed wet meadow that is traversed by ditches and small pools, ideal for a hunting Grey Heron. The usual range of riparian birds can be expected with the occasional Snipe and Redshank on passage. Lapwing have bred and Yellow Wagtail pause briefly while on migration. In autumn, the pastures can attract winter thrushes.

WEST HYDE GRAVEL PITS
(OS ref. TQ 036 910)

Just south of Maple Cross, to the east of the A412, lie a series of old gravel pits on the county boundary with Buckinghamshire and Middlesex. Coppermill Lane runs from the Fisherman's Tackle pub to the Fisheries

Inn on the Grand Union Canal, with pits north and south of this dividing line. The two waters to the north are both private but limited viewing can be gained from the entrance to Lynsters Farm. The more established Troy Mill Pits and Helycon Pit to the south are well served by public footpaths with access along the remnant watercress beds along the back of some of the older houses in the village.

The usual variety of riparian species can be expected with the open water attracting terns on passage. Winter brings a good sprinkling of wildfowl and regular watching throughout the year would undoubtedly yield a rarity or two. Up until the 1960s the once extensive watercress beds in this part of the valley used to regularly hold small numbers of Water Pipit amongst the numerous Meadow Pipit and Grey Wagtail; today only the latter species occurs with any regularity.

59 COLNE VALLEY PITS – UPPER TYTTENHANGER GRAVEL PITS

(OS ref. TL 195 053)

Habitat

To the south-east of St Albans, in the Upper Colne Valley, lies a series of gravel pits, some still being excavated, that have an uncertain future when wildlife conservation is considered. Three pits have already been landscaped and are administered by Bowmans Farm for intensive coarse fishing and are of limited value for birds; however, in a dry summer the lakes soon show muddy edges, attractive to passage waders. To the east of the River Colne there are several more abandoned pits and meres, which are suitable for waders and a variety of wetland species. Garden Wood, on the southern flank of the complex, although private (used for paintball games), is a mature Oak wood and harbours the usual range of woodland species.

When sand and gravel extraction is complete there are plans to turn a section of the site into a nature reserve with particular attention to a wader scrape and maintaining the large Sand Martin colony already present.

Access

The Bowmans Farm complex is due to reopen in 2002 following extensive redevelopment work. Parking will then be available at the farm shop with waymarked footpaths towards the fishing lakes and the proposed nature reserve. Vehicular access is off Coursers Road, near junction 22 of the M25. For those who fancy a pleasant 30-minute walk to the pits, park in Lowbell Lane, London Colney, opposite the Bull pub, or by the church car park, and take the public footpath north-east along the river, under the A1081 for about 0.7 km (1 mile) until a wooden bridge takes the path over the river and into the pits.

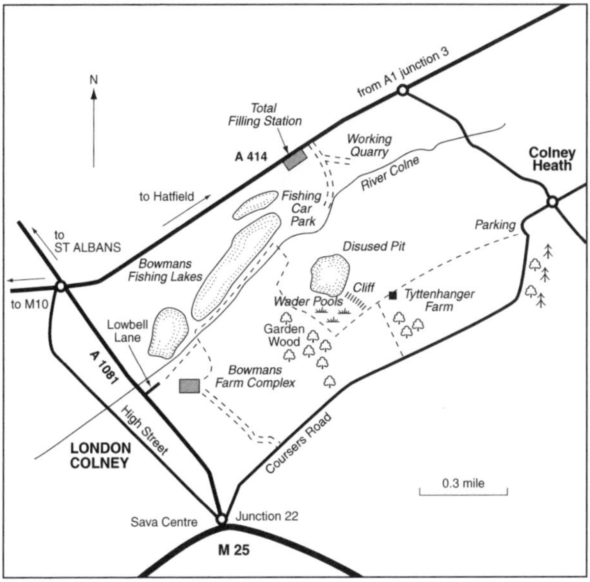

An alternative entrance point is off the A414 North Orbital, near the Total Filling Station, where a public footpath and track lead down to the lakes, alongside a lorry access road into the quarry. When the gate is closed only cars have access, due to a height restriction. There is limited parking for fishermen, but several local birders have an agreement with the water bailiff to park on site with a £5 annual permit available from the lakeside hut or the bailiff. Further details can be gleaned from the fishermen's noticeboard by the entrance.

Another access point is possible from Colney Heath (TL 198 058) where there is limited parking at present but this should improve in future. Follow the footpath, which is convenient for viewing the Sand Martin colony, towards the pits.

Species

Tyttenhanger Gravel Pits, in recent years, has been one of the best sites in Hertfordshire for waders. Little Ringed and Ringed Plovers, Redshank and Lapwing have all bred and if the site's open aspect can be maintained then Oystercatcher should be added to that list. Passage can bring Snipe, Common, Wood and Green Sandpipers, Dunlin, Ruff and Greenshank; local rarities in recent years have included Avocet, godwits, Curlew, Whimbrel, Spotted Redshank, Little Stint and Curlew Sandpiper.

The winter scene centres mainly on the open water of the fishing lakes with resident Grey Heron, Great Crested and Little Grebes joined by increasing numbers of the unpopular Cormorant. Wildfowl numbers can be high with the majority Pochard, Tufted Duck, Mallard and Coot joined by a scattering of Wigeon, Shoveler, Gadwall and Teal. Goldeneye and the sawbills are generally scarce here. Garden Wood should not be overlooked, with regular sightings of woodpeckers and Sparrowhawk, while passerine flocks should be checked for Tree Sparrow dispersed from a nearby breeding colony.

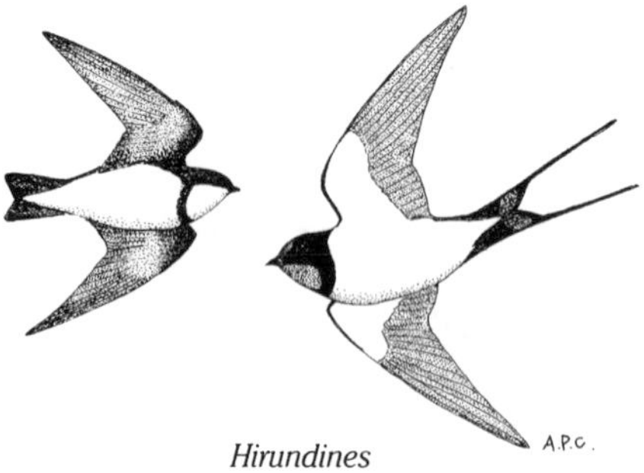

Hirundines

Spring is heralded by the early arrival of Sand Martin over the water, Wheatear on open ground and Chiffchaff in the wood. Large numbers of hirundines and Swift move through and all the common warblers breed around the site. Whinchat are noted on passage, perched on wire fencing, while Cuckoo quickly check out the availability of Reed Warbler nests in the many small reedbeds. Turtle Dove and Yellow Wagtail were both regular migrants that formerly stayed to breed, but now, typically, nest infrequently. Common Tern fish the open water and may nest if rafts are provided, while Black Tern are noted on passage in May when weather conditions are favourable, typically an easterly airflow with rain showers. Wildfowl numbers decline as spring progresses but Shelduck are regular and have bred, while Pochard and Teal have both summered.

Summertime is abuzz with breeding activity, centred on the Sand Martin colony, while Sedge and Reed Warblers are busily raising young around the pit margins. Grey Wagtail and Kingfisher can be seen along the river and Goldfinch are common. Hobby regularly patrol the site feeding on large flying insects and martins, and Sparrowhawk find easy pickings amongst the many juvenile finches and tits. Returning waders can be noted from mid-June with Lapwing and Green Sandpiper in the vanguard, followed by Common Sandpiper into August, when just about anything can occur if the water levels are low.

Into September wildfowl numbers increase on the fishing lakes, as thousands of hirundines move through. Stints and other rare waders tend to turn up now, and Snipe numbers build up into October. Scrub warblers are abundant as they prepare for the long haul south, and the site is alive with juvenile resident species. October is noted for an overhead passage of Skylark, pipits, wagtails, thrushes and finches. Tit flocks are soon joined by Goldcrest while Garden Wood is well used by roosting corvids and pigeons.

Tyttenhanger Gravel Pits has a good track record for rarities, e.g. Short-toed Lark, Red-backed Shrike and Lesser Scaup, but its main qualities are the wide cross-section of species on offer. If the planned reserve becomes a reality it has the potential to be one of the region's top wetland sites.

Calendar

Resident: Little and Great Crested Grebes, Grey Heron, common wildfowl, Green Sandpiper (rare in June), Sparrowhawk, Kestrel, Red-legged Partridge, Stock Dove, Tawny and Little Owls, Kingfisher, Green and Great Spotted Woodpeckers, Grey Wagtail, Mistle Thrush, winter thrushes, Stonechat, Tree Sparrow, common tits, finches and buntings.

December–February: Cormorant, Bittern and Merlin (rare), common diving duck, Ruddy Duck, Wigeon, Teal, Gadwall, Shoveler, occasional Goldeneye and sawbills, Lapwing, Snipe, Jack Snipe (rare), Meadow Pipit.

March–May: Shelduck, Hobby, wader passage – Redshank, Oystercatcher, ringed plovers, sandpipers, Dunlin, Ruff, Common and Black Terns, Turtle Dove, Cuckoo, Swift, hirundines, Wheatear, Whinchat, common warblers.

June–July: Peak breeding activity, Sand Martin colony, Hobby.

August–November: Outgoing warbler passage, Whinchat, Stonechat, larks, wagtails, pipit and finch passage, Goldcrest.

ADDITIONAL SITES

Broad Colney Lakes (OS ref. TL 177 033)

A series of small flooded gravel pits with peripheral damp woodland near London Colney. The HMWT manages a 5-ha (13-acre) reserve with an adjoining car park beside the British Legion club in Shenley Lane. There is much disturbance from the public and the water is heavily fished but a screen hide affords good views over a wooded marsh. There are small numbers of wildfowl in all seasons with an increase in the winter with Goosander preferring this site to nearby Tyttenhanger. The wood supports Willow Tit, Treecreeper and breeding warblers.

Park Street Pits (OS ref. TL 165 025)

Limited views can be obtained across a landscaped tip, a fishing lake and an active quarry. The large open field with vent stacks can be good for Lapwing, Skylark, pipits, wagtails and finches while the mature lake attracts common wildfowl and breeding warblers during the summer. Take Old Parkbury Lane, off the A5183, at Colney Street and park on the industrial estate by the private road to Springfield Farm. Follow the road, on foot, over the railway line and down towards the pits, where the field when wet can attract passage waders, including once a Black-winged Stilt.

Another series of pits in this complex worthy of attention is at Frogmore in the Ver Valley. Park in Hyde Lane, off the A5183, at TL 151 031. Public footpaths lead down to the river and through a small woodland. The usual wetland species occur, including Grey Wagtail and Kingfisher, plus breeding warblers.

Follow the Ver–Colne walk south to Moor Mill and Waterside crossing Bricket Wood road. The rough fields north of the M25 can hold Short-eared Owl in winter, while the willow carr alongside the river is favourite for roosting thrushes and corvids.

Vale of St Albans

An area of low-lying arable land, susceptible to flooding during the winter, between Shenleybury (TL 180 025) and Colney Heath (TL 205 057). Easy access off junction 22 of the M25. Check the fields from lay-bys either side of the roundabout at the junction of the B556 and B5378, near the M25. During the winter it is a reliable site for winter thrushes, Golden Plover, Lapwing and gulls.

Another good area is the fields south of Coursers Farm (TL 204 047) where a public footpath leads south towards the M25 at Redwell Wood (TL 212 025). In winter the stubble fields attract Skylark, finches, buntings and pipits, corvids and pigeons. Brambling are often noted in game cover and a nearby Tree Sparrow colony on a private site adds interest; check all sparrow flocks for this declining species. The nearby woods are worth scanning for Common Buzzard.

Ver–Colne Valley Walk

An 18-km (11-mile) long footpath between St Albans and Watford along the Ver and Colne river valleys. Special waymarked arrows take the walker through some pleasant countryside that is good for common birds. A fair cross-section of wetland species can be expected, especially during spring when the warblers arrive. A few Snipe and Lapwing are noted in winter. Although not part of the official walk, the watercourse north-west of St Albans, between Redbourn and where the river meets the A5183 (old A5), is of interest. A public footpath follows the north bank of the Ver. The area around Pre Mill is good for Water Rail and Grey Wagtail in winter and wetland warblers in summer. The fields to the west of the A5183 can hold large wintering flocks of Lapwing and Golden Plover.

Watford Link Pits (TQ 118 972)

A series of new flood lagoons along the River Colne accessed off Radlett Road or Bushey Mill Lane, Watford. Breeding Reed and Sedge Warblers, Reed Bunting, Kingfisher and common wildfowl. Occasional records of Black-necked Grebe.

Lairage Local Nature Reserve (TQ 102 952)

Also associated with the River Colne, this newly created reserve in the centre of Watford has the usual range of common wetland species including Little Grebe and Kingfisher. Good public access off Vicarage Road, Watford past the hospital and football ground.

60 HILFIELD PARK RESERVOIR

OS ref. TQ 155 960

Habitat

The whole site encompasses 79 ha (195 acres) of which 46 ha (115 acres) is open water. The reservoir, completed in 1955, has only one artificial bank on the western side, while the three remaining margins are well vegetated during the summer with a variety of marshland plants, including some small, but important, reedbeds. A mixture of deciduous and coniferous trees covers much of the adjacent land, along with areas of long grass.

Although owned by Three Valleys Water Services, an agreement was established with the Hertfordshire County Council for the creation of a

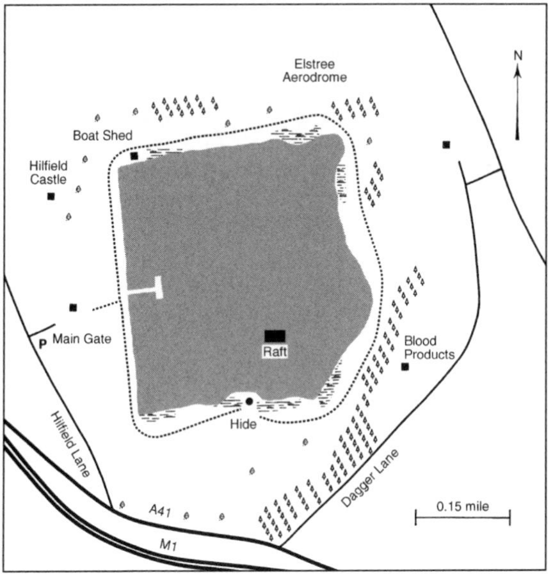

Local Nature Reserve. The Wildlife Trust performs the necessary management and has erected a hide on the southern bank and tern rafts on the water.

The rank growth along the natural margins is ideal for aquatic insects, particularly dragonflies with 14 species recorded, while 20 species of butterflies abound in the long grass and scrub.

Access

Hilfield Park Reservoir is situated just to the east of Watford, north of the A41 Watford by-pass and only 3 km (2 miles) from junction 5 of the M1 motorway. Limited viewing can be obtained from the A41, Dagger Lane to the east and a footpath running alongside nearby Elstree Aerodrome. Access into the site is by permit through the Wildlife Trust headquarters at St Albans and keys are needed for entry via the main gate (see Useful Addresses for details).

Once in, walk up the concrete steps and scan along the sloping bank for resting wildfowl, waders and wagtails. Keep checking the water for diving duck whilst heading for the hide. A full circuit should only take a couple of hours, eventually leading back to the pumping station.

The unique aspect of Hilfield Park Reservoir is that water sports and fishing are not permitted. Therefore, birders have the place pretty much to themselves, conjuring up a feeling of isolation despite the traffic noise from the nearby motorway.

Species

The reservoir was created a Local Nature Reserve because of its value as a wildfowl refuge in late autumn and winter. As it is a deep water, diving ducks predominate with Tufted Duck and Pochard the most numerous, usually peaking at around 200 each during late summer. Small numbers of Goldeneye are present and the most likely sawbill is the

Ruddy Duck

Goosander with one or two noted most winters. On the nearby London Reservoirs, Smew are a regular winter visitor but here only one or two are recorded annually. Coot can number up to 300 birds with about 20 pairs staying to breed amongst the marginal vegetation. Dabbling ducks peak in late autumn with Shoveler and Teal scattered along the shallow margins near the hide, where Water Rail are regularly noted in the winter months. Mallard and Gadwall average around 50 each, with the latter species recently breeding for the first time.

Great Crested and Little Grebe numbers peak at around 50 and 30 respectively in autumn. The most regular of the rare grebes in recent winters has been the Red-necked, with infrequent visits from Slavonian Grebe. Black-necked Grebe are more likely during spring and autumn passage; however, in 1990 a pair bred, constituting the first county breeding record since 1928 at Tring Reservoirs, and this beautiful grebe has continued to summer ever since.

One of the phenomenons of recent years has been the large numbers of wintering Ruddy Duck. Counts of over 200 make Hilfield one of the most important waters in the region for this curious, and currently controversial, species of North American duck; irregular breeding has also occurred since 1986.

A large gull roost features predominantly Black-headed, Common and Lesser Black-backed Gulls with regular sightings of Mediterranean Gull and the occasional Kittiwake. White-winged gulls should be checked for, and from late summer onwards Yellow-legged Gulls are now regularly recorded.

As spring approaches, duck numbers quickly decline although parties of Shelduck may be noted moving through. Attention is drawn to passage migrants from warmer climes, the concrete bank being the most likely spot to see the few waders that briefly stop off. Common Sandpiper are the commonest with up to ten on occasions 'teetering' at the water's edge. Little Ringed Plover arrive, some non-breeders remaining through the summer, and small numbers of Redshank and Dunlin appear. A few Wheatear show along the bank, and on the short turf parties of Meadow Pipit. Yellow and Pied Wagtails are regular in spring with a couple of pairs of the latter breeding among the buildings; an odd White Wagtail is sometimes found in the flock.

During April, especially following strong winds, the occasional Little Gull or Kittiwake may briefly appear. A more regular passage of Common Tern commences with flocks of c.20 sometimes noted during May and the autumn; a few pairs now remain to nest on the rafts. Arctic Tern arrive, a few at a time, and occasionally in flocks of over 20, but tend to be scarcer on the return passage. Black Tern are sporadic, but annual visitors, in small numbers, usually in May and September.

Hirundines filter over the reservoir, building up to several hundred by the summer; with several records of the rare Red-rumped Swallow, a close check of all swallows is recommended. Large numbers of Swift wheel and tumble noisily over the water feeding on flying insects.

The plantations contain the usual breeding tits, including Coal Tit, a few Goldcrest and the predatory Jay. Willow Warbler, Chiffchaff, Blackcap, Garden Warbler and Whitethroat all breed and the reedbeds harbour nesting Reed and Sedge Warblers, plus Moorhen and grebes. Kestrel, Hobby and Sparrowhawk are regular hunters with a pair of the former breeding nearby. Woodpeckers are scarce with Green the most likely, and Stock Dove breed on nearby Hilfield Castle. Little Owl are regularly noted and breed locally.

As summer wears on, a return wader passage is only of note if the water level has receded following a period of drought. A few Greenshank should be fairly obvious, delicately probing the exposed shingle, along with several Green Sandpiper, Snipe and the occasional Ruff. Terns move through and duck numbers build up to complete the year's comings and goings; post-breeding flocks of Pochard and Tufted Duck have attained national importance over past years. Kingfisher are more likely to be seen in late summer during their post-breeding dispersal.

For further details on this site, reference to the following paper is highly recommended: The Birds of Hilfield Park Reservoir, GS Elton, London Bird Report, No. 57. The Wildlife Trust also produces an annual Bird Report.

Calendar

Resident: Great Crested and Little Grebes, Cormorant, Grey Heron, Mute Swan, Mallard, Gadwall, Tufted Duck, Pochard, Sparrowhawk, Kestrel, Coot, Stock Dove, Green and Great Spotted Woodpeckers, Little Owl, Kingfisher, Coal Tit, Treecreeper, Jay, Pied and Grey Wagtails, Mistle Thrush, Goldcrest, finches, Reed Bunting.

December–February: Grebes, Cormorant increase, Wigeon, Ruddy Duck, Goldeneye, Goosander and Smew scarce, Water Rail, Lapwing, gull roost including Mediterranean Gull, chance of Kittiwake, winter thrushes, Siskin.

March–May: Shelduck, Little Ringed Plover, Dunlin, Common Sandpiper, Little Gull, Common, Arctic and Black Terns, Hobby, Cuckoo, Swift, hirundines, Yellow Wagtail, Wheatear, Meadow Pipit, Chiffchaff, Blackcap, Willow Warbler, Sedge and Reed Warblers, Whitethroat, Garden Warbler.

June–July: Breeding passerines and wildfowl, Black-necked Grebe, Hobby, Swift and hirundine flocks, Green Sandpiper end of July.

August–November: Waders if water level low, tern passage, ducks and grebes increase, chance of Rock Pipit and Whinchat.

61 LEMSFORD SPRINGS

OS ref. TL 223 123

Habitat

Lemsford Springs Nature Reserve was purchased in 1970 by the Wildlife Trust as a former commercial watercress bed covering 3.7 ha (9.27 acres). It is perhaps a microscopic site in size but high in the quality of fauna and flora it supports and a supreme example of how correct management can yield rich rewards for both wildlife and naturalist alike.

The River Lea runs south-east, bisecting a series of lagoons and marshes where once watercress was cultivated. The lagoons are fed by natural springs bubbling out of the chalk supporting some 50 species of molluscs in the unpolluted waters. A rich flora proliferates in the marsh, sustaining such local rarities as the Star-of-Bethlehem. Trees include pollarded willows bordering the Lea, a small coppice wood and peripheral hedgerows; one of which contains 17 species of trees. Patches of grassland and scrub complete the diversity of habitats.

The combination of water and wood encourages many insects including the rare Butterbur Moth. Mammals regularly noted are Water Vole, Water Shrew and Stoat with the occasional Fox passing through.

Access

The Springs are situated west of Welwyn Garden City near northbound access (junction 5) of the A1(M) just off the roundabout leading to Lemsford Village, where residential street parking is available. The nearest train station is in Welwyn Garden City which is a 30-minute walk to the reserve. The Springs are accessible to everyone, but a key is required, obtainable from the honorary warden who lives nearby, next to the reserve entrance. Contact: Barry Trevis, 11 Lemsford Village, Welwyn Garden City, Hertfordshire, AL8 7TN (telephone 01707 335517), or the Wildlife Trust headquarters (see Useful Addresses).

Once inside, follow the track south, past the toilet and huts, to the hides for views across the main lagoon. Alternatively, cross over Meadow Bridge to explore the marsh and Willow Wood. Most birds are best viewed from the hides (this causes less disturbance too), some approaching close enough to allow photography.

Species

Lemsford Springs has historically played host to a concentration of wintering Green Sandpiper and since 1982 has been the subject of a special study. Nearly 100 sandpipers have been colour-ringed and anyone seeing one of these birds is requested to fill in a form located in the hide. Sadly, in recent years numbers have declined in the county, and at Lemsford, but a few birds are present during the colder winter months. Excellent views are obtainable from the hide as they feed completely at ease only a few metres away. Water Rail can also be seen from the hide, occasionally out in the open but retiring into thick cover when alarmed; two or three are on site most winters. The muddy edges can attract groups of Snipe with perhaps a Jack Snipe and sometimes a Woodcock amongst them. The latter two species are extremely elusive birds when on the ground but here the opportunity exists for a detailed study of their cryptic plumage and secretive habits. A few Lapwing may probe

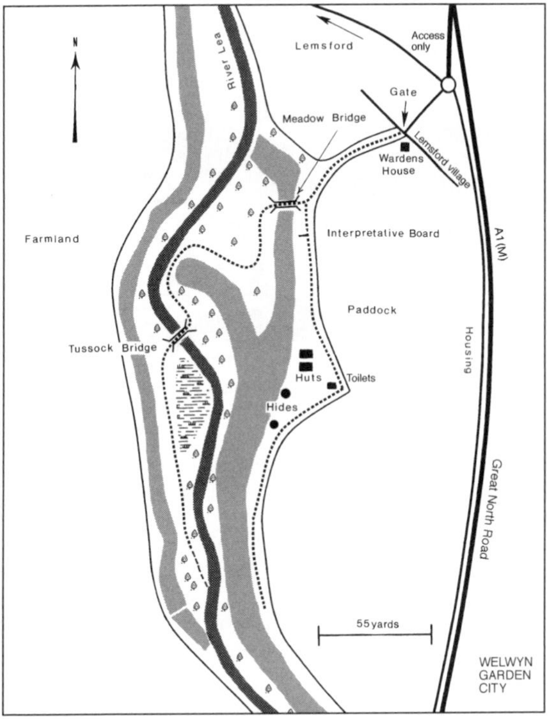

the alluvial silt alongside a solitary Grey Heron with a scattering of Teal and Mallard dabbling in the shallows, and Sparrowhawk are regularly seen from the hides flying low over the lagoons. The sharp piercing call of the Grey Wagtail is regularly heard, mixed in with the flatter note of Pied Wagtail. The former breeds regularly and is present throughout the year.

Breeding residents include a pair of Kingfisher which have a strategically-placed perch just outside the hide to entice them within camera range. Small numbers of Mallard and Moorhen are typical riparian breeders seen daily in all seasons, and occasionally a Mandarin plus ducklings appear on site. The scattered timber attracts Willow and Long-tailed Tits, within sporadic roving flocks, while Siskin and other small finches can be seen on the Alders beyond Meadow Bridge during the colder months. Woodpeckers sometimes stray from nearby Brocket Park, Great Spotted and Green being the most likely. A pair of Kestrel have taken up residence in a purpose-built nest box opposite the hide. Other parkland strays noted regularly are Jay and Treecreeper.

Hirundines are the most obvious spring migrants, passing low over the marsh to feed on flying insects. Most of the common warblers are recorded on passage with a few pairs of Whitethroat, Sedge Warbler, Garden Warbler and Blackcap breeding. Night Heron is the only national rarity to have appeared but perhaps more interesting are several occurrences of the European race of Dipper. Even stranger was the attempted breeding of a Pied Flycatcher, when an infertile clutch was laid in a nest box in 1988.

Green Sandpiper

Lemsford Springs is a fascinating little site, as most former cress beds usually are, and well worth a visit in winter for riparian specialities with the added bonus of being ideal for photography. It may be worth remembering when planning a visit to this site that there is a far greater chance of seeing numbers of birds during a prolonged freeze-up, particularly waders, as the lagoons are fed from artesian bores and therefore never ice over completely; Redshank and Dunlin have occurred in severe weather. Incredibly, due to regular coverage, the Springs boasts a site list of 122 species.

Calendar

Resident: Grey Heron, Mallard, Moorhen, Kestrel, Sparrowhawk, Kingfisher, woodpeckers, Pied and Grey Wagtails, Goldcrest, Willow Tit (irregular), Long-tailed Tit, Pied Wagtail, Reed Bunting (irregular).

December–February: Teal, Water Rail, Lapwing, Snipe, Jack Snipe, Green Sandpiper, Siskin, Redpoll, Goldfinch.

March–May: Chiffchaff, Blackcap, Whitethroat, Sedge, Willow and Garden Warblers, hirundines, occasional Common Sandpiper.

June–July: Riparian breeders.

August–November: Tit and finch flocks, Water Rail from September onwards, Snipe and Green Sandpiper late November.

62 LEE VALLEY GRAVEL PITS

Stretching from Ware in the north to Tottenham in the south, the Lee Valley Gravel Pits straddle the Hertfordshire and Essex county boundaries, before finishing in the London metropolitan area. The lower Lee Valley, south of the M25 is not included in this account as it lies completely outside the county. The main Hertfordshire sites are given full coverage with passing references to adjacent good sites in Essex, north of the M25, including Fishers Green, now made famous by its regularly wintering Bitterns. The valley is a popular birding area as the annual Winter Bird Race of 2001 proved with over a thousand participants.

The gravel deposits of the valley, which were left behind by retreating ice at the end of the last Ice Age, have been extensively exploited, drastically changing the landscape from one of predominantly wet meadows and marshes to many irregular-shaped lakes and large reservoirs nearer London. Small marshes and meadows do still exist, such as

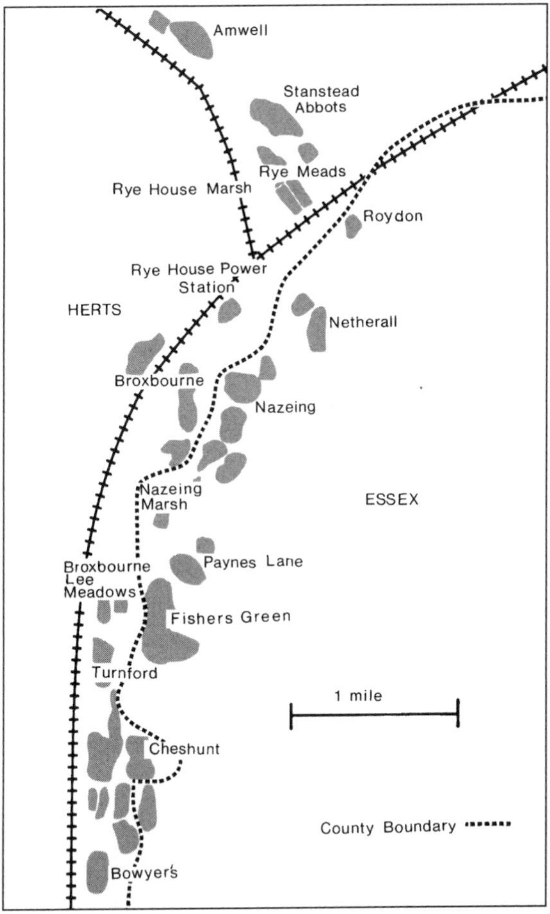

the RSPB reserve at Rye House and the meadows at Rye Meads, but are few and far between. The more barren pits still being worked (mainly in Essex around Nazeing) lure down some passage waders, especially if a low spit or island is retained, but most simply pass overhead. The new wader area, with associated hide opened in 1999, at Cornmill Meadows should go some way to redress the balance. Some workings have even been returned to arable farmland where they attract birds such as gulls, Canada Goose and Lapwing in the winter. In a recent survey it was estimated that the mosaic of wetlands in the Lee Valley attracts over 10,000 wintering waterbirds.

Woodland is scarce although the more established pits do have patches of mature trees, typically willows and Alder, encouraging typical water-tolerant passerines. Peripheral scrub growth bordering the lakes harbours breeding warblers and, in winter, finches and buntings feed on weed seeds. The lagoons at Rye Meads Sewage Works are good for wintering duck and passage migrants and are extensively studied by a ringing group. The development of Amwell Pit for wildlife is particularly exciting as it is attractive to waders, with an adjacent wood combining to afford a variety of habitats in a small area. The Cetti's Warbler is attempting a comeback from its virtual extermination during several hard winters in the 1980s and occurs irregularly along the Lee Valley. Finally, the River Lee itself is of interest along with its Navigation, flood channels and streams giving rise to luxuriant plant growth and banks suitable for riparian breeding birds.

The Lee Valley Project Group was formed by local naturalists concerned with nature conservation in the Lee Valley who considered that the wildlife should be recorded as an entity. It was envisaged that the recording would form a useful means to monitor the status of wildlife within the valley and the changes effected by development. This would allow the group to advise local authorities, including the park authority, on proposed developments likely to affect local wildlife. A report, Birds in the Lee Valley, is produced annually and is available at the RSPB Rye House Marsh Reserve. A number of highly informative leaflets and booklets are available from the Lee Valley Park Authority who administer a number of the pits and walks in the valley, not only for general recreational purposes but also specifically for wildlife. For further information on any aspect of the Lee Valley Park, contact the Lee Valley Park Information Centre, Abbey Gardens, Waltham Abbey, Essex, EN9 1XQ (telephone 01992 702200).

As we found earlier with the Colne Valley sites – with which there is much in common – the River Lee sites are too numerous to detail completely. So, we choose for further investigation Cheshunt Gravel Pits, Amwell Gravel Pit and Kingsmead, the Rye Meads area, with supporting notes on Fishers Green, which although partly in Essex, form an integral part of the upper Lee Valley, north of the M25.

CHESHUNT GRAVEL PITS & HALL MARSH SCRAPE

(OS ref. TL 370 030)

Habitat

Cheshunt Gravel Pits consist principally of five areas of water known as Hook's Marsh Lake, Bowyer's Water, (North Met Pit and Fishers Green, discussed as additional sites) and Police Pit, with the River Lee

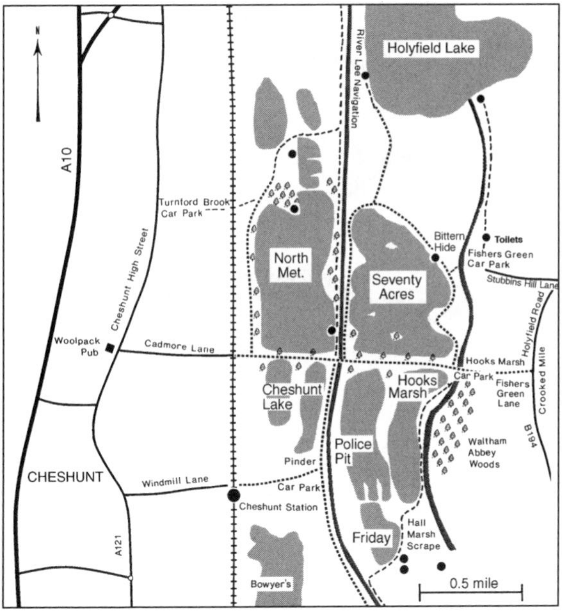

Navigation flowing between them. Police Pit and Bowyer's Water are more open, attracting good numbers of winter wildfowl while Hook's Marsh with its overgrown islands is a haven for breeding birds during the summer. A small wooded area is attractive with plenty more willow and Alder scattered along the river and around the lakeside margins. To the south of Friday Lake is Hall Marsh Scrape, an area of shallow water and marsh which was especially created in 1986 and greatly adds to the diversity of wetland habitats in the valley. The Marsh is served by three hides, aptly named Plover, Teal and Snipe. Patches of scrub and briars grow on the drier parts with more luxuriant plant growth such as willowherb and nettle flourishing nearer water.

Access

Being a part of Lee Valley Park, access is fairly unrestricted with plenty of well-signed tracks surrounding both lakes. Four car parks serve this area: Hook's Marsh and Fishers Green (toilets) car parks, west off the B194 Crooked Mile, 2.5 km (1.5 miles) north of Waltham Abbey; Pindar car park, just east of the level crossing at Cheshunt railway station, Windmill Lane (toilets); and Turnford Brook car park just north of Cadmore Lane.

Disabled persons should use Highbridge, Pindar and Fishers Green car parks, where the toilets and access to the hides are suitable along surfaced footpaths. In addition an annual permit and key can be purchased from the Lee Valley Park Information Centre, Abbey Gardens, Waltham Abbey, Essex, EN9 1QX. For further details telephone 01992 702200.

The nearest railway station is Cheshunt at the end of Windmill Lane, which is only five minutes walk away from the site. (For train information telephone 08457 484950.)

Common Tern

Species

Being one of the older pits in the valley the site has had time to develop and diversify, resulting in an area that is attractive to a great number of bird species. Spring passage is the best time of year to see the maximum number of species as the summer migrants mingle with the last of the wintering wildfowl making a possible checklist of 80 species for a morning's birdwatching, although the greatest variety of wetland birds occur during the winter months.

Ducks are present in all seasons with the autumn/winter period witnessing a peak of Mallard, Tufted Duck, Pochard, Shoveler and Gadwall; the latter sometimes numbering over 100, making Cheshunt one of the region's strongholds for this species. The odd Goosander and Goldeneye dive for food and small numbers of Smew are noted most winters, alongside increasing numbers of Cormorant which breed in large numbers at Walthamstow Reservoir. Gulls roost on the larger waters and, while the Black-headed is commonest, rarer Mediterranean and white-winged gulls regularly occur.

Seasonal visits from Bittern have made the valley an important wintering site for this secretive species and, while they can be seen almost anywhere, the watchpoint at Fishers Green, with its purpose-built hide overlooking Seventy Acres Lake, is a favoured spot. Long-eared Owl (roosts of one or more in waterside willows have become an attraction in recent winters) are logged most years, while the more regular Water Rail can be found skulking around Seventy Acres or among the reeds bordering the wood. Up to ten may winter with the occasional pair staying to breed. Finches abound with the occasional Brambling seeking out dead weed seeds or spilled grain alongside the more numerous Chaffinch, Greenfinch and Linnet. The smaller and more arboreal Siskin, Goldfinch and Redpoll haunt the lakeside Alders. Check out the hides at Hall Marsh Scrape for Shoveler, Teal, Grey Heron, Snipe and Kingfisher. Chiffchaff winter in small numbers. All three species of woodpecker are resident with Lesser Spotted easier to see or hear in late winter when drumming commences.

Early spring brings a few passage Shelduck, mainly on North Met. Pit, with Sand Martin skimming the surface and Chiffchaff calling from the willow tops. The farmland near the electricity station attracts small numbers of Wheatear as well as Lapwing to pause a while beside the more sedentary Red-legged Partridge. Most waders pass high overhead although Little Ringed Plover, Redshank and Common Sandpiper will settle on some of the more stony islands on Seventy Acres Lake or Hall Marsh Scrape.

The latter half of April is generally the peak migration period across the region and the Lee Valley is no exception. This is an exciting time at Cheshunt Gravel Pits as Common Tern stream up the river course along with the main arrival of hirundines and warblers; several pairs of Common Tern now breed on purpose-built tern rafts. Yellow and Pied Wagtails and Meadow Pipit can be heard and seen on the more open areas west of Police Pit accompanied by a handful of Cuckoo whose repetitive call rings out across the entire site. Late spring migrants include Hobby arriving with the Swift and ever decreasing numbers of Turtle Dove and Spotted Flycatcher.

May is an excellent time to study the warbler tribe as the combination of minimal plant growth and much territorial singing allows ideal and sometimes close viewing. The western side of Seventy Acres can at a pinch yield eight species of warbler to the patient observer. Reed and Sedge Warblers occur along the river with Willow Warbler and Chiffchaff in the mature stands of timber. Blackcap and Garden Warbler favour the Salix scrub while Whitethroat prefer the drier bramble patches. Lesser Whitethroat are often noted singing from the more isolated thickets along the summit of the river bank. A possible ninth species could be a Grasshopper Warbler which is occasionally heard 'reeling' from thick cover. Nightingale can be heard most years at Cheshunt GPs but Fishers Green and Holyfield Lake are more reliable sites.

Summer is a time of high activity for adult birds but, due to the lushness of the plant growth, much goes on unseen. Common Tern are far more visible fishing among hordes of Swift attracted to the legions of flying insects. The season drifts by as the return wader passage commences towards the end of July.

Autumn is a time of plenty with an abundant food supply for all. Wildfowl numbers increase and the odd Pintail puts in an appearance. Grey Wagtail call along the stream and Kingfisher numbers peak. Returning passerines may well include a Whinchat in late summer, perched prominently on a wire fence. The now silent warblers exit south in contrast to the arrival of the first winter thrushes which noisily chatter overhead, and Goldcrest filter down the valley in tit flocks.

Calendar

Resident: Little and Great Crested Grebes, Mute Swan, Grey Heron, Cormorant, Mallard, Tufted Duck, Gadwall, Wigeon, Pochard, Sparrowhawk, Kestrel, Moorhen, Coot, Kingfisher, three species of woodpecker, Grey Wagtail, Long-tailed Tit, Treecreeper, finches and buntings, Cetti's Warbler (rare).

December–February: Wintering ducks including Gadwall, Smew, Goldeneye and odd Goosander, rare grebes, gulls, Brambling (scarce). Siskin and Redpoll, Long-eared Owl and Bittern, Water Rail, Goldcrest, Chiffchaff.

March–May: End March Shelduck, Sand Martin, Chiffchaff, Wheatear. April for Little Ringed Plover, Common Sandpiper, Redshank and chance of other passage waders on scrape, warblers, wagtails, hirundines, Hobby, Cuckoo, Meadow Pipit, Common Tern, large waders overhead. Swift, Turtle Dove, Spotted Flycatcher.

June–July: Breeding riparian birds, returning waders end of July.

August–November: Bittern and Water Rail from October, duck numbers increase, Pintail in November. Finch flocks, warblers depart, Whinchat, Grey Wagtail, winter thrushes from October, Goldcrest.

RYE MEADS AREA

(OS ref. TL 388 100)

Habitat

Situated east of Hoddesdon the Rye Meads complex can be split into two administrative sites. At Rye House Marsh the RSPB has a small 6-ha (15-acre) reserve that comprises a number of wetland micro habitats. The south scrapes are both overlooked by hides where open shallows and mud are bordered by willow and poplar scrub, Alder and typical marshland vegetation such as sedge and reed. The creation of this area in front of the hide allows the maximum number of bird species to be seen with minimal disturbance. Further north are a small flood-meadow, sections of Glyceria marsh and reed fen and the North Hide that looks across a small shallow lagoon with willow scrub at the rear. A

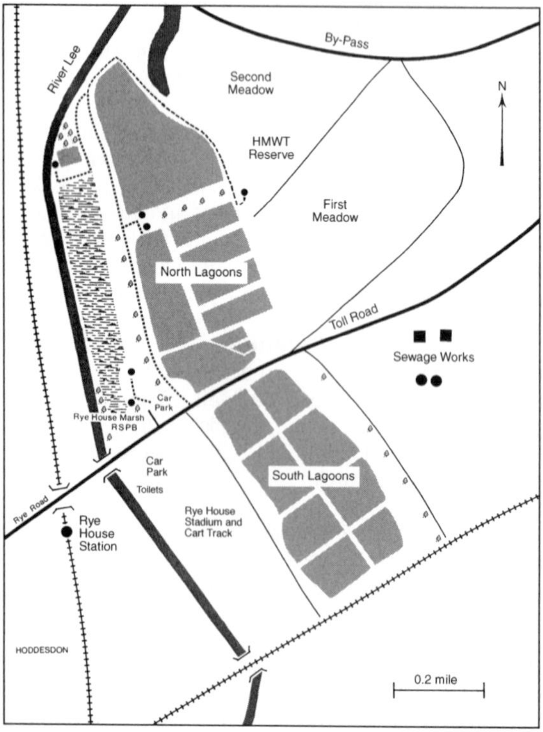

ditch separates the reserve from the sewage works' lagoons to the east, and the River Lee passes down the western perimeter.

Rye Meads is owned by Thames Water and St Albans Sand and Gravel Company and comprises mainly the North Lagoons and the South Lagoons and an old flood-meadow (the Meads), either side of the Toll Road. The Wildlife Trust leases the meadow from St Albans Sand and Gravel Company and influences the management of the adjacent Thames Water meadow. The tree-fringed North Lagoons are provided with rafts for breeding Common Tern and two hides, supplied by the RSPB, that afford ample viewing over the two larger pools. The tern rafts are maintained by the Rye Meads Ringing Group. The private grazed meadows, further east, along with clumps of Phragmites, bramble patches and scrub can only be viewed from a hide accessible via the RSPB reserve. South of the Toll Road are eight roughly symmetrical lagoons with surrounding drains and a ringing hut. The sewage works buildings are out of bounds.

Plant life includes the scarce Marsh Marigold, Comfrey, bedstraw and the delicate pink Ragged Robin. Water Vole and Water Shrew are present and the dykes hold many species of coarse fish as well as eels and freshwater crayfish.

A new information centre should open in the spring of 2002 with improved walks, linked to the Lee Valley Cycleway network, and three new hides overlooking the Wildlife Trust reserve.

Access

For Rye House Marsh take the Rye Road, east of Hoddesdon, towards the railway station, over the river bridge and turn left into the reserve car park. If full, parking is available on the opposite side of the road at the stadium, along with toilet facilities (sometimes closed). The WAGN railway line at Rye House Station is within easy walking distance of the reserve.

Access to both the HMWT and RSPB reserves is via the information centre and southern hides; follow the signs from the car park. Members of either organisation gain free access to the reserves, otherwise there is a small entrance fee. The Marsh is open to the public daily from 09:00 to 17:00 hrs except Christmas Day and Boxing Day. The information centre incorporates a classroom and display area from which experienced staff conduct classes from primary to university level. For further details contact the warden on 01279 793720.

Access onto the remainder of the complex is severely restricted and is through the Rye Meads Ringing Group. Keen birdwatchers interested in joining should contact the secretary of the group whose address is in the annual ringing report, available at the RSPB information centre or the ringing hut. The hut is usually manned at the weekends, when permission must be sought to look round the South Lagoons.

Species

Rye Meads is perhaps best known ornithologically as the site of the county's first recorded nesting of Cetti's Warbler in 1978. However, due to a number of severe winters in the 1980s the entire population was wiped out and they are now recorded only sporadically. More typically, however, is the importance of the complex in offering safe sanctuary to migrant birds that pass along the valley during spring and autumn and a variety of habitats for the 50 or so species that regularly breed.

Winter is possibly the best season to visit the marsh at Rye House where close views of both species of snipe and Green Sandpiper, probing the mud for invertebrates are almost guaranteed. Good numbers of Teal, 30 to 40, dabble the shallows while Water Rail slink around the margins alongside the more numerous Moorhen. A couple of Water Pipit may be present here or on the meads but are often difficult to detect in the long grass. A slight spring passage is of note when the males exhibit a pinkish flush on the breast and are generally more active. Solitary Grey Heron are scattered over the site and most winters Bittern are recorded. Bearded Tit are no longer an annual visitor but when they do occur can often be seen in small parties, most sporting coloured leg rings as they are easy 'prey' for ringers and are much studied. Mixed flocks of Siskin, Goldfinch and Redpoll seek out the waterlogged Alders and at dusk numbers of Reed Bunting and Yellowhammer roost in the reed swamp and scrub. The buntings are joined by winter thrushes, finches and Meadow Pipit on the meadows.

A visit to the North Lagoon hides will be rewarded by numerous Cormorant loafing on the tern rafts and a variety of gulls, mainly Black-headed, on the water. The deep water attracts many diving duck with several hundred Tufted the most abundant. Lesser numbers of Pochard, about 100, are joined by up to 500 Coot and single figures of the two common grebes. Sawbills are quite rare and even Goldeneye are unusual here. Dabbling ducks are represented by 50 or so Shoveler, with the occasional pair staying to breed, alongside good numbers of Mallard and a sprinkling of Gadwall. Winter geese records normally refer to the Canada Goose, with sightings of wild grey geese a rarity. The meadows sometimes entice a roving Short-eared Owl to hunt awhile in the short daylight hours but beware of falling into the trap that all diurnal hunting owls at this time of year are of this species; Long-eared do occasionally crop up.

Spring passage sees a variety of migrants moving north along the valley with a few Green Sandpiper stopping at Rye House Marsh and Common Sandpiper flitting over the lagoons. Small numbers of Little Ringed Plover are noted every spring and throughout the summer as they breed on adjacent gravel pits. Sporadic visits of larger waders such as godwits and Curlew relate to birds moving overhead calling. Chiffchaff and Willow Warbler are soon filtering through the site searching for insects which are attracted to the sweet-smelling willow catkins. Sedge Warbler also arrive early along with Blackcap. Out on the lagoons Common Tern start arriving, noisily wheeling overhead and plunge-diving for small fish. They spend many hours preening and resting after their long migration and as many as 40 pairs have bred here, raising young on the specially-prepared rafts where they enjoy a high fledgling success rate. Other terns such as Black or Arctic are rarely noted at Rye Meads.

Early Sand Martin are soon joined by other hirundines skimming over the surface of the water as small numbers of Yellow Wagtail and Wheatear move through the meadows. Stock Dove occur here along with one or two Whinchat flicking along the fence posts. The main arrival of warblers takes place at the end of April with good numbers of Sylvia warblers spread throughout the site. Reed Warbler arrive late accompanied by a handful of Cuckoo and the occasional Grasshopper Warbler, the latter 'reeling' from the reed swamp or amongst brambles on the meads. Spotted Flycatcher nest in the Ivy-covered trees at Rye House Marsh and small numbers of Turtle Dove summer, reflecting the improving habitat of willow scrub and mature bushes preferred by this species.

The summer scene is typified by hundreds of Swifts and hirundines swirling over the complex with the appearance of a Hobby enough to scatter the flocks skywards. Finches nesting in surrounding scrub include Bullfinch, Greenfinch, Chaffinch, Goldfinch, Linnet and occasionally Redpoll. The North Lagoons are busy, as adult Common Tern ferry in fish for their voracious youngsters in contrast to the ducklings of Mallard, Tufted Duck and Coot which obediently follow their parents around the margins, hurriedly scurrying for cover when danger threatens. Kingfisher young disperse in late summer and become more apparent, often frequenting the area in front of the south hides.

Returning waders seek out any muddy patches with the usual sandpipers and Greenshank most likely, calidrids such as Dunlin or Little Stint are irregular. Single Garganey and Pintail in eclipse plumage are almost annual autumn visitors to the lagoons as duck numbers build up for the winter. A passage of Sylvia warblers is noted in the willow scrub as migrant Skylark, Meadow Pipit and Yellow Wagtail mainly pass overhead. Finches and buntings seem to be everywhere, compensating somewhat for the warblers which surreptitiously depart south. The year turns full circle with the arrival of Grey Wagtail and Green Sandpiper to the marsh and the chance of a Stonechat on the meads.

Due to intensive watching and netting at the complex over the last 30 years well over 200 species have been recorded, including recent rarities such as Little Bittern, Great Snipe, Wryneck, Serin and Marsh Warbler. Keen birders wishing to develop their skills and contribute to ornithology would do well to join the Rye Meads Ringing Group (see Useful Addresses) which operates one of the most dynamic inland ringing stations in the country.

Calendar

Resident: Great Crested and Little Grebes, Cormorant, Mute Swan, Grey Heron, Mallard, Tufted Duck, Gadwall, Shoveler, Kestrel, Sparrowhawk, Moorhen, Coot, Kingfisher (increase in July and August), Stock Dove, three woodpeckers, Pied and Grey Wagtails (increase in winter), finches and buntings.

December–February: Bittern irregular, Wigeon occasional, Pochard, Teal, sawbills rare, Water Rail, Lapwing, Snipe and Jack Snipe, Woodcock occasional, Green Sandpiper, gulls, Short-eared and Long-eared Owls irregular, Meadow and Water Pipits, Grey Wagtail, Stonechat irregular, winter thrushes, Chiffchaff, Bearded Tit irregular, Siskin and Redpoll, bunting roost in reedbeds and scrub.

March–May: End March Chiffchaff, Wheatear, Sand Martin. April for Little Ringed Plover, Common and Green Sandpipers, Common Tern, other tern species scarce, Cuckoo, hirundines, Yellow Wagtail, Sylvia warblers, Sedge, Grasshopper and Willow Warblers. From May, Hobby, Whinchat, Reed Warbler, Turtle Dove, Spotted Flycatcher.

June–July: Hobby, Swift, breeding activity.

August–November: Wader passage, sandpipers and Greenshank, Whinchat, Yellow and Grey Wagtails, Sylvia warbler passage in August, Garganey and Pintail occasional, duck numbers increase, passage Skylark, finches, pipits, wagtails, Goldcrest, thrushes.

AMWELL GRAVEL PITS

(OS ref. TL 374 134)

Habitat

Situated in the northern section of the Lee Valley, a short but interesting walkway has been created by the park authority on a stretch of the Buntingford railway branch line. Amwell Gravel Pits are owned by St Albans Sand and Gravel Co. Ltd, who are currently developing the site as a nature reserve in conjunction with the Amwell Conservation Volunteers. The combination of nearby Easneye Woods, gravel pit wetlands, the River Lee, farmland and scrub make for one of the best birding areas in the valley.

Access

The site is 1.5 km (1 mile) north-west of Stanstead Abbots and although the gravel pits and wood are private the pits are viewed from the Amwell Walkway, which is a surfaced public footpath maintained by the Lee Valley Park Authority and suitable for wheelchair users. The good views across the valley make this an ideal site for observing passage migrants moving through the area.

Access is either by walking north along the Lee Navigation towpath from Stanstead Abbots or south from Ware. Alternatively, access can be gained from Hollycross Road, 1.5 km (1 mile) south-east of Ware or Amwell Lane (limited parking), 0.4 km (0.25 mile) east of Great Amwell. A viewpoint looks across the scrape and shallows while a nearby public hide overlooks a reedbed.

At Stanstead Abbots there is a car park, toilets and several good pubs (the Jolly Fisherman is recommended). There is also a regular train service from London Liverpool Street to St Margaret's on WAGN railway and Green Line buses from Heathrow to Harlow.

Species

Due to the open aspect of this site it is a good place to scan for resident birds of prey. Kestrel and Sparrowhawk can be seen throughout the year and increasingly Common Buzzard over Easneye Wood, while Little Owl are sometimes encountered on nearby farmland. Kingfisher frequent the river together with typical riparian species such as Reed Bunting and

Egyptian Goose

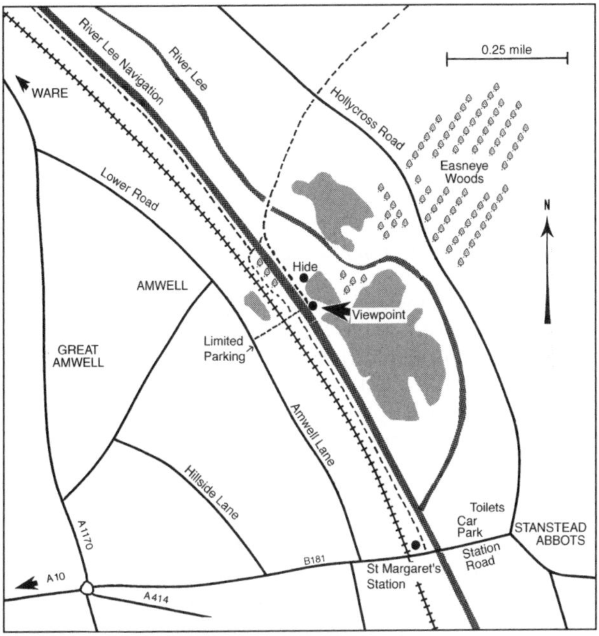

Moorhen while the more open waters of the gravel pits attract the usual range of wildfowl. The presence of nearby woodland ensures regular sightings of tits, woodpeckers, thrushes and finches, along with that Hertfordshire speciality the Hawfinch. It is now only rarely seen, flying over, in late winter or spring from nearby Easneye and Post Woods.

In winter, small flocks of Siskin, Goldfinch and Redpoll feed on the riverside Alders, while out on the open gravel pit waters good numbers of Cormorant and gulls are present. The gulls are worth checking as Yellow-legged, Glaucous, Iceland and Mediterranean Gulls have all been recorded in recent years. The two common species of grebe can be found amongst the regular wintering wildfowl which include variable numbers of Wigeon, Gadwall, Shoveler, Teal, Pochard and Goldeneye. Occasionally, an unusual visitor can be encountered such as a Red-necked Grebe, Red-crested Pochard, Pintail, Ferruginous Duck, Scaup or one of the sawbills; Smew and Goosander have been regular in recent winters. Snipe numbers can be as high as 50 in early winter, with one or two Jack Snipe. Water Rail are easily seen from the public hide, which overlooks a reed-fringed pool, and there is a good chance of a Bittern in late afternoon coming in to roost. Winter thrushes are often noted on farmland fields from November onwards along with finches and buntings.

Spring is usually heralded by a Sand Martin flicking low over the water or Chiffchaff singing from a willow, although the latter may be an over-wintering bird coming into song. March waders include the noisy Redshank and the more surreptitious Ringed and Little Ringed Plovers, all of which breed locally. Amwell has recently established a reputation for being one of the best sites in the county for passage waders and with regular coverage during April and May Common and Green Sandpipers, Dunlin and Greenshank can reasonably be expected. Oystercatcher,

Ruff, Wood Sandpiper and Turnstone are a typical irregular supporting cast, with the larger godwits and Curlew mainly passing overhead. As the valley now holds the largest number of breeding Common Tern in the county a steady movement northwards is noted from mid-April with several pairs nesting in most years. Passage Arctic and Black Terns are scarce with the latter more regular in May and numbers usually dependent on the intensity of easterly winds and rain showers. The main body of wagtails, warblers, hirundines and Cuckoo move through in late April followed by Swift, Hobby, Turtle Dove and Spotted Flycatcher throughout May; records of Osprey migrating along the watercourse have shown an increase recently.

Summer birding at Amwell is dominated by breeding birds, from the more obvious Common Tern to the furtive ringed plovers and chattering warblers. Breeding wildfowl can include Egyptian Goose, Shoveler, Pochard and Ruddy Duck. An evening visit in late summer should yield a Hobby, hunting insects or hirundines for a brood nearby.

The first returning sandpipers appear in July and the protracted autumn wader passage continues into September when species similar to spring occur, but often in greater numbers and with the chance of something rare such as a stint. Returning terns have included a Little and Sandwich Tern in recent years amongst the Commons and scarcer Black Tern. Garganey are often noted at Amwell having recently bred in this part of the Lee Valley. Migrant Grey Wagtail, hirundines and warblers are on the move and a late autumn passage of Skylark, pipits, finches, Goldcrest and thrushes is often noted.

Calendar

Resident: Little and Great Crested Grebes, Grey Heron, common wildfowl, Kestrel, Sparrowhawk, Common Buzzard, Coot, Little Owl, Kingfisher, woodpeckers, Nuthatch, Treecreeper, tits, Grey Wagtail, occasional Chiffchaff, finches including Hawfinch, Reed Bunting.

December–February: Chance of rare grebe or duck, Cormorant, Bittern, Gadwall, Shoveler, Teal, Pochard, Wigeon, Goldeneye, Smew, Goosander, Snipe, Jack Snipe, Water Rail, gulls, winter thrushes, Siskin, Redpoll.

March–May: Shelduck, Little Ringed and Ringed Plovers, Redshank, Green and Common Sandpipers, Dunlin, Hobby, Common Tern, Swift, Cuckoo, hirundines, Turtle Dove, pipits, wagtails, Wheatear, warblers including Grasshopper, Spotted Flycatcher, chance of Black Tern, Osprey, or scarce wader.

June–July: Breeding waders, wildfowl - Pochard, Ruddy Duck, Shoveler, Egyptian Goose, and passerines, Common Tern, Hobby.

August–November: Passage waders (chance of stint), terns (possible rare Little or Sandwich or irregular Black), passage warblers, wagtails, pipits and thrushes, Goldcrest, finch flocks.

LEE VALLEY – ADDITIONAL SITES

Fishers Green (OS ref. TL 377 033)

To the north of the Cheshunt Gravel Pits complex and within the Lee Valley Park is the Fishers Green Countryside Area, much of which lies within the county of Essex. The area includes open water, marsh, scrub and farmland owned and managed by the park authority. Holyfield Lake (not in Herts.) is one of the largest gravel pits in the Lee Valley and the open fields of Holyfield Hall Farm to the east form an interesting contrast. Access to the four hides (Waverley, Wren, Grand Weir and Grebe) around the site can be gained from the Fishers Green Car Park down Stubbins Hall Lane (also signposted to Hayes Hill Farm) off the B194, 3 km (2 miles) north of Waltham Abbey. Toilets and car parking facilities are suitable for disabled birders as is access to the hides. For details on the Fishers Green Bittern hide, that overlooks Seventy Acres Lake, refer to the Cheshunt Gravel Pits site account.

Winter is particularly good at Holyfield Lake, which attracts large numbers of gulls and ducks, including Goldeneye and quite often Smew and Goosander. A large Cormorant roost is of note among the wooded islands together with pigeons and crows, and Grey Heron can be seen well from the hides; Bittern have also occurred in recent winters. Kingfisher, Water Rail, Snipe, Grey Wagtail, Siskin and Redpoll are all present and the 'goose fields' usually contain large numbers of Canada and other feral species. The farmland should be checked for Little Owl, partridges and Golden Plover amongst the more numerous Lapwing.

Spring passage brings many of the species already mentioned in the previous Lee Valley sites plus Grasshopper Warbler and Nightingale to the scrub and woodland area. Waders are best viewed from Grand Weir hide and passage chats and wagtails haunt the open fields.

King's Meads, Ware (OS ref. TL 340 135)

At the northern end of the Lee Valley between Ware and Hertford lies King's Meads, a low-lying area between the two arms of the river which regularly floods during winter and spring. It can be worked from public footpaths that run alongside the river giving views across wet meadows and fields. Part of the Meads is now a HMWT reserve and Thames Water also carry out conservation works.

In winter Wigeon, Shoveler, Teal, Lapwing and Snipe are noted, but good numbers of each are dependent upon the water levels. Stonechat are often recorded on the rough pasture by the railway line. Garganey have bred in the past and passage waders are present when water levels are suitable, e.g. Little Ringed Plover, Green Sandpiper and Greenshank. Sedge and Reed are typical summering warblers and Yellow Wagtail occur.

63 NORTHAW GREAT WOOD

OS ref. TL 285 045

Habitat

At 162 ha (400 acres) Northaw Great Wood is a remnant of the extensive forests that centuries ago covered much of Hertfordshire. Although most of the wood was clear-felled before the Second World War, much replanting and management has taken place, making The Great Wood one of the best in the county for woodland birds.

A good selection of deciduous trees is found with Oak, Beech, Hornbeam, Birch and Ash predominating. Each species produces a rich harvest of seeds and supports the vital diversity of insect life necessary to maintain a varied breeding bird population. There are open glades carpeted with bluebells during the spring, 12 ha (30 acres) of coppice Hornbeam and chestnut, a Beech stand, Blackthorn thickets, a row of pollarded Limes, Ash alongside the brook and, above all, Oak. Amongst this feast of trees is a flora typically associated with an ancient woodland. Both Badger and Fox find safe refuge here along with Muntjac Deer.

Declared a SSSI in 1953 and a Country Park in 1968, Northaw Great Wood is managed between Welwyn Hatfield District Council and English Nature.

Access

Situated to the north-west of Cuffley, The Great Wood is reached along The Ridgeway or B157, which runs east to west between Cuffley and Brookman's Park. The road borders the southern perimeter of the wood with signposts to the car park at the western end where a small parking fee is payable (£1). Visitors should check the closure times as they vary throughout the year; generally the wood is open from 08:00 hrs to sunset. There are toilets on site, an information centre and a resident warden (telephone 01707 872213). Organisations wishing to visit as a party are requested to apply in advance to the Welwyn Hatfield District Council (see Useful Addresses).

An area of 117 ha (290 acres) is open to the public. Woodlands to the north of Cuffley Brook and to the west of Boundary Banks are private property. These, together with the school camp, are not open to the public. Within the wood there are three waymarked paths of various lengths. These are: Yellow 2.5 miles (4 km), Blue 2.1 km (1.25 miles), Red 1.1 km (0.75 mile). Walks and paths are not rights of way and it is occasionally necessary to re-route them to prevent damage or disturbance to wildlife.

Species

In winter, woodland birdwatching is a case of finding a flock and staying with it. Tits make up the nucleus of these flocks along with Goldcrest, Treecreeper, Nuthatch and the odd Lesser Spotted Woodpecker. Their incessant contact calls aid their location throughout the wood. Great Spotted and Green Woodpeckers range widely at this time of year, some leaving altogether to feed on bird tables in nearby suburban

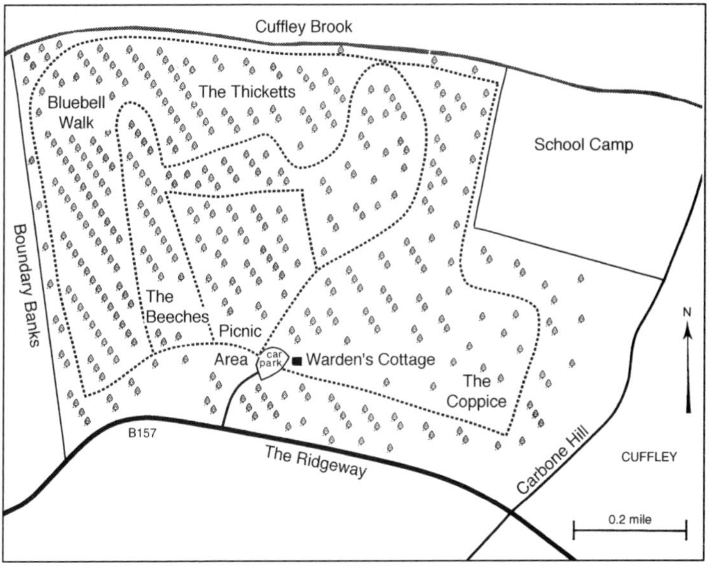

gardens. Goldfinch flock together with immigrant Siskin and Redpoll to feed on the plentiful supply of Birch seed. Chaffinch and Brambling (irregular) hunt out the Beech, working their way through the litter in search of mast. Hawfinch are sometimes recorded and are slightly easier to see in winter, especially in the vicinity of Hornbeam. Sparrowhawk are resident and increasingly Common Buzzard are noted in line with their eastwards range expansion. Tawny Owl are never easy to see but a healthy, and vocal, population exists across the wood.

Due to a continuing planned management programme the Great Wood is in a class of its own in the springtime, meeting the various habitat requirements for the specialised summer visitors. Good numbers of Willow Warbler, Chiffchaff, Whitethroat, Garden Warbler and Blackcap breed, adding variety to the resident bird song from late March onwards. Nuthatch, Treecreeper, Marsh Tit, Goldcrest, Green and Great Spotted Woodpecker are all present, but Willow Tit and Lesser Spotted Woodpeckers are proving increasingly difficult to find and are best searched for in early spring before the canopy is in full leaf.

Sadly, Redstart, Wood Warbler and Nightingale are only sporadic visitors but should be searched for from late April into May. Small numbers of Redstart formerly bred in the more mature Oaks while Wood Warbler preferred the Birch scrub and Nightingale the Blackthorn scrub and coppice areas of the wood. Tree Pipit too have declined and today are only irregularly heard singing from exposed songposts in the numerous glades. A few Spotted Flycatcher can still be found, sallying forth from perches in pursuit of insects.

Woodcock and Grasshopper Warbler, both active at dawn and dusk, are present in varying numbers, the former regularly seen 'roding' over the canopy; the latter, an occasional passage migrant, sometimes staying on to breed in small numbers. The smaller passerines have to be very alert during the breeding season as Jackdaw and Jay prey heavily on any unguarded nest. Nevertheless, come the end of the summer there always seem to be large numbers of juveniles hunting the abundant supply of insects.

The Great Wood is most productive in April and May when a dawn visit should easily reward the patient observer with over 40 species. An early morning trip is strongly advised as later on the wood becomes busy with dog-walkers.

Calendar

Resident: Kestrel, Sparrowhawk, Common Buzzard, Woodcock, Tawny Owl, Stock Dove, Green, Great Spotted and Lesser Spotted Woodpeckers, Mistle Thrush, Goldcrest, Long-tailed Tit, Marsh and Willow Tits, Nuthatch, Treecreeper, Jay, Magpie, Jackdaw, Redpoll, Bullfinch, Hawfinch.

December–January: Increase in Woodcock, Siskin, Redpoll and Brambling (irregular), tit flocks.

March–May: Chiffchaff, Whitethroat, Garden Warbler, Blackcap, Chiffchaff, Willow Warbler, Cuckoo, Spotted Flycatcher. Tree Pipit, Redstart, Wood Warbler, Grasshopper Warbler and Nightingale, all irregular visitors.

June–July: Passerines rearing young.

August–November: Juveniles finding their way around, warblers leave, Starlings move in to roost at dusk.

64 OUGHTON HEAD COMMON

OS ref. TL 168 303

Habitat

At 6 ha (15 acres) Oughton Head Common is ideal for a morning's birdwatching, combined with more general natural history interests such as botany. The Alder/willow woodland to the north of the River Oughton is managed by the county wildlife trust while the remainder of the site is owned by Hertfordshire County Council and used as an educational nature reserve.

Keeping the Sycamore under control is one of the main management tasks, along with scrub clearance to allow bog plants to flourish. The River Oughton bubbles out of the chalk to the west of the site and meanders across the common creating its own unique habitat. The water is sparklingly clear and well oxygenated, supporting a wealth of aquatic insect life and fish. Along the banks in the summer plant growth is thick and luxuriant. The common proper, south of the river, is a mixture of marshy ground with small reedbeds and willows, rank Tussock

Sedge, Hawthorn scrub, a Beech stand and thick hedgerows. The paddock and small wood near the mill are also of interest.

Conditions are ripe for a rich marsh flora and insect population, including many species of dragonflies. Mammals to look out for along the river include both Water Shrew and Water Vole, with Muntjac Deer in the woodland.

Access

Take the A600 north out of Hitchin heading towards Ickleford. Turn left at the Angel's Reply pub down Red Hill Lane. Park at the end of the lane and a narrow track leads to the south side of the common near the Beech stand. Alternatively, from Ickleford head west along the old Icknield Way, or West Mill Lane. Turn off at West Mill Farm, where only limited parking is available; care must be taken not to restrict access to the farm. Continue on foot down the lane, which is also a public footpath, through the mill yard, over the river and turn right towards the common.

Access to the woodland north of the river is by permit from the HMWT headquarters and is subject to seasonal variation, but the reserve can be viewed from a footpath opposite. The common proper has a footpath around the perimeter allowing good views across the whole site. A track also runs along the south side of the river to the springs and then heads back east across farmland, eventually meeting Red Hill Lane.

Species

Early morning visits nearly always pay dividends. Winter is the best time to find a Grey Heron stalking the marsh or river's edge before the dog-walkers are about. Teal are present in small numbers, along with Snipe, which when flushed, zigzag and tower away out of sight. Jack Snipe are occasionally noted, but are silent and more difficult to flush, only flying a short distance before disappearing into thick cover. Water Rail are

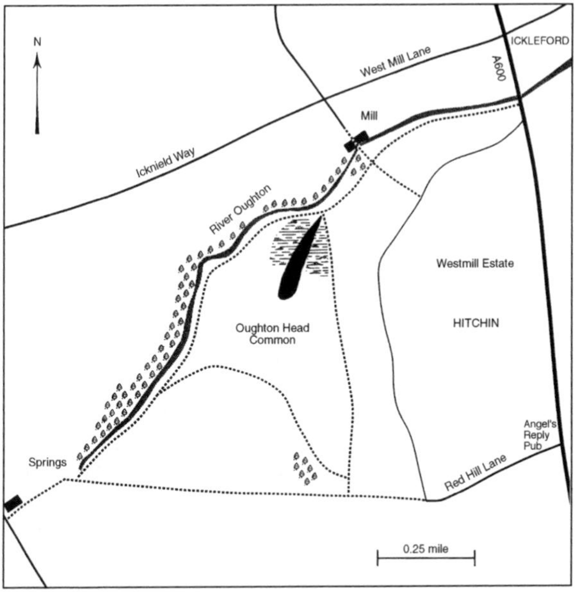

sometimes seen crossing open mud between reed patches or amongst rank grass, although they are more likely to be heard. The marshy area to the north-east is the best spot to look for them. Winter thrushes invade the scrub at this time of year in search of berries of Hawthorn, Sloe, Guelder Rose and, later on, Ivy. The familiar resident thrushes also join in the harvest with the larger Mistle Thrush being particularly aggressive, sometimes defending a favourite bush against all comers.

Both Long-eared and Short-eared Owls have been recorded in winter, the latter easiest to see as they hunt in the daylight hours, but neither are regular. Tawny Owl are resident and are heard reasonably often, especially in late winter. A large mixed flock containing Siskin, Redpoll and Goldfinch winters on the common feeding on the riverside Alders, their flight notes a valuable location aid. Wintering Woodcock haunt the wooded area in variable numbers but are difficult to find unless flushed.

The Chiffchaff is the first spring visitor, calling frantically from the larger trees around the farm and along the river. Most are just passing through but several pairs stay on to breed in the wood. Blackcap and Willow Warbler move through in good numbers in early spring with many pairs of each staying to breed. In fact the common is superb for warblers, with hordes of insects to feed upon and plenty of nesting sites amongst the rank growth. Sedge Warbler seem to be song-flighting everywhere and are probably the most numerous warbler, while a few pairs of Reed Warbler nest in the small patches of reed; even scarcer is the Grasshopper Warbler, now only an occasional passage visitor whereas once it bred regularly. The scrub-loving Garden Warbler and Lesser Whitethroat generally inhabit the drier part of the common and are quite plentiful, with Whitethroat frequenting the surrounding hedgerows.

Cuckoo and Turtle Dove both breed, the former regularly, the latter now only occasionally. Hirundines migrate over the common with Swallow breeding in the farm buildings. Sparrowhawk hunt the cover and Kestrel hover over the grass searching for small mammals. Sometimes a Hobby makes an appearance, usually towards dusk, to hawk the larger flying insects or dash after a Swallow. The occasional pair of Spotted Flycatcher breeds along the wooded riverbank, or around the mill yard paddock, where Ivy-covered trees provide ideal nest sites.

Resident passerines breed everywhere, intricately marking out their territories and singing to mark the borders. Reed Bunting breed in the marsh, Yellowhammer in the scrub, with Skylark overhead and finches nesting in any available bush or thicket. The wood holds the commoner tits, Treecreeper, Green Woodpecker and the two spotted woodpeckers, although Lesser Spotted are now rarely found. Grey Wagtail is a regular breeding species along the river or around the mill yard.

As summer passes and the flycatcher returns south, Kingfisher are more active as the adults chase away their offspring to establish a winter territory. Listen out for the distinctive flight call along the Oughton. Plenty of passerines are on the move now as large flocks of Meadow Pipit, Skylark, Chaffinch and Starling stream overhead. Goldcrest start to reappear, warblers and hirundines leave and large numbers of Goldfinch flock together.

Calendar

Resident: Mallard, Sparrowhawk, Kestrel, Pheasant, Moorhen, Tawny Owl, Kingfisher, Great and Lesser Spotted Woodpeckers, Skylark, Treecreeper, Jay, buntings.

December–February: Grey Heron, Teal, Water Rail, Jack Snipe a few, Snipe, Woodcock, Long-eared and Short-eared Owls irregular, winter thrushes, Brambling irregular, Siskin, Redpoll.

March–May: Cuckoo, Turtle Dove, Yellow Wagtail overhead with Meadow Pipit, hirundines, Blackcap, Sylvia warblers, Sedge Warbler, Grasshopper Warbler occasionally, Reed Warbler, Willow Warbler, Chiffchaff, Spotted Flycatcher.

June–July: Peak fledging period for warblers. Hunting Hobby.

August–November: Warblers depart early, Grey Wagtail, Goldcrest, tit, finch and bunting flocks.

65 TRING RESERVOIRS

OS ref. SP 920 135

Habitat

Situated in the Tring Gap in the Chilterns at about 100 m (330 ft) above sea level, Tring Reservoirs were created in the early nineteenth century to provide a regular water supply for the Grand Union Canal. In 1955 the four reservoirs were declared a National Nature Reserve under the auspices of the then Nature Conservancy Council who formerly managed 19 ha (47 acres) of banks and surrounding woodlands. The reservoirs are owned by British Waterways with the conservation management now undertaken by the Friends of Tring Reservoirs, who have filled the vacuum left by English Nature and, at Wilstone, by the Wildlife Trust. Birdwatchers who regularly use the reservoirs can make a positive contribution to the preservation of this valuable wetland by subscribing to 'Friends'. For further information on Friends of Tring Reservoirs log on to www.tringreservoirs.btinternet.co.uk/ or contact Judith Knight, 381 Bideford Green, Linslade, Leighton Buzzard, Bedfordshire LU7 7TY, telephone 01525 378161.

Wilstone is the largest of the reservoirs with open water and concrete banks in the north contrasting with natural well-vegetated margins either side of Drayton Bank. Fresh water from a nearby spring feeds a small marsh and wet meadow, harbouring some interesting relics of a once prolific marsh flora. Exposed mud can sometimes be found in late summer around the hide and in front of the poplar wood, attracting waders. Mature woodland, a reedbed, scrub thickets along the abandoned canal and arable farmland make for probably one of the best birdwatching sites in the region.

Tringford is much smaller and shallower, with at times an even more dramatically fluctuating water level. An open hide is positioned strategically amongst natural cover, enabling close studies of wildfowl. A damp wood near the hide is of interest, as are the peripheral meadows and paddocks.

Startop's End and Marsworth are bisected by a causeway affording good views over a reedbed at the latter. The former is more open with steep banks and occasional exposed mud in late summer; it also has a wheelchair-friendly hide. Adjacent to Marsworth is a sewage farm with a hide overlooking an old settlement lagoon (Lagoon Hide); access is only for members of 'Friends'.

Tring Reservoirs is one of the region's premier sites and is rated a SSSI. It is also a scenic location with views along the wooded Chiltern scarp and the plateau of the Three Hundreds of Aylesbury to the south.

Access

For Wilstone take the B489 off the A41 at Aston Clinton, heading towards Dunstable. Park alongside the reservoir in the car park just south of Wilstone village, taking care to secure your vehicle against the increasing spate of car thefts and break-ins.

A more central position for access to all reservoirs can be found near the Cemetery in Little Tring Road, with parking for about half a dozen cars. Cross the lane following the track across the field to the stile, turning right for views across the water and reedbed. A circular walk takes in the full range of habitats, including the Drayton Bank hide and the wood behind the reedbed.

For the other three reservoirs continue along the B489 to Startop's End using the pay and display car park (50p all day) by the canal. Information boards abound and a leaflet on the reservoirs is available at 20p. Either of the two pubs, the White Lion and Angler's Retreat, are worthwhile for refreshments. Once up on the bank, check out the meadows across the canal in spring for Wheatear and wagtails. Turn right towards a farm checking the water along the way. To reach Tringford carefully cross the lane and follow the footpath through the wood to the hide. The path turns sharp left by the pumping station, eventually leading back to the lane near the mill. Return to Marsworth checking the sewage farm lagoon from the hide, if a member of 'Friends'.

A point to bear in mind when visiting the reservoirs is that they are extensively fished during the season causing some disturbance, and that the Rothschild Estate still exercise their shooting rights during the winter months.

Species

Tring Reservoirs are steeped in ornithological history, commencing in the nineteenth century at the time of the beleaguered Great Crested Grebe population, subsequently studied by Julian Huxley. Other milestones have included England's first record of breeding Black-necked Grebe in 1919 and, in 1938, the first pair of Little Ringed Plover to breed in Britain. Today, neither breed regularly but both occur on passage. The reservoirs hold a good range of species the year round and being the only significant stretch of open water for miles about consistently attract migrant waders and seabirds.

The winter scene is dominated by wildfowl with large numbers of Mute Swan, Mallard, Tufted Duck, Pochard, Wigeon and Coot scattered

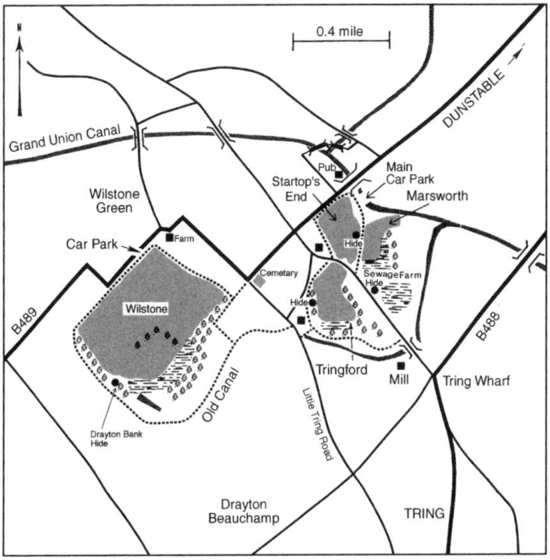

over all four waters with the majority residing on Wilstone. Lesser numbers of Shoveler, Teal, Gadwall, Goldeneye and Ruddy Duck are also present. Sawbills are erratic visitors in small numbers and Scaup occur most winters. Rare grebes occasionally turn up among Great Crested and Dabchick, although Black-necked Grebe are more likely on Wilstone during autumn passage.

The place to be in late afternoon is the causeway overlooking Marsworth reedbed. Wintering Bittern are often at their most active and can sometimes be seen commuting between here and Wilstone reedbed; late winter 'booming' may be a pointer to future breeding. Bearded Tit have also wintered here. Depending on the water level Water Rail become reasonably visible as they occasionally stray from the safety of the reeds to feed along the margin. As dusk approaches many birds fly in to roost, in particular a sizeable bunting flock, consisting mainly of Reed Bunting with up to 100 Corn Bunting.

Other, much larger roosts are gulls (mainly Black-headed) on Startop's End (pre-roost only) and Wilstone, plus hordes of Starling in surrounding scrub. Large species of gull are generally unusual, apart from Lesser Black-backs, and Mediterranean Gull are regularly noted. A nearby crow roost on the downs is also of interest. In early winter the sewage farm, depending on the water level, normally holds a few Snipe and Lapwing. Little Owl can often be seen on farmland surrounding Wilstone, while the woods still attract Willow Tit and more rarely Lesser Spotted Woodpecker, which are easier to locate when drumming from February onwards.

Early spring Chiffchaff and Blackcap are usually wintering birds that have found their voices prior to the main arrival in early April. Warblers soon move into their respective habitats as migration peaks towards the end of the month. A Sand Martin hawking low across the water is often the first harbinger of spring, usually by mid-March, with larger numbers of Swallow arriving a little later; although House Martin are noted in

April, the main passage occurs in late May. Parties of Yellow Wagtail and Meadow Pipit occur on the grassy tops of the concrete banks at Wilstone and Startop's End, while early waders such as Common Sandpiper and Little Ringed Plover flit around the edges. Any exposed mud could yield a passing Green Sandpiper, Redshank or Dunlin, but larger waders such as Curlew or godwits normally pass straight overhead.

Out on the water, duck numbers diminish as the majority disperse to their breeding grounds; however, a few Goldeneye often stay late, frequently displaying. Small parties of Common Scoter sometimes occur in April and Shelduck are more obvious. Startop's End and Wilstone attract varying numbers of Common, Arctic and Black Terns on both passages, with occasionally large flocks of the latter two; Sandwich and Little Tern should be checked for. Visiting seabirds include a scattering of Little Gull, mainly in April, and maybe a Kittiwake or two. Occasionally a local rarity turns up, such as a Red-necked Phalarope, Gannet, Eider or perhaps a party of Common Scoter, usually as a result of persistent onshore winds. More regular spring rarities are Osprey and Marsh Harrier, the latter favouring the reedbed at Wilstone, but most years something unexpected turns up in early May.

One of the highlights of spring is the large numbers of Hobby attracted to the reservoirs, particularly Wilstone, for the mayfly emergence. Up to 20 individuals have been noted swooping low over the water and taking insects off the surface. Hirundines are disregarded as the falcon plunders this abundant food source.

Reed Warbler and Spotted Flycatcher are the last migrants to arrive with substantial colonies of the former at Marsworth and Wilstone reedbeds. An early morning visit is vital during this season as most bird activity tends to peter out approaching midday. Riparian breeders abound, from the abundant Reed Bunting to a large heronry at Wilstone and summering Cormorants. Kingfisher can be encountered almost anywhere with Tringford and Startop's End being particularly favourite haunts.

The late summer wader passage is reliant upon the amount of exposed mud around the reservoir margins; normally, the hotter the summer the lower water levels, as water is pumped out to top up the canal. A steady flow of the commoner sandpipers and plovers is regularly enlivened by parties of Greenshank, and sometimes Whimbrel or Curlew calling overhead. Ruff, Dunlin, Wood Sandpiper, Oystercatcher and the two godwits are all typical autumn migrants in variable numbers, while visits by rarer calidrids such as Curlew Sandpiper and Little Stint usually occur in September. There have been many exciting waders to grace Tring Reservoirs over the years including Pectoral Sandpiper, Solitary Sandpiper and Long-billed Dowitcher.

As wildfowl numbers increase with the season's crop of juveniles, Garganey may appear en-route south to spend the winter in Africa; they favour the wooded edges of Wilstone. Check out the open water for passage terns. Migrating Whinchat frequent suitable fencing on adjoining farmland as a steady stream of wagtails, pipits, finches and Skylark moves through. Check out the overflow corner at Startop's End for warblers in August and Goldcrest amongst the tit flocks.

Late autumn gales occasionally bring in storm-blown pelagics such as skuas, Leach's Petrel or Grey Phalarope. The year turns full circle with the arrival of winter thrushes and roosting gulls.

Hobby

Calendar

Resident: Little and Great Crested Grebes, Grey Heron, Cormorant, Canada Goose, Mallard, Ruddy Duck, Gadwall, Pochard, Tufted Duck, Sparrowhawk, Kestrel, both partridges on farmland, Water Rail increase in winter, Moorhen, Coot, Tawny and Little Owls, Kingfisher, Green, Great Spotted and Lesser Spotted (rare) Woodpeckers, Skylark, Pied and Grey Wagtails, Willow Tit (rare), Treecreeper, finches and buntings including Corn Bunting.

December–February: Chance of rare grebe, Bewick's Swan possible, Cormorant, Bittern, Wigeon, sawbills erratic, Gadwall, Teal, Pochard, Ruddy Duck, Goldeneye, Lapwing, Snipe, gull roost, winter thrushes, Bearded Tit (rare), Siskin and Redpoll, corvids, Starling and Corn Bunting.

March–May: Shelduck, wader passage, e.g. Common Sandpiper, Redshank Little Ringed and Ringed Plovers, Little Gull, possible Kittiwake, tern passage – includes Common, Arctic, Black and rarely Little or Sandwich Terns, Hobby, Osprey, Marsh Harrier, Cuckoo, hirundines including Sand Martin, Wheatear, Meadow Pipit, Yellow/Blue-headed and White Wagtails, Chiffchaff, Blackcap, Reed Warbler, Spotted Flycatcher.

June–July: Riparian breeders including Grey Heron, hunting Hobby, Swift over water, late July returning waders.

August–November: Water levels allowing, or on reservoir banks early in day: Green, Wood and Common Sandpipers, Dunlin, Ruff, Greenshank, Curlew, Whimbrel, chance of inland rarity, e.g. Avocet, Pectoral Sandpiper. Terns, possible Garganey, Hobby, warblers, Whinchat, ducks build up, pelagics during late autumn gales, Black-necked Grebe, hirundines, finches, Goldcrest.

ADDITIONAL SITES

Aldenham Country Park (OS ref. TQ 170 955)

A Hertfordshire County Council site consisting of a reservoir with peripheral woodland and fields, close to junction 4 of the M1. It has typical country park facilities and is well used by the public. Limited wintering wildfowl with a tern passage most years. The Alder and Birch often attract flocks of Siskin and Redpoll in winter. Check the woodland for warblers during the summer and breeding Ruddy Duck in the marshy area. Close to Hilfield Park Reservoir.

Astonbury Wood (OS ref. TL 277 213)

A large, predominantly Oak and Hornbeam wood with coppice areas and natural glades formed by the gales of 1987 and 1990. The wood is owned by Hertfordshire County Council Education Department and access is by permit only from the Herts. Environment Centre, Lonsdale Road, Stevenage, telephone 01438 316102. Take the A602 from Stevenage to Hertford and turn left just before Bragbury End towards Aston. The Field Centre is situated down a private drive 300 m (330 yds) on the right, off the lane to Aston. The usual range of broadleaf woodland birds are present, including the declining Hawfinch.

Balls Wood (OS ref. TL 345 105)

A mixed woodland owned by the Forestry Commission with the HMWT managing some 55 ha (137 acres). Nearby Hertford Heath is also of interest and both sites can be reached by parking along the B1197 Hertford to Hoddesdon road.

The wood supports a fine cross-section of woodland species including all three woodpeckers and occasional Hawfinch. Check the heath for warblers in summer and finches and buntings in winter.

Bramfield Woods (OS ref. TL 285 168)

A complex of mainly coniferous Forestry Commission woods, scattered around the village of Bramfield. Park along the lane north of the village and follow the tracks into the woods. Woodcock, Redpoll and Goldcrest are resident. Check the clear-felled patches in summer for warblers and Tree Pipit.

Bricket Wood (OS ref. TL 130 010)

Most of the common land is now overgrown but some areas have survived with open bracken and scattered Birch. The majority of the wood consists of deciduous trees with the best Oak stand sandwiched between the M1 and the railway line. Access is good with parking along the lane from Bricket Wood village. The woodland holds the usual resident birds and is particularly good for Lesser Spotted Woodpecker. Wet meadows at nearby Munden Ford are worthwhile checking for the odd wader or two.

Brocket Park (OS ref. TL 215 125)

A country estate in the Lee Valley west of Welwyn Garden City comprising a landscaped lake with surrounding parklands and woods. Park in the lay-by along the A6129 and follow the track through the wood. The weir is a good spot to watch from for riparian birds, especially in early morning. A particularly good site for seeing woodpeckers as opposed to just hearing them. Kingfisher and Grey Wagtail frequent the river. Check the fields west of the main road in the winter for Golden Plover.

Cassiobury Park (OS ref. TQ 090 970) and Whippendell Woods (OS ref. TQ 075 977)

A large municipal park close to Watford town centre with some attractive wetland habitat alongside the River Gade. The damp Alder/willow wood and cress beds harbour a wide range of species at all seasons. Parking is available in nearby side roads and at points around the park with Watford Metropolitan Underground station within easy walking distance. A large car park is situated at the end of Gade Avenue, just inside the park gates, off the A412 Rickmansworth road. Particularly good in summer for warblers and resident breeders such as Kingfisher and Grey Wagtail. In winter Snipe, Grey Heron and Water Rail are attracted to the cress beds, where Bearded Tit and Water Pipit have been noted.

Whippendell Woods is a large block of mainly deciduous woodland that can be worked in conjunction with Cassiobury Park. There is good public access and two large car parks. To avoid disturbance, visit early morning. The usual broadleaved woodland species occur, including Hawfinch, although numbers are now low. In winter, check the wide bridleways as Hawfinch often feed on fallen beechmast or Hornbeam seeds.

Croxley Moor (OS ref. TQ 082 948)

A recently recognised SSSI close to the conurbation of Watford and Croxley Green. An open grassy moor in the Gade Valley alongside the Grand Union Canal. Good for a variety of common wetland species such as Kingfisher, Grey Wagtail and Reed Bunting and a regular site for Whinchat and Stonechat during migration. From Croxley Met. Station take the waymarked Mill Lane, where a footpath leads over the watercourse and across the moor.

Hatfield Aerodrome (OS ref. TL 205 090) and Beech Farm (OS ref. TL 195 085)

The famous old British Aerospace plant at Hatfield (which spawned the Comet), is now largely derelict and awaiting development. Some of the airfield has already been built on and another part is used as a film set; but there are still some decent areas of grassland remaining, attractive to the likes of Lapwing, Kestrel, Barn Owl, Skylark, Meadow Pipit, partridge, sparrows, finches, and buntings. During the winter months Golden Plover are present, with occasional records of Stonechat and Short-eared Owl. Sections of the airfield near Hatfield Garden Village can be viewed from roads on the Business Park but the best approach is from Beech Farm.

For Beech Farm, park in the small lay-by in Coopers Green Lane at TL 188 090 and take the public footpath eastwards, past the farm. A series of active gravel pits can hold spring waders such as Little Ringed Plover and Common Sandpiper on passage and Snipe during the winter. The south-western corner of Hatfield Aerodrome can be overlooked for passerines and migrants; check out any sparrows as a small and declining colony of Tree Sparrow does breed nearby.

Little Egret

Knebworth Park (OS ref. TL 230 210)

Classic parkland associated with Knebworth House to the south-west of Stevenage.

Approach off junction 7 of the A1(M) or the minor road from Old Knebworth and explore from the waymarked public footpaths across the estate and Newton Wood to the north. All the common woodland and parkland species are present including three woodpeckers, Nuthatch, Spotted Flycatcher and Hawfinch, although the latter two species are in decline.

Panshanger Estate (OS ref. TL 282 130)

A mixture of private woodlands, either side of the Mimram Valley to the east of Welwyn Garden City bisected by a public footpath. New pits are being created as gravel extraction continues; while wet meadows, reedbeds and marginal habitat along the river add to the interest. Typical wetland birds can be expected, including Kingfisher, Grey Wagtail and Little Ringed Plover around the new workings. Check the woodland canopy for Common Buzzard and Hobby during the spring.

Prae Wood, St Albans (OS ref. TL 125 065)

A large block of private woodland on the outskirts of St Albans. Definitely no public access but views across the canopy can be obtained from nearby lanes. The small lay-by near Windridge Farm, at TL 125 059, is probably best; approach off the A4147 Hemel Hempstead Road down Bedmond Lane. Common Buzzard breed in the wood and are often noted soaring over the treetops, particularly in early spring, along with Sparrowhawk and Kestrel. Goshawk have occurred and Hobby are present during the summer. Good views over the wood are also possible from a footpath that runs from the Roman Theatre to Prae Mill and links to the Ver Valley walk.

Pryors Wood (OS ref. TL 266 265)

An 11-ha (26-acre) mixed woodland nature reserve managed by the wildlife trust on the outskirts of Stevenage. The best point of access is from Cartwright Road opposite the Sunblest factory. There is a small parking area and the reserve entrance is directly south of this point following Dixon's perimeter fence. Resident species abound including the elusive Hawfinch, all three woodpeckers, Spotted Flycatcher and warblers in summer.

Purwell Ninesprings (OS ref. TL 206 293)

A compact but diverse reserve of wetland habitats, close to Hitchin town centre and managed by the HMWT. The reserve is best accessed from the Gypsy Lane bridleway which joins the junction between Kingswood Avenue and Purwell Lane at its north end and Wymondley Road at the south. At the Kingswood Avenue end there is a small car parking area, and the reserve is always open. A good winter site with Redpoll and Siskin in the Alders and a mixed thrush, finch and bunting roost in the reedbed. Snipe, Jack Snipe and Green Sandpiper are sometimes noted in the wet meadow or along the River Purwell.

Sawbridgeworth Marsh (OS ref. TL 492 159)

A wildlife trust reserve of some 12 ha (30 acres) situated in the Stort Valley south of Bishop's Stortford. A fine marsh consisting of small reed and sedge beds, open meads, Salix scrub and pollarded willows. Accessible at any time from the Sawbridgeworth railway station to Little Hallingbury road; there is limited roadside parking. The reserve is jointly owned by the HMWT and the Essex Wildlife Trust.

In summer, breeding colonies of Reed and Sedge Warblers with the occasional Grasshopper Warbler. Water Rail, Snipe and Grey Wagtail winter, with the latter species occasionally breeding. Wintering finches and thrushes feed on weed seeds and berries respectively and Jack Snipe are sometimes flushed from the marsh. Also during the winter months check the fields around nearby Trim's Green for flocks of Golden Plover.

Sherrards Park Wood (OS ref. TL 230 137)

An ancient, predominantly Oak wood containing some particularly fine old specimens, west of Welwyn Garden City. Managed by Welwyn and Hatfield District Council, access is good with numerous footpaths throughout the wood. A high breeding density of woodpeckers, tits, Treecreeper and especially Nuthatch. Summering warblers abound along with Spotted Flycatcher.

Stanborough Reed Marsh (OS ref. TL 231 105)

A small yet important 3 ha (7 acre) reed marsh managed by the HMWT south of Welwyn. Park by the sailing lake and follow the track on the north bank of the River Lee towards the railway line. The reserve supports a good population of Reed and Sedge Warblers as well as other typical wetland species. Bearded Tit have wintered in the past and on several occasions have even bred.

Stortford Park (OS ref. TL 470 212)

Throughout the 1990s this former medieval deer park to the west of the town of Bishop's Stortford has regularly recorded Ring Ouzel on spring passage in mid-April. The ancient deer pasture has been replaced by seeded turf, cut for commercial purposes, but still attracts Wheatear and Whinchat on passage. Access is via public footpaths.

Therfield Heath and Royston Hills (OS ref. TL 335 400)

A Local Nature Reserve and, at 169 ha (417 acres), the county's most important area of chalk downland, famous botanically for its Pasqueflowers during April. A car park is available at the Royston end of the heath along with access from the A505 and Therfield roads. Typical downland birds such as Skylark, Meadow Pipit and Corn Bunting breed with a passage of Wheatear and possibly chats in spring and autumn. Winter brings the odd Short-eared Owl or, rarer still, Hen Harrier, and Golden Plover frequent the surrounding arable land.

The rolling arable lands from Ashwell and around Royston are worthy of attention throughout the year. The lanes from Therfield via Reed and onto Barley can be productive in winter for Golden Plover, Lapwing, raptors, owls, partridges, pigeons, finches and buntings. In spring check out the sparsely planted fields of pea and bean for Wheatear, Whinchat and Yellow Wagtail. The open fields around Barley, and the southern edge of the Cambridgeshire fens, are traditional stop-off points for Dotterel, although flocks of Golden Plover are more likely. Stone Curlew and Quail are irregular and rare breeders but Corn Bunting are still common on the Barley prairies. Worth a visit on a fine spring morning or evening in May.

Weston Hills (OS ref. TL 245 323)

An extension of the Chilterns stretching from the outskirts of Hitchin via Wallington (TL 290 338) eventually leading to Royston and Therfield Heath (see above). The area is well served by public footpaths, including the Icknield Way and Hertfordshire Way, and a network of lanes.

The large arable fields attract resident partridges, wintering plovers, thrushes, pigeons, larks, pipits and finches, with the occasional raptor sightings – Common Buzzard are most frequent, but Merlin, Goshawk and Rough-legged Buzzard have been noted. In spring check out pea and bean fields for passage Golden Plover, Yellow Wagtail, Wheatear and Whinchat.

OXFORDSHIRE

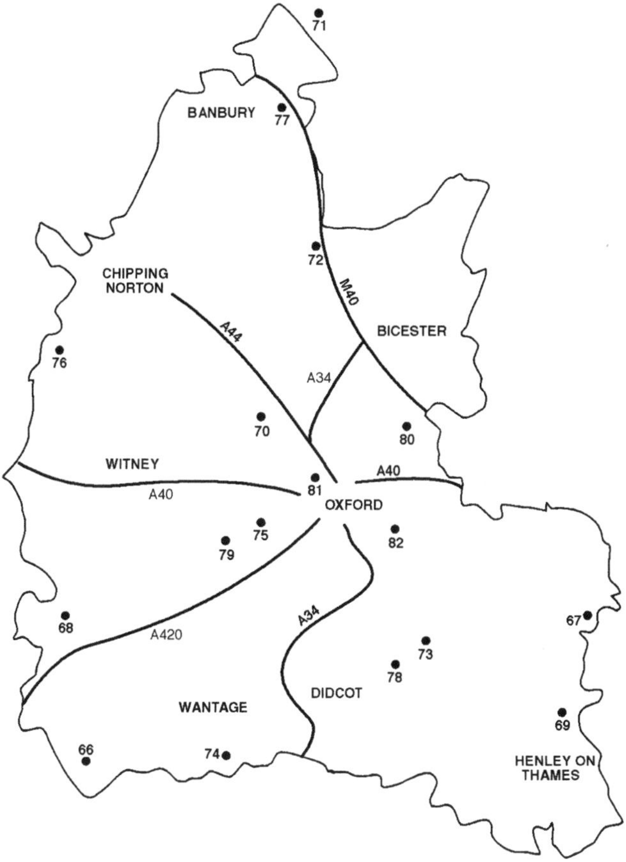

66 ASHDOWN ESTATE

OS ref. SU 284 823

Habitat

The fine grounds of the seventeenth-century Dutch-style Ashdown House have been extensively regenerated and maintained by the National Trust (01793 762209), and the house and formal gardens can be visited at set times of the week in the summer season. However, the 500-acre wood, together with the sloping downland opposite, ensures a variety of habitats attractive to birds.

The woodlands open to birdwatchers are Middle and Hailey Woods, whilst the treescape south of the main house, Upper Wood, is closed to the public. Middle Wood is mainly deciduous, with areas of shrubs and bracken, whereas Hailey Wood is more of a mix of coniferous and deciduous species. The main ride, perimeter trails and joining tracks are rich in grass species and attract numerous butterflies. Viewing points on the west of the woodland trails afford stunning views of the western downs whilst the eastern edge overlooks rabbit-grazed pastures sloping steeply down towards the estate, ridged with a conifer shelter-belt just right for soaring raptors.

The Estate presents an oasis of woodland in an arable and downland setting. Badgers are present, and Hares abound along with Fallow and Muntjac Deer, so it is not just birds that will ensure an enjoyable walk round the estate.

Access

The Estate nestles just where Oxon., Berks. and Wilts. converge, alongside the B4000 from Lambourn to Shrivenham. Travelling in that direction, the entrance to the car park is on the left 5 km (3.5 miles) from Lambourn at the above grid reference and, even if the gate to the main house is open, it is preferable to turn right just before the gate to use the small car park available to non-house visitors; this avoids getting locked in! Access is from dawn to dusk daily except on Fridays when maintenance work is undertaken. Although the rides and tracks are formally laid out, the feel of the woodland is very natural. In addition to woodland paths, a track passes along the entire western and northern edges and other footpaths on the eastern side of the B4000 facilitate the exploration of Kingstone Down and the Estate's meadows on Weathercock Hill.

Species

The car park places the observer right onto the first of the many grassy tracks which zigzag through the woodland, and it is possible to walk all the compartments in a few hours. The north-going trail from the car park gives occasional views of the sloping meadows where groups of Mistle Thrush, occasional Wheatear or even passage Stone Curlew might be possible. In spring and summer, the trees and bushes resound to the sips, peeps and contact calls of young birds, with family parties of Nuthatch most prominent. Dozens of young brown-headed Long-tailed Tit sweep through the vegetation, and yellow-faced Great Tit juveniles maraud through the Oaks and Ashes mimicking their parents' feeding techniques. Both Willow and Marsh Tits are to be seen, although the latter is more common. Treecreeper, more likely heard

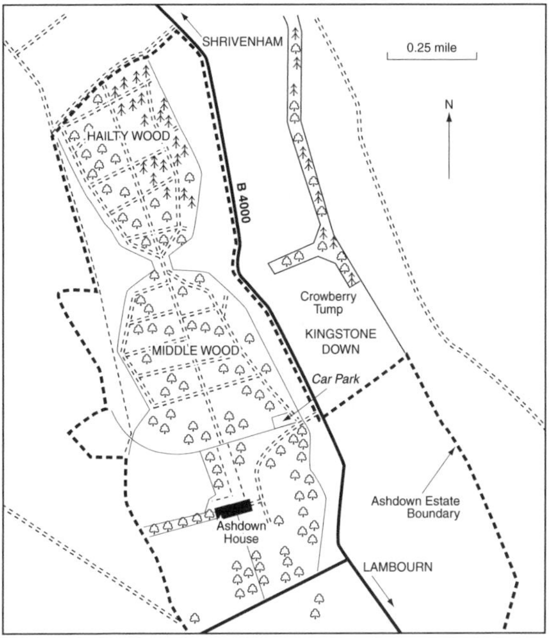

before being spotted, are common, as are woodland Wren and Robin.

Those areas which suffered from the damaging storms of recent winters have created spinneys, with ferns and bracken now well established, and Whitethroat, Willow Warbler and Chiffchaff favour these clearings as well as taller songposts adjacent to the main rides. Wild Honeysuckle is a major draw to butterflies and insects and in turn becomes a café for feeding tits and warblers. Wherever the combination of shady glades and open sunny trails occur, Spotted Flycatcher are likely to be found along with Blackcap and Garden Warbler. Any passing Wood Warbler on its way to its breeding grounds would be well advised to rest up here for a day or two, with some suitable-looking habitat being available. The evergreen stands, particularly in Hailey Wood, are home to Goldcrest and Coal Tit, feeding together in groups in winter, when Redwing and Fieldfare move in to shelter from hard weather.

The woods are not so remote that Tawny Owl would fail to find them, with up to three day-time calling males at different points confirming their territories. Beyond the formal parkland to the west of the house, sightings of Barn Owl have encouraged the erection of Barn Owl nest boxes. There may also be Little Owl in these more open parkland areas. Woodcock are recorded and presumably spend the day in the denser bracken-covered compartments, or perhaps in the ridge of conifers above Kingstone Down.

This same ridge is also a good place to look for Common Buzzard over the park or soaring over any of the high ground on the western or northern horizons. Kestrel too are common over the surrounding crops and Sparrowhawk can be expected rifling along the rides. As with anywhere else in the downland region, Hobby should be looked for around the periphery of the woods, and soaring harriers are a passage possibility. Surrounding farmland guarantees plenty of singing Skylark and Yellowhammer, and perhaps a few Corn Bunting, with huge numbers of Swallow, House Martin and Swift swooping over the crops for flying snacks. Meadow Pipit are more plentiful in winterl, when Chaffinch, Goldfinch and Linnet flock in reasonable numbers.

Wintertime sees the familiar formation of mixed feeding flocks of tits, finches, Nuthatch and Treecreeper, foraging corvids and roosts of winter thrushes on Weathercock Hill. Great Spotted Woodpecker become more obvious as they move from tree to tree in search of sustenance, and reduced foliage improves the chances of catching up with Lesser Spotted Woodpecker. A day in the region seeking typical downland species would be much enhanced with a visit to this island of woodland.

Calendar

Resident: Common Buzzard, Sparrowhawk, Kestrel, Woodcock, Little and Tawny Owls, Green and Great Spotted Woodpeckers, Skylark, Meadow Pipit. Three thrush species, five tit species, Nuthatch, Treecreeper, corvids, Chaffinch, Greenfinch, Bullfinch.

December–February: Prospect of Short-eared Owl, winter thrushes, Brambling, Siskin, Redpoll. Meadow Pipit flocks on adjacent arable land.

March–May: Chiffchaff, Blackcap, Garden Warbler, Willow Warbler, possible Wood Warbler or Nightingale on passage, Whitethroat, Lesser Whitethroat, Cuckoo. Other passage migrants: Whinchat, Wheatear, Ring Ouzel.

June–July: Peak breeding season.

August–November: Winter thrushes and Brambling arrive later in period. Siskin and Redpoll usually evident, tits and finches and Mistle Thrush flock together, Coal Tit particularly evident.

67 ASTON ROWANT NNR

OS ref. SU 731 966

Habitat

In the year 2000, the RSPB opened an office in Princes Risborough to launch the 'Red Kites in the Chilterns' project, sharing facilities and objectives with the equally new 'Chilterns Area of Outstanding Natural Beauty' initiative by local councils (the Chilterns Conference). The Aston Rowant NNR embodies all the features that the Chilterns Conference was established to celebrate and promote. Managed by English Nature as a National Nature Reserve, the site itself covers a total of 134 ha (331 acres) although other woods nearby extend the interest and value of the area.

On the highest parts of the reserve, where the chalk is capped first with 'clay with flints' and then with clay, are found typical Chiltern

Red Kite

woodlands. Towering Beech is the dominant species but there is a good complement of Ash, Rowan, Hazel and Oak with Hornbeam and Wild Cherry also seen. These woods give a very shaded understorey and floristically are at their best in spring when shade tolerant species such as Bluebell, Wood Sorrel, Wood Anemone and violets make an attractive display. The reserve management involves the maintenance of this high level of diversity which represents typical Chiltern succession of grassland, followed by scrub and then woodland. On the reserve's steep, west-facing slopes is typical chalk grassland, its short sward, rich in flowering plants, being maintained by Rabbit and sheep grazing. Also on these slopes is a considerable area of scrub, primarily of Juniper, Privet and Dogwood, with Ash, Hawthorn, Blackthorn, Yew, Field Maple, Whitebeam and Wayfaring Tree all present.

The reserve was unfortunately severed in two by the construction of the M40 which cuts through this part of the Chilterns in a deep 21 m (70 ft) canyon. It is from this stretch of road that many reports stem from non-birders who mention incredulously that 'I could have sworn I saw a Red Kite up there'. Adjacent to the reserve are two other areas of woodland worthy of a visit. To the south is Cowleaze Wood, a 30-ha (75-acre) working plantation of Larch, conifer and mixed deciduous timber, planted by the Forestry Commission between 1957 and 1966, and managed by Forest Enterprise. And enterprising it is with numerous works of woodland art located throughout the site along the 'Sculpture Trail'. To the north-east is the characteristic Beechwood landscape of Aston Wood, owned by the National Trust. Encompassing the whole area are grazing pastures and arable fields.

In addition to the fine flora and insect fauna of the area, Fallow and Muntjac Deer are common and Fox, Badger, Stoat and Weasel are also frequently noted. English Nature has recently purchased an adjacent 100 ha of land to create still more chalk grassland.

Access

The car park is the most convenient starting point from which to explore the reserve (SU 731 966). From the M40 at the Lewknor interchange (junction 6), proceed north-east for 600 m (660 yds) and turn right onto the A40. After 2.5 km (1.5 miles) and at the top of the hill, turn right, drive for a further 600 m (660 yds) and turn right once more into a narrow, metalled lane (care required) continuing to the far end where parking is available for up to 25 cars.

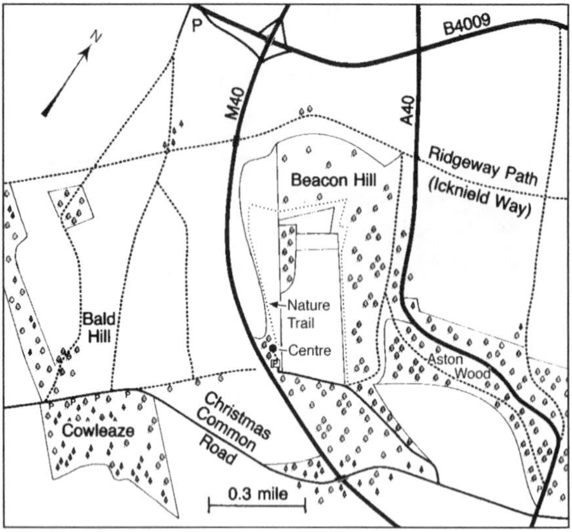

Access on the reserve is limited to the nature trail and one other public right of way. As mentioned earlier the reserve has been split in two and although the section south of the motorway can be reached from the north using the Ridgeway path (which can be reached along a permitted footpath from the reserve), it is best to park at Cowleaze Wood, which has some 70 car spaces (SU 726 957), and to follow the footpaths onto the reserve from here. Cowleaze Wood itself is crossed by many paths and, as Forest Enterprise land, has free access along them. The site is used regularly by the Red Kite Office for guided walks to see this magnificent bird of prey. It is also a favourite site for picnickers and is best avoided at likely peak times.

Aston Wood can be reached from the car park at the Rowant nature reserve but a lay-by on the A40 at the top of Aston Hill gives more immediate entry and a number of tracks lead through the Beeches. Facilities exist for visits by parties but contact the site manager (telephone number given on site) beforehand to make the necessary arrangements. Dogs are not allowed. Aston Rowant, diverse and interesting as it is, is not the only Chiltern site worthy of ornithological observation and the reader is urged to visit other sites in the area they cover. (See Additional Sites.)

Species

The first species to look out for in the car park is Marsh Tit, a bird which thrives in this locale. The reserve has much varied habitat to offer; from the car park, use the obvious viewpoint to scan the distant horizon and the sky in between for soaring raptors. At any time of year, there will be Common Buzzard and Red Kite circling at varying heights, several of which will be just overhead, or along the slopes ahead. Drawn to be nearer these birds, the visitor will soon be in the 28 ha (70 acres) of mixed scrub that exist, this mixture providing many suitable nesting and feeding sites and, where interspersed with larger trees, convenient songposts. In summer, all the common warblers can be found, many staying to breed, to the continuous accompaniment of the song of Skylark. In winter, it is much more a scene of Redwing, Fieldfare, woodpeckers, Chaffinch, and occasional Brambling. Wren and Dunnock are amongst the most numerous of the resident species, nesting alongside Long-tailed Tit, Robin, Blackbird, Song Thrush and Mistle Thrush. Several finches breed, Chaffinch and Greenfinch being the most obvious. The flash of a white rump and the quiet piping call will betray the presence of a Bullfinch, several of which can be found, while Linnet and Goldfinch complete the list of resident finches.

Although becoming more scarce, Turtle Dove and Tree Pipit may be seen on passage or during the summer. If present, the latter is likely to be the more conspicuous, especially as it performs its display flight, and whilst the former remains hidden from view, its purring calls do reveal its whereabouts. Cuckoo also haunt these scrublands.

As one moves from scrub into woodland there is a change in the species encountered, although some birds will be found in both habitats. Species such as Nuthatch, Treecreeper and Great Spotted Woodpecker are common in the woodland but the Green Woodpecker, whilst nesting here, is more usually noted as it feeds on the ants on the open grassland. Marsh Tit tend to be found more in the woodland than the scrub but, as with most erstwhile suitable sites in the Thames Valley, Willow Tit are becoming more infrequent. In previous years, Wood Warbler has joined the list of species breeding at Aston Rowant, but now a glimpse of a bird on passage is all that could be hoped for. Another bird that one might hope to encounter is the Hawfinch as this species has a particular fondness for Hornbeam. But the bird is now extremely scarce in the county so anticipation needs to be applied thinly. Woodcock, beautifully camouflaged against the leaf-litter, nest on the ground in the mature woodlands.

Of the birds of prey, the aforementioned Common Buzzard and Red Kite tend to steal the show, but Hobby may be seen hunting in summer, even at eye level, and sightings in the region of Peregrine have increased in recent years, so 'eyes to the skies' is a good motto here. It is even proving worthwhile nowadays checking corvid flocks for wandering Raven, perhaps being drawn into the Chilterns by increased numbers of Common Buzzard. Tawny Owl are found almost exclusively within the woodland, using it for both nesting and hunting. Sparrowhawk nest in virtually any of the area's woods including the conifer plantations but hunt woodland edges and rides, and over scrub and hedgerow. Little Owl and Kestrel nest at the woodland edge but feed over the grassland. This grassland is the breeding domain of Meadow Pipit and Skylark in summer, but occasionally becomes good hunting ground for Short-eared Owl in winter. Huge numbers of Woodpigeon roost in surrounding trees.

Whilst the conifer woodland of Cowleaze Wood does not show quite the same range of breeding species as elsewhere, a very pleasant walk can be had seeking out Robin, Chaffinch, Blue Tit, Chiffchaff, Willow Warbler and Goldcrest. Coal Tit are particularly abundant here and Crossbill are sometimes seen. Wintertime can be quiet but the diversity of habitat usually means that something of interest can be found. Redwing and Fieldfare gather in large flocks as they greedily devour berries of the scrub and hedgerow; Hawthorn and Whitebeam being particularly relished. Pheasant cough loudly to one another and a Woodcock may jump up and tower almost vertically to escape the dense tangle of branches. Brambling may join the mixed flocks of foraging finches and small parties of Siskin and Redpoll can also be tracked down. The RSPB Red Kite Office runs guided walks around this wood as it offers yet again opportunities for observing the kite as it wafts above and below the eye-line in the valleys viewed from the outskirts of Cowleaze. And there are always those mysterious sculptures to look out for on the way round.

As at virtually any point along the Chiltern escarpment, Aston Rowant can be a great place to view migrating birds. In April, Wheatear feed boldly over the grassland anthills and Whinchat bob nervously on fence posts. In April and May, every 'Blackbird' should be checked out as a potential Ring Ouzel. These same species appear, albeit with less regularity, in autumn. The vantage point that the escarpment presents enables active migration to be observed and, during either passage period, particularly early in the day, birds can be watched as they move along or across the slope. At any time of the year, reasonable weather, coupled with a certain amount of luck, may just create one of those 'best birdwatching days'.

Calendar

Resident: Red Kite, Common Buzzard, Sparrowhawk, Kestrel, Woodcock, Little and Tawny Owls, Green and Great Spotted Woodpeckers, Skylark, Meadow Pipit. Common thrushes, Goldcrest, common tit species plus Marsh Tit, Nuthatch, Treecreeper, corvids, Chaffinch, Greenfinch, Bullfinch.

December–February: Possible Short-eared Owl, winter thrushes, Brambling, Siskin, Redpoll, possible Crossbill.

March–May: Chiffchaff, Willow Warbler, Blackcap, Garden Warbler, Whitethroat, Lesser Whitethroat, Cuckoo, Turtle Dove, Tree Pipit. Passage migrants: Whinchat, Wheatear, Ring Ouzel, possible Wood Warbler.

June–July: Peak breeding season.

August–November: Winter thrushes and Brambling arrive later in period. Siskin and Redpoll usually evident, tits and finches flock together, Coal Tit particularly evident, occasional Stonechat.

68 BADBURY FOREST & COXWELL WOOD

OS ref. SU 260 960

Habitat

Lying to the west of Faringdon, these two woodlands occupy adjacent areas of rising ground separated and surrounded by open arable fields and improved grazing pasture. Badbury Forest, the larger area rising to 120 m (395 ft), is owned by the Forestry Commission and consists primarily of mixed conifer plantations, dense in parts but with blocks of mixed and deciduous woods of predominantly Oak, Birch and Hazel.

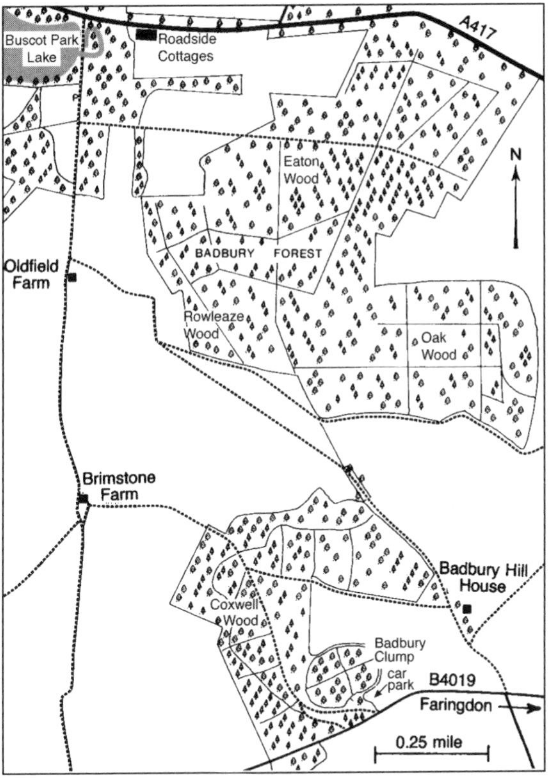

Paths transect the area quite extensively, some forming quite wide rides.

The smaller area, Coxwell Wood, rises to 160 m (525 ft) and is also owned by the Forestry Commission. Tree species here include Scots Pine, Larch, Oak, Ash, Birch, Hazel and Wild Cherry, all interplanted in attractive confusion. The wood here is much more open with a dense understorey, providing the better area for the visiting birdwatcher.

However, a visit to the northernmost woods can be combined with a visit to Buscot Park Lake which, as part of the 7500-acre Buscot and Coleshill Estate, has a more varied treescape, increasing further the selection of avifauna likely to be seen. Adjacent to Coxwell Woods is Badbury Clump, originally the earthen ramparts of an Iron Age settlement. Now it is a Beech plantation owned by the National Trust and renowned for its fine display of Bluebells and other springtime woodland flowers. The woods as a whole have a rich flora and a good complement of butterflies and other insect life. Fox and Badger breed and Muntjac Deer are present in some numbers, often allowing good views as they feed along the grassy rides of Badbury Forest.

Access

To explore the woods to the south of the site, take the B4019 out of Faringdon signposted to Highworth. After approximately 2.5 km (1.5 miles) there is a National Trust car park on the right-hand side of the road with space for 50 cars. For views over Buscot Park Lake and the northern block of woodland, take the A417 Lechlade Road out of Faringdon. After 4 km (2.5 miles), on the left and just beyond Eaton Hastings, is a concealed gateway with large concrete posts, opposite a footpath sign, providing access to a metalled road leading past the lake. Park on the roadside verge alongside the cricket pitch, but do so slowly as drainage ditches cross this verge.

Within Badbury Forest and Coxwell Wood the Forestry Commission allow pedestrian access on all paths unless notices indicate otherwise. Similarly, Badbury Clump has open access and footpaths exist on the land surrounding the woods. From this elevated location, excellent views across the Thames Plain are offered, with the vast hangers and RAF Tri-Stars of Brize Norton dominating the distant north, and the rapidly-developing Fairford Aerodrome to the west; a good place to be birdwatching on air show days!

Buscot Park is strictly private and the only access, apart from the public path next to the lake, is on days when Buscot House and grounds are opened by the National Trust. A notice giving details is at the main entrance to the park approximately 1.25 km (0.5 mile) further west on the A417.

Avoiding the business of Sundays and Bank Holidays, in order to take in all aspects of the site's habitats, a typical visit would probably begin with a good exploration of Coxwell Wood and Badbury Clump before taking the short walk across open country to the larger forest. From here one would make one's way to view Buscot Park Lake, returning via Oldfield and Brimstone Farms for further views over the fields and hedgerows. Alternatively, explore the southern woods and then drive around to the opposite end of the site to check out the lake and adjacent woods.

Species

As noted elsewhere in this book, the woodlands of these five counties are at their best in spring and summer. To demonstrate this fully, pay a visit to Coxwell Wood early on a calm sunny spring morning in May to witness a truly fine dawn chorus. All of the breeding species will be apparently trying to out-sing each other with perhaps members of the thrush family being the star performers. Robin and Blackbird, Song Thrush and Mistle Thrush are all common here and perch conspicuously, setting up their territories and attracting mates with their songs. Determined to make their presence felt, the Wren's explosive trill and the rather scratchy but nonetheless spirited song of the Dunnock will also be heard. Chaffinch, Greenfinch, Blue Tit and Great Tit are other residents that contribute, whilst of the summer visitors Blackcap, Chiffchaff and Willow Warbler all play their parts. Garden Warbler are less regular and Nightingale may only be heard occasionally. Other birds of the site, less tuneful but just as entertaining, are Green and Great Spotted Woodpeckers, both nesting in holes in mature or dying trees. Treecreeper are common throughout and a few Nuthatch nest, particularly in the older trees surrounding Badbury Clump. In the woods close to the lake and on the lower slopes of Coxwell Wood will be found Marsh and Long-tailed Tits. Within the conifers Coal Tit are found in good numbers, but are probably not as common as the Goldcrest whose thin, shrill notes are often the only sound to be heard in the denser stands of conifer. There are also records of Firecrest and with so much apparently suitable habitat available it would be very surprising if these birds were not breeding here.

Jay, Magpie, Stock Dove, Woodpigeon and Carrion Crow are other common woodland residents with Tawny Owl and Sparrowhawk being the commonest birds of prey, though challenged by Common Buzzard of late. Cuckoo and Turtle Dove complete the list of summer visitors.

By comparison, winter in the woods is the more usual scene of roving parties of mixed tit and finch flocks providing the main interest. These woods may have greater numbers of birds in winter than others in the area since feed put out for Pheasant rearing attracts species besides this gamebird. In some years, Crossbill and Redpoll have been seen in the woods and they too could be breeding in the vicinity.

Buscot Park Lake adds another dimension to the site for the visiting birdwatcher. The main interest is in the breeding season and in particular the good-sized heronry, allowing excellent views. Built mainly in Oaks on the northern bank but with others scattered around the lake, the nests are huge, untidy affairs and prone to wind damage. The birds spend much time rebuilding and refurbishing at the start of each season, ready for the long period of incubation and rearing of young. Grey Heron may hunt for prey many miles away but a few can usually be found stalking the lakeside or resting in some of the lower trees below the nest platform. Other breeders on the lake include Coot, Moorhen and Mallard, Great Crested and Little Grebes, and a colony of Canada Geese. Pied Wagtail feed at the water's edge or on the cricket pitch most of the year and hirundines hawk over the water in summer. The lake in winter is less vibrant with only Teal, Pochard, Tufted Duck and Black-headed Gull joining the resident species.

Further interest is found in the open fields surrounding the woods. Most are arable and, except for Skylark and Red-legged Partridge, offer few nesting opportunities, but hedgerows and woodland edges do allow Whitethroat, Yellowhammer, Linnet and Bullfinch to breed. In winter the resident hedgerow birds are joined by Redwing and Fieldfare whilst in the now bare fields flocks of Skylark, Lapwing and more Black-headed Gull feed.

Whilst perhaps not generally regarded as a local birdwatching hot spot, and probably underwatched, the variety of habitat is distinctive in an otherwise farmland environment. Such a large and relatively undisturbed area is always likely to produce something unusual, maybe breeding, maybe on passage, but even if only the regular species are present it is always worth a return visit.

Calendar

Resident: Great Crested and Little Grebes, Grey Heron, Canada Goose, Mallard, Sparrowhawk, Common Buzzard, Red-legged Partridge, Pheasant, Moorhen, Coot, Tawny Owl, Green and Great Spotted Woodpeckers, Skylark, Pied Wagtail. Commoner thrushes, tits and finches, Goldcrest, possibly Firecrest, Nuthatch, Treecreeper, Jay, Magpie, Yellowhammer.

December–February: Redwing, Fieldfare, Redpoll, Crossbill, possible Teal on lake.

March–May: Chiffchaff, Willow Warbler, Blackcap, Garden Warbler, Cuckoo, Turtle Dove, possible Nightingale. On passage: Pied Flycatcher, Wood Warbler.

June–July: Height of breeding season, heronry active.

August–November: Arrival of winter thrushes, Skylark, Lapwing and finch flocks.

69 BIX, THE WARBURG RESERVE

OS ref. SU 720 880

Habitat

Owned and managed by BBOWT, the Warburg Reserve is undoubtedly the Trust's showpiece. Named after the eminent botanist and conservationist Dr E. F. Warburg, it was purchased in 1967 and is the only one of the Trust's reserves to have a full-time warden living on site.

Nestling in the dry valley of Bix Bottom, and occupying 106 ha (261 acres), the reserve lies totally on the upper and middle chalk between 90 and 152 m (300 and 500 ft). For the birdwatcher its prime importance is as a woodland site with much of it having been so since before 1768. A system of broad rides and open grassland totalling 9 ha (22 acres) greatly adds to the interest.

A diverse woodland, the steepest slopes of the valley comprise mainly Beech, including a good area of coppiced timber. There are blocks of conifer plantation, the rest being predominantly Oak, Ash, Silver Birch and Hornbeam, much with an extensive and well-developed understorey. Areas of scrub are to be found, mainly of Hawthorn, Hazel, Dogwood, Rose, Wayfaring Tree and other species which, when open and associated with areas of grassland, supports a rich chalkland flora and fauna. Indeed, the whole reserve with its degree of diversity boasts a wonderful flora (including 15 species of orchid) and this floristic richness is reflected in the overall quality and range of animal life to be found; from the insects of all forms (including over 30 butterfly species) to a fine collection of vertebrates. Fallow and Muntjac Deer can be seen or heard on most visits and Stoat and Weasel are common. On an evening visit Badgers and Foxes can be expected. Adders, Grass Snakes, Common Lizards and Slow-worm, are also to be found in good numbers.

The reserve is actively managed in such a way that maximum diversity is maintained with a continuous age structure within each habitat type. Sheep-grazing is used to maintain the grassland habitat and keep down scrub and rank vegetation, encouraging a wealth of flowering plants. Coppice and scrub management is undertaken in selected areas of the reserve.

Information on the reserve and its wildlife is contained in the Warburg Reserve Species Handbook and its Supplement, available from the visitors centre.

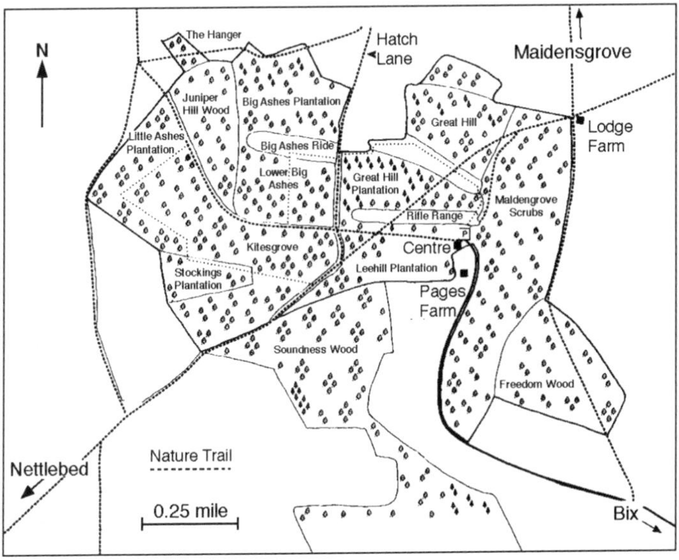

Access

The main point of access to the reserve is from the car park situated opposite the visitors centre at the northern end of the unclassified road joining the B480 at Middle Assendon and the A4130 at Bix village. All roads are very narrow and care must be taken. Additionally, footpaths lead to the reserve from Nettlebed and from Maidensgrove Common. The latter route is well worth attempting since panoramic views of the reserve and the surrounding countryside are to be obtained as one descends to the valley bottom.

The reserve itself has good accessibility along a number of public footpaths and rides, and a nature trail (guide book available on site) has also been laid out taking visitors to all areas of interest on the reserve. Straying from these paths is unnecessary and potentially damaging to the flora and fauna. To prevent too much disturbance upon the reserve, groups wishing to visit should telephone the warden (01491 642001) to book beforehand. The narrow nature of the lanes leading to the reserve does however mean that access for coaches is difficult. Whilst visits from individuals and groups of all kinds are encouraged (one of the main values of the reserve is its educational role), visitors are requested to consider making a donation towards the reserve upkeep.

There is an information centre at the reserve explaining the work being undertaken, describing the plants and animals to be found and showing the valuable work of BBOWT. Information is available about what has been seen and what is currently on the reserve. The presence of sheep on the reserve requires that dogs are kept on leads at all times. In some areas there is no access for dogs at all.

Species

From the birdwatcher's point of view, the prime importance of a visit to Warburg lies in the large number and variety of woodland species likely to be encountered. As with most woods, the best time to visit is during spring and summer whilst the breeding season is in full swing and the birds are most active and vocal.

Probably the most widespread birds are the titmice. Six species can be seen here, all in good numbers with Blue and Great the most numerous. Long-tailed Tit are also frequent, building their intimate enclosed nests in areas of coppice and scrub, although occasionally at Warburg nests will be built high up on the branches of mature trees. The reserve gives opportunity to identify and distinguish between the frequently confusing Marsh and Willow Tits. Song and call of the two are the best means of separation. The sixth and smallest species, the Coal Tit, is associated with coniferous woodland and is accompanied by the tiny Goldcrest whose high-pitched call notes from the dense coniferous canopy betray its presence. It is suspected that its rarer relative, the Firecrest, once nested on this reserve, and after an absence of many years, was recorded again in February 2001.

The three species of British woodpecker are all present with Green and Great Spotted being seen and heard on most visits. The Lesser Spotted Woodpecker is not found in such good numbers but Juniper Hill Wood, The Hanger or Big Ashes Plantation do offer a good chance of a glimpse of this, the most diminutive of woodpeckers. The other woodland specialists, Nuthatch and Treecreeper, thrive within the reserve.

Of the finches, Greenfinch and Chaffinch are very common whilst Goldfinch and Linnet will nest in areas of scrub such as is found within Freedom Wood. Yellowhammer also nest here. Scrub and coppice, particularly coppiced Beech, provide nest sites for Bullfinch. Redpoll and Crossbill have probably bred on the reserve, the former being associated with Birch, the latter with Larch.

Boxes installed in the mature woodland provide nest sites for up to ten pairs of Tawny Owl, which are more often heard than seen. Long-eared Owl have also nested. Red Kite are frequently seen soaring overhead and sightings of Sparrowhawk are regular, whilst Common Buzzard are now breeding again after an absence of several decades. The boundary of the reserve provides nest sites for Kestrel and Little Owl, both of which are more likely to be seen hunting over the adjacent open fields.

Woodcock are quite common at Bix although, because of their amazing camouflage, they are almost impossible to find when on the ground but are often put up when walking through the woods. Dusk, when birds 'rode' their territories uttering their curious croaking calls, makes them far more visible and often one does not have to go any further than the reserve car park to witness this behaviour. Most of the common resident birds are to be found at Warburg and in good numbers. Songsters such as Robin, Blackbird and Song Thrush can make Warburg seem alive with song. Somewhat less tuneful but adding life with their colours, Magpie and Jay are also common. Regrettably, the Golden and Lady Amherst's Pheasants were last regular in the 1980s, since when numbers reduced to very low levels and both became hybridised out.

From April onwards resident species are joined by a good number of summer visitors. Commonest are Chiffchaff and Willow Warbler whose springtime songs can really make one believe that summer is just around the corner! Shortly afterwards come the Blackcap and Garden Warbler. Small numbers of Turtle Dove favour areas of younger woodland, and Spotted Flycatcher might be found, though in reducing numbers. In many respects, the woodland looks ideal for Redstart, Tree Pipit, Pied Flycatcher, Grasshopper Warbler or even Wood Warbler, but few have been recorded recently, possibly through lack of observer coverage. Nightingale, Snipe, and Wheatear have been occasional of late.

During winter months woodlands can be very quiet with most activity concentrated within large mixed flocks of tits and finches, Goldcrest, Nuthatch and woodpeckers. Roaming throughout the woods and scrub searching for insects and berries, they commonly feed upon the ground amongst the beechmast crop. Many resident birds do move outside the reserve, particularly since it lies in something of a frost hollow and, at times, the wood can be very quiet indeed. Some birds do appear on the reserve only during the winter months; Siskin and Redpoll feed amongst the Birch and conifer and Redwing and Fieldfare may forage in noisy mixed parties on the periphery of the reserve.

In the not too distant past, Barn Owl, Stone Curlew and Nightjar all bred in the vicinity of the Warburg Reserve. For now, whilst we hope for their return, there is still much to offer the birdwatcher in what must be the most attractive woodland site in Oxfordshire.

Calendar

Resident: Red Kite, Common Buzzard, Sparrowhawk, Kestrel, Woodcock, Tawny and Little Owls, Pheasant, six tit species, three woodpecker species, Goldcrest, Nuthatch, Treecreeper, Chaffinch, Greenfinch, Bullfinch, Linnet, Jackdaw, Jay, Magpie.

December–February: Winter thrushes, Siskin, Redpoll. Food and bathing stations near hide very active.

March–May: Chiffchaff, Willow Warbler, Blackcap, Garden Warbler, Cuckoo, possible Redstart, Tree Pipit and Pied Flycatcher on passage.

June–July: Turtle Dove, Spotted Flycatcher (rare). Possible wandering Hobby and, more recently, occasional Goshawk.

August–November: Mixed flocks of tits, finches and other species congregate, Redwing, Fieldfare, possible Brambling.

70 BLENHEIM PARK

OS ref. SP 440 160

Habitat

Built in the early-eighteenth century at the behest of a nation grateful to the victorious Duke of Marlborough at the battle of Blenheim in 1704, Blenheim Park and Palace provides a wonderfully historic setting for one of Oxfordshire's finest birdwatching sites. With a total area of some 960 ha (2,400 acres) there are a number of distinct habitat types giving a very varied landscape and associated flora and fauna.

The focus of attention is supplied by the lakes which were created in the 1760s by damming the River Glyme, their formation being the brainchild of Lancelot 'Capability' Brown who, at that time, attempted to naturalise the formal layout designed by John Vanbrugh (architect for the palace) and Henry Wise. Brown was also responsible for planting most of the trees around the lakes and elsewhere, including the clumps of Beech and the impressive selection of cedars.

The water is in three parts. Queen Pool is the shallowest and takes water from the River Glyme. It covers some 16 ha (40 acres) and apart from the very shallow north end with its scrub and Glyceria beds, bankside vegetation is sparse. The largest area, The Lake, covering some 32 ha (79 acres), is the deepest water. It is fringed with stands of Glyceria and has woodland running to its edge. Downstream, the long and narrow Bladon Water has an area of 8 ha (20 acres) and an abundant bankside and emergent vegetation.

Perhaps the most attractive woodland, of greatest importance for breeding birds, is High Park. Predominantly Oak, and a relic of the ancient Wychwood Forest, it has quite an open nature, encouraging a rich ground flora. Oaks are also featured in Lower Park, scattered throughout the area of permanent pasture. In the north, the Great Park is arable land and permanent grassland. Elsewhere there are further arable fields, blocks of conifers, areas of shrubs, small thickets and woodland, the latter managed commercially but with landscape and conservation in mind. Continuous, selective felling and replanting maintains a mixed age structure whilst replanting has also been necessary since the Dutch Elm disease of the 1970s led to the loss of the species that was so very much a feature in the park. Summer droughts have also killed off many of the Beech trees but the replanting policy will restore the park to its former glory.

Access

The main access to Blenheim Park is at Woodstock, 9.5 km (6 miles) north of Oxford on the A44. Parking is possible in the grounds although a charge is made. Free parking is available in Woodstock (check the time limit) from where it is just a short walk to the main gate; a small admission fee is payable. Entering at this point gives immediate views over Queen Pool.

There are three free entry points for the pedestrian: at Bladon, the Ditchley Gate and at Combe Lodge. From Bladon there is an entrance adjacent to the White House pub in the village, 1.5 km (1 mile) west of Woodstock. For Ditchley Gate turn left off the A44 at the filling station 2.5 km (1.5 miles) north of Woodstock. Proceed along the B4437 for 600 m (660 yds) where the gate is to be seen on the left. The entrance at Combe Lodge is from the village of Long Hanborough, 5 km (3 miles) south-west of Woodstock on the A4095. Take the unclassified road to East End, Combe, turning right at the top of the hill. Parking at these three entrances is rather restricted and not so convenient for viewing Queen Pool and the lake.

Many footpaths cross Blenheim Park and whilst large areas of Great and Lower Park are freely open to the public (unless notices indicate otherwise), access elsewhere is restricted to roads and footpaths. This includes the woodland of High Park. There is no access to the buildings and grounds in the immediate vicinity of Blenheim Palace, and very occasionally sections of the grounds may be closed for shooting or special events. On the eastern corner of the palace complex are the Pleasure Gardens, with a restaurant, butterfly house, children's play area, maze and a number of other attractions. Toilets are available here and also near to the Grand Bridge, and in Woodstock. Since sheep are pre-

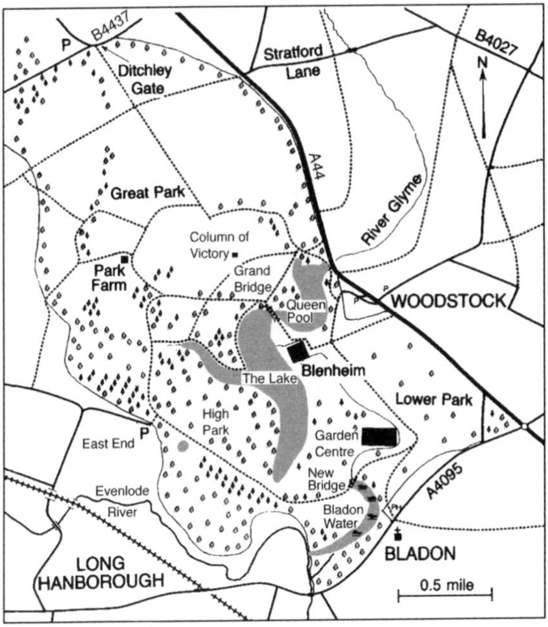

sent most of the year and there is extensive Pheasant rearing, dogs must remain on leads.

The palace and its grounds are a honey-pot for thousands of tourists and walkers. Whilst the park is large enough to absorb these visitors without undue disturbance to wildlife, the birdwatcher who enjoys peace and quiet would be well advised to pay an early morning visit.

Species

The grounds are of great value all year round for their ability to produce a very large number and variety of species. In recent times over 150 species have been recorded here – almost half of this figure being breeding birds.

Perhaps the most popular birds of the Blenheim pools are the Great Crested Grebe whose elaborate spring courtship displays can provide much fascinating and enjoyable watching. Nests are built in the reedbeds and those built on Queen Pool afford good views. Other breeding species include Coot and Moorhen, Little Grebe, Mallard, Tufted Duck and Mute Swan. Canada Goose also breeds and there is usually a sizeable flock of non-breeding birds present, occasionally including a few escapees from wildfowl collections and a regular feral flock of Snow Geese. Other species of 'interesting' origin which have visited in recent times include Mandarin, Wood Duck, Ruddy Shelduck, Red-crested Pochard, Ringed Teal and even a Canvasback. In 1975 Gadwall was added to the list of Blenheim's breeding birds whilst 2000 saw another addition when a small heronry developed on the main island.

In autumn, the breeding birds are joined by individuals which use Blenheim as a wintertime feeding and roosting site. They are also joined by good numbers of Pochard, Teal, Wigeon and Shoveler. Gulls, mainly Black-headed, are always present. Occasionally, winter visits

Gadwall

will produce treats such as Black-necked Grebe or Smew, whilst during periods of passage Garganey and Shelduck may put in an appearance.

Unless there is a significant drop in water level, the fringes of the pool generally provide little in the way of feeding opportunities for waders. Common Sandpiper do appear on passage, and a few Snipe may occur but, apart from a few wintering Lapwing on the pastures, waders are not a regular feature of Blenheim's birds. An early morning visit in winter might be rewarded with a Water Rail, especially near the Glyme Bridge, and having overwintered at least once, Bittern may be found using the area. Kingfisher are regularly seen, particularly in winter when the rivers are in spate. Check all likely perches over the lakes, especially around the Queen Pool. In the breeding season, birds of the water's edge will include Pied and Grey Wagtails, favouring the area around the Grand Bridge, which also has colonies of House Martin and feral pigeon. Common Tern will be present in summer, any passage Black Terns already having moved on. For anybody who has never had good views of Reed Warbler, Blenheim can be very useful; on a still evening in June, stand on New Bridge overlooking Bladon Water, scan the reedbeds nearby and watch as they feed or perform their courtship displays. Their presence guarantees sightings of Cuckoo. Sedge Warbler and Reed Bunting also nest close to New Bridge, utilising dense, bankside vegetation.

Blenheim Park presents plenty of opportunities for observing a good range of our woodland birds. Great Spotted and Green Woodpeckers, Nuthatch and Treecreeper are common wherever there are wooded areas and a few pairs of Lesser Spotted Woodpecker are also to be found. Often the more isolated clumps present the best views of these species with birds easy to detect as they fly from one stand to another. The conifer plantations are noted for Coal Tit, Goldcrest and Chaffinch with the majestic cedars having similar breeding species but are also frequented by Mistle Thrush whose nests, built early in the year, are found on the thick branches of these huge evergreens. All of the woodland tit species are present and in winter form mixed wandering flocks often in the company of large numbers of Chaffinch and Greenfinch, foraging amongst the beechmast. Check these flocks for Brambling as the Blenheim Beeches are probably the most convenient place in the county to observe these delightful finches. For Long-tailed Tit, the area around Combe Lodge is usually the most productive.

Warblers are more usually encountered in and around High Park. Here there is more ground and scrub cover providing nest sites and songposts for Chiffchaff, Blackcap, Garden Warbler and Willow Warbler. Wood Warbler have nested in the past and occasionally appear in spring. Spotted Flycatcher hunt the more open areas, especially near to the pool, another place where Little Grebe, Moorhen and Mallard may nest. Other woodland species include large numbers of Jackdaw (nesting in tree holes all over the park), Jay, Tawny Owl and Sparrowhawk. Hawfinch have been a specialty here but have been irregular recently. Sightings in 2001 were mainly in the vicinity of the palace gardens.

The large areas of open pastureland are probably the least exciting areas of the park. The resident Kestrel may hunt over them, particularly around the margins, coveys of both species of partridge are usually present, and Rook and Jackdaw feed here. Red Kite are still to make regular visits but Common Buzzard may now be breeding here for the first time in decades. Sightings of Osprey are almost an annual occurrence, and with recent records of Red-necked Grebe, Red-breasted Merganser and those elusive Hawfinch to seek out, regular visits to Blenheim should be high on the birdwatcher's list of things to do.

Calendar

Resident: Great Crested and Little Grebes, Grey Heron, Mute Swan, Canada Goose, Gadwall, Mallard, Tufted Duck, Sparrowhawk, Kestrel, Pheasant, Moorhen, Coot, Stock Dove, Little and Tawny Owls, Kingfisher, Green and Great Spotted Woodpeckers, Goldcrest, Nuthatch, Treecreeper, Jay, Jackdaw. Commoner finches, thrushes and tits, Reed Bunting.

December–February: Increased numbers of winter duck, possible Smew or rare grebe, possible Bittern and Water Rail. Large corvid flocks, possible Lapwing flocks. Wandering Hawfinch easier to see in reduced foliage.

March–May: Early in period: migrating Garganey and Shelduck. Reed and Sedge Warblers, Blackcap, Garden Warbler, Chiffchaff, Willow Warbler, Grey Wagtail, Spotted Flycatcher.

June–July: Common Sandpiper, Cuckoo. Breeding season at its height.

August–November: Black-headed Gull, Pochard, Teal, Wigeon, Shoveler. Roaming tit and finch flocks including Brambling, numbers of Siskin and Redpoll rise steadily.

71 BODDINGTON RESERVOIR

OS ref. SP 496 530

Habitat

One of the most substantial bodies of water in the region, Boddington was built in 1805 to replace Byfield Reservoir as a feeder lake for the South Oxfordshire Canal system. Now designated a Nature Reserve, the 5 m-deep lake is some 30 ha (80 acres) in size, situated at the northern sector of the Cherwell Valley and surrounded by wet meadows, rough grassland and numerous rivers and ditches. Exposed mud banks and large frame boulders provide suitable habitat for waders, wagtails and

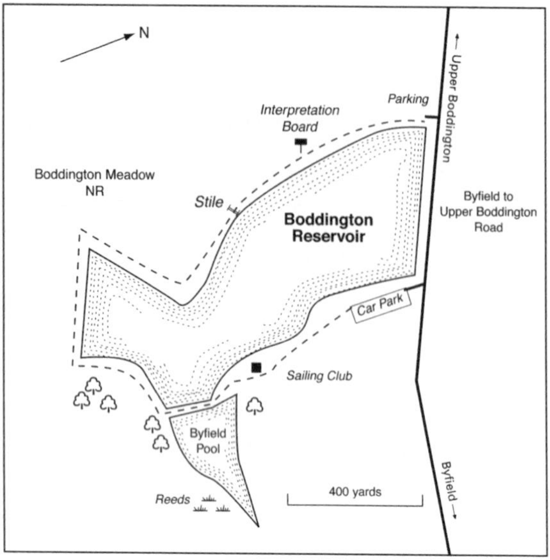

pipits, whilst the adjacent Byfield Pool has a reasonable Phragmites reedbed and abuts further grassland and areas of scrub, attractive to warblers and grebes.

To the west is the nearby small Wildlife Trust Nature Reserve of Boddington Meadow whilst to the east, in the area of the Sailing Club facilities, further flood-meadows and mature hedgerows are a draw for passage and farmland species.

Access

The site is about 12 km (8 miles) north of Banbury and lies just east of the A361 at its junction with the village of Byfield. Driving 2 km to the east in the direction of Upper Boddington brings one to the reservoir car park with space for 30 vehicles. Although lying just on the Northamptonshire side of the county boundary, and looked after by Northants Wildlife Trust (01604 405285), the Banbury Ornithological Society has undertaken the bulk of the observations and site monitoring.

Species

The main body of water attracts a fairly typical range of wildfowl with Canada Goose, Coot, Tufted Duck and Mute Swan always present. Bewick's or occasional Whooper Swan can be expected infrequently to join the large numbers of other birds which can provide a real winter spectacle. The Canadas may be responsible for drawing in small numbers of feral Greylag, and any Barnacle Geese found may have equally uncertain credentials. Shelduck might be seen, though in smaller numbers than a decade ago, but Goldeneye are an annual addition to the impressive sight of hundreds of Wigeon, Teal, Gadwall and Pochard feeding, loafing or simply decorating the water. Elegant Pintail may be present, shadowing groups of Shoveler across the water. The controversial Ruddy Duck is present most months but one wonders for how much longer.

Some of the more unusual species have included both Red-necked and Black-necked Grebes, Scaup, Common Scoter and Goosander. Both Little and Great Crested Grebes breed here, the latter in good numbers, when non-breeding individuals move off to find their own over-summering waters, (possibly Willen Lake) before returning to boost numbers overall in autumn. Water Rail is spotted from time to time and undoubtedly breeds here too. Some of the commoner gulls, passing on their daily movements around the valley, will visit for a preen and rarer species on seasonal passage will also be attracted in. One of the more notable such occurrences was a brief stopover by a possible Franklin's Gull in March 2001, and recent records of Mediterranean Gull make it worth checking the four or five thousand Black-headed specimens, just in case! With up to 1,500 Common Gull and perhaps 500 Lesser Black-backs to eliminate first, patience is essential. Dozens of Common and Arctic Terns stop over on passage, as indeed do occasional Black Tern, no less than 65 being counted here on one occasion. The water's edge, and surrounding meadowlands, will hold Pied and Grey Wagtails whilst Yellow Wagtail will be seen on passage. Kingfisher will more likely be found on the adjacent pool and river systems whilst Snipe is the most likely wader in the wet meadows and exposed muddy banks, which become far busier in passage seasons. Summer months in most years are graced with passage Ringed and Little Ringed Plovers, numerous Lapwing and varying numbers of Green Sandpiper. Several Common Sandpiper may be present in autumn, when Ruff, Dunlin, Curlew Sandpiper, Little Stint, Sanderling and Spotted Redshank become possible encounters to look forward to.

Winter wader movement signals the chance of finding additional species and important visitors have included such notables as Red-necked Phalarope, Spotted Redshank, Turnstone, Pectoral Sandpiper and the area's only ever sighting of Black-winged Stilt in a previous era, but Jack Snipe, Little Stint, Whimbrel and Curlew Sandpiper are more likely nowadays. The warmer months bring hundreds of Swift and hirundines to the aerial feasting table above the water, with the prospect of Hobby being attracted. Major excitement ensues should one of the occasional visits of Osprey coincide with your own and eyes to the skies may be rewarded with sightings of one or two Common Buzzard, an occasional Peregrine Falcon or an infrequent Merlin.

The now mature vegetation and hedgerows around the perimeter of the reservoir are significant for both passage and breeding summer migrants, notably including Turtle Dove (though in reducing numbers of late). Chiffchaff and Willow Warbler, Whitethroat and Lesser Whitethroat bring the warming sounds of summer song and Grasshopper Warbler may well be heard reeling, though their status in the region has plummeted over the last twenty or so years. Reed and Sedge Warblers breed here, the former using the reeds on Byfield Pool, and being at least partly responsible for any Cuckoo seen in the vicinity. Wagtails abound, and a huge group of 160 Yellow Wagtail was once recorded a decade or so ago. Reed Bunting can be found the year round and Tawny Owl can be heard as dusk approaches. Other possible owl species are occasional Short-eared Owl, Barn Owl hunting over nearby meadows and Little Owl. Long-eared Owl roosted in the scrub area near Byfield Pool on one occasion, in numbers approaching double figures.

Lesser Spotted Woodpecker has frequented Byfield Pool, and other scrubby areas are worth checking for Stonechat, often seen atop the tallest piece of vegetation. That other family member, the Whinchat, may also be found on its journey elsewhere. Any pipits espied in autumn should be checked for Rock species, recorded in most years, and as winter leans in, some of the largest flocks of Greenfinch, Goldfinch and Linnet in the region are likely to be found here, Tree Sparrow also having been noted.

Over recent decades, the reservoir has enjoyed a reputation for rare visitors, which have included Red-throated Diver, Leach's Petrel, Purple Heron, Spoonbill, Eider and Garganey. Arctic Skua and Kittiwake have called in previously, as have Sabine's Gull and an area first in the form of a Yellow-browed Warbler in 1993. Spotted Crake were present in 1999 as was Caspian Gull, and yet another first for the region: a fine Aquatic Warbler. Two years running, Red-backed Shrike called in briefly and a group of no less than13 Great Skuas passed through in September 2001. However, it is not even the very good prospect of finding a rarity at Boddington Reservoir that entices the birdwatcher here but the excellent variety of British birds that are drawn to this important part of the region's natural heritage (even if some of it is man-made!)

Calendar

Resident: Great Crested and Little Grebes, Grey Heron, Mute Swan, Canada Goose, Gadwall, Mallard, Tufted Duck, Sparrowhawk, Kestrel, Water Rail, Pheasant, Moorhen, Coot, Stock Dove. Little and occasional Tawny Owls, Kingfisher, Green and Great Spotted Woodpeckers, Goldcrest, Jay, Jackdaw, Crow. Commoner finches, thrushes and tits, Reed Bunting.

December–February: Increased numbers of winter duck, a few Goldeneye and Goosander, possibility of Pintail. Water Rail may be more obvious. Large mixed gull flocks, particularly Black-headed and Common. Chance of wandering Little and Mediterranean Gulls. Increasing possibility of Yellow-legged and Caspian Gulls. Large gatherings of Greenfinch, Goldfinch and Linnet.

March–May: Early in period: migrating Ringed and Little Ringed Plovers, Ruff, Redshank, Dunlin, Little Stint and Curlew Sandpiper. Parties of Snipe, occasional Jack Snipe. Common, Arctic and Black Terns on passage. Reed and Sedge Warblers, Blackcap, Garden Warbler, Chiffchaff, Willow Warbler, Grey Wagtail, Spotted Flycatcher, possible Redstart.

June–July: Common Sandpiper, Cuckoo. Large gatherings of Swift. Breeding season at its height.

August–November: Build up of Black-headed Gull, Pochard, Teal, Wigeon, Shoveler. Passage waders including Little Stint, Greenshank or Spotted Redshank. Wandering tit and finch flocks. Possible Rock Pipit and Yellow Wagtail on return migration. Large numbers of Fieldfare in the area.

72 CHERWELL VALLEY

OS ref. SP 490 300

Habitat

Flowing slowly on a bed of clay, from its Northamptonshire origins to the Thames in Oxford, the River Cherwell runs parallel to the Oxford Canal, its good emergent and bankside vegetation guiding it along a broad valley given over almost entirely to fields of arable crops and improved grazing pasture. Though its level in summer may be reduced, in winter it is very liable to flood, turning adjacent fields into an area attractive to a range of species, depending upon the timing and duration of flood. Whilst inundation may occur anywhere within the valley, the system of flood-meadows covering 360 ha (900 acres) between Somerton and Nell Bridge is the most productive and is designated a Local Nature Reserve. However, the same range of bird species may be encountered elsewhere along the valley.

Access

Limited access includes one or two footpaths across the meadows, but observations are best from the towpath of the Oxford Canal, a public right of way and well above the level of the floodplain, offering good views right across the valley. Venturing off the towpath is unnecessary and will disturb the wildlife and jeopardise the existing agreement.

Three roads cross the valley and limited roadside parking is found close to where these roads cross the river and canal towpath.

Species

Whereas the main interest in the Cherwell Valley lies outside the breeding season, its remoteness from major roads and conurbations makes it deserving of a spring or summer visit. Whilst the waterways have nesting Mute Swan, Little Grebe, Moorhen, Mallard and Kingfisher, bankside scrub and vegetation alongside the canal attracts Reed Bunting, tits, finches and warblers including Reed and Sedge Warblers and occasional Grasshopper Warbler. The scrub and hedgerows will hold Yellowhammer and, in mature trees, Little Owl, Great Spotted and Green Woodpeckers. On the meadows breed Skylark, Yellow and Pied Wagtails, both species of partridge and, in undisturbed sites, Curlew and Lapwing, another valid reason for not wandering from permitted rights of way.

But it is in winter, especially following prolonged heavy rain, that the valley may turn up high number of birds making the most of the feeding opportunities that the floodwaters present. But should the area become frozen, birds move away rapidly making the timing of a visit crucial. It is interesting to consider a typical winter's day: cold but not freezing and the area well covered by shallow floodwaters. Of the wildfowl likely to be present, the majority will be Mallard, Teal and Wigeon, dabbling and grazing at the water's edge, with up to 200 birds of each species distributed along the valley. There may also be smaller numbers (never usually more than 20) of Gadwall, Shoveler and Pintail. In pools of deeper water Pochard, Tufted Duck and even Great Crested Grebe may be seen. Canada Goose numbers may rise dramatically in these wet conditions, possibly attracting some wild grey geese such as White-

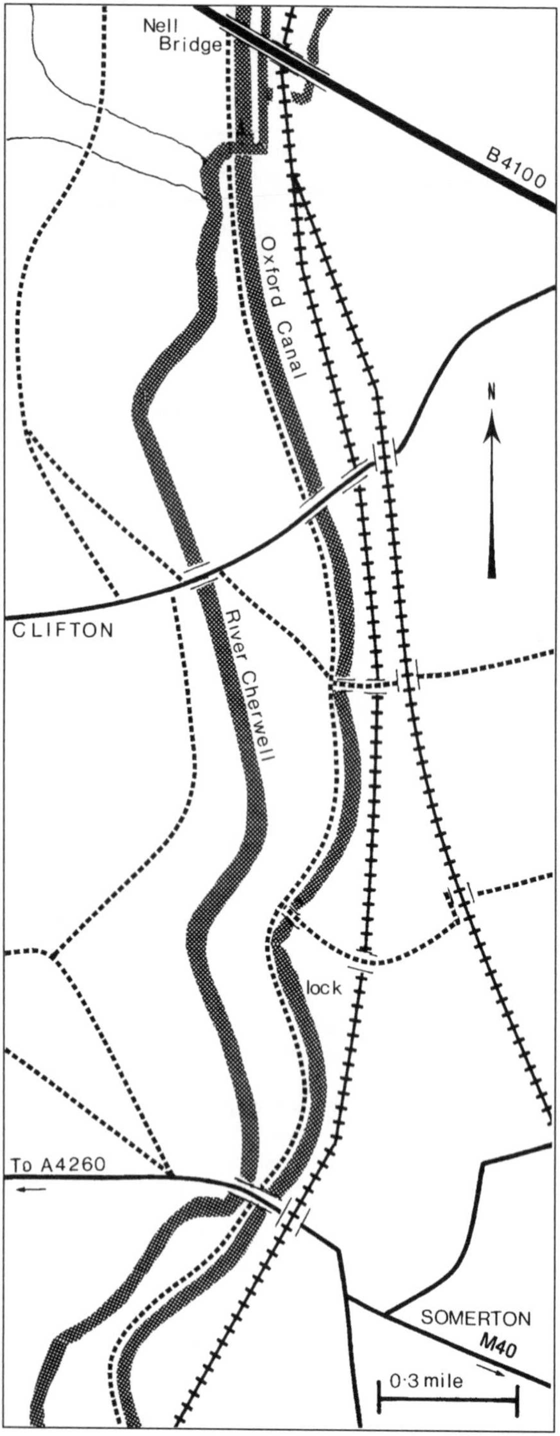

Nell Bridge
B4100
Oxford Canal
N
CLIFTON
River Cherwell
lock
To A4260
SOMERTON
M40
0·3 mile

fronted or Pink-footed and potentially a few Shelduck. Mute Swan in loosely-knit herds make an impressive sight, especially when they wing their way along the valley, occasionally accompanied by small numbers of Bewick's Swan.

In this season, other species have the capability of forming huge flocks in the valley; Black-headed Gull are usually present in reasonable numbers in any weather, but in wetter periods have exceeded 2,000. On drier ground, mixed flocks of Woodpigeon and Stock Dove may congregate, occasionally in excess of 1,000 birds. Redwing and Fieldfare gather on the numerous Hawthorn hedges and bushes, usually accompanied by a few Mistle Thrush and Blackbird. The greatest avian accumulations are, however, created by Lapwing; flocks of 1,000 birds have occurred but twice this number may be seen, with maximum numbers reached towards the end of winter as they range widely in the Cherwell Valley, following the activities of the flood and the plough. They are often in the company of the well marked, but rather less conspicuous, Golden Plover and up to 250 birds have been recorded. Other waders found are Dunlin, Redshank, Ruff and Snipe, counts of the latter reaching over 100. One or two Jack Snipe are also regularly recorded. Towards the end of winter and through into the spring migration, and where suitable feeding ground is available, Ringed Plover, Grey Plover and Whimbrel may make brief stopovers.

The winter floods also attract a number of Pied Wagtail, Meadow Pipit, Linnet and Reed Bunting. Yellow Wagtail, Whinchat and Wheatear join them during the spring migration, sometimes returning via the site in September. Such gatherings of small birds may draw in a Peregrine.

The Cherwell Valley also has the potential to attract a few rarer species. In the past Avocets have appeared, usually in March and April as they return to their breeding grounds, and Bittern have occasionally overwintered.

Calendar

Resident: Little Grebe, Mute Swan, Canada Goose, Mallard, Kestrel, partridge, Moorhen, Lapwing, Curlew (possible), Little Owl, Kingfisher, Green and Great Spotted Woodpeckers, Pied Wagtail. Great, Blue and Long-tailed Tits, commoner finches and thrushes, Yellowhammer, Reed Bunting.

December–February: Meadow Pipit, Woodpigeon, winter thrushes, Lapwing, Golden Plover and Stock Dove flocks. Possible Whooper or Bewick's Swans and White-fronted Goose. If wet, Teal, Wigeon, Gadwall, Shoveler, Pintail with possible Tufted Duck, Pochard and Great Crested Grebe. Dunlin, Redshank, Snipe, Ruff and possible Jack Snipe.

March–May: Passage: Ringed Plover, Grey Plover, possible Whimbrel and Avocet. Wheatear, Whinchat, possible Garganey and Shelduck. Reed and Sedge Warblers, Yellow Wagtail, occasional Turtle Dove.

June–July: Possible Hobby.

August–November: Return movement of Whinchat, Wheatear and a few waders. If wet, build-up of species as for December–February.

73 DORCHESTER GRAVEL PITS

OS ref. SU 580 950

Habitat

Some 10 km (6.5 miles) to the south of Oxford, in the area of countryside separating Dorchester-on-Thames and Berinsfield and bounded by the Rivers Thame and Thames, is a group of flooded, worked-out gravel pits. This network of six lakes has shown itself to be a fine site for birds during both summer and winter. Orchid Lake and Dorchester Lagoon are well landscaped and for angling and boating. Both have islands and a rich bankside vegetation comprising reeds, scrub and overhanging willows. Along its southern edge, Orchid Lake has a small reedbed and area of fen vegetation with willows, Birch and Alder. Queenford Pit is the largest body of water and the prime site for waterfowl, gulls and terns. Its banks do not have such good cover as the other lakes but a recently constructed earth bund in the centre is already interesting waders. (To assist the reader in relating the text to the associated map, letter references are used in the following paragraphs.)

Further east is the medium-sized Drayton Road Pit (A), surrounded by rank vegetation and with sprawling Bramble and hedgerows beyond. To the south of Queenford pit on the opposite side of the Dorchester by-pass, A4074, is a smaller and much older lake (B) much used by anglers. It has a thick hedgerow along its southern and eastern aspects and a bankside with dense cover and many mature trees, mainly willows. Allen Lake has matured and now attracts most of the common waterfowl species.

Unless there is a drop in the water table following periods of drought, the Dorchester Gravel Pits provide little in the way of islands and sand bars; waders therefore tend to be found scattered along the shorelines and terns only use the pits for feeding.

In addition to these features there are hedgerows, mainly of Hawthorn, ringing the lakes, the STW just north of Orchid Lake and, to the north of Queenford Pit, a waste disposal site. The future of Queenford Pit itself is a little unclear.

Access

The pits are to be found just south of Berinsfield on the A4074, some 10 km (6.5 miles) south of Oxford. For views over the lakes to the east of the A4074, park in the lay-by on the left approximately 1 km (0.75 mile) beyond the Berinsfield roundabout and just before the footbridge. Queenford Pit can be viewed from the roads around its boundary and also from the footpath along its western edge. The smaller pit to the east is privately owned and viewing is possible only from the road along its western shore. Cross over the by-pass for the third, smaller pit around which there is a well-worn path.

For Orchid Lake and Dorchester Lagoon turn right at the Berinsfield roundabout (signposted for Abingdon) and then left (for Dorchester) after 300 m (330 yds). Access is forbidden to these lakes, but views are possible through the hedge.

Allen Lake can be viewed from its northern tip or, for a challenge, 'scoped from the top of Little Wittenham Hill when visiting this latter site.

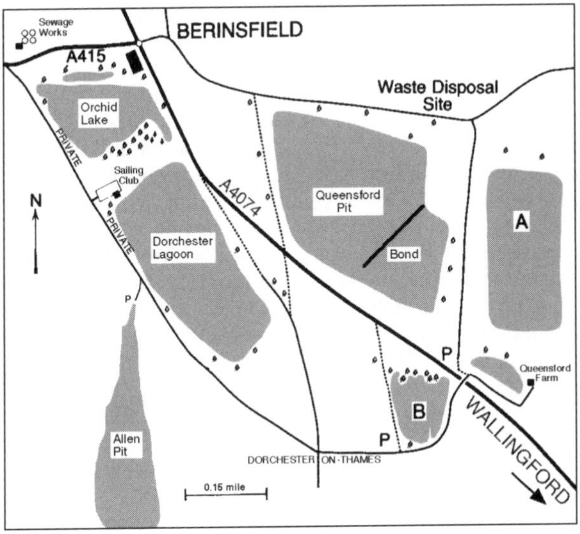

Species

Wintering wildfowl are undoubtedly the main attraction to this area. During winter, Dorchester Gravel Pits is one of the favourite haunts in the county for Goosander. Over 40 may be present and, if not disturbed, small groups will be found on all the pits, the majority on Queenford. The drake stands out clearly amongst other species present, with extensive white plumage both in flight and on the water.

Another species particularly noted here is Ruddy Duck. Whilst found on any of the Oxfordshire waters during winter, Dorchester has always been a favoured haunt and became the first still-water breeding site in the county. Of course, the controversial culling exercise may have had an effect on numbers. Duck species found all year include Mallard, Tufted Duck and Pochard, with maximum numbers being reached in the autumn. During the winter, Wigeon form the largest flocks on the pits when up to 500 birds may be present, especially on Allen Lake. On the same water, Shoveler, Teal and Gadwall will be present in smaller numbers but with Goldeneye completing the list of regular winter visitors. Less regular but seen most winters are Pintail, Shelduck and Smew, and exotic escapees such as Red-crested Pochard or Mandarin may occur. Avocet and American Wigeon are among the more prized visitors to this lake.

Common grebes are present all year on all of the lakes but in winter those on Queenford Pit may be joined by Black-necked, Red-necked or Slavonian Grebes or maybe even a Great Northern Diver. Coot take the prize for the most numerous waterbird on the complex, with winter counts over the area exceeding 1,500. Mute Swan and Canada Goose breed on any of the lakes but outside of the breeding season there is a dramatic increase in numbers with as many as 60 Mute Swan and up to 1,000 Canada Geese present, and it is worth checking for Bewick's and Whooper Swans. Grey Heron is another frequent visitor to the pits, quietly stalking the shallows, while at the water's edge Pied and Grey Wagtails flit busily along the margins.

Having stated that the area is not a prime site for waders, small numbers do use the complex although visits tend to be brief. Most visit in the autumn, when the water level has dropped and Greenshank, Green Sandpiper, Ruff and Little Stint may be seen. Redshank and Lapwing are present most of the summer, although in recent years nesting has become sporadic. The best places to seek waders would be the bund on Queenford, the edges of Allen Lake at low water and the temporary scrapes and flashes near Days Lock, a site responsible for Green-winged Teal, Garganey, Kentish Plover, Temminck's Stint, Whimbrel and Wood Sandpiper in its time. Another pool forms in very wet weather on the opposite side of the Thames above Days Lock (locally known as the River Scrape) and if the towpath is not too busy, Common and Green Sandpipers, Ringed and Little Ringed Plovers, Ruff, Redshank, Golden Plover, Dunlin and Snipe are all prospects; a Pectoral Sandpiper visited here on one occasion. Wild (and probably less than wild) geese also frequent this patch in winter, Bean and White-fronted having featured as well as feral species such as Bar-headed and Egyptian Geese.

Both passages are times to look out for Black, Common and Arctic Terns. They may stop at the lakes for several hours, working their way over the water surface in search of small fish. Little and Sandwich Terns have been recorded. Before spring terns move through, many summer migrants will already be on site. Earliest will be Sand Martin and Chiffchaff, joined later by Sedge and Reed Warblers and Whitethroat. In April, small numbers of Wheatear, Whinchat and Yellow Wagtail move through the site, some of the latter staying to breed, taking their place alongside the resident Reed Bunting and Yellowhammer, tits, finches and Treecreeper. Where trees are to be found, Great Spotted and Green Woodpeckers nest, with the latter being particularly evident around Orchid Lake. Small numbers of the Lesser Spotted Woodpecker also occur. Of the resident birds of prey Kestrel, Sparrowhawk and Little Owl all nest locally and remain active throughout the year, joined occasionally in winter by Merlin.

As well as a broad spectrum of wintering and breeding birds, the pits do draw a few rarities. On autumn passage, Wryneck, Red-backed Shrike and Pied Flycatcher have all been recorded, usually in quieter areas of scrub and hedgerow. In autumn, Little Gull may feed over the water whilst the moderate gull roost has included Glaucous Gull, and will probably involve Yellow-legged Gull. With some 190 species to its credit, this complex of water bodies, meadows and rough areas deserves exploring in most seasons.

Calendar

Resident: Great Crested and Little Grebes, Mute Swan, Canada Goose, Mallard, Ruddy Duck, Sparrowhawk, Kestrel, Moorhen, Coot, Little Owl, Kingfisher, all three woodpecker species, Pied Wagtail, common tits and finches.

December–February: Rarer grebes, Pintail, Smew all possible. Large numbers of Canada Goose, with other goose species often present, Wigeon and Coot. Gull roost, mainly Black-headed and Lesser Black-backed but Glaucous possible. Goosander, Teal, Tufted Duck, Pochard, Ruddy Duck, Shoveler, Gadwall, Merlin. Flocks of Golden Plover.

March–May: Sand Martin, Chiffchaff, Wheatear, Cuckoo in first half of period followed by Swallow, Swift, Sedge Warbler, Reed Warbler, Sylvia

Golden Plover

warblers and Yellow Wagtail. Terns and a few waders on passage. Possible Redshank, Dunlin, Ringed and Little Ringed Plovers, Lapwing, Common Sandpiper.

June–July: Most species at height of breeding season. Swift and hirundines over the lakes.

August–November: Main wader passage with possible Little Stint, Ruff, Greenshank, Green Sandpiper. Much movement of finches and warblers and chance of rarities. Waterfowl and gull numbers increase.

74 DOWNLAND OXFORDSHIRE

Habitat

The Downlands of Oxfordshire form part of the large band of chalk that stretches in a huge, sweeping arc from Yorkshire south to Wiltshire. This chalkland manifests itself quite dramatically within the Oxfordshire landscape in two rather contrasting fashions. East of the River Thames it forms the elegant, wooded Chiltern Hills whilst on the opposite side of the river is the far more open countryside of the Wessex Downs. The Downs run westwards as far as Ashbury in Oxfordshire and thence on to Salisbury Plain.

From the Thames Valley and the Vale of the White Horse at 60 m (200 ft), the hills rise in a steep, north-facing escarpment to an altitude of over 220 m (720 ft). Beyond the scarp they slope away gently southwards in a landscape dissected by an intricate system of mainly dry valleys.

The Downs possess a number of contrasting habitats each having a bearing upon the wildlife encountered. Before the Second World War

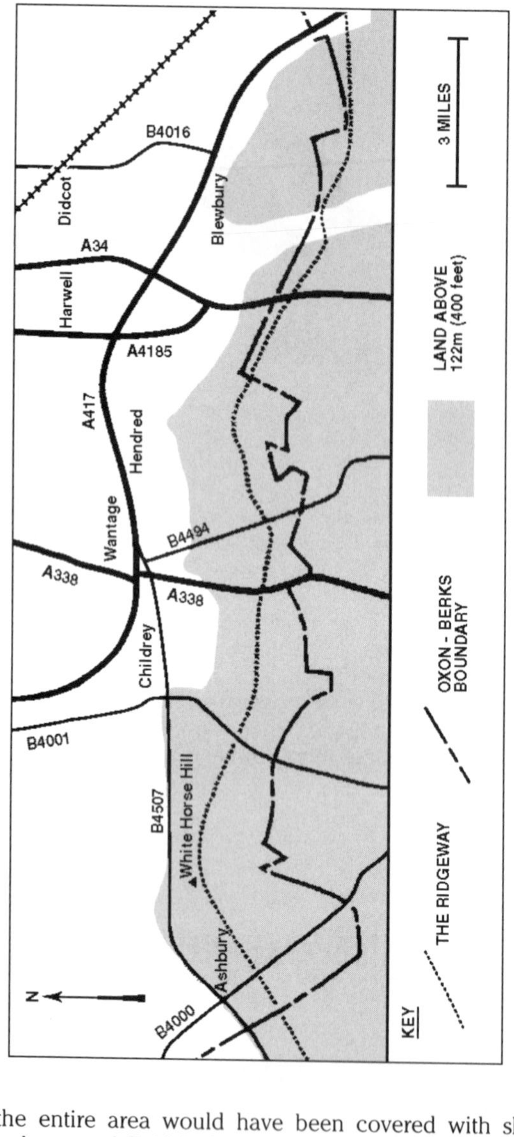

virtually the entire area would have been covered with short turf, grazed by sheep and Rabbits but without application of fertilisers or herbicides, and with areas of Hawthorn and Juniper scrub. This combination creates a rich habitat for a range of wildlife. Today, whilst this traditional scene can still be witnessed in some localities, much of the landscape has been converted to intensive cultivation with subsequent impoverishment of wildlife. As some recompense for this loss of traditional grassland, the presence of several horse racing stables in the vicinity has created areas of permanent grassland (in places fringed with scrub) for training gallops. Whilst less rich floristically, they add another dimension to the available habitat for birds, providing feeding areas for corvids, Starling and partridge.

The Downs are criss-crossed by lanes and tracks, many being ancient rights of way, wide, rich in flowers and insects, often with isolated bushes dotted along their length and sometimes lined by hedgerows. In places the open atmosphere of the Downs is further broken by stands of trees and shelterbelts. Beech and conifers are the main species but a few Oak woods can be seen. These wooded areas provide shelter for Fox and Badger and Roe, Fallow and Muntjac Deer; the early morning observer will often see them feeding out on nearby fields.

The area is very dry, with few ponds or streams on the high ground. Whilst restricting the species to be found, it does mean that the wet areas are something of a magnet for wildlife. In summer, a sizeable puddle can often be worth watching whilst small reservoirs and areas around farms, especially pig farms (e.g. Churn Farm) should always be checked.

Since the Downs are essentially a very open area, windy, stormy conditions can lead to an apparent dearth of birds. In these conditions they head for shelter in the valleys or around the villages at the foot of the escarpment. Here the greater amount of vegetation and man-made cover creates a less hostile environment for wildlife.

The hills straddle the Oxfordshire–Berkshire border and, but for a boundary change in the 1970s, would remain within Berkshire. Hence, even today, the whole upland area is still known traditionally as the Berkshire Downs.

Access

Throughout the year, but especially in winter and at periods of passage, the entire length of the Downs can be very rich in birds. However, because at these prime times birds can be rather localised, birdwatching can involve a fair amount of luck in order to find some of the most interesting species. It would therefore be rather artificial to describe individual downland sites alone since this may imply that the remainder has reduced ornithological value when this is far from true. Thus, this chapter will refer to sites across all of the Oxfordshire Downland and give details of access to areas where a good range of birds and habitat types can be encountered.

As they pass through Oxfordshire, the Wessex Downs are well served by road, footpath and bridleways, making access relatively uncomplicated. However, do not be tempted to stray from the beaten track into field or woodland; most are in private ownership and as well as disturbing wildlife, the action could jeopardise existing rights of public access.

CHOLSEY HILL

(OS ref. SU 578 878)

Not the highest hill in the region, but with excellent views in all directions, affording the site the reputation as something of a raptor viewpoint. Approximately halfway between South Moreton and Cholsey, parking on the minor road at the highest point overlooks The Lees woodland to the south-west and the marshy area of Mackney to the north.

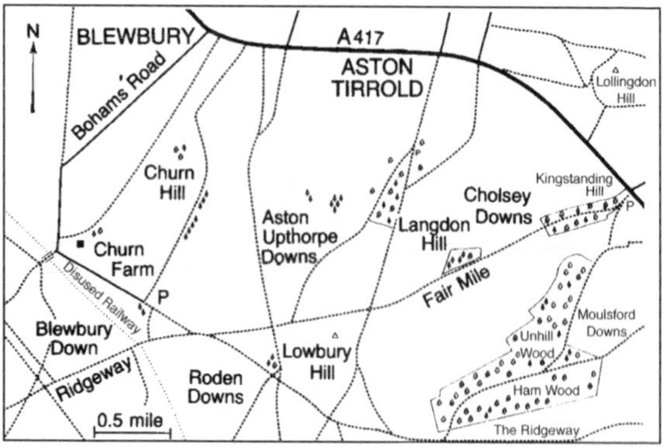

CHURN & THE FAIR MILE

(OS ref. SU 520 828)

This area at the eastern end of the Downs is favoured by local birdwatchers and does turn up a good selection of migrating birds. The area is mainly arable but Moulsford and Aston Upthorpe Downs retain typical chalk grassland. Racing gallops feature and rights of way are wide with bushes and hedgerow. Further interest is added by mixed woodland at Unhill and Ham Wood and by scrub and woodland at the eastern end of the Fair Mile.

There are a number of access points. From Kingstanding Hill on the A417, access at SU 573 838 where car parking is available at the end of the Fair Mile. From Streatley, take the A417 north and after 6.5 km (4 miles), opposite the turning to Aston Upthorpe, turn left and follow the track south, parking at SU 550 843. From Blewbury, turn off the A417 south into Bohams Road on the western edge of the village. Continue to the end of the lane, bearing left to Churn Farm and following the straight, concreted road to the Field Studies Centre car park.

The final route is probably best for birdwatchers limited by time, whilst for those wishing to explore the area at a more leisurely pace, any of the given points can be used as the start of some very interesting and not too taxing circular routes.

THE WARREN & GINGE DOWN

(OS ref. SU 418 841)

Whilst lacking in the traditional grassland habitat this is another area much favoured by locals and in addition to the usual range of breeding birds is always likely to turn up a few less common species, e.g. Wood Warbler. Access is centred upon the Ridgeway but there are many footpaths creating circular routes and allowing views over the mixed woodland of the Warren, some extensive gallops and a number of shelterbelts. The most convenient point for access is from the B4494, 4 km (2.5 miles) south of Wantage, where it is crossed by the Ridgeway. Ample car parking is available here.

Species

The open nature of most of Oxfordshire's chalk downland is reflected in the composition of its bird communities with ground and scrub nesting species the most obvious and more frequently encountered. Of these, Chaffinch, Yellowhammer and Corn Bunting are common, using patches of scrub or any of the bushes that dot the landscape as convenient songposts. The thick vegetation along the edges of tracks provides nest sites. Meadow Pipit are plentiful, the Oxfordshire stronghold for the species being in this region. Whilst their feeble piping calls seem to be everywhere it is a thrill to watch them perform their display flights, rising high in the air and then descending, parachute-like, uttering rapid shrill notes. These four species are abundant throughout the year, often forming large flocks in winter as they feed on fields of stubble or newly planted crops. Another bird present all year, similarly forming larger winter flocks, is Skylark. Their airborne songs throughout the spring and summer months help to create the atmosphere that is so typically Downland.

Red-legged Partridge are common residents, nesting along field edges and feeding on the gallops, lanes and arable fields, whilst the Grey Partridge is less frequently seen. Game-rearing, especially in the vicinity of the Warren, ensures that Pheasant is abundant. In summer the list of gamebirds is added to by the arrival of Quail, a bird more often heard than seen and from May onwards its deceptively ventriloquial calling, especially at dusk, is worth listening out for. In a good year they may be encountered anywhere, but when they are more thinly distributed, the area of Nutwood Down, south of Letcombe Bassett is a good place to visit (SU 365 825).

The ground-nesting species are completed by the waders. The Lapwing, whilst having declined in numbers over the years, is found in areas of sheep-grazed grassland, where arable fields have been left fallow for a while, or on fields of late-sown corn. Springtime, when the birds are displaying and holding territory, can provide some memorable birdwatching. Outside the breeding season, Lapwing form huge flocks of up to several thousand birds, often accompanied by Golden Plover, roaming extensively, even to areas below the scarp such as Aldfield Common (SU 465 877). The lack of water precludes visits by other wader species, but some waterways at the foot of the hills provide sites

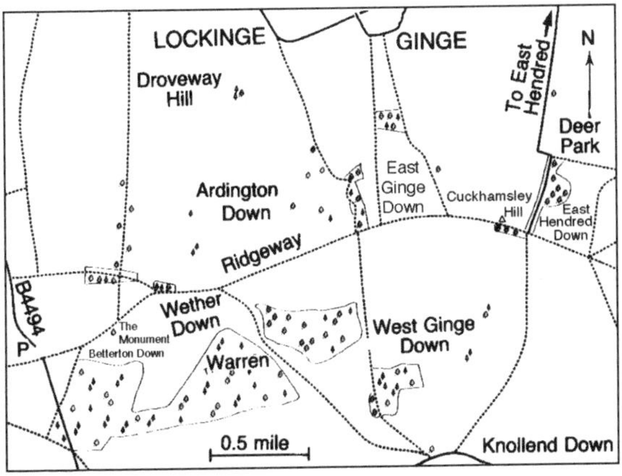

for Snipe, whilst the woodlands (e.g. Unhill Wood or the Warren) may harbour Woodcock.

These Downs were once the place for Stone Curlew in good numbers. Sadly their numbers have declined but it is still worth keeping eyes and ears open during the summer, particularly over fallow ground or land which has been sown late in the season, since it is always possible that they may appear at new sites.

Where the open ground changes to patches of denser scrub and hedgerow, the associated bird community also alters. Chaffinch and Greenfinch, Goldfinch and Linnet now become common and, perhaps something of a surprise in the absence of water, Reed Bunting are often found in the scrub along the gallops, where Little Owl are also seen. In summer, Chiffchaff, Willow Warbler, Blackcap and Whitethroat occupy hedgerows and scrub, while Spotted Flycatcher are regularly noted. A similar range of species is found within the Downland woods, added to by Great, Blue and Coal Tits, Great Spotted and Green Woodpeckers, Jay, Nuthatch and Treecreeper. Tawny Owl and Sparrowhawk are also found here, the latter more often seen as it hunts over scrub and hedgerow for unsuspecting passerines, or soars high overhead on summertime thermals.

It is probably the birds of prey which receive most attention from the Down's birdwatcher, particularly in winter. Typical birds would be Short-eared Owl and Hen Harrier, providing exciting watching as they hunt over any rough grassland. Again, Churn is perhaps the most consistent site for both species with Hen Harrier often seen at dusk hunting along the disused railway line. Both can, however, turn up almost anywhere, probably moved around by weather and disturbance over the feeding and roosting sites. Marsh and Montagu's Harriers are also recorded occasionally. Wintertime can turn up the occasional Merlin, preying upon the flocks of pipits or finches (including Brambling) which wander the area, whilst Kestrel and Sparrowhawk are found all year, nesting within woodlands on both high and low ground. Also seen throughout the year are Common Buzzard, these magnificent raptors observed hunting over grassland for their small mammal prey or, during summer, soaring majestically overhead riding the thermals. Summertime will also find Hobby in the area, particularly in late summer when drawn to prey upon hirundines that gather along the escarpment prior to migration. These species have been recorded also at Cholsey Hill, where Peregrine may be added, and where Quail might be heard in summer.

Either passage period can provide some of the best birdwatching experiences on the Downs. The north-facing escarpment seems to act as a line of travel for birds allowing them to be observed either during flight or on the ground as they make a brief stopover. As emphasised elsewhere, the point of stopover can be anywhere, but the Churn area can be the most productive. During springtime Wheatear are the first visitors to drop in, arriving from mid-March, whilst later, Whinchat and Ring Ouzel visit and, with the chance of Dotterel or Nightjar, this can be quite a lively time of year. Autumn passage sees the return movement of these birds, in particular Whinchat and Wheatear, as well as the first incoming winter visitors such as Redwing and Fieldfare. Meadow Pipit, gulls and waders are also 'on the move' during September and October.

Birdwatching on the Downs can be rather frustrating and one should not be put off if a blank is drawn on the first visit. Periods of passage, both spring and autumn, undoubtedly provide the best birdwatching days and if there has been a clear night, followed by cloud, areas of scrub can be alive with migrants forced down in the course of their long-distance travels.

Wintertime too can give many memorable moments and whilst timing is all important, a certain amount of luck is involved; but with patience, the Downs will eventually reveal just why they are one of Oxfordshire's most exciting birdwatching areas.

Skylark

Calendar

Resident: Sparrowhawk, Kestrel, partridges, Lapwing, Little Owl, Meadow Pipit, Skylark, Corn Bunting, Yellowhammer, Reed Bunting. Scrub and woodlands: usual tits, woodpeckers and finches, Nuthatch, Treecreeper, Goldcrest, Woodcock, Jay and possible Common Buzzard.

December–February: Short-eared Owl, Hen Harrier, possible Merlin. Large Golden Plover and Lapwing flocks.

March–May: Migrating species especially during April: Wheatear, Whinchat, Ring Ouzel and Meadow Pipit, possible Nightjar and Dotterel, Tree Pipit, commoner warblers, Cuckoo, Turtle Dove, Spotted Flycatcher. Possible Nightingale.

June–July: Quail, possible Stone Curlew, Hobby.

August–November: Early in period, Whinchat and Wheatear on passage. Build-up of hirundine numbers. Finches and tits flock together, possible Brambling.

75 FARMOOR RESERVOIRS

OS ref. SP 450 064

Habitat

These two huge concrete bowls, comprising some 153 ha (378 acres) of Thames Water's estate, represent without doubt one of the 'must visit' birding sites in the county. Since completion in 1976, the two west-Oxford reservoirs have afforded birdwatchers some of their 'best birding days', with many county firsts being found here and the site has proven a consistent draw to rarer birds which visit the region. The reservoirs' importance to birds is on two counts: firstly, during the winter period (October–March) as a feeding, resting and roosting site for large numbers of waterfowl and gulls, and secondly as a site for those birds resting and feeding on migration.

The vast open areas of water incorporating both Farmoor I and Farmoor II are at a high elevation providing an ideal landmark for interested species. Although at first sight the lakes seem devoid of bankside vegetation or muddy feeding areas, with no available bankside breeding opportunities, the area just beyond the perimeter of the works does provide some recompense. Earlier tree planting of the grassed areas beyond the embankment has begun to mature but the single most important feature has been the creation of two small reserves, nestling between the Thames floodplain and the western edge of the basins. Pinkhill Meadow Nature Reserve has existed for a few years now but another 4-ha (10-acre) reserve, opened in May 2000, has enhanced the overall species richness of Farmoor tremendously. This reserve was named The Shrike Meadow following the historic visitation of a fine Great Grey Shrike during the winter of 98/99. These two potential hot spots for a wide variety of birds, were developed with assistance from the Environment Agency to create a rich mosaic of ponds, ditches, wet grassland, reedbed and scrub, all with good viewing opportunities. The hide at the 4-ha (10-acre) Pinkhill has been augmented with another at The Shrike Meadow, both with wheelchair access. The River Thames (to the west of the reservoirs) and its associated flood meadows, shrubs and bankside trees is widely used by breeding birds, as is the area of fields and mixed woodland to the south.

Access

The reservoir complex is situated just south of Farmoor village. From Oxford proceed west along the B4044, turning left onto the B4017 immediately upon reaching the village. The main entrance and car park are on the right, approximately 750 m (800 yds) from this junction.

Access to the reservoir embankments is by permit only, available from the gatehouse (£1 for day visitors, £8 for one year) or by writing to the senior warden. (See Useful Addresses.) The gates are open from sunrise until half an hour after sunset although they may be subject to change. Due to a limit set on the number of birdwatchers using the reservoir, any parties wishing to visit should inform the warden in advance (01865 863033). Toilets are available and a birdwatchers' log book is kept in the last building on the right overlooking Farmoor II, just past the sailing club. Here one can preview the birds likely to be encountered and, at the end of the visit record one's own observations. The permit allows

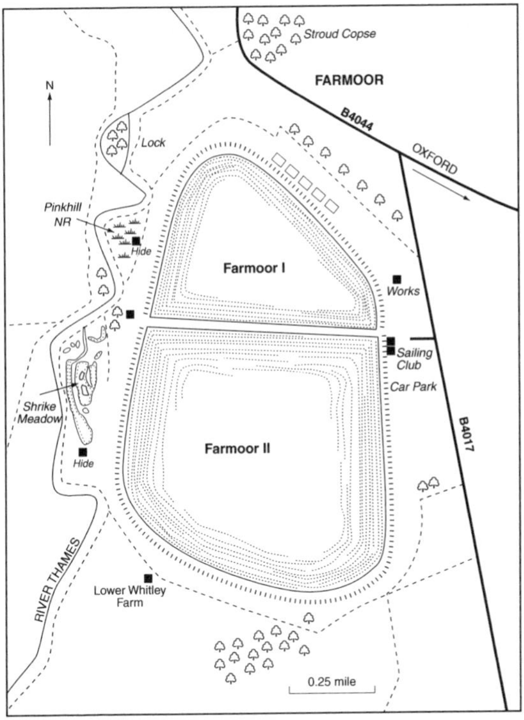

access only to the embankment and does not allow the holder to wander around the works or the sludge tanks at the north of the site, but these can be viewed from the northern causeway, perhaps on a return route for the energetic birder after utilising the central causeway to scan both waters and to visit the new reserves. A telescope is essential here and warm clothing is advisable since a bitter wind can blow across the water and ruin a visit if unprepared. Dogs are not permitted.

Windsurfing, sailing and angling are pursued, the first two mainly confined to Farmoor II where they cause a certain amount of disturbance to the birdlife but Farmoor I is seldom disturbed to the same extent. Angling, primarily fly-fishing, takes place along most of the embankment and though disturbance to birds on the open water is minimal, bankside feeders such as waders, wagtails and pipits may be more mobile. Anglers may actually pose greater problems to birdwatchers – more than one local birder has found himself impaled by a fishing hook and in need of some first aid, victim of an angler's back-cast!

Access to the hides at Pinkhill and The Shrike Meadow is also restricted to keyholders, and keys are available at the warden's gate for £3 per day. Please do not walk along the service road between the reservoir and the small reserves as this not only contravenes Thames Water rules, but tends to flush everything off the two sites you are about to look at!

Species

The gravel pits that were to be destroyed to create these reservoirs in the 1960s had provided some of the finest bird records imaginable for such

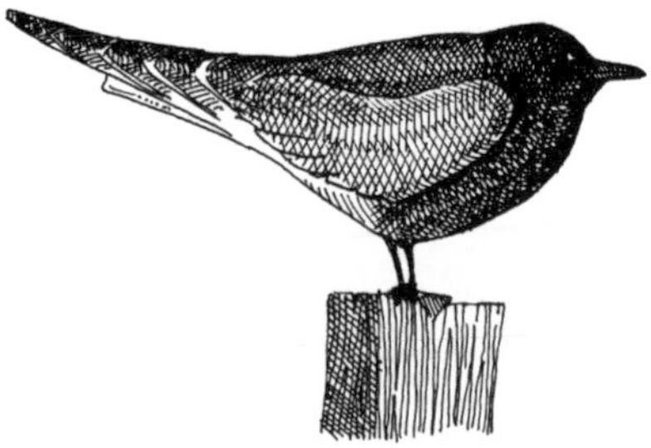

Black Tern

a landlocked county as Oxfordshire. However, the quality and variety of birds visiting the site has remained at least as good as before, if not better. Some exciting and spectacular species, as well as very high numbers of birds, can be enjoyed at Farmoor.

Gulls have generated a form of millennium madness amongst birders with 'new' species to hunt for in the midst of Farmoor's impressive gull roost, such as Yellow-legged and Caspian Gulls. Numbers start to build up on the site from early September, at first perhaps no more than a few hundred birds – mainly Black-headed but accompanied by Lesser Black-backed and a few Herring Gull. By December and January numbers have swollen to be in excess of 10,000 birds. Well over half will be Black-headed with up to 2,500 Lesser Black-backed and 2,000 Herring Gull, and since birds of all ages and plumages will be among them, one has plenty of opportunity to polish up one's gull identification techniques. Two hours before dark is a good time to arrive for this spectacle, when the air is full of crying, screaming gulls, arguing and fighting their way to roost. Even as darkness falls, formations of gulls are still arriving, their calls filling the air as one departs. With so many gulls present, it is advisable to double-check in the hope of a Glaucous, Iceland or Mediterranean Gull, or Little Gull which has become regular in recent years. Usually, only small numbers of this last species occur but it is readily identified by its agility, small size and, most notably, by the way it feeds tern-like over the water. Indeed, it may well be found in the company of Black and Common Terns, and occasionally Arctic Terns, as they pause to feed at Farmoor. The terns occur at both ends of the breeding season and have included White-winged Black Tern. The provision of rafts has enabled birds to rear young and has added an extra dimension to the local avifauna. Gull-watching is not the favourite pastime of all bird enthusiasts, but persistence may be rewarded with something special, such as the Gull-billed Tern found in July 1999, or the Bonaparte's Gull discovered in May 2000.

The high, wide and handsome waters of Farmoor also attract maritime species. Gannet, Arctic and Long-tailed Skuas, Manx Shearwater, Kittiwake, Surf Scoter and even a Leach's Petrel have all been recorded, usually as a result of violent gales. A visit after one of these storms can be most rewarding. All three divers can be anticipated in winter, and the same applies to the rarer grebe species. Large numbers of Cormorant have earned the ire of the angling fraternity.

Even prior to the creation of the two adjacent scrapes, it is remarkable how many waders were to be seen here. April and May provide the greatest variety and number of birds with Grey Plover, Knot, Whimbrel, Greenshank, Sanderling and both godwit species making stopover visits most years. Ruff, Turnstone, Oystercatcher and Spotted Redshank may call in, these also making regular visits on the return migration in August and September. Purple Sandpiper and Little Stint are most likely to be seen during the autumn passage. Little Ringed Plover are often around throughout the summer whilst Dunlin, Redshank and Ringed Plover are recorded at all times of the year and represent Farmoor's commonest waders. The Pinkhill Meadow NR provides additional feeding for waders and it is hoped that as the site develops, opportunities for nesting. From July, Water Rail, Greenshank and Common Sandpiper, sometimes in double figures, may be found in front of the hide. Very occasionally, birdwatchers will be rewarded with real gems; an Avocet perhaps, or maybe a Grey Phalarope, a Whimbrel or Purple Sandpiper – all of which have visited in recent times.

Passage birds also include a number of passerine species. Wheatear are common during March to May and again in August and September, seen darting along the causeway, often accompanied by Whinchat, although the bushes and fences between reservoir and river can be the better site for this typically moorland bird. Some Meadow Pipit overwinter at the site and flocks occasionally include Rock and Water Pipits among their ranks. Wagtails are abundant, feeding along the water's edge, the causeway and around the treatment works. Pied Wagtail, which nest on the works' buildings, form quite large flocks in winter; at migration periods check for White Wagtail as one or two appear most years. In spring, some Yellow Wagtail are seen, but in August large post-breeding flocks with many young birds amongst them congregate at the reservoir, creating a bright and lively scene. In spring, look out for the handsome Blue-headed race of Yellow Wagtail. On the larger side, Osprey are becoming almost an annual visitor at this time of year.

For sheer numbers of birds, Swift, Swallow and martins create quite a spectacle as they feed on the hordes of flies rising from the water. Large numbers of Swift congregate here soon after arrival in Britain and from the tail-end of April up to 3,000 birds scream and wheel over the waters. Ahead of them a steady stream of hirundines replenish food reserves utilised on migration, while local birds of all these species use the reservoir as a summer feeding area. A few House Martin actually nest on the buildings of the treatment works, and with large numbers feeding, Hobby attempt to cash in on this abundance of prey. Looking for Red-rumped Swallow in this throng is a daunting task, but has been proven worthwhile.

There is a rapid turnover of birds and no sooner have summer visitors left than the winter ones begin to arrive, which at Farmoor primarily involves waterfowl. Late September and early October will see the first Goldeneye, small numbers at first but rising to as many as 60 by January. Tufted Duck, Pochard and Mallard numbers also rise steadily, birds flying in to join the flocks of non-breeders that have summered here, with each species peaking at around 400 birds. Smaller numbers of Teal, Gadwall and Shoveler join the flocks, but by far the most numerous species is the Wigeon with up to 1,000 birds present. Of the other regular species the Goosander is probably the most conspicuous, the bold, predominantly white plumage of the drake being instantly recognisable even at some distance, while the elegant, upright posture of the Pintail is another frequent sight.

Total numbers of waterbirds present vary according to weather and local floods, with maxima being reached in very cold spells, Farmoor usually being the last of the local waters to become ice-bound. Birdwatching can then be most memorable as birds concentrate into small areas of open water. At these times, and also during migration, one can expect species such as Scaup, Common and Velvet Scoters, Smew and Long-tailed Duck; birds that are more likely to be seen off the coast during the winter. There seems to have been a trend in recent years for these birds to remain at Farmoor for several days or weeks rather than just a fleeting visit as used to happen.

Apart from the birds found on the water, Farmoor reservoirs are relatively quiet in the colder months. Some passerines such as Meadow Pipit, Pied Wagtail, Linnet and Goldfinch are usually present and may be joined by 'goodies' such as Snow Bunting and Black Redstart. Red-breasted Merganser, Merlin and Bittern have warmed up previous winters. In the surrounding area, particularly along the river, species of the open field, hedgerow and woodland can be found. On winter floods, flocks of Canada Geese gather to graze, often with local feral Greylag. Lapwing also use the area and, if it is very wet, Curlew may feed. Species such as Wigeon and Teal commute between the meadows and the reservoirs, while Grey Heron hunt the pools and ditches. The extensively varied habitat of Pinkhill and The Shrike Meadow ensures an increase in birds of scrub and reedbed, and therefore, at any time of year, these areas are well worth investigating.

Farmoor's reputation as one of the county's top birdwatching haunts is thus not without good reason. The number and variety of bird species, and the reservoirs' close proximity to Oxford, certainly make it the most watched site, with the constant possibility of something else to add to the extensive bird list. A visit is thoroughly recommended.

Calendar

Resident: On and around the reservoirs: Pied Wagtail, Tufted Duck, Mallard, Coot, Mute Swan and Little Grebe. On surrounding area: partridges, Water Rail, Moorhen, Kingfisher, Reed Bunting, Yellowhammer.

December–February: Gull roost at peak, occasional Snow Bunting, Black Redstart; possible Great Northern Diver or rarer grebes, winter duck numbers at peak with Goosander, possible Scaup, Common Scoter, Smew, Long-tailed Duck.

March–May: During March and April, Wheatear, Whinchat, Yellow Wagtail, Sand Martin, Meadow Pipit. April–May is the main passage period with terns and Little Gull, and maybe Garganey. Possible Kittiwake, Knot, Grey Plover, Whimbrel, Ringed and Little Ringed Plovers. Swallow, House Martin, Swift.

June–July: Swift and hirundines over water, Hobbies, a few non-breeding duck, swans and grebe, Common Sandpiper.

August–November: Early in period, build-up of Yellow Wagtail, hirundines and Swift numbers, possible Hobby. Migrating waders – Little Stint, Ruff, Oystercatcher, Turnstone. Build-up of Cormorant and gull numbers. Return of winter duck, e.g. Wigeon, Teal, Shoveler, Goldeneye, possible Red-throated Diver, Red-breasted Merganser, Redshank, Common Sandpiper.

76 FOXHOLES

OS ref. SP 254 206

Habitat

This quiet and inconspicuous BBOWT reserve lies close to Oxfordshire's boundary with Gloucestershire, on the west bank of the River Evenlode. The 64 ha (160 acres) site is part-owned, part-leased by the Wildlife Trust and its tranquility stems from being part of a sizeable estate, much of which is undisturbed, and its distance from major roads and developments. Another reason for its undoubted attractiveness is the variety of habitat in and around the reserve boundaries. At the lowest altitude, 100 m (330 ft), is the River Evenlode. Its course follows a quite intensively arable valley but at Foxholes the reserve includes an attractive, unimproved base-rich wet meadow. From the river, the reserve slopes gently through woodland and open grazing meadow to reach a plateau at 140 m (460 ft). A remnant of the once vast Wychwood Forest and generally quite wet, the lower limestone area comprises Oak, Ash and Beech woodland with a good shrub layer of Hawthorn, Bramble and Hazel, some of which is coppiced. On higher ground, the more acid soil encourages Bracken, some heather and a more open woodland with Oak and Birch dominant. Part of the plateau is given over to a sizeable Larch plantation.

The quietness of the reserve makes it a superb site for mammal watching, even in daylight, with Fox, Stoat and Weasel, Fallow, Muntjac and the occasional Roe Deer. The reserve is noted for its flora (it is rather picturesque at Bluebell-time) and is particularly renowned for its fungi.

Access

Foxholes lies close to Bruern Abbey between Milton-under-Wychwood and Bledington. Proceeding north out of Burford on the A424 towards Stow-on-the-Wold, take the third turning on the right. Head north-east along the unclassified road to Bruern for 3.5 km (2 miles). Just before

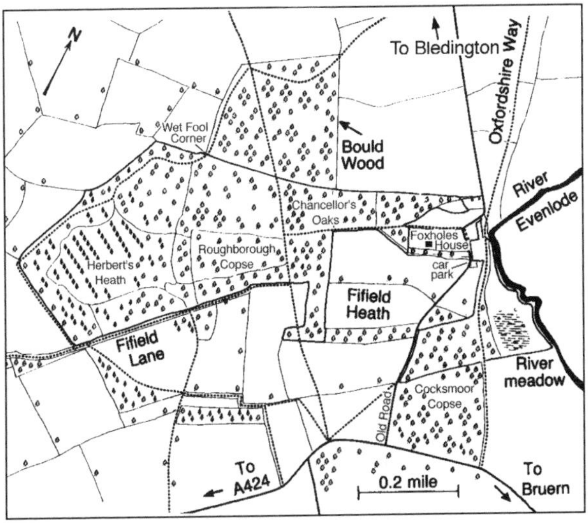

Bruern, turn left along the rough track following the edge of Cocksmoor Copse. After 750 m (820 yds), and just before reaching the farm buildings, there is a small car park on the right. A number of bridleways and footpaths cut across the reserve giving good access to all areas of interest; BBOWT members though have access along a number of other tracks and rides including the wet meadow, allowing an even greater appreciation of the reserve. Wellingtons are advisable in winter.

Species

A good place to start would be the river and wet meadow close to the car park, which increases the variety of species, particularly in spring and summer. This area provides nest sites for Mallard and Moorhen as well as Reed Bunting, species that are present all year, as are Grey Heron. Snipe, which often overwinter in the meadow, may breed in some years. Mute Swan and Canada Goose are seen in all months either on the river in summer or grazing the fields adjacent to the reserve in winter. Along the river itself, Little Grebe breed – very wary birds quickly diving below the water if one approaches incautiously, surfacing silently beneath overhanging vegetation. The high, steep river banks allow Kingfisher to nest and at any time there may be a couple of pairs in the area.

Adjacent grazing meadows, the largest being Fifield Heath, are usually too disturbed to provide nest sites, except for Skylark or the occasional Lapwing, but are used as regular feeding areas by Rook, Mistle Thrush, Green Woodpecker, Kestrel and Little Owl, all of which breed on the reserve and are found all year round. Significant numbers of Jackdaw are present and a wandering Raven joined the throng on one occasion in 2001. In winter, Lapwing may gather in small flocks in these fields, and it may be worth looking out for occasional Golden Plover. The numerous Oak trees around the farmland are always worth checking for Lesser Spotted and Great Spotted Woodpeckers, which are present in good numbers over most of the reserve. More at home in the woodland are Treecreeper and Nuthatch, the latter more likely within the Beech woods.

The dampness of the reserve and the presence of so much dead timber means that hole-nesting species are well represented. Marsh, Great and Blue Tits are very common, and Willow Tit are still present, whilst Jackdaw, Starling and Tawny Owl add to the list of hole-nesters. Of the other members of the tit family, Long-tailed Tit is more likely in the Hawthorn scrub at the north-west of the reserve and the Coal Tit often associates with Goldcrest in conifer stands at the southern end. The wetness of the site also creates ideal conditions for that secretive woodland bird, the Woodcock.

All over the reserve, typical breeding finches are Chaffinch and Greenfinch, with Goldfinch and Bullfinch nesting in areas of scrub. Wintertime may find a few Siskin and Redpoll using the reserve, particularly around Birch trees, and while foliage cover is reduced, this may be a good time to look for the occasional visiting Hawfinch.

Significant numbers of summer visitors provide good watching and listening on the reserve. Chiffchaff, Willow Warbler, Blackcap and Garden Warbler are the most common in the woods whilst Whitethroat is found along the woodland edge and in nearby hedgerows. Foxholes House and its outbuildings provide good habitat for nesting Spotted Flycatcher, Swallow and House Martin, the latter forming a draw for infrequent Hobby. In

Goldfinch

spring, species such as Redstart and Wood Warbler may pass through and with breeding conditions here seeming ideal for both species, it could be just a matter of time before they decide to make a longer stay.

The good numbers of passerine species, coupled with the general open nature of the area, provide ideal hunting conditions for Sparrowhawk, which nest high in the canopy, particularly in Bould Wood or in the plantation upon Herberts Heath. Increasingly, Common Buzzard are using the wood as their range expands throughout the region. Being situated on high ground, the woods, especially in winter, can be a little on the quiet side and it pays to be patient in seeking out flocks of mixed species, such as tits, Goldcrest and Treecreeper. Winter also sees the influx of visiting thrushes, Redwing and Fieldfare, often present in large mixed flocks (including some Blackbird and Song Thrush) feeding on Hawthorn and other berries within the wood or on adjacent fields and pasture.

Even in the absence of any rarities, Foxholes can give some very pleasurable birdwatching moments: Sparrowhawk feeding recently fledged young, a Willow Tit noisily and industriously chiselling away its nest hole, a displaying Lesser Spotted Woodpecker, a Common Buzzard calling from a woodland perch or a glimpse of a passage Redstart.

Calendar

Resident: Woodcock, Kestrel, Sparrowhawk, Common Buzzard, Little and Tawny Owls, Great Spotted, Lesser Spotted and Green Woodpeckers, Goldcrest, all six tit species, Nuthatch, Treecreeper, Jackdaw, Rook, Carrion Crow. Common thrushes, Bullfinch, Chaffinch, Goldfinch, Greenfinch, Linnet, Hawfinch (possible). On wet meadow and river, Little Grebe, Mute Swan, Canada Goose, Mallard, Moorhen, Kingfisher, Skylark, Reed Bunting. Possible Lapwing and Snipe.

December–February: Redwing, Fieldfare, Siskin, Redpoll, increased numbers of Woodcock, occasional Golden Plover.

March–May: Yellow Wagtail, Nightingale, Blackcap, Garden Warbler, Chiffchaff, Willow Warbler, possible Redstart and Wood Warbler, Spotted Flycatcher, House Martin, Swallow.

June–July: Breeding activity at peak.

August–November: Summer migrants in large parties before departure. Resident tits and finches form flocks.

77 GRIMSBURY RESERVOIR **OS ref. SP 458 417**

Habitat

Whilst small in size at 6.5 ha (16 acres), and leaning hard against the bustling town of Banbury, Grimsbury Reservoir and the surrounding area provides sufficient diversity of habitat to be of importance at a county level.

Created in 1966 and owned by Thames Water, the 5 m-deep reservoir itself has a concreted shoreline lacking in vegetation and so is of limited use to nesting birds. Fishing and sailing also take place, bringing further restriction for birds, but a voluntary exclusion zone between April and September brings some respite. Above the shoreline, the banks have a covering of dense herbage and, if they remain unmown, offer shelter to nesting passerines. To the east of the reservoir runs the River Cherwell, its banks generously lined by coarse vegetation and reeds with scattered Alder, Birch and Hawthorn trees. Other, more recent tree planting has taken place. To the east and north-west, and bounded by the Oxford Canal, are areas of permanent pasture composed of rough grasses and rushes. A stream, lined by willow and Hawthorn, crosses this area and as a consequence these fields can be very wet in winter. To the north is the Woodland Nature Reserve, created in 1967 by Thames Water and Banbury Ornithological Society. The dominant species were Alder and Corsican Pine, but ensuing work has resulted in many of these being replaced with native tree species such as Hazel, Holly, Wild Service and Oak. Field Maple, Buckthorn, Dogrose and Hawthorn have also been planted to attract insects.

Other improvements to the plantation have included the creation of more open areas and a pond, maintenance of the stream that runs through it, and the installation of a series of bat boxes. A nature trail exists around the site, incorporated into the Banbury Fringe Circular Walk.

Access

The reservoir lies on Banbury's northern edge and is reached from the A422 link road joining the A423 with the A361. Turn off at the roundabout situated approximately 500 m (600 yds) east of the junction with the A423. The reservoir and water treatment works are signposted from here with parking for about 40 vehicles available on the left-hand side of the lane almost opposite the main gates.

From the main entrance, a footpath takes one around the reservoir along the River Cherwell and through the plantation. Good views over the adjacent meadows are obtained from the path but no rights of way exist over these pastures. The public are permitted along the canal towpath although for most of the way tall, thick hedgerows prevent good viewing.

Species

The site is definitely at its best in winter and during periods of bird migration. Disturbance and the general nature of the reservoir means that there is little scope for breeding waterfowl but an evening or early morning visit during the nesting season can still be profitable. Along the

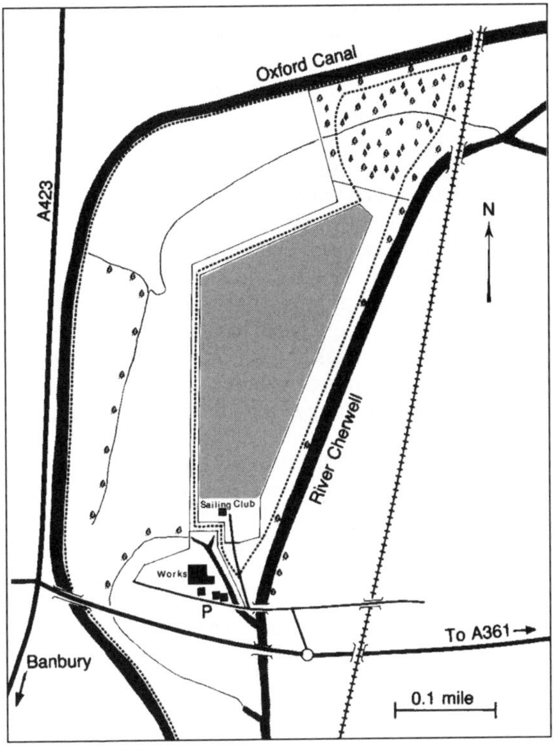

river, Moorhen and Mallard are common and Little Grebe and Kingfisher may breed, with Wren, Reed Bunting and Sedge Warbler making the most of the dense bankside vegetation. Garden Warbler, Blackcap and Willow Warbler are all likely along the banks of the Cherwell. In the woodland, and in other trees and shrubs, nest the resident finches and thrushes as well as the more usual warblers. Goldcrest, Treecreeper and a number of tit species breed within the plantation. Both Green and Great Spotted Woodpeckers will be found, whilst Pied Wagtail are present all year, nesting on the buildings of the treatment works. During the breeding season, birds to be found upon the open fields will depend on the level of grazing disturbance and upon how wet it is, following recent drainage work. Lapwing may breed and Golden Plover are a possibility, with Skylark usually seen or heard, but partridges are now rare. In the pollarded Willows, Little Owl nest and Kestrel may be encountered, whilst a Sparrowhawk can often be watched hunting the hedgerow by the canal or through the woodland. In late summer these fields, and the reservoir, may draw hirundines to feed which in their turn may attract the attention of a hungry Hobby or two; and Common Buzzard are being seen with increasing regularity.

A visit in early spring may be rewarded by the presence of one of a number of species which utilise the reservoir as a stopping-off point on their migration. Wheatear are the most frequent, feeding boldly on the open grassy banks around the reservoir or in the nearby meadows, and Yellow Wagtail also pass through. Though the reservoir is small and has been subjected to cleaning out, removing most of the muddy bank, a number of wader species are seen during passage, notably Ringed Plover, Dunlin and Common Sandpiper. Oystercatcher, Turnstone and Sanderling were always less common, and may be all the more so now the muddy patches have gone, but one may still be lucky. Garganey have been recorded and a Red-necked Grebe favoured the water in 2001.

Many spring migrants return at the end of summer when the flocks comprise family parties with young individuals. During August and September some species form large congregations as local birds flock together. Swallow, for example, chatter noisily over the site, roosting with Yellow Wagtail, Reed Bunting and Pied Wagtail. Of course two of these move on to overwinter in continental Africa, but the latter two remain all winter and in recent years Pied Wagtail have formed roosts with numbers reaching a peak during December; White Wagtail is a possibility in subsequent spring. As autumn progresses, Meadow Pipit arrive in small numbers, feeding across the site in the company of Pied Wagtail and Linnet. A few Grey Wagtail and occasionally a Stonechat may also overwinter, and Chiffchaff is another species staying through, accompanied in 1999 by a fine male Firecrest.

With Alder trees in abundance it is hardly surprising that, in winter, the Siskin is one of the most conspicuous birds of the location, over 100 being recorded on at least one occasion. They probe the cones acrobatically for seeds and are occasionally joined by Redpoll. In winter, resident birds show more social tendencies forming mixed flocks; tits, Treecreeper and Goldcrest group together and Chaffinch and Greenfinch forage widely in search of food. On areas of rough ground, and especially where thistle and teasel heads still stand, more Linnet, Goldfinch and Redpoll may be found.

Provided the water remains undisturbed and does not become icebound, a selection of wildfowl take up winter residence on the site, using both the reservoir and the fields if flooded. Mallard and a few Tufted Duck are the commonest but in small numbers, whilst Wigeon and Pochard may call in occasionally. Shoveler and Teal have become more infrequent but Great Crested Grebe are usually present. Although too small a site to regularly attract many of the less common duck, Goosander, Mandarin and Shelduck have all been recorded, and there is always the hope that a passing Goldeneye or Scaup, on their way to Farmoor, might call in.

In common with the majority of English reservoirs, gull roosts are a feature of Grimsbury, although the congregations here are more likely to be pre-roosting flocks which move off to join larger overnight roosts elsewhere. Forming at dusk, numbers are never huge and Black-headed Gull make up the majority with Lesser Black-backed and Herring Gull also possible. Small groups of Common Gull may join the flocks and one year a Glaucous Gull was a notable visitor. If making an evening visit for gulls, use the occasion to check neighbouring fields for owls. It is a little while since Short-eared Owl or Barn Owl were recorded here, but who knows, as near to the town as this site is, it is the sort of place that might add an odd surprise to end a good day's birdwatching.

Calendar

Resident: Moorhen, Mallard, Little Grebe, Kestrel, Sparrowhawk, Little Owl, Kingfisher, Pied Wagtail, Goldcrest, Blue, Great and Coal Tits, Treecreeper, Chaffinch, Linnet, Skylark, Reed Bunting.

December–February: Best time for winter duck especially Pochard, Tufted Duck, Mallard and Wigeon, and occasional Goldeneye and Goosander. Peak time for gulls, Grey Heron, Great Crested Grebe. Overwintering Chiffchaff, Siskin and Redpoll.

March–May: Passage: Wheatear, possible Redstart or Whinchat, hirundines. Occasional Ringed or Little Ringed Plovers, Dunlin, Common Sandpiper, Sanderling, Common and possibly Arctic Terns, Yellow Wagtail.

June–July: Riparian breeders.

August–November: Build-up in hirundine and wagtail flocks. Occasional Hobby, Stonechat, Siskin, Redpoll. Finch and tit congregations. Small rafts of duck, Great Crested Grebe and commoner gull species.

78 LITTLE WITTENHAM NATURE RESERVE

OS ref. SU 570 930

Habitat

Since being acquired by the Northmoor Trust in the first half of the 1980s, county naturalists have continued to enjoy this 100-ha (250-acre) site bordering the River Thames, whilst children have learned about the countryside in the reserve's education centre.

Little Wittenham supports a good range of wildlife habitats. Of foremost importance, particularly so far as breeding birds are concerned, is Little Wittenham Wood, recently granted SSSI status and awaiting SAC accreditation. Sloping down to the river's edge it is an ancient woodland site of 53 ha (130 acres) with some fine old Oak trees and areas of coppice. Unfortunately much had been replanted with dense conifer stands and mixed timber plantations. Significant areas of scrub are found and there are two woodland ponds. To the west of the wood and on the same steep slope is an area of open grassland, towered over by a group of ancient Beech trees atop Round Hill from where panoramic views over the Oxfordshire countryside can be obtained. Just to the south-east of Round Hill is Castle Hill, the site of an Iron Age hill fort dating back 2500 years. These two neighbouring hills are known locally as the Wittenham Clumps.

The third facet of importance to the naturalist is the River Thames and the adjacent flood meadows. Worthy of special mention is the length of bank where the woodland runs down to the river's edge and which remains relatively undisturbed, offering quiet breeding sites for the typical riverside birds and other wildlife. A new area including ponds and a hide is being created next to the Thames below the wood.

Whilst a relative newcomer to the nature reserves of Oxfordshire, the site has enormous potential and much active work is being undertaken

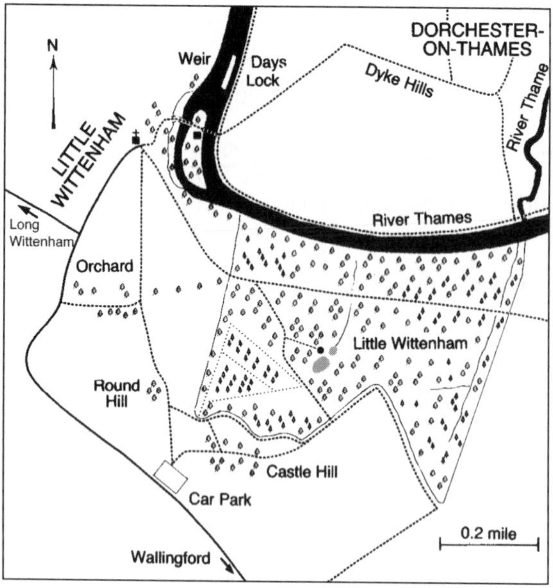

by the Northmoor Trust to create and maintain the widest diversity of habitat. This management includes removal of conifers, opening of broad rides and coppicing of timber within the wood, and also the improvement of chalk grassland by sheep-grazing and wildflower planting. Many of the magnificent Beech trees on Round Hill are unfortunately dying and a replanting scheme has been initiated.

Much survey work has been done to assess the status of the site's flora and fauna and to look at changes as management plans are put into operation. Additionally, a bird ringing group operates on the site.

Access

The reserve is east of Little Wittenham village and a car park is provided, close to Castle Hill, reached from the unclassified road between Little Wittenham and Brightwell-cum-Sotwell. An information board is located near this car park. The grassland of Round Hill stretching down to the river and including Castle Hill is designated a Country Park and the public has free access over it. Through and around the woodland is a public footpath and bridleway, offering some access. From the highest point on the reserve, a wonderful panoramic view of the wider area is offered. The Trust has also opened up a number of other 'permitted paths' along which the public may walk. Please note that there is no public access around the woodland ponds, primarily in an attempt to prevent disturbance to breeding wildlife, but a hide has been provided to aid observation.

The river can be viewed from the towpath running along its north bank and a footpath from Days Lock leads across the fields to Dorchester-on-Thames. Groups wishing to visit the reserve should telephone the Trust beforehand (01865 407792). This is to prevent excessive disturbance and also, if necessary, to arrange for one of the Trust's staff to act as a guide.

Species

Whilst a good range of species has been recorded, the birds seen in this locality depend upon the season and, according to the time of the visit, the birdwatcher's attention is best directed to one particular part of the reserve. Winter for instance sees the main avian activity centred upon the river and adjoining flood meadows. Snipe and Redshank feed on the edges of pools and flocks of Starling and Lapwing haunt the drier areas. Black-headed Gull also move in, noisily harrying the Lapwing. Small groups of Herring and Lesser Black-backed Gulls will also be seen. Meadow Pipit and Pied Wagtail frequent these fields and the lucky observer may be rewarded with the sight of a hunting Short-eared Owl.

Duck are mainly represented by Teal and Wigeon, feeding around the floodwaters, and there may be a few Shoveler. On the river, small parties of Tufted Duck and Pochard may congregate. Canada Geese gather in the fields around Days Lock and are always worth a second glance since they are sometimes joined by small numbers of Pink-footed and White-fronted Goose. If very cold weather ensues and still waters freeze then, as well as an increase in the birds present, other species of wildfowl may move on to the Thames or the deeper parts of Allen Lake, with Goldeneye, Goosander and Red-breasted Merganser all being possible.

Mallard, Moorhen and Coot, together with Mute Swan and Great Crested Grebe, are resident whilst Grey Heron feed along the river. Kingfisher are also around most of the year, nesting close to Days Lock, as do Grey and Pied Wagtails, while passage Yellow Wagtail has been seen in numbers up to 60 in recent times, especially in the area of Church Meadow. Warm summer days are embellished with Swift, Swallow and House Martin swooping to feed on insects rising from the river and wet meadows. All breed in the nearby villages but nests of the latter are clearly visible on the lock keeper's house just below the weir. During passage the weir pool or lakes beyond the lock may prove attractive to Common or Arctic Terns, gracefully dipping and diving into the waters.

In summer, the main interest shifts to Little Wittenham Wood and the good variety of woodland species that it supports, aided by a significant nest box scheme, with some 120 in place. A Constant Effort ringing station has been set up here, and amongst the less common species ringed have been Brambling, Redpoll and Firecrest. Nuthatch are few but this is compensated for by a good woodpecker population. Great Spotted are the most obvious and as many as nine pairs may be present, their noisy drumming and loud calls allowing birdwatchers to locate them with relative ease. The ringing, laughing call of the Green Woodpecker is another common sound and the opening of broad grassy rides in the wood will improve the chances of sighting this bird, as some five pairs breed around the reserve. One or two pairs of the smallest native woodpecker, the Lesser Spotted, have nested in the wood and are also occasionally seen near the orchard which abuts the reserve. Other residents include good numbers of Treecreeper, Wren, Jay, Magpie, Robin and Blackbird, a good population of Goldcrest (in the conifer plantations) and the usual titmice including Marsh, Willow Tit having disappeared from the area now. Of the finches Chaffinch is very prolific and Bullfinch regularly seen. Both Common Buzzard and Hobby have bred here previously and Red Kite is becoming a regular visitor too. Sightings of Goshawk have increased in recent times and Merlin has been noted.

In the more open areas of the wood, Mistle Thrush and Dunnock

Sparrowhawk

thrive. Up to five pairs of Tawny Owl and one or two pairs of Sparrowhawk can be expected. If for no other reason than their song, Chiffchaff, Blackcap, and Willow Warbler are the most prominent summer visitors, with a few Garden Warbler. Small numbers of Whitethroat breed and a few Lesser Whitethroat nest in the locality, while around the village Spotted Flycatcher may be seen. The Cuckoo, widespread and common in the area, and the Turtle Dove concludes the list of summer visitors. The area in the vicinity of the woodland ponds often acts as a focus for passerine birds, providing feeding and drinking opportunities as well as some nest sites. Species such as Moorhen, Mallard and Little Grebe nest on the ponds, and Grey Heron may feed. At periods of passage, Green and Common Sandpipers have been noted on these ponds and along the river.

The area of open chalk grassland is perhaps less productive, though both species of partridge might be found, nesting on the tops of the hills or along hedgerows, with Little Owl noted in similar areas. Kestrel can often be seen, hovering gracefully, ever watchful for potential prey below. Later in the year, Rook and Jackdaw feed on these grasslands where in winter, flocks of Meadow Pipit take up residence. Various finch flocks may move into the area in winter and parties of Linnet, Goldfinch, Chaffinch and Greenfinch may be present, and it is well worth looking out for Brambling.

An extremely pleasant visit can be assured as The Northmoor Trust continues its management programme at this important piece of Oxfordshire's natural heritage.

Calendar

Resident: Woodcock, Sparrowhawk, Tawny and Little Owls, Pheasant and partridge. Three woodpecker species, Skylark, Treecreeper, typical woodland corvids, thrushes etc. Common tits and finches, Goldcrest, Yellowhammer. On and around river: Great Crested Grebe, Mallard, Canada Goose, Mute Swan, Moorhen, Coot, Kingfisher, Pied Wagtail, Reed Bunting.

December–February: Snipe, Redshank, mixed gull flocks, Starling, possible Short-eared Owl, Meadow Pipit, winter thrushes. If floods persist Teal, Shoveler, Wigeon, Tufted Duck, Pochard, possible wild swans and geese, occasional Goldeneye, Goosander.

March–May: Passage: possible Wheatear. Lesser Whitethroat, Whitethroat, Blackcap, Garden Warbler, Chiffchaff, Willow Warbler, Yellow Wagtail, House Martin, Swallow, Swift, Cuckoo, Turtle Dove.

June–July: Spotted Flycatcher, Hobby. Much breeding activity.

August–November: On passage: Green and Common Sandpipers, possible terns. Flocking of many resident species. Influx of wintering species as outlined for December–February.

79 LOWER WINDRUSH VALLEY GRAVEL PITS

OS ref. SP 405 045

Habitat

Spread over the general area of Stanton Harcourt, Hardwick and Standlake, and straddling the River Windrush, is a sprawling complex of pits created by gravel and sand extraction. Something like 35 pits, most of them now lakes, are found in this complex, making it the largest in the county and of great importance to wildlife. The pits show considerable variety ranging from shallow dry scrapes, some still undergoing extraction, to deep, established lakes with well-developed bankside vegetation. Many of the worked pits have been landscaped and used for sailing, powerboating and angling. Unfortunately the disturbance created by some of these activities does limit breeding birds. However, in winter when disturbance is reduced, most pits are worth a visit as the entire complex becomes important for wintering wildfowl. It is not the bodies of water alone that are of interest as the land around is a varied landscape of open fields, 'waste ground', scrub and hedgerows with mature trees.

The area is likely to be worked for gravel for many years to come. New pits will be dug, worked-out ones reclaimed or landscaped for leisure activities. As long as a diversity of form exists among the pits with some remaining undisturbed then the wildlife interest will be retained.

Access

With many of the pits still being actively worked or held in the hands of private groups using the lakes for recreation, full access to the site is not possible. However, virtually all the waters can be seen from roads or footpaths which traverse the area. Additionally, many of the landowners (if approached tactfully) will grant access to individuals or groups, but check before entering.

To visit all of the pits and study them properly would be a huge undertaking. Hence, in order for visiting birdwatchers to be a little more selective in their choice of pit to watch, the ornithologically most important and the ones with easiest access are now given.

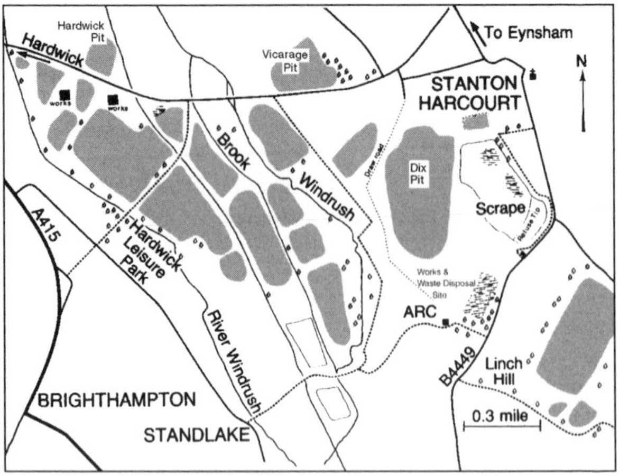

Vicarage Pit (OS ref. SP 403 057) A 9.2-ha (23-acre) pit lying alongside the road between Hardwick and Stanton Harcourt. Park at the side of the road from where adequate views can be obtained, or view from the hide located in the south-east corner of the pit.

Linch Hill Complex (OS ref. SP 416 039) Three lakes (Willow, Christchurch and Stoneacres) managed by Hanson's for leisure activities such as fishing and sailboarding. Admission is free although a charge is made for parking. Entrance to the lakes is approximately 2 km (1.25 miles) south of Stanton Harcourt on the B4449. Check for wider access to 'fishermen only' areas at the café.

Dix (or Devil's Quoits) Pit (OS ref. SP 409 045) A large deep-water pit with two islands and good bankside vegetation. Recreational disturbance is limited on this pit, a notable fact since this water is probably the single most important of the complex for winter wildfowl. Limited views are obtainable from the road leading to the refuse disposal site (gate is locked when site not in use) but bankside viewing is possible courtesy of a special visitors car park provided by Hanson Ltd (see Useful Addresses) in front of the offices near the gravel workings. Check what time the gates will be locked.

Heyford Lakes south-east of Hardwick are best explored form the footpath, with parking at SP 392 048.

The pits of the area are constantly changing, their status altered and birds may need to move from one to another. Footpaths over the area are often rerouted but if in doubt check with the owners first.

Species

With such a large complex of water bodies, it is hardly surprising that a wide range of waterfowl will be encountered here. Tufted Duck and Pochard remain all year, a few pairs of Tufted, and Ruddy Duck, breeding on the deeper waters (e.g. Dix Pit) but groups of non-breeders are also usually present. From September onwards the numbers of these species rise dramatically so that by the end of the year several thousand will be seen. Wigeon, Teal, Shoveler and Goldeneye are winter visitors and may be accompanied by up to 150 Pintail, dozens of Gadwall, and several Goosander and Shelduck. Of the larger species of wildfowl, the most obvious is the Canada Goose, though Brent Goose has visited. Mute Swan are present all year with pairs nesting on any of the less disturbed waters. In some winters, a few Bewick's or Whooper Swans will stay briefly, sometimes in the company of White-fronted Geese. The highest numbers of Goldeneye, perhaps 50 or more, may however be found at the ski lake or Oxlease Pit on the Heyford Lake complex.

Tagging on to parties of any of these waterfowl may be an array of feral birds and escapees from wildfowl collections. At times, Dix Pit can look like a mini-Slimbridge with Bar-headed, Snow, Greylag and Barnacle Geese joining up with other geese, whilst amongst the flocks of duck, Mandarin, Wood Duck and Red-crested Pochard have been present during the winter period. Coot and Moorhen are common breeding birds and on some waters Great Crested and Little Grebes nest. In winter, numbers increase as individuals move into the area to find shelter and food. Close scrutiny of the birds on the deeper waters may also reveal regular winter visitors such as Black-necked or Slavonian Grebes. Scaup is possible, but beware of the TuftedxPochard hybrid which has roamed the county in recent years.

Towards dusk, whilst many gulls fly over towards Farmoor, sizeable roosts build up on the large waters here at Dix, adding to those spending the day on the rubbish tip. Black-headed, Lesser Black-backed and Herring Gulls are the most numerous with fewer Great Black-backed and Common Gulls. As with any roost a close check should be made for other species since Mediterranean, Iceland, Glaucous and especially Yellow-legged Gulls have all been noted. In recent years more and more gulls have been found in the area in the summer months and Black-headed Gull now breed, producing up to 30 or so young. The Cormorant is another species that is constantly commuting between pit and reservoir, depending upon disturbance, with numbers at Dix Pit rising to over 90 birds, often using the two islands where Grey Heron breed.

The pit complex is famed for its status in attracting waders. In either passage period check the edges of any water but pay particular attention to dry and shallow pits for Ruff, Dunlin and godwit, Knot, Sanderling and Whimbrel. A visit at any time of day can be worthwhile but early morning offers the best opportunities of catching those birds that have made an overnight stay. The autumn passage is probably better for Wood Sandpiper, Curlew Sandpiper, Greenshank and Little Stint. Redshank are present all year, nesting in the shelter of bankside vegetation. Lapwing also breed, particularly in the dry pits and on nearby fields. In winter this species may be found in large flocks, accompanied by a few Golden Plover. Common Sandpiper are present in summer, bobbing characteristically along the wave-washed shoreline. Some overwinter joining other regular winter visitors such as Snipe and Green Sandpiper. Patience (and a telescope) can work wonders and with 'gems' such as Turnstone, Avocet, Grey Phalarope or Pectoral Sandpiper always possible, the exercise can be well worth the effort.

Passage times do not just mean waders. Any of the terns are likely, particularly at the end of April and in early May. Osprey and Garganey are likely and passerines such as Meadow Pipit, Pied Flycatcher, Whinchat, Wheatear and Yellow Wagtail (check for individuals of the Blue-headed race) all visit. The surrounding area attracts virtually all the commoner species associated with open fields, hedgerows, scrub and waterways. The commoner tits, thrushes and finches, Skylark, Yellowhammer, occasional Corn Bunting, and numerous Reed Bunting, Stock Dove, Kingfisher, Great Spotted and Green Woodpeckers are all likely with the list further extended by Kestrel and Sparrowhawk, Little Owl and Barn Owl.

Among the first wave of summer visitors is the Sand Martin. In the past, large colonies have built up along open sand faces on some of the pits near to Stanton Harcourt. Problems encountered in the wintering grounds lead to numbers decreasing dramatically during the 1980s but the population is showing signs of recovery. Large numbers of hirundines and Swift feed on insects over any of the waters with the largest gatherings noted in late April and early May and again in early September. Pied Wagtail are particularly numerous. Other summer visitors make use of the hedgerows and scrubland. The common Sylvia and Phylloscopus warblers are very numerous whilst, amongst the dense vegetation bordering pit and river, the chattering, rattling song of the Sedge Warbler can be heard. A few Nightingale may frequent the area, Cuckoo are widespread and the gentle purring of Turtle Dove may be heard.

Overlapping with departing summer migrants, wintering birds start to move in. Many are wildfowl but the adjoining countryside attracts Brambling and Meadow Pipit, Fieldfare and Redwing and often increased numbers of the resident species. With always a good chance of a wintering Short-eared Owl or Merlin using the area, and with Pied-billed Grebe, Common Scoter, American Wigeon, White-headed Duck, Red-breasted Merganser and even White Stork recorded, there is never a lull in the avian activity of this varied gravel pit complex.

Calendar

Resident: Great Crested and Little Grebes, Mute Swan, Canada Goose, feral Greylag, a variety of exotic escaped wildfowl, Mallard, Tufted Duck, Coot, Moorhen, Sparrowhawk, Kestrel, Barn and Little Owls, Redshank, Lapwing, Kingfisher, Skylark.

December–February: Occasional Bewick's Swan, possible Black-necked and Slavonian Grebes, large flocks of Lapwing and Golden Plover. Short-eared Owl and Merlin.

March–May: Passage: Dunlin, Ruff, godwit, Knot. Possible Whimbrel, Garganey and Osprey, Wheatear, Whinchat, Meadow Pipit, Yellow Wagtail. Sand Martin, Turtle Dove, Nightingale, Cuckoo, common warblers.

June–July: Non-breeding birds on water, feeding hirundines and Common Tern, Hobby, Common Sandpiper present, heronry in use.

August–November: Passage waders: Little Stint, Curlew and Wood Sandpipers, Greenshank, Ringed Plover. Gradual rise in wintering duck: Pochard, Teal, Wigeon, Shoveler, Tufted Duck, Goldeneye, possible Mandarin and Red-crested Pochard. Snipe, Green Sandpiper, Brambling, Meadow Pipit, Fieldfare, Redwing.

80 OTMOOR

OS ref. SP 570 126

Habitat

Situated approximately 11 km (7 miles) north and east of Oxford, Otmoor is a flat plain lying 60 m (195 ft) above sea level, sitting upon layers of either alluvium or Oxford clay, combining to produce an area with immense water-retaining qualities and contributing significantly to the nature of Otmoor. Indeed, had this account been written 150 years previously the whole area would have been a vast expanse of moorland and open pools, probably of national importance for wildfowl and waders. Even just five years ago, improved drainage technology had degraded the area so that much had become agricultural land. Today, however, part of the site is being returned to its former glory and value to wetland birds due to a huge investment by the RSPB. Many areas are now wet all year and a new reedbed and reservoir have been created, with two open-topped hides. Furthermore, local farms have agreed to ensure high water levels throughout spring over an extended area around the reserve. This entire area therefore, including the rifle range, is now managed for water level control and many of the large well-established drainage ditches bordering the arable fields also retain water and attract a number of birds and other animals for feeding and nesting.

Although dry, much of the centre of Otmoor still remains unimproved with large fields of coarse grasses, sedges and rushes, and areas of

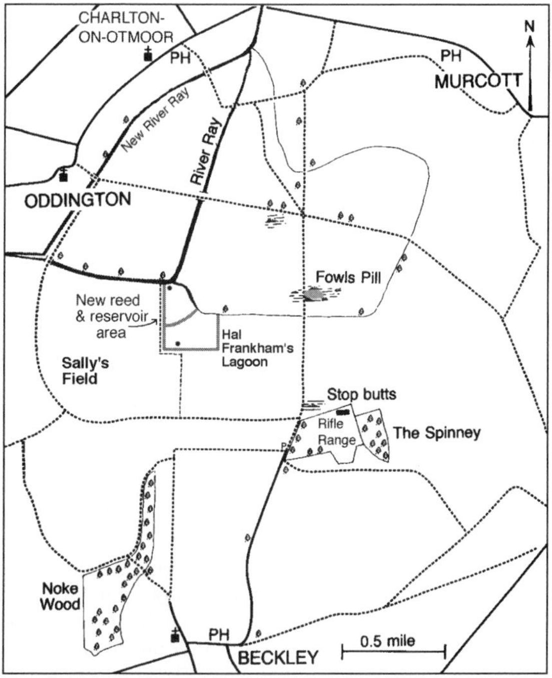

invading scrub. There are extensive hedgerows, primarily Blackthorn and Hawthorn with occasional mature stands of Oak and willow. On higher ground and running down to the plain are remnants of the forest once surrounding the moor and now represented by Noke Wood. Although small, a good variety of wildlife is supported beneath its mainly Oak canopy. The Spinney, the small pool known as Fowls Pill, and the adjacent rifle range (used daily apart from Monday and Thursday) are managed operationally, but sympathetically to conservation. (Access is by permit only, but a footpath runs along the southern edge.)

The area as a whole is rich in all forms of plant and animal life and part of Otmoor is designated an SSSI. Dragonflies are well represented and a good range of butterflies is to be found. Muntjac, Roe and Fallow Deer, Hare and Fox are all seen. Grass Snakes are common; look for them along any of the waterways or whilst they bask on sheltered banks during periods of sunshine.

Access

The area is well served by footpaths from which much of Otmoor's wildlife can be viewed. Access can be gained at various points, with paths leading from each of the villages that ring the moor. The most convenient for pedestrians are from Oddington and Charlton-on-Otmoor.

Vehicular access to the reserve car park (SP 570 126) is at the end of Otmoor Lane in Beckley but care is needed as the lane is narrow and regularly used by dog walkers, families and horse riders. When the rifle range is in use, a red flag flies from the Stop Butts and warning notices are to be found. Otmoor is vast and walks are long, even to the hides east of the main water bodies. A circular walk around the periphery is possible, but allow lots of time!

Species

Whilst Otmoor has been one of the most exciting places in the county for the birdwatcher, the recent transformation stands to make it even more so. Parties of ducks, once numbered in tens, are now surpassed with recent peaks of 2,200 Wigeon, 2,000 Teal, 396 Pintail and 170 Gadwall. Lapwing has reached 4,500 and Golden Plover may total 2,500. As colder weather arrives, small flocks of White-fronted Geese may appear occasionally and both Bewick's and Whooper Swans have been known to make brief visits.

With much vegetation, and a network of ditches, ducks and waders can be well concealed but Snipe may be found, the fast erratic flight of the bird when flushed from underfoot usually the best view one can expect. Any Snipe perceived, however, need checking as both Woodcock and Jack Snipe are possible. In past winters a number of Short-eared Owl would take up temporary residence, but perversely there may be too much water for them now. On the other hand, sightings of Hen Harrier, Merlin and Peregrine have become regular and there are always prospects of Common Buzzard soaring overhead. These raptors join Sparrowhawk and Kestrel, both of which are resident all year round. Of the other birds of prey, the Little Owl is most frequently encountered, particularly at home in pollarded willows along the River Ray. Often seen in daylight hours, they are vocal throughout much of the year and on a clear, still evening can be heard calling right across the plain.

The hedgerows in winter hold noisy gatherings of Fieldfare and Redwing, mixed flocks of tits accompanied by Treecreeper and Goldcrest

Snipe

and also finch and bunting flocks, which journey out to the fields where food has been put out for cattle, or to sites where grain has been put down for gamebirds and around farm buildings. From March to May, Otmoor is a good place to search for migrating species using it as a stopover site for feeding and resting. Waders recorded at this time have included Whimbrel, Ruff and Wood Sandpiper. Marsh Harrier are regular as too is Garganey, a duck which has in the past bred on Otmoor. Snipe also breed on the open fields, up to eight birds seen performing the territorial display flights and heard 'drumming' over and around the marshier areas. Lapwing breed here too, a few pairs nesting on the spring-sown arable fields. Contributing to the feeling of remoteness that is so much part of Otmoor's character will be the bubbling, liquid trilling of the Curlew. Up to twelve pairs may nest, although unless one visits early in the day or at dusk the birds can remain rather elusive. Redshank, not recorded as a breeding species for some years, are already up to 20 pairs. The recently-constructed screen-hides afford good views of waders throughout the seasons and the MOD-owned 100-acre field and pool has also proven important for wildfowl and waders, attracting Stone Curlew and Spotted Crake in recent years.

Meadow Pipit, Skylark and Reed Bunting are all doing well and the Yellowhammer is common, but Corn Bunting has suffered a major decline even here. Willow Warbler, Chiffchaff, Blackcap and Whitethroat are all widely distributed and quite common. Lesser Whitethroat are also present but easily missed unless one is familiar with the rather monotonous rattling song. They are probably more numerous across the site on autumn passage. Sedge Warbler have become more numerous, frequenting the river banks wherever dense bankside vegetation will permit, although increasingly found in drier locations close to the rifle range, where Nightjar and Firecrest have also been noted. The Grasshopper Warbler, though scarce, is most usually found in the hedgerows along the access lane from Beckley and particularly in the scrub, hedges and rank vegetation near the rifle range. A warm, still evening in May is the best occasion to listen to its curious 'reeling' song and perhaps glimpse this most retiring of birds. Nightingale and Tree Pipit are less likely to be found nowadays but Spotted Flycatcher are regularly seen in the villages, often feeding in the lanes leading to Otmoor, and Turtle Dove nest deep in hedges though are more usually seen on trees and telegraph wires. Yellow Wagtail and Hobby are most evident late in the season when young birds are off the nest.

The woodlands hold Treecreeper and all the woodpeckers. Most finches are numerous, with Otmoor being one of the best places locally to see Bullfinch. Water Rail has bred in recent times in overgrown ditches, whilst Mallard nest at sites all over Otmoor. Little Grebe are found along the River Ray most of the year, nesting under the shelter of a well-vegetated bank, and in good numbers on the reserve itself. Also along the river, Kingfisher are frequently seen. Late July and August is a relatively quiet period with very little song or activity as birds are undergoing moult. From mid-August, parties of Whinchat and Wheatear move through in discrete family parties, with occasional Redstart. Waders will by then also be making brief visits.

Declared an Environmentally Sensitive Area in 1995, and in part an RSPB reserve since '98, Otmoor is becoming more and more a premier birdwatching site, with almost 200 species now recorded. Recent rarities include Ring-necked Duck, Blue-winged Teal, Bean Goose, Osprey, Lesser Yellowlegs, American Wigeon, Spoonbill and even Arctic Skua. The common waders encouraged back to the site to breed have been joined by Wood and Pectoral Sandpipers and Temminck's Stint. But visitors will want to luxuriate in the open wildness of this restored wetland, and the myriad bird, plant and insect species attracted to such habitat, before wondering about the more unusual guests. As recently as April 2001, yet another 47 ha (117 acres) of land has been added to the reserve thanks to the RSPB and the Heritage Lottery Fund, so the 'good news' story continues to run for Otmoor.

Calendar

Resident: Little Grebe, Mute Swan, Mallard, Sparrowhawk, Kestrel, Common Buzzard, partridges, Pheasant, Moorhen, Coot, Water Rail, Snipe, Lapwing, Woodpigeon, Stock and Collared Doves, Little and Tawny Owls, possible Barn Owl, Kingfisher, Green and Great Spotted Woodpeckers, Skylark, Meadow Pipit. Commoner tits, corvids, finches, thrushes, and Yellowhammer. Tree Sparrow and Corn Bunting are rarely encountered, however.

December–February: On pools: Mallard, Teal and Wigeon and possible Shoveler, Pintail, wild geese and swans, Snipe, Lapwing, Golden Plover, possible Jack Snipe. Mixed flocks of finches and buntings, mixed tit, Treecreeper and Goldcrest flocks, winter thrushes, possible Short-eared Owl, regular Hen Harrier, occasional Merlin, Stonechat.

March–May: On passage: Wheatear, Whinchat, waders including occasional Whimbrel, Garganey. Hen and Marsh Harriers. Meadow Pipit, Tree Pipit, Lesser Whitethroat, Whitethroat, Sedge Warbler, Chiffchaff, Willow Warbler, Blackcap, Garden Warbler, Grasshopper Warbler, Nightingale (now rare), Cuckoo, Turtle Dove (though fewer), Redstart, Spotted Flycatcher, Yellow Wagtail, Curlew.

June–July: Much breeding activity, regular Hobby.

August–November: From August to September: return passage of Wheatear and Whinchat, Redstart. Build-up of dove and pigeon flocks. Resident species become more wide-ranging in their movements and flock together more. Influx of Redwing and Fieldfare.

81 PORT MEADOW **OS ref. SP 495 095**

Habitat

Any big city would be enriched by such a large parcel of common land beside its metropolitan boundary, as is the case with Port Meadow, a 167-ha (418-acre) low-lying urban common owned by Oxford City Council. Following a long and rich history, these unimproved grazing meadows have remained as they were today. Despite disturbance the scale of this open green prairie-land and its propensity to flood in the wet season, guarantees a wide range of species during the different seasons of the year.

The River Thames to the west and the Oxford Canal to the east afford gravelled and muddy shores as attractive feeding places, and beyond the Thames is a patchwork of permanent grazing land dissected by hedgerows and ditches. On the canal side, a different patchwork of habitat exists, including allotments, reeds, small unimproved meadows, linear tree-lines and hedgerows. The southern edge of Port Meadow is bounded by the Castle Mill Stream, a tree-lined sidestream of the Thames with good bankside vegetation of reeds, Meadowsweet and willowherb. This channel also forms the northern edge of Fiddler's Island, a particularly interesting area of lush vegetation and scrub. Alder, Osier and pollarded willow are found here, tree species which border much of Port Meadow and the towpath of the Thames. The common is somewhat less grazed in the south leaving patches of nettle-bed for butterflies and insects, and in this sector may still have small pools of open water after wetter winters.

From Wolvercote Common in the north, tracks lead onto the adjacent Burgess Field Nature Reserve, a huge open grassland with outcrops of young Hawthorn, Cherry and Oak, planted ten years ago on a reclaimed rubbish tip. The grass grows to near shoulder height in summer, attracting large numbers of Marbled White and other butterfly species. Regarding the entire site, local city-dwellers in particular have opportunities for a quick, pre-breakfast visit, but several hours are needed to explore every nook and cranny of this pleasant piece of wilderness.

Access

By car from the centre of Oxford, proceed north along Walton Street turning left after approximately 0.5 mile (1 km) into Walton Well Road, to the car park at the far end. Alternatively, drive north out of Oxford on the Woodstock Road, turning left at the Wolvercote roundabout. Drive for 1.6 km (1 mile) where, just before a river bridge, there is a car park

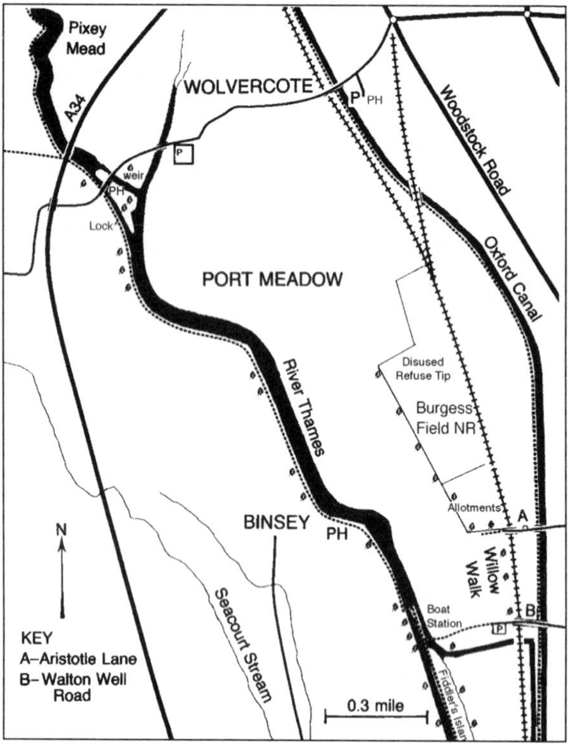

on the left, with toilets. One can walk out onto the meadow from this point or walk further along the Godstow Road, passing The Trout public house to join the towpath along the other side of the river.

Annual flooding of the meadow makes it impossible to negotiate the southern part, but approaching the floodwater from the north is more likely to disturb the birdlife. At these times, amongst the most exciting from an avian perspective, it is better to view from the west bank towpath of the Thames or from the vicinity of the metalled road joining Walton Well Road with Aristotle Lane. A telescope is a near necessity, so if you do not own one, visit with someone who does! Towpaths alongside the Thames and Oxford Canal are accessible from either car park. Views over the area can be obtained from either of the bridges that cross the railway or from Willow Walk in the meadow's south-east corner.

The meadow is best visited, summer or winter, early in the day before the dog-walkers arrive and birds disperse to feeding grounds elsewhere. Provided it is not too hot, the areas around the meadow can be visited most times of day. If one is able to spend perhaps a morning exploring the site then a final stop at one of the riverside inns (The Perch at Binsey or The Trout at Godstow) can round off a trip nicely and of course allows a check of one's notebook and the results of the morning's activities.

Species

Springtime at Port Meadow can be a frustrating affair, as anything might be anywhere on this large area. Waders such as Ruff, Spotted Redshank, Whimbrel, Curlew and Sanderling, which occur most years, will be easy to find if the meadows remain wet, but passerines such as Whinchat, Wheatear and Yellow Wagtail might use any part of the meadow and could escape notice.

In summertime, however, the meadow loses most if not all of its surface water and muddy feeding grounds, and the surrounding areas come into their own. Mallard, Moorhen, Coot and Mute Swan breed along the waterways, finding nest sites on secluded backwaters, and despite disturbance along its banks, the river may provide much entertainment. The scene will be of stalking Grey Heron and families of ever-present Pied Wagtail, performing their aerial dance for water-side midges, whilst their ashy-backed progeny watch from overhanging branches or jog along the beaches. By June, Common Sandpiper can be found whilst Black-headed Gull feed over the water, squabbling over whatever scraps they can find, with their newly arrived juveniles in their splendid chocolate mantle and scarf. Common Tern will be seen patrolling with a nodding action as they alternately look down for morsels and ahead to see where they are going. Groups of young Mallard will be whelping from cover and a raft of 200 to 300 geese will adopt a section of bank which will be liberally littered with their moultings. Many will have had their origins in Greylag stock and there will be Canada Geese too, but a good proportion will show strains of more than one species. Kingfisher are occasionally seen, more usually along the quieter backwaters than the main river. Hirundines and Swift wheel overhead and a Skylark may be singing amongst them, vainly seeking a quiet corner to nest.

The thick bankside vegetation of the Castle Mill Stream and Fiddler's Island should be checked for resident Reed Bunting and Dunnock or summer visitors such as Chiffchaff, Whitethroat and Sedge Warbler. Cuckoo will be watching closely, searching for suitable nests in which to deposit their eggs. The patchwork of gardens, allotments, scrub and waste ground between the meadow and the canal allows Goldfinch, Linnet and Bullfinch to thrive alongside Greenfinch and Chaffinch. Later in the year, when these birds group together more, Redpoll and Yellowhammer may also be found. Small numbers of Tree Sparrow have been noted previously and may still be worth looking for, especially in the pollarded trees along Willow Walk (a site also favoured by Treecreeper), whilst in winter, they might frequent the car park at the end of Walton Well Road. The same Willow Walk can offer respite from the heat of a midsummer day and can be rewarded with a serenading Garden Warbler, its song containing a little Lesser Whitethroat, a hint of Nightingale and a lot of Blackcap! Aristotle Lane could be good for a pair of Spotted Flycatcher.

Continuing northwards on the canal side, and just beyond the allotments, one can cross over to Burgess Field, a huge area of open grassland interspersed with bushes and brambles, which resounds to the repetitive calls of several male Reed Bunting and the more melodic song of numerous Whitethroat and a few Willow Warbler. The area has held Nightingale and also Grasshopper Warbler so keeping an ear open may pay dividends. More Jack Snipe than are actually seen no doubt spend the mid-winter months here, and the same field has often been used by hunting Short-eared Owl and even Barn Owl, while Peregrine have been noted. Of the birds of prey occurring here, Sparrowhawk and Kestrel are the most likely to be encountered, but summertime presents an enticement to opportunistic Hobby, so 'eyes to the skies' is the motto. Stonechat are noted here, mainly in the winter months.

And it is in wintertime that Port Meadow itself really comes to life. Recent mild but wet winters ensure that the flooded river or heavy rains create a large shallow pool towards the southern end and render part of the remainder a marshland. Dabbling ducks such as Mallard are the most conspicuous and as winter progresses, Wigeon and Teal can be found in rapidly increasing numbers, typically 1,000 of the former and 100 of the latter. When they choose to do an aerial circuit or two, they make a magnificent sight wheeling over the meadow, whistling and calling in an excited flurry. The larger and colourful Shoveler can be found and a careful scan across the flocks can usually reveal the presence of several Gadwall. As many as 50 or so of that most elegant of the ducks, the Pintail, may be present between December and March and although by no means annual, the equally striking Garganey has visited. Resident species such as Mute Swan, Coot and Moorhen are attracted to the floodwaters and one can occasionally find them joined by small parties of White-fronted Goose and Bewick's Swan. Flocks of gulls are usually in the area, Black-headed the most numerous, with a few Lesser Black-backed Gull. In recent years less common species such as Little and Mediterranean Gulls have been noted, and Yellow-legged Gull are nowadays reported almost as often as Herring Gull, so check the flocks carefully.

If it is sheer numbers of birds that gives delight, then Port Meadow will not disappoint. First there are the Canada Geese, common birds in the county but winter flocks in excess of 1,000 birds may form on the meadow, spread along its length, often avoiding the wettest parts. Together with the resident feral geese, they often draw in other wandering species such as Egyptian Goose and Shelduck. There are also Lapwing; the number often reaches 500 but flocks of over 1,000 birds have been noted, including one exceptional count of over 10,000 birds. Large, mixed flocks of corvids add to the numbers. Should a passing Grey Heron, Sparrowhawk or even Peregrine disturb the flocks, the ensuing panic created among all these birds is an impressive sight. Other raptors infrequently recorded have included Merlin, Red Kite, Marsh and Hen Harriers, all perhaps taking time out from the far more suited habitat of nearby Otmoor.

Perhaps less conspicuous is the Snipe, feeding across the wet, marshy meadow, beautifully camouflaged from predator and birdwatcher alike. With careful scanning, up to 100 can be located in autumn, though more usually a couple of dozen may be lurking. Golden Plover on the other hand gather in huge numbers, perhaps up to 2,000 – when one at first thought the meadow was bare! Other waders, including Redshank, Ruff and up to a couple of dozen Dunlin, are also present in winter, often feeding between river and flood such that viewing from the west bank of the Thames offers better views. Bar-tailed and Black-tailed Godwits may join the other waders, which have included Oystercatcher, Grey Plover, Curlew, Knot and Avocet, whilst along sheltered margins such as Fiddler's Island, a wintering Water Rail might be seen feeding. A number of passerine species also exploit the feeding opportunities created by the floods with Pied Wagtail, Linnet and Meadow Pipit

Grey Heron

being common and Grey Wagtail occasional visitors. During winter, especially if the still waters freeze, the Thames is always worth investigating. Many of the surface-feeding ducks (Teal, Mallard, etc.) will congregate here and small teams of Goosander play against the river's flow, occasionally alongside the odd Goldeneye. Even a Ring-necked Duck called in one autumn.

In modern-day England, more and more reserves are having to be created to try and hold on to our natural heritage. It is all the nicer, therefore, to be able to visit a 'natural' reserve such as this and see much of our birdlife in all its glory.

Calendar

Resident: Grey Heron, Mute Swan, Canada Goose, Mallard, Sparrowhawk, Kestrel, partridge, Moorhen, Coot, Little Owl, Linnet, Goldfinch, Bullfinch, Treecreeper, possible Tree Sparrow. Reed Bunting and Yellowhammer.

December–February: When wet: Wigeon, Teal, Shoveler, Gadwall, possible Pintail, occasional Bewick's Swan, Dunlin, Redshank, possible Golden Plover, large congregation of Snipe, Lapwing, Canada Goose. Merlin, Peregrine, Short-eared Owl, Meadow Pipit, possible Grey Wagtail, occasional Goosander, Goldeneye, Water Rail.

March–May: Passage: Garganey, Common Sandpiper, Ruff, Whimbrel, Spotted Redshank, Sanderling, Yellow Wagtail, Whinchat, Wheatear. Breeding: Chiffchaff, Whitethroat, Sedge and Grasshopper Warblers, Cuckoo, Nightingale, Reed Bunting.

June–July: Feeding hirundines, breeding warblers, patrolling Common Tern.

August–November: Occasional Hobby, possible terns and Common Sandpiper on river. As meadow becomes wet, duck and wader numbers rise.

82 SHOTOVER COUNTRY PARK

OS ref. SP 565 055

Habitat

Owned and managed by Oxford City Council, Shotover Country Park is situated just outside the city ring road and occupies 164 ha (410 acres) of Shotover Hill's south-facing slopes. The park represents one of the remnants of the Shotover Royal Forest which, prior to its deforestation in the mid-seventeenth century, covered some 2,300 ha (5,750 acres). Despite this size reduction, today's park remains immensely diverse and, with the wealth of wildlife that flourishes, is designated an SSSI.

The slopes of the hill are predominantly a mixture of grassland, scrub, bracken and open woodland. Horseshoe Field is a good example of how scrub will invade when grassland is left unmanaged for, up until the Second World War, this area was in agricultural use. The field is mainly Hawthorn and Gorse scrub, with areas of bracken and acid grassland. Almost all the more mature trees are relatively young and include Pedunculate and Turkey Oak, Ash and three species of Sorbus: Whitebeam, Rowan and Wild Service. To the west of Horseshoe Field is Johnson's Piece, an interesting sector of open woodland and bracken, edged with old pollarded Oaks, the wood itself dominated by Ash, Birch and Pedunculate Oak. The same three Sorbus species are present, together with Crab Apple, Wild Cherry and a variety of maples and conifers, in an old informal arboretum. The Sandpit Field comprises mainly scrub and acid grassland, a scene also noted in Mary Sadler's Field. The scrub here is mostly Hawthorn and Oak with smaller amounts of Elder and Sycamore. The western edge of the slope was a Larch plantation, and has reverted to bracken and mixed scrub. At the foot of the hill are two areas of woodland. Brasenose Wood is a fine example of Hazel coppice with an over-canopy of Oak – a traditional style of woodland management dating back 800 years. Still managed in

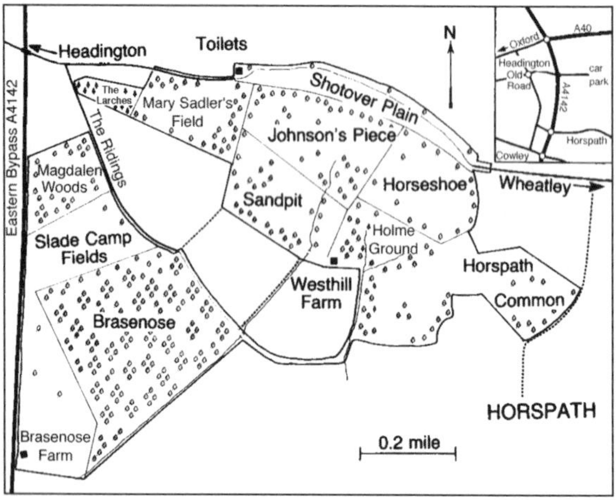

this way, selected areas are coppiced in rotation such that a range of age classes of Hazel are present at any one time. With an extensive system of grassy rides, the wood has an open feel, resulting in a diverse wildlife and good viewing of the woodland birds found here. Magdalen Wood is much smaller and because it is younger and more enclosed, does not exhibit the same diversity as Brasenose.

Between the two woodlands and west of Brasenose is an area of grassland and scrub known as Slade Camp Fields which were once used for post-war army dwellings. The wide range of bushes and shrubs here (mainly Blackthorn and rose) encourage much invertebrate activity. The northern field has been planted with a mixture of native tree species.

Other features include patches of heathland (currently undergoing restoration and recovery from encroachment by Birch) and areas of marsh and wetland created by springs emerging in Johnson's Piece and Holme Ground. Adjoining the country park to the north and east are open pastures and arable fields bounded by hedgerows, giving the whole area a very rural feel, despite being so close to Oxford's urban sprawl. Farmland also extends eastwards towards the imposing Stokenchurch communications tower which dominates the horizon.

Oxford City Council has a positive conservation policy at Shotover so that, while catering for numerous recreational activities, the intent is to maintain, and if possible increase, the diversity of habitat available for wildlife. In addition, the council run various countryside events, many of them centred around Shotover.

Access

The Park is very popular with dog-owners, runners, orienteers, picnickers and casual walkers, all out to enjoy the countryside and the marvellous views from the higher points of the hill. For anybody wishing to avoid the multitudes, a visit on a weekday or at either end of the day is recommended.

Ample car parking is available on Shotover Plain which is approached either from Wheatley or Old Road, Headington. Note, however, that there is no direct vehicular access from the ring road (A4142). There are three waymarked nature trails within the park, and a leaflet describing the Park and the work of Shotover Wildlife (01865 715830) is available at the car park noticeboard.

Species

Anyone wishing to learn about or observe woodland and farmland birds will be well rewarded by a visit here. Throughout the year there is much to see but it is during spring and early summer that bird activity reaches a peak, especially just after summer visitors have arrived. The descending musical song of Willow Warbler embellish the woodland edges whilst the repetitive disyllabic tones of Chiffchaff extend deeper into the park. A little later arriving are Blackcap and Garden Warbler. Whilst easy to separate if seen well, it is their songs that are so similar, but by visiting the park early in the season both are easier to see providing ample opportunity to directly compare their songs. Also vocal early in the season will be the Cuckoo and, whilst encountered almost anywhere, the best views are obtained on Slade Camp Fields. Here there is dense cover, in which species such as Dunnock and Whitethroat nest, with plenty of bushes and fences to use as songposts or vantage points. Other visitors to note include Lesser Whitethroat, nesting in areas of scrub perhaps near the well-established gardens, and Spotted Flycatcher – usually found in open areas of Brasenose Wood.

Other songsters such as Blackbird and Robin are plentiful around the site although the range and musical quality of the Song Thrush are even more notable. The Wren, another noisy if rather less tuneful bird, is common all over Shotover, its loud explosive song apparently out of all proportion to its size. The raucous calls of Jay and Magpie are common and a significant colony of Jackdaw has established itself in Brasenose, the black-and-grey adults shepherding increasing numbers of sooty-brown youngsters between suitable feeding places. Woodcock are probably more common than the infrequency of sightings suggest.

Arguably, it is Brasenose Wood that is best for birds, particularly in the breeding season. In this relatively small tract of woodland, 18 ha (45 acres), some 34 species breed, and in good numbers. This is the place in which to find Nuthatch and the woodpecker species including the often elusive Lesser Spotted Woodpecker, views of which are best early in the year when birds are 'drumming' and the Oaks not yet in full leaf. There are ample nest sites available for all the woodpeckers and larger holes (natural and excavated) are readily taken by Stock Dove, Jackdaw and Tawny Owl. Treecreeper nest in Brasenose but are likely to be found wherever medium and large trees exist in the park. Nightingale continue to be heard on occasions.

The tit family is well represented on Shotover. Most can be found nesting throughout the areas of scrub and woodland, although Coal Tit are more usual in the Larches along with Goldcrest. Check also for Firecrest which have been noted. Of the birds of prey, Kestrel is frequently seen, hovering over areas of grassland, and Sparrowhawk haunt the woods and hedges for small birds. Despite the proximity of the city, Red Kite are being recorded more and more often in the vicinity and Common Buzzard too is seen more frequently. On most evenings, Tawny Owl can be heard calling from the woods and from some of the large wooded gardens on the hill, whilst on the periphery of the park and along the nearby hedgerows Little Owl may be seen.

It is always well worth checking the surrounding fields for species not present in the park itself. Skylark and Red-legged Partridge are common and Yellowhammer occasionally nest in scrub cover within Shotover's boundary (e.g. Horseshoe Field), often in the company of Linnet, Chaffinch and Whitethroat.

The elevation of the site provides a convenient stopover point for birds to rest. In spring, Wheatear and Wood Warbler have been recorded. In September or October it is a useful place to stage a 'migration watch'. Birds such as pipits and finches move past on their way to winter quarters on the coast. Late Swallow move through on their way to Africa and early Redwing and Fieldfare fly over. Many of these thrushes will remain for the winter, making the most of the plentiful food and shelter in the park and nearby gardens. Also present in winter will be Redpoll and Siskin, hanging upside down to feed on the Birch and Larch seeds, or maybe, in the case of the latter species, on a convenient bag of nuts! In some years, Crossbill frequent the park's hillside, the result of irruptions from the Continent when food becomes short, usually seen from July onwards and small flocks remain in the general area until the following spring. An excellent site in any season.

Calendar

Resident: Sparrowhawk, Kestrel, possible Common Buzzard and Red Kite, Red-legged Partridge, Pheasant, Woodcock, Little Owl, Stock Dove, Magpie, Jay, Jackdaw, Wren, Skylark, common tits, finches, thrushes and woodpeckers, Nuthatch, Treecreeper, Yellowhammer.

December–February: Increasing numbers of Siskin, Fieldfare, Redwing, Redpoll.

March–May: Willow Warbler, Chiffchaff, Blackcap, Garden Warbler, Lesser Whitethroat, Whitethroat, Spotted Flycatcher, Cuckoo, possible Nightingale. Passage: possible Wheatear, Wood Warbler, Meadow Pipit.

June–July: Height of breeding season. Occasional Hobby.

August–November: Crossbill, Redpoll, Siskin. Passage: hirundines and winter thrushes overhead, Meadow Pipit. Tits and finches.

ADDITIONAL SITES

Bicester Wetland Reserve (OS ref. SP 578 211)

A new 6-ha (15-acre) nature reserve created by Thames Water resulting in reedbeds, scrapes and ditches alongside the STW. Excellent for waders, including Jack Snipe, and wildfowl. A hide exists alongside the car park and a raised viewing point has been constructed at one side of the reserve. Access is for BOS members only and a key is needed, so becoming a member not only gains access to the reserve but means you can help in the essential work of mapping the ornithological picture throughout their area.

Bladon Heath (OS ref. SP 485 022)

Misleadingly named, Bladon Heath is actually a piece of woodland at Bladon, south of Woodstock. A mixture of deciduous and coniferous stands, with sectors of Hawthorn, Oak and Sycamore thicket and other more open Birch, pine and Sycamore spinneys. Access from the north is via the A4095, turning off at Lamb Lane which leads to Heath Lane, at the end of which is a bridleway heading off between the row of garages and the houses. (Not the one behind the garages, which merely crosses open fields.) This track passes through the northern section of the wood before opening onto an uncultivated meadow between the wood and the village of Begbroke. Return is via the same route, but a southerly 4-km circular walk skirting Begbroke Wood and farmland is possible using footpaths shown on the OS map.

The woods are excellent for both birds and butterflies, the former including Great and occasional Lesser Spotted Woodpeckers, Goldcrest, Nuthatch, Jay, Bullfinch and Marsh Tit. Woodcock and Tawny Owl are present and wintertime draws in Siskin and Redpoll. Roe and Muntjac Deer roam freely and Wood White and White Admiral butterflies are seen in summer. The open meadows host Yellowhammer and winter Meadow Pipit, whilst the hedgerows attract both Whitethroat and Lesser Whitethroat in summer. Common Buzzard and Sparrowhawk will often be seen overhead and the many Swift and hirundines sweeping the fields for insects occasionally result in Hobby being encountered.

Lashford Lane Fen (OS ref. SP 468 013)

Situated to the west of Wootton, near Abingdon, this BBOWT reserve is well worth a visit at any time. At 7 ha (17 acres), it comprises a mosaic of habitats including fen with reedbed, scrub, woodland, dense Hawthorn thicket and grassland. A stream runs through the site and there are several small pools, and an excellent hide overlooking the reedbed and a feeding station. Many paths are very boggy and pass through enclosed sections of dense woodland.

A good range of resident birds, typical of the habitats present, are aided by a selection of nest boxes. During summer, a number of Chiffchaff, Willow Warbler and occasional Spotted Flycatcher breed here while in the wetland areas, Reed Bunting, Sedge and Reed Warblers nest. In the winter months, birds are attracted to the site for feeding and roosting, including Fieldfare and Redwing, and a roost of Reed Bunting. The provision of peanuts and grain at the feeding station attracts finches and tits, including Marsh Tit, together with Great and Lesser Spotted Woodpeckers and Nuthatch. From the hide one might glimpse Water Rail, which may take up temporary residence, an occasional Kingfisher, and possibly Tawny Owl making use of suitable nest boxes.

The entrance to the site is in Lashford Lane, 400 m (440 yds) south of its junction with Besselsleigh Road. There is a small car park at the entrance and visitors are asked to use this rather than the road. The reserve warden (see noticeboard in the car park for details) can arrange guided walks and provision can be made for additional car parking for groups.

Merton Borrow Pit (OS ref. SP 570 170)

This is the small lake visible from the M40 motorway near junction 9 but access from there means travelling south-west on the A34 towards Kidlington and turning off to Islip, following signs to Oddington and Charlton-on-Otmoor, and parking near the gate on the right just before the bridge over the motorway. But the jaunt may prove worthwhile, especially if one observes from this point rather than walking round the lake edge, which is certain to flush waders such as Redshank and Common Sandpiper and ducks such as Shelduck, Pintail, Pochard, Tufted Duck, Ruddy Duck and Mute Swan. A visit might simply be rewarded with a good number of these commoner species, but might as easily coincide with one of the star birds that have used this small site. They have included Ruddy Shelduck, Scaup, Peregrine, Bewick's and Whooper Swans, Brent Goose, Black-tailed Godwit and Greenshank. Other waders noted have been Little Ringed and Ringed Plovers, Golden Plover and Oystercatcher. Major interest was caused by the short stay of a female Red-footed Falcon in 1997, which seemed a sickly bird on arrival but which perked up after regular feeding by local birders. Other significant star performers have been Ring-necked Duck, Grey Phalarope and even Gannet. Who knows what might turn up next, especially with Otmoor so close.

Oxfordshire Chilterns

Extending for some 80 km (50 miles) from the River Thames at Goring, running across the south-east corner of Oxfordshire, on through Bucks., Herts. and Beds., is the ridge of chalk which forms the Chiltern Hills. Rising in a steep, west-facing scarp, up to 265 m (870 ft) and sloping away gently eastwards, they give a general impression of a long string of rounded hills with grassy downs, wooded escarpments and ridges with many valleys beyond the scarp. Most valleys are dry but on the western slope where clay meets chalk, a spring line emerges, often providing man-made ponds, cress beds, etc. attractive to birds.

Access is very good with many miles of well-marked footpaths, including the Icknield Way/Ridgeway path, all of which, thanks to the commendable efforts of the Chiltern Society and various landowners, allow a greater appreciation of this designated Area of Outstanding Natural Beauty (AONB). And of course, there has been the amazing success story of the re-introduction of Red Kites into the Chilterns. Some 90 kites were imported into the area between 1989 and 1993, and pairs first started breeding in 1992. With currently 100 pairs producing nearly 200 young each year, it has been possible to relocate some of these birds into schemes elsewhere in England and Scotland.

Two Chiltern sites have already been described in this book. However, these are not the only sites within the Oxfordshire Chilterns where a birdwatcher may gainfully spend many hours, particularly in the spring, summer and during periods of migration when the species found are much the same as at Aston Rowant and Warburg. Hence, a brief account of each additional site is now given, commencing in the north and moving south-west.

Chinnor Hill (OS ref. SP 766 002) This 28-ha (70-acre) site is owned by BBOWT and exhibits each typical Chiltern habitat. Oak and Ash woodland exists at the south-west of the reserve where the chalk is capped by clay, while on the chalk escarpment Beech woodland dominates. Except for a small area of grassland, the remainder is scrub, dense in parts, and mainly of Hazel coppice, Cherry, Whitebeam and Hawthorn, but Juniper, Yew, Silver Birch, Field Maple and Wayfaring Tree also feature. Good views are to be obtained over the escarpment, making it particularly worth watching during passage. The hill was the county's last known breeding site of the Cirl Bunting.

To reach the reserve leave Chinnor on the unclassified road up the escarpment following the signs for Bledlow Ridge. Approximately 2 km (1.25 miles) from Chinnor, turn left into Hill Top Road. Car parking is available at the end of the lane. Access to the reserve is by way of several established footpaths allowing views over all types of habitat and the birds within.

Ewelme and Swyncombe Downs (OS ref. SU 680 910) These rather open areas of the Chiltern escarpment mostly include chalk grassland and scrub, but sadly most have been converted into arable fields. This was once a stronghold of the Stone Curlew, now unfortunately very rare in the district, but still worth watching out for. The rolling landscape may attract occasional Common Buzzard and harriers in winter, roosting in the nearby woods. Interesting walks, following the Ridgeway and other public footpaths, begin at Park Corner on the B481 Watlington to Nettlebed Road, or from the unclassified road leading west from Cookley Green further along the same road.

Queen, Fire and College Woods (OS ref. SU 715 932) Park on the roadside just east of Christmas Common and follow the broad Hollandridge Lane south-east. From the lane, one is free to explore these Forestry Commission-owned woods using any of the rides and waymarked paths.

Primarily of interest in the breeding season, these woods support a good variety of species, particularly where areas of more open scrub prevail.

Shotridge and Blackmoor Woods (OS ref. SU 713 935) Park on the right-hand side of the road leading north from Christmas Common and in the vicinity of the radio mast. From here, footpaths lead eastwards, down through a superbly-wooded valley. One first negotiates an area of Oak wood with a good scrub layer and then on into an area of Chiltern Beech woodland.

Following the track down the valley one then comes into a wetter area, with Salix and Birch scrub – ideal habitat for warblers and titmice. After 2.5 km (1.5 miles) from the starting point, one bears south-west, climbing the steep escarpment through Blackmoor wood to Northend. Here, there is an area of well-drained acid soil with thickets primarily of Gorse, just right for Yellowhammer and warblers, Linnet and other breeding finches. By rejoining the road and turning right, the route returns to the starting point.

Watlington Hill (OS ref. SU 711 936) In the safe hands of the National Trust, this 38-ha (96-acre) site on the west-facing scarp, with superb views of Oxfordshire (and migrating birds), is a favourite with walkers and picnickers. Visits should therefore be timed to avoid the usual busy periods. Much of the Hill is chalk grassland and scrub, providing nesting and feeding sites for many bird species. Some Beech woods exist but the bulk of the wooded area is the Great Yew Wood, very dense and believed to date back to the time of the Napoleonic wars.

The dense cover prevents a good ground or shrub flora but breeding species, including Coal Tit, Goldcrest, Robin and Mistle Thrush thrive. Winter can bring Hawfinch and Crossbill whilst Red Kite are numerous throughout the year. Raven and Common Buzzard are increasingly noted and Peregrine is an occasional possibility.

Parking is available at the top of Watlington Hill approximately 2 km (1.5 miles) from Watlington village. There is open access to most of the grassland areas and numerous paths run through the blocks of scrub and woodland.

Parklands of Oxfordshire

Blenheim Park has been awarded its own section in this book by virtue of its size, reputation and well-recorded ornithological history. However, many species of parkland bird can equally be found at a variety of similar, albeit smaller, parks around the county, with the added bonus of free, and particularly in mid-week, almost exclusive access. Several permit no public access, but those below have public footpaths through or around them. Parkland scenery is the playground for flocks of Jackdaw and winter thrushes, Little Owl bounding between well-separated mature trees, hooting Stock Dove, at least two, if not all three, of the woodpecker species, and around the grand houses and outbuildings, opportunities for Spotted Flycatcher and nesting Swallow. Most parks also have a lake or pool facilitating the study of common waterfowl, often overlooked in more 'exciting' environs. Unlikely the sources of many rarities, Oxford's parks offer the beginner an unparalleled stage to learn on, and the accomplished birder the challenge of finding all the species expected whilst enjoying pleasant and quiet surroundings. Taking with you OS Sheet 164 for navigation, why not visit these charming parts of our natural heritage.

Barton Abbey (OS ref. SP 448 248) This site consists of parkland and formal gardens with arable surroundings. The wooded areas are good for Tawny Owl, Green and Great Spotted Woodpeckers, Nuthatch, Treecreeper and Marsh Tit, with Siskin in winter. The lake supports Kingfisher and breeding Little Grebe, with Chiffchaff, Blackcap and Garden Warbler in summer, whilst Spotted Flycatcher favour trees near the main buildings. Check the formal areas for Bullfinch and Pied Wagtail, the open parkland for owls and woodpeckers and possible Turtle Dove and the farmland for Yellowhammer, partridges and corvids. Sparrowhawk and Kestrel breed locally, Common Buzzard is regular, and Hobby is possible. Park opposite the church, utilising the path through the cemetery to gain access to the footpaths leading through the grounds, a circular walk being possible by using the minor road from Whistlow to Steeple Barton.

Bletchingdon Park (Os ref. SP 505 178) Parking at this point, follow the footpath to the church, checking the enclosed woodland and hedgerows for warblers, thrushes and Dunnock. After looking for any Spotted Flycatcher or Tawny Owl, follow the path to the left past the residences. This leads out onto open fields where several footpaths are available. From this elevated point, one can scan the farmland to the north-east for raptors or watch the parachuting over Weston-on-the-Green. The path to the left passes patches of woodland where Goldcrest, Marsh Tit and Treecreeper can be seen, with Common Buzzard overhead and Hawfinch at least once recorded. The fence line at the bottom of this field has several stiles leading into a pleasant creation of pools and reedbeds, where Reed and Sedge Warblers will be found, along with more Treecreeper, breeding Kestrel, and Coot, Moorhen and Grey Heron around the water. Time permitting, one can continue north to visit Kirtlington Park and complete a circular walk via the Oxfordshire Way, or return to your vehicle via the outward footpath.

Cornbury Park (OS ref. SP 357 166) The main park itself is closed to the public, though one footpath does run from Finstock through the north-eastern edge of the formal grounds to Charlbury. Of more interest to the birdwatcher, however, is the only other available footpath passing through the grand mixed and mature woodland of Wychwood Forest. This large mass of treescape is one of the most significant to the north-west of the county and potentially a good stopover point for passage Redstart or Wood Warbler, as well as hosting all three woodpeckers and most likely, all six tits. Occasional Hawfinch and Nightingale have to be possibilities but with this limited access, the site is underwatched and the status of many species uncertain, so regular visits would be enjoyable for the observer and valuable to the County Recorder. The footpath passes one of the lakes and then describes an arc through the wood from the grid reference above to its other end near Leafield, from where a return walk along the lane also takes in 2.5 km of the woodland edge and farmland opposite.

Ditchley Park (OS ref. SP 380 205) The whole area east of Charlbury contained within the triangle of the A34, B4437 and B4022 is worthy of exploration, with a variety of tracks and semi-metalled roads and a complex of footpaths facilitating a number of circular walks. Vehicular access through the centre of this private park is not possible but paths which pass through the area can be picked up having parked at the above reference point, at the end of the 3.2-km metalled road from Charlbury. Walking through the Model Farm leads to a conifer belt hosting Goldcrest, Coal Tit and winter Siskin. The adjacent deciduous compartment is good for Chaffinch, Great Spotted Woodpecker and common tits. The next stile leads to the open parkland where Jackdaw, Stock Dove, Mistle Thrush and Nuthatch will be found, with the prospect of spotting resident Little Owl. This more open aspect may be a good spot to look for roding Woodcock in season. To the right of the main residence at the far side are paths leading around the house to the north of the lake, from where return trails can be picked up, through farmland echoing to the songs of Skylark, Yellowhammer and Whitethroat. The lake itself is mainly secluded and has relatively little variety of birdlife, but a sneak view can be obtained via a well-worn trail through the hedgerow at SP 384 214. In summer, Hobby range widely over the estate, and a regular look over Shilcott and Deadman's Riding Woods to the north, and Out Wood to the east will be rewarded with Common Buzzard which breed here, and occasional Sparrowhawk. Red Kite have been recorded, and Raven has also been noted.

Glympton Park (OS ref. SP 423 215) Parking here, opposite the main gates on the B4027, a pedestrian-only footpath leads to the church at the centre of this private estate, along a more formal parkland which nonetheless hosts many of the expected species, including Goldcrest, Treecreeper, Nuthatch and Goldfinch. As the estate is based upon Pheasant shooting, at least this species will be encountered! Chiffchaff and Blackcap are common in summer, followed by flocks of thrushes and corvids in winter. Around the church, and the small lake at the lowest point in the park, Spotted Flycatcher are present in summer and Tawny Owl are heard calling by the staff. The parking area between the church and the Estate Office can be used if preferred, accessed by the track at SP 426 223. This may be useful if one intends extending the walk to nearby Kiddington Hall, looking out for partridges on the way. In winter, farmland around Glympton village should be checked for flocks of Yellowhammer and Corn Bunting.

Great Tew Park (OS ref. SP 395 295) A large area of mixed woodland, excellent for all usual species plus Common Buzzard, Lesser Spotted Woodpecker and Little Owl. Regrettably, available footpaths only circumnavigate the wood with no access to the centre; nonetheless, most species can be encountered on such a walk and in winter, significant flocks of Linnet, Goldfinch and Siskin occur. Slightly to the north, an area of farmland and somewhat more dilapidated parkland (SP 398 313) attract more winter finch flocks, and breeding Spotted Flycatcher. The hedgerow on top of the hill here may be worth checking for passage warblers such as Chiffchaff, Willow Warbler, Lesser Whitethroat and Blackcap accompanied by mixed finch and tit flocks. A free car park exists in the village just off the B4022 to Enstone.

Heythrop Park and College (OS ref. SP 374 296) A group of woodlands, interspersed with grassland and farmland, with footpaths through several areas, including the lake which has historically hosted many species until Mink disrupted this recently. Kingfisher and Grey Wagtail have remained and other species will return in due course. Tawny and Little Owls are present and Barn Owl may occur. Hedgerows attract Bullfinch and summer warblers, hirundines are numerous, especially from mid-August, and the conifers near the college (being converted to an hotel) have attracted Crossbill. Woodcock has been recorded. Parking outside the entrance on the minor road near Little Tew Grounds Farm, the walk down to the lake has the novel attraction of a zoological collection, adding Penguin, Peacock and Pelican to the day's list! The south-eastern woodland block, abutting a tributary to the River Glyme, is best explored on a circular walk from Enstone, returning via farmland and a disused quarry, looking for Grey Partridge, Yellowhammer and Little Owl. Nearby, Enstone airfield will be worth checking for winter gatherings of corvids, gulls and Lapwing, and occasional passage waders or overwintering Golden Plover, whilst Glyne Farm, to the south-east of Chipping Norton (SP 325 264) has a good reputation for Corn Bunting and occasional Short-eared Owl.

Kiddington Hall (OS ref. SP 412 229) Another family estate but with a footpath through the centre and another around the western edge, and walkable from nearby Glympton for an extended session. Parking is allowed near the church at the centre, accessed from the minor road to Kiddington off the A34. The usual species will be encountered, with Spotted Flycatcher more likely near the main house. The lake is severed by the pathway, one half being tree-lined and with a somewhat 'ornamental' feel to the species present. The other half is more open, with breeding Mute Swan, passing Kingfisher and ledges all round suited perhaps to passage Common Sandpiper and feeding Pied Wagtail. Hirundines sweep the skies above the estate tempting Hobby in during summer. Hawfinch has occurred.

Kirtlingon Hall (OS ref. SP 502 192) Parking considerately here gives access to the footpath entrance to this sizeable private estate. Mainly a fairly open scenery, and with Beech and Oaks, both lone and in clumps, plus some fine Cedar of Lebanon near the church, corvids, Woodpigeon, Stock and Collared Doves and Green Woodpecker are likely to be the first noticed. From July, groups of Mistle Thrush work their way across the grazed areas, joined by Redwing and Fieldfare later in the year. Mature hedgerows near the mid-way cattle grid are used by Yellowhammer, Goldfinch and Linnet, and just occasionally Tree Sparrow, whilst summer warblers and occasional Turtle Dove can be heard singing in adjacent thickets. The area around the main building and estate offices regularly holds Spotted Flycatcher with nesting Swallow and House Martin. The lake beyond is mostly obscured but the antics of young Moorhen, Mallard, Tufted Duck and Canada Geese can be observed, and Kingfisher, Snipe and Redshank have been recorded here. Both Little and Tawny Owls are present, and small groups of Common Buzzard occasionally soar overhead. The polo pitch hosts family parties of Pied Wagtail in summer, winter thrushes later, whilst Kestrel hunt over the surrounding rough grassy areas.

Oxford University Parks (OS ref. SP 513 071) Despite proximity to the city centre these parks offer excellent birdwatching throughout the year. Laid out in a rich mixture of native and ornamental trees, areas of herb-rich, rough grassland and formal flower beds and lawns, there is the added attraction of the tree-lined River Cherwell. New Marston Meadows adjacent is a SSSI.

Most of the typical woodland species can be found, including Nuthatch, common warblers and tit species and Spotted Flycatcher. It is one of Oxfordshire's best sites for observing all three species of woodpecker. Pied Wagtail and resident thrushes feed on open grassed areas and commoner finches can be seen. Mallard, Mute Swan, Coot, Moorhen and Little Grebe may breed on the river. In winter, the Parks offer shelter to most of the aforementioned resident birds, joined by good numbers of Redwing and Fieldfare, especially on the Meadow, and occasional Redpoll and Siskin. Floods on adjacent meadows attract gulls, waders (such as Snipe and occasional Redshank) and an increased number of duck. Periods of passage, especially in spring, may be profitable with Redstart, Pied Flycatcher and Wood Warbler all recorded. Kestrel and Sparrowhawk are regular whilst Common Buzzard and Hobby are occurring more frequently.

The parks are only open during daylight hours from 08:00 hrs, the main gates being in Parks Road. Footpaths across the river facilitate exploring of the Cherwell, its banks and additional meadows. The university also owns Wytham Wood (OS ref. SP 460 080), using it as a field study area for biological research. Subjects include Sparrowhawk, Tawny Owl and members of the tit family, and probably more is known about the birds of this tract of woodland than any other in the region. Its rich birdlife has included Nightingale, Tree Pipit and Grasshopper Warbler, but access is only by application in writing to the university land agent. (See Useful Addresses.)

Ryecote Park (OS ref. SP 670 050) Comprising areas of mixed woodland, arable fields and pasture, plus two reed-fringed lakes, this private park has several footpaths crossing the area, allowing views over all aspects of the site, which is generally quite boggy. A car park near a memorial chapel in the centre of the park is open during various seasons and details are available from English Heritage (01483 252000).

The lake usually supports common breeding duck and grebe and is a regular haunt for Grey Heron, whilst Reed and Sedge Warblers breed in the lakeside vegetation and Kingfisher are frequently seen. Recent dredging will disrupt this situation for a while however. Skylark and Lapwing nest on the open fields whilst the hedgerows hold both species of Whitethroat, Yellowhammer, Linnet and Little Owl. Yellow Wagtail, Stock Dove and Cuckoo may also be seen. The woodland is home for the three woodpeckers, Treecreeper, Spotted Flycatcher, Marsh and Willow Tits, thrushes and warblers. There is a sizeable rookery. Winter is rather quiet but gulls and a few wintering duck may return to the lake whilst winter thrushes forage on adjacent fields and hedgerows. More gulls, together with Lapwing and possibly Golden Plover may gather on the golf course south of the A329, and nearby Fernhill Wood to the east is also good for general woodland species.

Shelswell Park (OS ref. SP 604 315) This site is a small estate north-east of Stoke Wood, with grazing parkland and a small lake. Most of the typical parkland species are present, reeds around the lake attracting Reed Warbler, with Grey Heron, Teal and common ducks on the water. Kestrel and Sparrowhawk are resident, Hobby probable and Common Buzzard regular. Marsh Tit use the garden areas whilst Tawny Owl,

Treecreeper, Nuthatch, Green and Great Spotted Woodpeckers occupy linear woodland around the periphery. Large mixed thrush and finch flocks occur in winter, bringing a prospect of Brambling, and with Raven reported more regularly in the county of late, the large corvid gatherings should be checked carefully. A small new plantation to the north-west of the park should interest Whitethroat and possibly Tree Pipit, the wood that abuts this sector being good for Siskin in winter. Parking at the entrance (per the grid reference given) allows access to the footpath network through the park.

Stonor Park (OS ref. SU 737 880) Situated midst the stunning Chiltern scenery of south Oxon, the rolling countryside surrounding Stonor beckons those hungering for views of Red Kite and Common Buzzard. The Park and House are only open to the public on Bank Holiday Mondays, Sundays April to September, and Wednesdays during July and August. However, the Chiltern Way passes through the park from the grid reference point above. The path follows the edge of the deer park through open parkland where Jackdaw and Nuthatch reside, climbing gradually up to more enclosed woodland where Spotted Flycatcher join resident tits and finches during summer. A conifer plantation, Balhams Wood, near the top of the gradient hosts Treecreeper, Goldcrest and Coal Tit whilst the denser thicket on the very top of the hill has Bullfinch and Marsh Tit, with Chiffchaff around its perimeter. Stock Dove can be heard 'hooting' from woods around the main house and both Kestrel and Sparrowhawk can be expected hunting in the valley.

Return by the same route emphasises the grandeur of the scenery, embellished by magnificent Red Kite, often just a few feet above one's head, with calls reminiscent of a shepherd whistling his dog. Up to 20 kites are possible on this walk, within the park confines or soaring over adjacent hills.

Turville Park (Os ref. SU 743 909) Strictly speaking, most of this walk lies within Bucks. but is included here for its proximity to Stonor Park. A much smaller, and private, park but with a footpath through the south-eastern sector and another through the woodland in the west. Parking at the grid reference given and following the footpath through the 'garden gate', leads into sheep and goat paddocks where Little Owl is possible amongst other birds of open parkland. Again the views around are compelling and more Red Kite and Common Buzzard are assured, whilst Marsh Tit are found in the wayside tree-line. The path continues south-west through farmland where Yellowhammer and Whitethroat are found. Picking up the north-going footpath and taking the right fork to pass through the estate's woodland, look for Nuthatch and more Marsh Tit whilst listening for woodpeckers and Tawny Owl. The path eventually exits the estate by Blundell's Farm where Skylark and hirundines are present, or finch flocks in winter. Turning right onto the lane leads back to the parking place.

NOTE – Please be aware that strictly no access is possible at Middleton Park. Eynsham Hall Park too is inaccessible but a footpath runs between the park and Cogges Wood to the west, running from the A4095 at SP 385 123 southwards to Hill Farm. Lesser Spotted Woodpecker is one of the prospects here.

Radley Gravel Pits (OS ref. SP 520 978)

In the area of countryside between Abingdon, Radley and the River Thames and split by the main Oxford to London railway line lies a collection of gravel pits. Black-winged Stilt and Pied-billed Grebe have helped give the site some fame, in addition to a good range of passage birds, e.g. Black Tern, and records include Mediterranean Gull, Purple Heron, Little Egret and Pied Flycatcher, plus Whinchat and wintering species such as Shelduck and Water Rail. Equally important is the area's ability to support a good list of breeding species. Indeed, during the course of the Atlas of Breeding Birds in Oxfordshire, Radley was the richest area in the county with over 80 breeding species, including Common Tern, Sand Martin and Reed Warbler. Cetti's Warbler has been noted, though less frequently of late, and the supporting cast includes all the common summer visitors, such as Grasshopper Warbler and Turtle Dove, which are something of a specialty here.

Access is rather limited, with only a single public right of way over the area although many people use the area freely. The lakes to the west of the railway are effectively inaccessible, but for access to the attractive waters on the Abingdon side, leave Abingdon on the Radley Road and turn right after 0.4 km (0.2 miles) into Thrupp Lane as one enters the village of Radley. (If you come to the railway station, you've gone too far!) Drive for approximately 1.2 km (0.75 mile) until reaching the newly laid National Cycleway, which runs off to the left. Limited parking is available here (SU 521 978), and the new tarmac surface makes for a pleasant walk through the complex of lakes, most of which can be seen from the track or are accessible from it. The main lakes are at SU 520 970 and in wintertime will host Goldeneye in double figures, good numbers of Dabchick and rafts of gulls in pre-roost gatherings later in the day, and quite high counts of Tufted Duck. Occasional Smew, Ruddy Duck and lots of Reed Bunting occur in winter and hawking Hobby in summer, with regular visits from Peregrine using nearby Didcot Power Station, being observed on one occasion failing to catch a very agile Green Sandpiper.

River Windrush

Rising in the Cotswolds, the River Windrush flows eastwards through Oxfordshire to join the Thames at Newbridge. Particularly to the west of Witney, it is a clean, fast-flowing stream (much favoured by trout anglers), with good emergent and submerged vegetation. Along much of the valley the adjacent meadows are of permanent pasture, much of it unimproved, and having good hedgerows and small copses along their boundaries. Many footpaths traverse the valley making it quite an accessible tract of countryside.

Most of the usual birds of hedgerow, open countryside and woodland may be encountered, including Barn, Little and Tawny Owls, Kestrel, Sparrowhawk, Yellow Wagtail, Cuckoo and Spotted Flycatcher. In winter, Redwing and Fieldfare forage widely and Siskin and the occasional Common Buzzard may take up residence. Along the river, its adjacent meadows and close to the many ponds that exist (for example, at Widford), one can find Pied and Grey Wagtails, Sedge Warbler, Kingfisher, Moorhen, Mallard and Mute Swan. Dipper bred in the past and may still have a tenuous hold in the general area. At undisturbed grassland sites Snipe, Lapwing, Curlew and more rarely Redshank may breed. During the winter when the valley floods, wader numbers, particularly Lapwing, rise and large flocks often including Golden Plover may be noted. Various wildfowl may also be attracted to the floods.

It is worth noting that all of Oxfordshire's waterways can be regarded as linear havens for wildlife and therefore potential birdwatching sites. All still have their undisturbed reaches with lush bankside vegetation and adjacent woods and meadows offering ample opportunities to birds. Most have good access along towpaths or public footpaths allowing views of a similar range of species as outlined for the River Windrush.

Sonning Eye (OS ref. SU 745 745)

The areas of interest at this location include the Thames floodplain at the end of the A329M, the adjacent Thames Valley Park and Henley Road Pits, the footpath to Sonning along the river, and Sonning Eye Gravel Pit. In summer, the entire area is a draw to tourists and little birdlife may be found on occasions. However, during winter flooding, large numbers of mixed gulls, ducks and geese appear, with Canada and Egyptian types on show. Snipe visit the boggy areas whilst flocks of Meadow Pipit, Skylark and Pied Wagtail gather. Winter thrushes reach impressive numbers, scattering when the occasional Peregrine turns up. Autumn passage produces Wheatear and Whinchat. During this time, the nature reserve will host Little Grebe, and Water Rail may be encountered calling from the reedbed. Various finches team up in small flocks.

Spring brings in most of the common warblers, Reed Warbler in particular breeding well, often accompanied by Sedge Warbler. Other breeders include Great Crested Grebe, Coot and Mute Swan. A summer walk from the car park behind the Lloyd Centre, where paths are suited to wheelchairs, will produce a variety of riparian species, with Swallow, Swift and martins overhead, occasionally drawing a hunting Hobby or two. This area in winter, however, will be impassable without wellington boots.

A towpath stroll towards Sonning will afford good views of Goldcrest and Long-tailed Tit in adjacent hedgerows, and Siskin feeding in riverside Alders. Arctic Tern pass through in spring, and Common Tern will patrol the river in summer. The Jackdaw colony on nearby farmland should be checked over as Raven was found in 2001. Huge numbers of House Martin congregate in the Sonning area in summer, and Kingfisher will be seen along the river. From this footpath, views over the Sonning Eye Gravel Pit are possible, with good numbers of Pochard (130) and Tufted Duck (200+), and up to 80 Goldeneye and c.400 Wigeon, with Red-breasted Merganser recorded also in 2001. Gadwall may be present in important numbers, up to 130, and breeding has been proven at the Henley Road lake, where Garganey, Goosander and Smew have also been recorded. Autumn sees good numbers of pre-departure Common Tern at Sonning Eye. In colder weather, large rafts of gull gather here, containing who knows what!

Stoke Wood (OS ref. SP 557 281)

A 35-ha (88-acre) mixed wood owned by the Woodland Trust, first opened to the public in 1993. Comprising large Oaks, Ash and Hazel Coppice, with some Corsican Pine, the wood supports a good range of species including all six tits, Treecreeper, Nuthatch, passage and summering warblers. A box scheme has encouraged breeding Tawny Owl, and Common Buzzard settled in recently. Open glades may draw Spotted Flycatcher. Surrounding farmland hosts Yellowhammer and occasional Corn Bunting whilst the adjacent landfill quarry attracts numerous gulls and corvids. The only access is from the B4100 near junction 10 of the M4 (no access from the service area), using the official car park from which a variety of waymarked trails cover all sections of the wood.

Stonesfield Common (OS ref. SP 390 165)

Lying on the west bank of the River Evenlode, this area of limestone grassland, damp meadow, scrub and hedgerow provides nesting and feeding opportunities for a wide variety of species. In the recent past, Grasshopper Warbler bred but probably no longer. Little Owl, Barn Owl and Kestrel use the area as a hunting ground throughout the year, whilst foraging parties of Redwing and Fieldfare are regularly seen in winter and occasionally Stonechat and Short-eared Owl may take up temporary residence. The adjacent narrow deciduous woodland strip hosts Nuthatch, tits and finches and nest boxes have been provided for resident Tawny Owl. Access to the area is along footpaths either from Stonesfield village or from the unclassified road between Stonesfield and North Leigh.

Stratfield Brake (OS ref. SP 495 120)

A new woodland and wetland creation project by the Woodland Trust in association with the Environment Agency, extending existing woodland on the western side of the A4260 south of Kidlington and sculpting a wetland area abutting the Oxford Canal. Completed in early 2002, an ideal site for local birdwatchers to monitor the effect of the project. Parking is by the playing field on the west of the dual carriageway.

Sutton Courteney Pools (OS ref. SP 504 941)

Embracing this small village on the B4016, two bodies of water are worth visiting. Small pits behind the church and The Swan pub can be accessed from the free car park near Churchmere Road and by walking down the lane, after checking the churchyard for winter thrushes, Spotted Flycatcher and Coal Tit, and then keeping an eye on garden feeding stations for other tits and Nuthatch. The lake on the right is somewhat open to the pathway and probably has few birds on it, but the one on the left is more enclosed and has seen Green Sandpiper, Kingfisher and Grey Heron. Beyond these two pools is an area of rough grass-land and hawthorn scrub, potentially attractive to Bullfinch, Reed Bunting, Cuckoo and Meadow Pipit. The resident Green Woodpecker play here, and Yellowhammer and Tree Sparrow are other possibilities. The more northern pool is the quintessential English village duck pond with many common species following walkers for bread, but Great Crested Grebe, Gadwall and Shoveler also use it. Great Spotted Woodpecker and even Turtle Dove might be found.

Sutton Pools, on the other side of the main road, are home to more Great Crested Grebe, Grey Wagtail, Moorhen and Kingfisher, and, when high water causes the Thames to pour into it, rough-water canoeing!

The slightly more 'wild' pools and scrapes further along the B4016 towards Appleford have produced such waders as Little Ringed Plover, Redshank, Green and Common Sandpipers and look suitable for Snipe or even Jack Snipe. The best place to park and observe from might be the pull-off on the bend at SP 520 937. Tree Sparrow and Corn Bunting have also been recorded in this general area and Mute Swan on floods in winter could draw rarer swans to them.

Tadpole Bridge (OS ref. SP 335 004)

A particularly interesting stretch of the Thames from Tadpole Bridge to Rushey Lock, with seasonal flood-meadows and willow-lined waterways. Turning north off the A420 at Buckland, Tadpole Bridge will be crossed after 3 km (1.5 mile) beyond which a lay-by can be used for parking. After checking the area around the bridge and the adjacent Trout Inn for regular Tree Sparrow, a westerly walk along the tarmac Thames Path embraces typical riverside habitat, with reeds attracting Reed and Sedge Warblers, Whitethroat and possible Grasshopper Warbler. Kingfisher and Grey Wagtail frequent this stretch of the river and Rushey Lock presents another opportunity for Tree Sparrow, especially in trees near the lock-keeper's cottage. By late summer, large numbers of Swift and hirundines gather to feed over the adjacent meadows here.

One can cross the river at this point and return via the fisherman's path, looking out for Willow Tit and Turtle Dove. Alternatively, one can continue westwards on the Thames Path where, in spring and summer, the evocative bubbling of breeding Curlew can be experienced. In winter, potential flooding enhances numbers of wildfowl and wader concentrations. Barn Owl is a possibility whilst Little Owl breed in pollarded willows along the banks and interestingly, regular records of Redstart on their autumn passage occur here, often accompanied by other returning species such as Lesser Whitethroat, Wheatear and Yellow Wagtail. Both Common and Green Sandpipers use the banks for feeding and wintertime brings groups of Snipe to the marshy vegetation alongside the river. A network of footpaths facilitates a variety of circular walks through the surrounding countryside, looking for Yellowhammer, Grey Partridge or winter flocks of Linnet and thrushes. Common Buzzard frequent the woodlands near Buckland to the south and often soar over the river. Aviation buffs will have the added bonus of the graceful VC10 tankers circuiting from nearby Brize Norton.

Whitecross Green Wood (OS ref. SP 600 150)

Designated a SSSI, this 62-ha (156-acre) ancient woodland is owned by BBOWT and a management plan of coppicing Hazel and replacing earlier conifers with native forest species is opening up the wood and attracting additional species. The wide rides encourage numerous dragonflies and butterfly species include Black Hairstreak and Purple Emperor. As cleared areas mature, birdlife changes accordingly, and species such as Nightingale, Grasshopper Warbler, Marsh and Willow Tits, Lesser Spotted Woodpecker and Sparrowhawk occur. Tawny Owl and Common Buzzard breed here and both Woodcock and Snipe are recorded, often on the rides themselves. Bullfinch are particularly plentiful. The presence of several small ponds enriches the habitat still further.

The reserve is situated approximately 1.6 km (1 mile) on the right-hand side of the unclassified road east of Murcot. A small car park is accessed by two gates along the track opposite a small cottage. There is public access along all rides but dogs are not admitted.

Witney Lake (OS ref. SP 355 087)

Through the foresight of Witney Town Council, this lake and adjacent wet meadows have become a managed nature reserve, part of which is designated an Environmentally Sensitive Area. Although bisected by the east–west A40, footpaths passing beneath the flyover facilitate a pleasant walk around this small and sometimes busy site. Parking is

Woodcock

available at the end of Avenue Two at the above map reference. Despite being very popular with the local community, species which might be expected include both Little and Barn Owls, Grey Wagtail and Reed Bunting and accompanying riparian species, always with the prospect of Common Buzzard soaring overhead. Winter visitors generally include Water Rail and Snipe, with Stonechat, Corn Bunting and Golden Plover to watch out for, plus Siskin and Redpoll to listen out for.

Summer water-side birds will include Sedge Warbler, Whitethroat and Lesser Whitethroat, Garden and Willow Warblers, Cuckoo and Common Tern. Passage birds have included Whinchat and Wheatear, whilst Redstart and Common Sandpiper can be expected. Yellow Wagtail add colour and a dashing Hobby may spring into view. Some interesting species have been seen amongst the 115 species totted up by one local observer, such as Red-necked Grebe, Wood Warbler and even Osprey.

Yarnton Gravel Pits (OS ref. SP 470 107)

Three pits north of the A40, which are viewable from the adjacent cycle track. Good numbers of winter waterfowl, including hundreds of Wigeon, dozens of Pochard, annual Smew and Goosander, half a dozen Goldeneye and occasional Red-breasted Merganser. Ruddy Shelduck and Red-crested Pochard represent the less kosher visitors whilst Great Northern Diver, Slavonian Grebe and White-fronted Goose have been recorded. Spring passage brings Ringed Plover, Wood and Green Sandpipers, occasional Oystercatcher or Turnstone and Temminck's Stint has been noted. Black Tern pass through but several pairs of Common Tern breed alongside Black-headed Gull and Redshank, whilst Hobby hunts in the evenings. Jack Snipe are occasionally seen in the area.

BIBLIOGRAPHY

Clews, B.D. *Cookham, its Birds, People and Places* (BCS, 1996)

Easterbrook, T.G. (ed.) *Birds of the Banbury Area 1972–1981* (B.O.S., 1983)

Fitter, R.S. (ed.) *The Wildlife of the Thames Counties* (Dugdale, Oxford, 1985)

Frankum, M. & R.G. *The Birds & Plants of Freemen's Marsh* (Private, 1970–1974)

— *The Birds & Plants of Freemen's Marsh 1975–1979* (Private)

— *The Birds & Plants of Hungerford Common* (Private)

Gladwin, T. & Sage, B. *The Birds of Hertfordshire* (Castlemead, Ware, 1986)

Harding, B.D. *Bedfordshire Bird Atlas* (Private, 1977)

Hobson, M.G. & Price, K.L.H. *Otmoor and its Seven Towns* (Private, 1967)

Kennedy, A.W.M.C. *The Birds of Berkshire & Buckinghamshire* (Private, 1868)

Lack, P. & Ferguson, D. *The Birds of Buckinghamshire* (Buckinghamshire Bird Club, 1993)

Mead, C. & Smith, K. *The Hertfordshire Breeding Bird Atlas* (Private, 1982)

Montgomery-Massingbird, H. *Blenheim Resisited* (Bodley Head, London, 1985)

O'Sullivan, S. *The Birds of Witneydale 1994-1996* (Simon O'Sullivan, 1998)

Radford, M.C. *The Birds of Berkshire & Oxfordshire* (Longman, London, 1966)

Sage, B . *The Birds of Hertfordshire* (Private, 1959)

Steel, D. *The Natural History of a Royal Forest* (Pisces, Oxford, 1984)

Trodd, P. & Kramer, D. *The Birds of Bedfordshire* (Castlemead, Welwyn Garden City, 1991)

Wiggins, R.H. *The Birds of Little Wittenham* (Northmoor Trust, 1985)

Youngman, R.E. & Fraser, A.C. *The Birds of Buckinghamshire and East Berkshire* (Middle Thames Natural History Society, 1976)

In addition to the works listed above, the annual reports of any of the bird clubs in the region make fascinating reading and provide an up-to-date assessment of the local birds. These reports may be obtained by writing to the secretary of the relevant bird club or organisation. (See Useful Addresses.)

INDEX OF SPECIES

Site number references are given here. Species mentioned in the Additional Sites sections are not included.